RE: DIRECTION

Re: direction is an extraordinary resource for practitioners and students of directing. It provides a collection of groundbreaking interviews, primary sources and essays on twentieth-century directing theories and practices around the world.

Helpfully organized into four key areas of the subject, the book explores theories of directing, the boundaries of the director's role, the limits of categorization, and the history of the theatre and performance art.

Exceptionally useful and thought-provoking introductory essays by editors Schneider and Cody guide the reader through the wealth of material included here. *Re: direction* is the kind of book anyone interested in theatre history should own, and which will prove an indispensable toolkit for a lifetime of study.

Rebecca Schneider is a member of the graduate faculty of Cornell University's Department of Theatre, Film, and Dance where she teaches Performance Studies, Visual Culture and Theatre History. She is the author of numerous works in theatre, performance art, and performance theory.

Gabrielle Cody is Associate Professor of Drama and Chair in the Department of Drama and Film at Vassar College, where she has taught since 1992. She received her M.F.A. in Directing from the University of Minnesota, and her Doctorate in Dramaturgy and Dramatic Criticism from Yale University.

WORLDS OF PERFORMANCE

What is a 'performance'? Where does it take place? Who are the participants? Not so long ago these were settled questions, but today such orthodox answers are unsatisfactory, misleading, and limiting. 'Performance' as a theoretical category and as a practice has expanded explosively. It now comprises a panoply of genres ranging from play, to popular entertainments, to theatre, dance, and music, to secular and religious rituals, to 'performance in everyday life', to intercultural experiments, and more.

For nearly forty years, *The Drama Review* (*TDR*), the journal of performance studies, has been at the cutting edge of exploring these questions. The Worlds of Performance Series is designed to mine the extraordinary riches and diversity of *TDR*'s decades of excellence, bringing back into print important essays, interviews, artists' notes, and photographs. New materials and introductions bring the volumes up to date. Each World of Performance book is a complete anthology, arranged around a specific theme or topic. Each World of Performance book is an indispensable resource for the scholar, a textbook for the student, and an exciting eye-opener for the general reader.

Richard Schechner
Editor *TDR*
Series Editor

OTHER TITLES IN THE SERIES

Acting (Re)Considered edited by Phillip B. Zarrilli
Happenings and Other Acts edited by Mariellen R. Sandford
A Sourcebook of Feminist Theatre and Performance: On and Beyond the Stage edited by
 Carol Martin
The Grotowski Sourcebook edited by Richard Schechner and Lisa Wolford
A Sourcebook of African-American Performance: Plays, People, Movements edited by
 Annemarie Bean
Brecht Sourcebook edited by Carol Martin and Henry Bial

RE: DIRECTION

A THEORETICAL AND PRACTICAL GUIDE

Edited by Rebecca Schneider and Gabrielle Cody

London and New York

First published 2002 by Routledge
11 New Fetter Lane, London EC4P 4EE

Simultaneously published in the USA and Canada
by Routledge
29 West 35th Street, New York, NY 10001

Routledge is an imprint of the Taylor & Francis Group

© 2002 editorial matter, Rebecca Schneider and Gabrielle Cody

Typeset in Times New Roman by RefineCatch Limited, Bungay, Suffolk
Printed and bound in Great Britain by
TJ International Ltd, Padstow, Cornwall

British Library Cataloguing in Publication Data
A catalogue record for this book is available from the British Library

Library of Congress Cataloging in Publication Data
Re: direction : a theoretical and practical guide / [edited by] Rebecca Schneider
    and Gabrielle Cody.
        p. cm. – (Worlds of performance)
    Includes bibliographical references.
    ISBN 0–415–21390–8 (alk. paper) – ISBN 0–415–21391–6 (pbk. : alk. paper)
    1. Theater – Production and direction.   I. Schneider, Rebecca.   II. Cody, Gabrielle
1956–   III. Series.
    PN2053 .D537   2001
    792'.0233 – dc21   2001019654

ISBN 0–415–21390–8 (hbk)
ISBN 0–415–23191–6 (pbk)

CONTENTS

Part IV   Montage, reiteration, revision

ILLUSTRATIONS

ACKNOWLEDGMENTS

Thanks are due to Talia Rodgers of Routledge for encouraging this project in every respect. We are also grateful to *The Drama Review*'s editor, also editor of the Worlds of Performance Series, Richard Schechner, for allowing us to take his journal and 'do as we think best' in our approach, choices, and organization of material. When he took issue with our perspective he always allowed himself to be convinced. We are also thoroughly indebted to editorial assistants Monika Gay, Magdalena Romanska, and Harvey Young of Cornell University for invaluable help with research, leg-work, and general editing, and also to Alexa Torgensen of Vassar for hours of scanning and spell-checking.

The following were first published in *The Tulane Drama Review* and are reprinted with permission of *TDR* (NB the prefix 'T' is a style used by *TDR*, denoting each issue not by volume and number but by individual issue): '*The Three Sisters* at the MAT' by M. N. Stroyeva, *Tulane Drama Review* 9, 1 (T25) 1964: 42–56 and 'Reality is not enough: an interview with Alan Schneider' by Richard Schechner, *Tulane Drama Review* 9, 3 (T27) 1965: 118–54.

The following were first published in *TDR: The Drama Review* and are reprinted with permission of *The Drama Review*: 'My Russian notebook, 1934' by Lee Strasberg was published as 'Lee Strasberg's Russian notebook (1934),' *TDR* 17, 1 (T57) 1973: 106–12; 'An interview with Okhlopkov' by Lee Strasberg and Sidney Kingsley, *TDR* 17, 1 (T57) 1973: 121–3; 'Meyerhold's production of *The Magnanimous Cuckold*' by Nick Worrall was published as 'Meyerhold's production of *The Magnificent Cuckhold*,' *TDR* 17, 1 (T57) 1973: 14–34; 'Brecht as director' by Carl Weber, *TDR* 12, 1 (T37) 1967: 101–7; 'The revolutionary moment' by Lee Baxandall, *TDR* 13, 2 (T42) 1968: 92–107; '*Paradise Now*: notes' by the Living Theatre, *TDR* 13, 2 (T43) 1969: 90–107; 'Antonin Artaud's *Les Cenci*' by Roger Blin *et al.*, *TDR* 16, 2 (T54) 1972: 90–145; 'Robert Wilson and therapy' by Bill Simmer, *TDR* 20, 1 (T69) 1976: 99–110; '*Vessel*: the scenography of Meredith Monk: an interview' by Brooks McNamara, *TDR* 16, 1 (T53) 1972: 87–103; 'Foreman's *PAIN(T)* and *Vertical Mobility*' by Kate Davy, *TDR* 18, 2 (T62) 1974: 26–37; 'An interview with Grotowski' by Richard Schechner, *TDR* 13, 1 (T41) 1968: 29–41; 'Eisenstein's *Wiseman*' by Daniel Gerould, *TDR* 18, 1 (T61) 1974: 71–6; 'Montage of attractions' by Sergei Eisenstein, *TDR* 18, 1 (T61) 1974: 97–106; 'Charles Ludlam's Ridiculous Theatrical Company' by Ron Argelander, *TDR* 18, 2 (T62) 1974: 81–6; 'Ridiculous Theatre, scourge of human folly' by Charles Ludlam, *TDR* 19, 4 (T68) 1975: 70. 'Family of the f.p.: notes on the Theatre of the Ridiculous' by Stefan Brecht, *TDR* 13, 1 (T41) 1968: 117–41.

The following were published in *The Drama Review: A Journal of Performance Studies* and are reprinted with permission of MIT Press: 'Stanislavsky: uncensored and unabridged' by Sharon Marie Carnicke, *TDR* 37, 1 (T137) 1993: 22–37; 'Invisible Theatre' by Augusto Boal, *TDR* 34, 3 (T127) 1990: 24–34; 'Tadeusz Kantor's journey' by Jan Klossowicz, *TDR* 30, 3 (T111) 1986: 98–155; '*Pearls for Pigs:* program notes' by Richard Foreman, *TDR* 42, 2 (T158) 1998: 157–9; 'AIDS and avant-garde classicism: Reza Abdoh's *Quotations from a Ruined City*' by John Bell, *TDR* 39, 4 (T148) 1995: 21–47; 'Woman, man, dog, tree: two decades of intimate and monumental bodies in Pina Bausch's Tanztheater' by Gabrielle Cody, *TDR* 42,2 (T158) 1998: 115–31; 'Talking with Peter Brook' by Richard Schechner, Jean-Claude Carrière, Joel Jouanneau, Georges Banu, *TDR* 30, 1 (T109) 1986: 54–71; 'Nomadmedia: on Critical Art Ensemble' by Rebecca Schneider, *TDR* 44, 4 (T168) 2000: 120–31; 'The Other history of intercultural performance' by Coco Fusco, *TDR* 38, 1 (T141) 1993: 143–67; 'Island hopping: rehearsing the Wooster Group's *Brace Up!*' by Euridice Arratia, *TDR* 36, 4 (T136) 1992: 121–42; 'Suzan-Lori Parks and Liz Diamond: doo-a-diddly-dit-dit, an interview' by Steven Drukman, *TDR* 39, 3 (T147) 1995: 56–75.

'The reign of the theatrical director' by Bettina L. Knapp was originally published in *The French Review* 6, 6 (1988) and is reprinted with permission of *The French Review*.

The selection from *Art in Everyday Life* by Linda Montano, Station Hill, NY: Astro Artz, 1981; 'Collective creation' by Theodore Shank, *TDR* 16, 2 (T54) 1972: 3–31; and 'Building up the muscle: an interview with Ariane Mnouchkine' by Josette Feral, *TDR* 33, 4 (T124) 1989: 97–106, are reprinted with permission of the authors.

'Is there a text on this stage?' was originally published in *Performing Arts Journal* 26/27 (1985) and is reprinted with permission of the journal.

'*Hamlet* at world's end: Heiner Müller's production in East Berlin' by Maik Hamburger is reprinted from *Shakespeare and Cultural Traditions*, edited by Tetsuo Kishi, Roger Pringle, and Stanley Wells, London: Associated University Presses, 1994. It is reprinted with permission of the Associated University Presses.

'Review of *Three Sisters*' by Rebecca Schneider was published in *Theater Journal* 49, 3 (1997): 365–7 and is reprinted with permission of the journal.

NOTE

Notes at the ends of chapters are by the author(s) of those chapters unless otherwise indicated.

GENERAL INTRODUCTION

Rebecca Schneider and Gabrielle Cody

The post-atomic, post-revolutionary, post-colonial decades of the latter half of the twentieth century generated a dizzying multiplicity of theatrical languages and performative possibilities. In an age of quickly accumulating 'posts,' we are less than ever post-performance. We have consistently borne witness to alterations in social proxemics – what bodies and objects mean in spatial relation – by negotiating those proxemics across our screens or on our stages. Cultural traditions, as well as spaces between cultures and their traditions, have been displayed, contested, buttressed, hybridized, and sometimes collapsed. So too have gender/race/ethnic/ sexual politics been negotiated and renegotiated. While this kind of negotiation is arguably the stuff of theatre as far back as we could hope to trace, certainly with late modernism the pitch and fervor of exchange, the tussle of myriad 'isms' and the opening out and boundary shifting of theatrical methodologies and aesthetic practices have only increased. Transculturalism, multiculturalism, interculturalism, not to mention feminism, critical race theory, poststructuralism, postmodernism have introduced a range of notions of how meaning is encoded and enacted on the body, between bodies, across words, and through space. If our experience of the globe has been shrinking in 'real' space, the available palette to any artist or director of virtual space – words and images, gestures and poses, media and method, flesh, celluloid, tape and digitalia – has increased with remarkable speed.

Indeed, performance could arguably be the medium most articulate of speed since live performance, unlike object art, passes in time and appears to 'vanish' – too quick, one might say, to leave itself behind. It is common to say that the theatre, and the performances through which it is articulated, is composed in temporal space, composed via repetition but unable to outlast the instances of its utterance. When a 'live' show or a run of a production closes, that production supposedly 'disappears' into the various documents which record it – film, photograph, video-tape, interview, playbill, play text, promptbook, ticket stub, costume, prop, review, memoir.

Yet, the documents and archived materials of production, as well as schools of training in the styles of various luminaries, clearly show that the 'liveness' in productions and production values have a definite resilience. Productions, directing styles, and acting methods cite each other across spaces, even reenact each other – via direct reproduction from a promptbook, or via quotation (as when Brecht adopts and adapts certain of Stanislavsky's techniques, and Boal adopts Brecht, etc.). Such quotation or citation may occur via parody or overt resistance to precedent as well. If Stanislavsky's groundbreaking assertion in 1913 that 'an actor alone, without outside help, cannot create a role' has served as a bible for the foundation of much modern theatre, it has also been fervently contested and overtly resisted by numerous strains in the avant-garde. That contest itself suggests ongoing interaction, an interaction that can be considered a kind of theatrical remain. The almost mythical role of the modern director, itself just over a century old, has been as changeable a category as any in the history of representational practice, yet that changeability is arguably evidence of discursive connection and exchange.

The interactions and connections we can chart in the history of directing extend beyond the bounds of theatre proper to more general venues and ventures of arts in the twentieth century, as multiple media negotiated the production and reproduction of 'meaning' in rapidly changing society. Gerald Rabkin draws a connection between theatre and literature in 'Is there a text on this stage?' an essay first published in 1985 in *Performing Arts Journal* (Chapter 37 of this volume). As Rabkin notes, 'The rise of "director's theatre" mirrors literary criticism's movement from the emphasis upon the immanent "meaning" of literary texts to the acceptance of the processes of reading and interpretation which determine meaning.' Similar mirrorings and cross-current connections can be charted in the visual arts and film, which were, of course, influencing as well as influenced by movements in literary criticism.

Therefore, we have assembled the essays in this book with one eye toward the ways in which theatre styles vanish in particular performances, and another toward the way theatrical styles remain in citation, reenactment, and adaptation within and across media. Our hope is that this collection can help to refract the traces of staged bodies, allowing readers to remark upon the patterns their interactions make across the landscape of twentieth-century Euro-American theatre. The tracks we follow here – of intersection and contest in directing practices – are, specifically, tracks left across forty years of the journal *The Drama Review*. These tracks, imprinted in *TDR*, were left by critics, spectators, photographers, performers, and the directors themselves: revolutionaries, auteurs, ensemble-leaders, and, even, performance artists. *The Drama Review* has been an extremely influential journal internationally, especially during the mid-1960s and 1970s when experimental 'director's' theatre as well as ensemble theater work was flourishing (notice the number of theatres in this collection alone that cite 1968 as the date of their founding).

Every journal, or course, has an editor. Therefore, the tracks in this book are also laid via the editorship of the journal – beginning with Robert Corrigan (1955–62), Richard Schechner (1963–9), Erika Munk (1969–70), Michael Kirby (1971–85), and then Richard Schechner again with associate editor Mariellen Sandford (1986–present).The conceptual approaches of these editors were quite distinct, and even the difference in approach between Schechner's first seven-year editorship (when he brought the journal to a considerable peak of influence) and his present sixteen-year editorship is noticeable.[1] The choices of these editors have been, of course, profoundly interpretive of the performance worlds they document. A similar culling from another journal would result in another set of intersecting tracks. But this in itself is fascinating, as the variety of styles of journals on performance and theater (from *Performing Arts Journal* (*PAJ*) to *Theatre Journal* to *High Performance* to *Theater* to *Performance Research*, etc., etc.) obviously contribute to maintaining a richly varigated, and often hotly debated, performance scene. Still, the fact that almost all of the directors represented in this volume also appear at different moments in their careers in conversation or interpretation in the pages of other journals weaves a lively cross-hatch of influence.

Combing through decades of *TDR*, selecting essays with occasional additions from other publications (such as Rabkin from *PAJ*, Knapp from *French Review*), our choices sometimes surprised us, and led us to include work by artists who seem quite far from directing as more commonly considered. For example, consider the occasional inclusion here of 'directors' who might more properly be called 'performance artists.' Though performance artists are seemingly 'directorless,' as we were reading the forty years of the journal it became apparent that when situated within the crucible of modernity and 'revolution' that birthed the modern director, even performance artists can be tracked as odd offspring of the impulse to orchestrate action, wrestle with vision, populate a *mise-en-scène*, or even telescope a 'slice of life.' Of course, to repeat, the 'scene' that emerged for us regarding Euro-American directing in the twentieth century was highly influenced by the particular journal which served as our focal point.

And yet, if performance artists are surprising inheritors of the impulse to direct, their inclusion here may not be a singularly odd inclusion in the history of defining directing.[2] The role of director, first associated with unifying the visual realization of a play text on stage, rather rapidly came to include not only those who approach the director's role as servicing the text, but also the contributions of auteurs who may abandon dramatic text altogether – Antonin Artaud, Jerzy Grotowski, Robert Wilson, among others. Though one would suspect that playwrights might begrudge this inclusion, it was playwright George S. Kaufman (who himself won a Tony Award for directing *Guys and Dolls* in 1950), who stated that 'Good plays have a way of being well directed' – suggesting that a good play hardly needs direction and that a director's role is most pronounced in the absence of what is still often taken to be the primary element of Western theatre proper: the 'good' script.

The script as 'pinnacle' of performance has been something *The Drama Review* has, from time to time, challenged quite vociferously.[3] The squabble over primacy of playwright or director, however, is evidence of a much deeper tangle of definition. As Rabkin wrote for *PAJ*, republished here, 'The question of the relationship between play and performance is at the center of contemporary theatre theory.' It is also a question with a long history. Evidence of the tangle of definition between actors, playwrights, and directors (not to mention unruly avant-gardes or their postmodern descendants, performance artists) is still quite lively, in part because the categories that separate them are historically porous and have included as much cross-pollination as definitional segregation. To remember that Stanislavsky was an actor, Brecht a playwright, Kaufman a director, or that Artaud was an actor and playwright, or that Foreman is a playwright or that Müller directed and LeCompte and Wilson and Kantor have performed should be evidence enough. But the category of 'director' (as opposed to 'actor' or 'playwright') has the added knotty spot of being quite newly minted on the scene – at least as a category with the solidity of a name. The opening sentence of the important anthology *Directors on Directing*, edited by Toby Cole and Helen Krich Chinoy in 1953 (revised in 1963 and again in 1976), reminds us of the relative youthfulness of the category: 'Less than 100 years ago the director was only an ideal projected by disgruntled critics of the chaotic Victorian theatre. He did not even have a name, for the terms "director," "regisseur," and "metteur en scène" had barely begun to acquire their present theatrical meaning' (1976: 3). When the director did emerge with a name, Chinoy describes his entering gesture as one in which he 'stamped his individuality' on what had, before him, been a more varied stage.

Indeed, the mark of the individual eye, the signature of an individual visual guide, is often cited as *the* element distinguishing the modern director from what Chinoy calls 'stage manager only' – referring alike to nineteenth-century actor-managers, medieval sticklers, or Elizabethan and French neoclassical dramatist-directors. While the notion of a 'stage manager only' is worth contesting on a number of fronts, it is true that the notion of a director 'in the modern sense,' as Oscar Brockett puts it (1999: 97; 314), is most often discussed in relation to the organization of disparate elements into something resembling a unified whole, and most often – in terms of the modern – a decidedly *visual* whole.

The argument as to the primacy of vision is one familiar to the theorizing of modernism generally (the rise of photography and film and the crisis of 'the copy' vis à vis mechanical and technological reproduction). And yet the importance of the scratching mouse in Stanislavsky's 1901 production of Chekhov's *Three Sisters* (Stanislavsky 1948: 373; see also Chapter 4 in this volume) or the gauze curtains scrimming Lugné-Pöe's 1983 direction of Maurice Maeterlinck's *Pelléas and Melisande* might invite us to think that vision was not always primary for the modern director, but sometimes precisely contested. Still, even in contest, it is nevertheless relative to the general Western habituation to the perspectival (or pictorial) stage that the earliest modern directors plied their newly named trade. Though scratching mice and blurring gauze may be said to contest pictorial primacy, it is still arguably relative to the inherited visual thrall to perspectivalism that we see the distinct appellation of 'director' congeal. If 'directors' existed before the nineteenth century, it was the late nineteenth to early twentieth century that ushered in what Bettina Knapp has dubbed 'The reign of the theatrical director' (Chapter 2 in this volume, and 1988).

But who were the earliest modern directors setting the stage for this so-called reign? In 1903, French director André Antoine claimed that his art was conceived immaculately, claiming that 'Directing is an art that has just been born. Nothing – absolutely nothing – prior to the last century prefigured its emergence' (in Whitton 1987: 49). While he does admit vague precedent in the nineteenth century, his resounding 'nothing' may be too heavy handed. In the category of early 'directors' often cited are eighteenth- and nineteenth-century English actor/managers such as David Garrick, Charles Kemble, W. C. Macready, and Charles Kean; playwright/producers such as Johann Wolfgang Goethe (1749–1832) in Germany and Victor Hugo (1802–85) in France; and the early ensemble-leading duo of producer Duke Georg II of Saxe Meiningen and his manager Ludwig Cronegk at the Meiningen Court Theatre (1866–90) in Germany.[4]

Certainly the late nineteenth-century confluence (and stand-off) of the styles of naturalism and symbolism in Europe had an impact on the rise of directing as these emergent play forms apparently demanded strikingly different stagings.[5] The crucible of symbolism and naturalism also saw the genesis of the theatrical avant-garde, which is often historicized as occurring first in France at the hands of a playwright/director, Alfred Jarry. Symbolists and naturalists filled Lugné-Pöe's Théâtre de l'Oeuvre at the opening of Jarry's *Ubu Roi* in 1896 – and rioted when Jarry's lead actor, mimicking the playwright/director himself, crossed to the front of the stage and said, '*Merde.*' Indeed, the 1896 scandal that reverberated well into the twentieth century had as much to do with the play's direction as with the play presented – but this can be said to be true of Victor Hugo's 'direction' of his own riot-inciting *Hernani* at the Comédie Française sixty-six years earlier.

As mentioned above, the stage for the 'reign' of modern directing was set not only by individual artists, but by an increasing emphasis on visuality in modernity. The orientation toward the laws of perspective, a science of sight indebted to the Western stage as far back as the writings of Vitruvius in ancient Rome, was integral to developments in technologies of vision such as photography and film – developments which in turn exacerbated the emphasis on vision (or the contest against it) on the theatrical stage. The increasing polarization between viewer and viewed, a byproduct of technologies of vision and 'alienation' in industrialized urban society, contributed to a drive toward a director who could produce a 'communal' experience (Cole and Chinoy 1976: 3) – either through visual unity or through ritual effects.[6] The language of integration or of 'primitive' communion became prevalent among artists as diverse as Edward Gordon Craig and Antonin Artaud (see Innes 1993). Eventually, the irony that the generation of 'communal' harmony should be sought through an individual director and his imposed singular 'point of view' led some directors, later in the century, to see their role not as individual artists but as strictly the spokesperson for a mutually generative ensemble (see Shank, Chapter 25 in this volume). Other directors, conversely, became so bent on individual process that their theatres shed semblance of the communal either to become solo performance art or to resemble, even with a large cast, snapshots of their own individual minds (see Davy on Richard Foreman, Chapter 19 in this volume).

The terrain, in other words, is complex – directors who might seem profoundly distinct from one another become closely related when read as reacting to similar stimuli. Therefore, rather than provide a compendium of historical landmarks and discrete directing methodologies organized chronologically, this book explores the exciting, often contradictory links between varying directing aesthetics across the twentieth century. Rather than champion a narrative of evolution, we have chosen to embrace the recurrence and interconnectedness of a number of aesthetic positions. We found that in organizing *Re: direction* into four overlapping categories, intended as interpretive tools, we were able to avoid imposing one historical lineage, one narrative of 'progress,' upon an incredibly complex field of work. Because some directors included here could appear in several of our categories, we encourage readers to look for intersections. The four parts are I) Directors of classical revolt; II) Auteur theatre; III) Theatres of community and transculturation; and IV) Montage, reiteration, revision. Each of these sections will be prefaced by an introductory articulation of the category.

In Part I, 'Directors of classical revolt,' we have assembled practitioners as diverse as Antoine, Lugné-Pöe, Stanislavsky, Strasberg, Schneider, Meyerhold,

Brecht, The Living Theatre, Montano, and Boal. This group of essays raises questions regarding changing assumptions about 'naturalism' and artistic 'revolution' across the century. The opening essay by Bettina Knapp on French directors Antoine and Lugné-Pöe illustrates what might be called revolutionary impulses in *fin de siècle* directors' naturalist and symbolist works. We chose this as a starting place in part because many students of theatre assume that 'naturalism' has always been a popular mainstream activity. That naturalism, particularly, could ever have been contestatory, could ever have necessitated a manifesto such as Zola's impassioned 1877 treatise 'Naturalism in the theatre' (1963), causes many students pause – a pause we hope will lead to critical thinking about the century of deployments and of reactions to naturalism(s) that followed.

Indeed, that 'the modern director' should have emerged via contested practices of production is a fascinating element of theatre history, leading to the question of whether 'directing' is best when, as at its birth, it contains the sparks of experimentation. Proto-directors Goethe and Hugo were questioning the tenets of classicism in the previous turning century. Indeed, it is not difficult to argue that 'directing' itself arose from a spirit of revolution against the literary regulations of classicism, just as revolution (or a continual thrall to the new) would become classic in itself in the hands of modern avant-garde directors (see John Bell, Chapter 21 in this volume). 'Directors of classical revolt' is a title which hopes to point both to the revolt against neoclassicism at the start of what would become modern directing *and* the ways in which revolt, or revolution itself, became a kind of classic modal signature of twentieth-century modernism in general. Thus we use the term 'revolt' here in mulitple senses. We cite the sense of revolution, or turning away from 'congealed' theatrical practice toward a purportedly more promising future for the art – much in the way that Georg Fuchs used the term in his 1908 *Revolution in the Theater* to argue for a revitalization, indeed a 'retheatricalization' of the theatre, an aim shared by many theatre visionaries early in the century. However, at times, a more literal sense of revolt is appropriate here – not only in terms of the (violent) political revolutions in the West that incited and flamed this spirit, but also in the literal sense of the disrupting or inflammatory potential in citing and inciting 'revolt' as the French trajectory from Hugo's revolt against neoclassisim to Jarry's more literally revolting citation of *merde* might illustrate.

An essay such as Baxandall's 'The revolutionary moment' (written, not insignificantly, in 1968), works well to weave together issues that resurface throughout the first section, if not the entire book. It is interesting that Baxandall could claim in 1968 that 'naturalism is far from dead in America and Europe.' Certainly this continues to be true thirty-three years later. Baxandall shows the relationship between naturalism and revolution to be an extremely complex one. However, in 1968, 'revolution' was still considered by many to be a potential and viable goal, as underscored by Baxandall's revolutionary zeal when he claims that the Living Theatre, wedding art to life, 'boldly stepped beyond naturalism.' Indeed, Julian Beck famously claimed in 1971: 'We are the revolution; it is happening and we are all participating' (in Stoehr 1990: 17). We think Baxandall's essay is a useful historical document, especially when read in relation to the articles on directing practices much later in the century, when 'revolution' as political promise is far more suspect, as evident in the essays on the Wooster Group's 1991 *Brace Up!* (a production of Chekhov's *Three Sisters*), Schechner's 1996 production of *Three Sisters*, Pina

Bausch's reworking of classical naturalism through postmodern practice, or Reza Abdoh's 1994 *Quotations from a Ruined City*.[7] We want to suggest that if the sense of the viable possibilities of revolution changed between 1968 and the end of the century, some of the 'postmodern' implications of 'post-revolutionary' theatre nevertheless continue to produce a theatre in revolt – except perhaps the 'pomo' sense of revolution is one now spinning on itself so intensely that John Bell can claim that Abdoh's quoting of precedent avant-garde motifs can be considered 'post-post-modernist.' Why not post post post post – pick up some rhythm in the repetition – like Liz Diamond and Suzan-Lori Parks's 'rep and rev' collaboration in this collection? Here, reiteration, recitation, repetition, revolution *with a difference* take on distinctly post-'68 (though much older African-American) valences.

Without going through each section in detail, a discussion of our choices in the first section will give a sense of the logic of our selection. Our first section follows a line from the experimental revolution of naturalism in its French incarnation, through Russian naturalism where theatrical 'revolution' met, as evidenced in the difference between Stanislavsky and his student Meyerhold, the pressures of political revolution. We then move to naturalism in its American translation – through the eyes of Method acting founder, director Lee Strasberg, as he traveled to Russia and encountered various Russian theatres, including Meyerhold's. We then encounter Brecht, well known for his strategic use of naturalist detail *and* his investment in dialectical materialism. Through Baxandall, we then turn to consider naturalism in a different modality: the blurring of the line between art and life in 1960s 'revolutionary' works like the Living Theatre's or the performance work of Linda Montano. Such work might be read as involved with the effort to approach the 'natural' of life in the blur between art and life at its base – however, the concern with 'reality' in the Living Theatre (if not for Montano) is one pitched less toward representing the natural than toward change. As Judith Malina says regarding the group's direction of *Paradise Now!* in this volume: 'In Paradise, reality changes.' The interest in approaching 'reality' is evident again, if again quite differently, in Boal's 'Invisible Theatre.' Still, if impulses toward a 'natural' or 'real life' or 'everyday life' were revolutionary in any historical instance, at the close of the third section of the book we are reminded by Coco Fusco that 'revolutions' in aesthetic representation, like political revolutions, have a tendency to settle into normativity and institute a blindness to their effects.

Fusco is an important inclusion in this anthology because, while less apparently engaged in 'direction' than others, she makes quite apparent some of the political implications of Euro-American parsings of the 'natural' and 'unnatural,' drawing our attention to the ways these categories have been delineated precisely by display – the direction of point of view – whether on the art stage or in the ethnographic museum. The often fetishistic tendency of the early naturalist attempt to locate 'truth' in 'authenticity' on stage (Antoine's onstage sheep carcass comes to mind here, see Knapp, Chapter 2 in this volume) is brilliantly turned on its head in Fusco and Gómez-Peña's performance work. Fusco's 'The Other history of intercultural performance' is a chronicle of her 1992 international tour with Guillermo Gómez-Peña in which the pair exhibited themselves in a cage as 'two undiscovered Amerindians,' commemorating the 500-year anniversary of Columbus's explorations west. Like the spectators at the turn of the century, who feared for their lives when they saw the lifelike image of a moving train on a screen, Fusco reports that upon viewing the caged couple, spectators in Australia, not recognizing the performativity of the display, began to apologize for taking their land away. The aims and effects of naturalism must, it appears, be reread in hindsight. As Fusco puts it, the presentation of anything 'naturalized' deserves critical attention:

> For Gómez-Peña and myself, the human exhibitions dramatize the colonial unconscious of American society. [. . . The] naturalized, fetishized representations of Otherness, mitigates anxieties generated by the encounter with difference.

This mitigation against anxiety was also arguably what Brecht warned against decades earlier, when he fought against the notion of 'natural' material conditions, or social fate, even as he employed, theatrically, a profound attention to specific naturalistic details in production. Under Brecht's direction the presentation of the 'natural' was not meant to fetishize that natural *as natural*, but to incite critical attention to the ways in which the natural was deployed socially and politically for specific ends.

Unlike Brecht, however, Gómez-Peña and Fusco manipulate their critique beyond the realm of the modern director. Or do they? They are auteurs, directors, performers, artists and designers in one – in other words, performance artists. By including their work, like the work of Linda Montano, we are in some senses posing a question: At the end of the century, what has become of the seemingly stable notion, articulated by Chinoy, that a director orchestrates a 'harmonious' relation between text and image, crafts an outside view, provides an unseen eye? One thing that this anthology should make clear is that the category and role of the director, while certainly powerful and certainly linked to image-making or display, has never been absolutely stable – not, that is, if stability resembles stasis. Experimentation has always been basic to the role. There have been recurrent and important historical exceptions to the 'outside eye' model of directing, from Jarry to Meyerhold to Kantor to Foreman, all of whom have either appeared on their own stages, or 'staged' their own appearances, troubling the seemingly solid demarcation between stage and house, director and performer, author and auteur. Nevertheless, the question remains posed here, if unanswered: Is a critique of high modernism necessarily a critique of removed or disinterested visuality, otherness on display, or passive spectator positioning? If so, does such a critique automatically critique *directing at all*? Which is to ask: Is 'the director' not only a product of but coterminous with modernity and assumptions of 'newness,' even 'conquest' and 'progress'? It was the extraordinary Max Reinhardt (1873–1943), modern director par excellence, who approached theatre in every instance as a '*new world*,' open to the 'direction' of his vision (Cole and Chinoy 1976: 51). What becomes of the forward gaze of 'modern directing' when 'new worlds,' like the potential of revolution, are troubled? Is repetition and reiteration, evident in the 'postmodern' directing discussed here, fundamentally different from earlier revolutionary models? Or is it not?

We would like to close this introduction with some words of advice to the reader. We have included the dates and place of each essay's publication under the author's name in each instance. These dates are extremely important. Editorially, we chose to make very few alterations in the texts as they stand as historical documents.

Some essays are quite dated – would Baxandall get away, today, with suggesting that Eleanor Marx died from indirect complications of naturalism? Or with claiming that John Reed 'got the girl' from Eugene O'Neill because he was *not* a naturalist director? Other essays are not fully footnoted. In our efforts to recover citation we encountered fascinating issues of the difference between scholarship in a digital age and scholarship when paper was paper – including shifting attitudes toward the fissure between academic authority and the critic's role as artist or witness. Gerald Rabkin put it to us this way regarding his reencounter with his 1985 *PAJ* article 'Is there a text on this stage': 'You are aware that this article was written almost twenty years ago for a journal that then abjured scholarly apparatus. In a pre-computer age one did not clutter up one's files with manuscripts once an article was published; hence, I have no access to a fully cited original. And with the passage of time the precise sources of the various quotations are no more available to me than they are to you' (Rabkin 2001). The move away from 'scholarly apparatus' was, indeed, something that *TDR* had been instrumental in provoking in the 1960s in the interest of freeing the study of performance from what Schechner then called its 'enslavement' to literature – a provocation that incited several scholars to view the journal as 'anti-critical' (in McNamara 1983: 8; see the comments and letters in *The Drama Review* T23 through T26). That the study of performance would, in the later 1980s, return to rigorous citational practices is indicative not of a return to 'enslavement' but of the fact that academic criticism in general had, via the impacts of structuralism and poststructuralism, taken performativity profoundly into account.

We have also been keen to include here a variety of textual approaches to the topic of directing: from interviews with directors, to manifestos, logs, and program notes by directors, to critical descriptions of directors, to theoretical analyses. Sharon Marie Carnicke's analysis of translations of Stanislavsky's writings is followed by S. M. Stroyeva's account of Stanislavsky's direction of Chekhov's *Three Sisters*. Stroyeva is in turn followed by Lee Strasberg's account of his visit to Russia where, perhaps surprisingly, this architect of American Method acting does not encounter Stanislavsky but discovers, instead, Meyerhold, Vakhtangov, and Okhlopkov. Daniel Gerould's essay on Sergei Eisenstein's production of Ostrovsky's *Wiseman* is followed by Eisenstein's own manifesto, and Lee Baxandall's theoretical musings on the Living Theatre is followed by a Living Theatre rehearsal log. In one case, a director's career is intersected at radically different points. Kate Davy's account of two very early Richard Foreman productions is followed by Foreman's own program notes to his recent production of *Pearls for Pigs*. There are *three* texts on Charles Ludlam, each of them extraordinarily distinct. Ron Argelander gives us a relatively straightforward account of the Theatre of the Ridiculous, followed by a brief Ludlam manifesto, followed by Stefan Brecht's 1968 engagement with Ludlam's techniques in what stands as a remarkably prescient piece of proto-queer theory.

Finally, we are pleased that this anthology contains three descriptions of *Three Sisters*. That is, the book includes analyses of directorial decisions regarding one play in particular – Anton Chekhov's *Three Sisters* – neatly rounding off the century and providing points for comparison. The first, of course, is Stanislavsky's 1901 production at the Moscow Art Theatre. Next we include Euridice Arratia's thick description of Elizabeth LeCompte's direction of the play in 1991. The book closes with a review of Richard Schechner's production at LaMama in 1997. This final inclusion is particularly apt, as Schechner's influence in twenty-three years of editing *TDR* runs through this volume like a memory of Moscow: ever present.

Ithaca, New York
December 2000

NOTES

1 For an in-depth account of the history of *The Drama Review* and its editorship, written in 1983 on the occasion of its 100th (or, in actuality, 109th) issue see McNamara 1983.

2 If it seems a stretch to include performance artists under the appellation 'director,' consider that semiotician and theatre scholar Marco DeMarinis went so far as to suggest that the spectator is the 'director' of any production (1993). Indeed, in the light of poststructuralism in general, our categories of inclusion might even be called conservative.

3 See, for example, Schechner's incendiary *TDR* 'Comment: toward the 21st century' which begins 'The great era of playwriting is over.' We do well to remember that editor Schechner was also the director of the theatre ensemble the Performance Group (1967–80). This group was extremely influential on the performance group that grew out of it – the Wooster Group – a group well known for what many would call textual irreverence (see Rabkin, Chapter 37 in this volume).

4 Some refer to this duo as a trio, including the Duke's third wife, actress Ellen Franz, as she was very active in ways that might be called 'directorial.' See Osborne 1988.

5 That naturalist and symbolist plays demand different directing styles was, even at the turning century, debatable. In Russia, for example, Chekhov criticized Stanislavsky for ignoring the symbolism in his (naturalistic) plays and Meyerhold staged Ibsen's arguably realist *Hedda Gabler* with techniques of stylization closer to symbolism.

6 We do not here mean visual unity simply through pictorial facsimile, but a unity of all the elements in the visual field, organizing and associating all the senses relative to the visual grid. This notion of unified vision is more in line with the ways in which Appia argued for a director (or 'word-tone-poet') to produce Wagnerian *Gesamtkunstwerk*. See Appia 1962.

7 On some of the complexities in thinking about 'revolutionary theatre' in the late twentieth century see Marc Robinson and Joel Schechter's introduction to a special issue of *Yale Theater* devoted to the topic of 'Theater and revolution' (1990). See also Birringer 1991.

WORKS CITED

Appia, Adolphe (1962) *Music and the Art of the Theatre*. Miami: Miami University Press.

Birringer, Johannes (1991) 'Repetition and revolution: theatre anthropology after Brecht.' In *Theatre, Theory, and Postmodernism*. Bloomington: Indiana University Press.

Brockett, Oscar (1999) *History of the Theatre*. Boston: Allyn and Bacon.

Cole, Toby, and Helen Krich Chinoy, eds. (1976) *Directors on Directing*, Indianapolis: Bobbs-Merrill.

DeMarinis, Marco (1993) *The Semiotics of Performance*. trans. Aine O'Healy. Bloomington: Indiana University Press.

Fuchs, Georg (1959) *Revolution in the Theatre*, trans. Constance Connor Kuhn. Ithaca, NY: Cornell University Press.

Innes, Christopher (1993) *Avant Garde Theatre: 1892–1992*. London: Routledge.

Knapp, Bettina (1988) *The Reign of the Theatrical Director: French Theatre 1887–1924*. New York: Whitson.

McNamara, Brooks (1983) '*TDR*: memoirs of the mouthpiece, 1955–1983.' *TDR* 27, 4 (T100): 3–21.

Osborne, John (1988) *The Meiningen Court Theatre*. Cambridge: Cambridge University Press.

Rabkin, Gerald (2001) Email correspondence with Gabrielle Cody. 5 January.

Robinson, Marc, and Joel Schechter (1990) 'Theater and revolution: revolution from 1789–1989.' *Yale Theater* 21, 1 and 2: 4–5.

Schechner, Richard (1993) 'Comment: toward the 21st century.' *TDR* 37, 4: 7–8.

Stoehr, Taylor (1990) 'Paul Goodman, the Living Theatre, and the great despair.' *Yale Theater* 21, 1 and 2: 17–22.

Whitton, David (1987) *Stage Directors in Modern France*. Manchester: Manchester University Press.

Zola, Emile (1963) 'Naturalism in the theatre.' In *Documents in Modern Literary Realism*, ed. George Joseph Becker. Princeton: Princeton University Press.

Part I

DIRECTORS OF CLASSICAL REVOLT

1

INTRODUCTION TO PART I

Rebecca Schneider

The 'reign of the theatrical director,' as Bettina L. Knapp refers to the late nineteenth and early twentieth centuries, occurred in a contested field. The split in focus between the material detail of the naturalists and the abstract dreamscape of the symbolists at the last turning century would fracture into the thousand 'isms' that would compose twentieth-century modernism. Meyerhold, for example, included here in one of his incarnations, was responsible across a single career for the deployment of numerous stylistic 'isms' ranging from symbolism to stylization to the grotesque to constructivism.

Using the spine of 'revolt,' as explicated in depth in the General Introduction, this section moves in and around naturalism and its discontents and ultimately explores the movement off the stage and into the house with the 1960s complication between art, life, ritual, and politics that groups like the Living Theatre provoked. To end the section with Augusto Boal's 'Invisible Theatre,' an early strategy in his Theatre of the Oppressed, has a certain ironic appropriateness – almost a full circle revolution – when read in a lineage with Antoine's decision to hang real carcasses of sheep in his 1888 production of Icres' *Les Bouchers* (*The Butchers*). If Antoine and Stanislavsky worked to have their actors and props be so realistic as to become invisible *as theatre*, one of the ironies of the twentieth-century move out of the theatre and into 'real' life was the discovery of the theatrical bases, the performativity, of real life at all times. The lineage of 1960s performative actions in the theatre is most often linked to the theatrical avant-garde, stemming from futurism and dada and resulting in Happenings and Fluxus. Without denying that lineage, the force of this first section is to suggest other alliances as well, such as the link with early naturalist environmental theatre.

In the 1870s Zola's agenda was, in some ways, the first theatre anthropology. He insisted that by observing ourselves as we exist 'naturally' in our social environments we could come to know ourselves, and to know ourselves would be, presumably, to better ourselves (1963). Audiences began, like anthropologists on boats to the 'wilds,' to travel to the theatre to view private lives (often conceived as our own 'primitivity') in public, to observe domesticity reproduced in detail – our parlors, our kitchens, servants' quarters, master bedrooms. The plan for the naturalist theatre was, together with modern science generally, to improve the world through observation and deduction. We can chart this effort to take on the affect of real life in order to effect real life from Zola and Antoine to Stanislavsky's work, to his student Okhlopkov's move off the stage in early environmentalism, through the life/art work of much 1960s and 1970s work and on to Boal's melding of the divide between spectator/actor into his 'spectactor.' The result of drawing such a set of alliances is to watch the 'a' of affect slip and slide into the 'e' of effect, ultimately questioning the grounds for distinguishing between the two words at all.

One aim of naturalism, then, to affect real life in order to effect real life, swings on a pendulum between visibility and invisibility in complex and fascinating ways throughout the century. The move onto the streets or across the magic gulf, disappearing the boundaries between performative action and 'real' political action, can be read alongside fourth-wall theatre and the naturalist director's aim to have the actor, through methodological skill at focusing his own attention (Stanislavsky 1989: 72–94), disappear as an actor and meet or find the truth of his character. At the Moscow Art Theatre, audiences were encouraged to blind themselves to the performative bases of the display (or at least momentarily forget or 'suspend'), allowing those bases to become invisible. With *Paradise Now!* or with Richard Schechner's *Dionysus in '69*, however, we might not have been able to discern which were actors, which characters, and which were 'real' people as spectators, beckoned to join the action, took their clothes off, danced with, and caressed the cast and each other in the playing space. Both the MAT and Living Theatre, then, blurred the line between stage and house – one, ironically, through buttressing the fourth wall, the other through literally dismantling it.

It seems odd that Brecht's alienated performer might fit into this mix, but the connection with naturalism can be drawn from another angle. Brecht's directing practice, like Meyerhold's before him, privileged visible theatricality. Brechtian performers wield the 'natural' detail (such as Courage's belt buckle) in order to underscore it or make it appear *as* performance, or as performative, social and conscious *act*. Here we have the effort to make the performative bases of action visible, in order to bring to visibility the political consequences of choices in everyday life. Brecht thus shares with early naturalism the faith in observation and the effort to make the familiar visible, even if the end product aims to insure that that 'natural' or familiar is denaturalized, made strange. That is, Brecht worked to foreground that which we forget about the familiar – its strangeness. Showing the unnatural side of the 'naturalized' is linked to bringing the invisible to visibility – showing that the invisible-through-habit is in fact right before our eyes. So, while it may seem odd to suggest that theatre which privileges acute observation (Brecht's 'uncongealed eye') might be linked to a theatre which disappears as theatre, or which blurs the boundary between stage and house, nevertheless the tangle of visibility and invisibility of the seeming natural binds the practices together.

As we made clear in the General Introduction, directing arose relative to the perspectival, or pictorial stage, and flowered alongside the birth and development of cinema. The need to orchestrate vision – to provide an 'angle of viewing' as Lee Strasberg has written (1948: 119) – thus seems to be endemic to the job of director, be the production naturalist, symbolist, constructivist, etc. Given this, can there be such a thing as a director of *invisible* theatre? In Boal's theatre of the oppressed, the director becomes a 'joker' whose focus is not on an end product in terms of an observable show, but on a never-ending 'rehearsal for revolution' (Boal 1985). Still, the links between director in production, joker in rehearsal, or performance artist in life/art installations may not be entirely bogus. Our opening section offers a genealogy that takes us from Antoine's external naturalism to Stanislavsky's radical inward move toward the subconscious life of the character/actor, through to a theatre which becomes invisible, at least to the degree that it troubles the distinction between performativity and actuality, or theatricality and everyday life.[1] The 'angle of viewing' became, early on, intimately bound to the 'angle of veiling.' As early as Stanislavsky, the director's attempt to angle vision had gained in complexity to 'angle' the invisible as well as the given to be seen.

Throughout this section the question of whether reality is 'enough' – as Alan Schneider puts it here – is key, as is the drive toward political change that splits naturalist theatres between a Stanislavskian effort simply to show life as it is or a more Meyerholdian effort to incite political activism (see Braun 1986: 22–8 on the apolitical aims of Stanislavsky as compared with Meyerhold). The conflicts between the dreamscapes of symbolism and the everyday life-scapes of naturalism at the 'revolutionary' beginnings of director's theater are never quite resolved, as we think these essays articulate. The push and pull between articulating utopian dream (the Living Theatre's 'paradise') or quotidian life is very evident in the Living Theatre notes for *Paradise Now!* (Chapter 11), for example.

And finally, throughout this section, the question of 'basics' in theatre is quite important to the artists – even when the 'basic' is not the naturalistic detail of everyday life but something far more basic (even natural) to the theatre itself – a *basic theatricality*, almost in the sense of Grotowski's 'poor theatre.' Consider the following excerpt from Nick Worrall's essay on Meyerhold included in this collection. According to Worrall, Meyerhold was concerned to offer what he saw as natural to the creative process of exchange in the theatre:

> a new kind of stage acting [that] was not, in the terms of someone like Artaud, a signaling through the flames of a destructive universe, but a communication of *basics* now that the inessentials, the accumulation of centuries, had been cleared from the stage, together with the canvas and the costumes, the scenery, the drapery, the masking, the footlights, the cyclorama, the borders, the whole paraphernalia that had served to frame the flow of history as it passed in steady sequence across the enclosed proscenium arch stage during the previous 300 years or so. What was being signaled was a *basic-ness* about a human condition and a setting as starting points from which meanings could be jointly created by actors and audience through means which acknowledged the creative powers of each.

The issue of the creative powers of exchange between actors and audience, important to Meyerhold's 'theatre of the straight line' positions the director as conduit to this exchange, not as sole coordinator of a primarily visual event (Meyerhold 1969: 50). Other essays in this section show very clearly that the issue of exchange between playwright and director is one that can 'acknowledge the creative powers of each,' as the interview by Richard Schechner with Alan Schneider about Schneider's choices as director of Beckett's plays suggests. Schneider interestingly finds himself in somewhat of a 'middle' between the 'basic' naturalism of Stanislavsky and the 'basic' theatricality of Meyerhold: 'my whole position, philosophical or aesthetic, if I have any – is that, to the theatricalist guys, I tend to be a realistic director, a Stanislavski-oriented director; to the Stanislavski guys, I'm a theatricalist director.' Schechner then asks him: 'Who are you to you?' To this Schneider replies: 'I think I'm in the middle. I think that's a weakness and a virtue.' While Schneider does not seem to be precisely in revolt, one can read his choices relative to the creative ferment of revolution that produced the category of 'director' which he fulfills.

NOTE

1 On the meaning of 'performativity' and its relation to performance see J. L. Austin (1959) and Sedgwick and Parker (1995).

WORKS CITED

Austin, J. L. (1959) *How to Do Things with Words.* Cambridge, MA: Harvard University Press.

Boal, Augusto (1985) *Theatre of the Oppressed.* New York: Routledge.

Braun, Edward (1986) *The Theatre of Meyerhold: Revolution on the Modern Stage.* London: Methuen.

Meyerhold, Vsevlod (1969) *Meyerhold on Theatre,* ed. Edward Braun. New York: Hill and Wang.

Sedgwick, Eve Kosofsky, and Andrew Parker, eds. (1995) *Performativity and Performance.* New York: Routledge.

Stanislavsky, Constantin (1986) *An Actor Prepares.* New York: Routledge.

Strasberg, Lee (1948) 'The director.' In *The Theatre Handbook,* ed. Bernard Sobel. New York: Crown Publishers.

Zola, Emile (1963) 'Naturalism in the theatre.' In *Documents in Modern Literary Realism,* ed. George Joseph Becker. Princeton: Princeton University Press.

2

THE REIGN OF THE THEATRICAL DIRECTOR
Antoine and Lugné-Pöe

Bettina L. Knapp

The French Review,[1] 1988

1887: the founding of the Théâtre Libre by André Antoine; 1893: the birth of Aurelien Lugné-Pöe's Théâtre de l'Oeuvre. Two memorable dates in the history of the performing arts. Two noteworthy theatres on whose stages France and the world were to witness not only innovative theatrical performances, but also the beginnings of the *reign of the theatrical director*. There had been, to be sure, directors of all types throughout the centuries in France. Molière, for example, was the greatest of them all. But since his time, few French directors had captured the attention of dramatists, performers, and the *tout Paris*; still fewer had created styles of their own, bringing fresh insights into the performance of multiple genres of international scope. Antoine enlarged the ideals, mission, and function of the theatrical director; so, too, did Lugné-Pöe.

A memorable date in French theatre was 30 March 1887. It marked the opening performance of Antoine's newly founded Théâtre Libre. On that momentous night, Antoine offered spectators a new brand of realism/naturalism: a *slice of life* production that brought audiences face to face with themselves and with their environment. Decors followed the patterns of reality. A revolutionary acting technique was also instituted on that night: actors and actresses no longer declaimed in stiff and studied ways, as was the style in state-subsidized and boulevard theatres. They walked and talked, comported themselves on stage as they did in shops, on the streets, and in their homes. [. . .] Nor did performers upstage each other. Antoine had abolished the star system. His company worked as a unit – a cohesive whole.

Not exclusively one-sided, Antoine's tastes were eclectic. He invited Parnassians, Symbolists, Decadents, and Humorists to contribute their dramas to his creative enterprise. One cardinal rule prevailed, at least at the outset of the Théâtre Libre: the works of mostly untried and unpublished authors would be staged, thereby giving a creative and motivated young person a chance in life. Broadminded in every way and an internationalist, Antoine was the first French director to produce plays by foreign authors, for the most part, Slavic, Scandinavian, and German.

[. . .] Antoine had sufficient energy to overcome the nearly insurmountable obstacles facing a person who went counter to the trends of his day. Commercial theatre, Antoine remarked numerous times, was vapid, arid, and sterile – it wallowed in mediocrity. He would change all this and create a theatre which would be meaningful to his audiences, stir and perhaps even shock them into a new state of awareness. Antoine produced 112 plays as director of the Théâtre Libre (1887–94). Although he offered audiences a preponderance of naturalistic, realistic, and psychological dramas (Zola, Goncourt, Alexis, Duranty, Hennique, Méténier, Porto-Riche, Curel, Brieux), lyrical, poetic, and symbolistic plays were also included (Bergerat, Villiers de l'Isle Adam, Banville, Mendès). His productions were performed only three times: a dress rehearsal, an opening night for invited guests, and a performance for subscribers.

I have chosen three of Antoine's most typical productions for review here: Emile Zola's *Jacques Damour*, Oscar Méténier's *En famille*, and Tolstoy's *The Power of Darkness*.

Although a much-admired novelist, Zola failed as a dramatist, his plays being overly static, devoid of poetry, paper-thin characterizations. *Jacques Damour* (1880), adapted for the stage by Léon Hennique, differed from the former: it was dramatic in essence, focusing on a man struggling against his 'evil' instincts.

Visibly influenced by Balzac's *Colonel Chabert*, Zola's drama tells the story of Jacques, a communard and fugitive, who was thought to have been drowned during his attempted escape from New Caledonia. Some time after his departure, a death certificate is given to his wife. She marries a butcher after which a daughter is born to them. A few years later, much to the astonishment of all, Jacques returns and wants to assume what he considers to be his rightful place as husband to his wife. His inner struggle becomes acute when he realizes that were he to yield to his wishes, he would be destroying a loving and harmonious household. After much soul-searching, he leaves, sacrificing his happiness for his wife's well-being.

Antoine portrayed Jacques as a stern and grim man: tragic, like many a Greek hero destroyed by destiny. Although pain is explicitly expressed in the part, Antoine underplayed the highly emotional situations on stage, thereby increasing the impact of his character's inner tension. His facial expressions ranged from euphoria, at the sight of his wife whom he has not seen in so many years, to dread, when he discovers she has married, to anger which takes hold when he wrestles with his own conscience. Antoine's controlled gestures and stance point up the protagonist's deeply pathetic situation. So deeply did he feel his character that he confessed to having been oblivious of the audience – even to his own nervousness. Another being inhabited him: Jacques Damour walked the planks at the Théâtre Libre.

[. . .] Antoine had also taken special pains with his *mise-en-scène*. Everything had to be just right. Without any funds to spare, Antoine asked his mother for permission to borrow her dining-room furniture (a table and chairs) to use for sets. She agreed. On the night of the dress rehearsal, after finishing his work at the Gas Company, a friend lent Antoine a hand-cart which enabled him to take the furniture himself down the tortuous streets to Krauss's theatre. Unable to afford real props and accessories, Antoine had to resort to *trompe-l'oeil* which he would rarely use in future productions. The backdrop for *Jacques Damour* depicted chunks of meat, immediately situating the drama in a butcher's shop (Roussou 1954: 69).[1]

Zola, visibly moved – 'enchanted' – by Antoine's production, expressed his admiration in no uncertain terms. When, right after the curtains rung down Hennique led 'le maître' on stage, Zola backed Antoine into a corner and told him point blank that his performance was very fine indeed, and that he would return the following night. Antoine was so shaken by the shock of it all that he could only stammer his gratitude (Antoine 1964: 81).

Antoine asked the future founder of the Grand Guignol, the ultra-naturalist Oscar Méténier, to produce his one-act prose play, *En famille* (1887). Already known for his volume of short stories, Méténier's dramatic work focuses on the *tranche de vie apache* style. Comparable in theme to the songs his contemporary, Aristide Bruant, performed in his café, Le Mirliton, *En famille* singled out the wretched of the earth – the prostitutes, drug addicts, murderers, prisoners, criminals – for description, for compassionate and dramatic reasons. Bruant, who had lived among the derelicts and the poverty stricken, and Méténier, as secretary to a police commissioner, knew well the complex feelings inhabiting these pariahs. The real and the evidential rang true, therefore, in *En famille*.

Thugs, cut-throats, rag-pickers, and receivers of stolen objects inhabited the stage of the Théâtre Libre, a fitting background for the sharply delineated characters. Antoine, playing Father Paradis, [the actors] performed with all the rage, hate and cruelty demanded of their roles; but also with the understanding and love buried beneath their sordid and brutal exteriors.

The decors featured a rustic wooden table upon which a whitish cloth has been placed; some glasses and plates. Four and sometimes five protagonists are seated around this central and focal object. All sorts of stolen objects are visible in the background of this den of iniquity. [. . .] Nor are audiences spared the coarse and vulgar vocabulary implicit in the dialogue of *En famille*: the argot of the drunken and besotted rejects of humanity crying out their despair – their disgust with the world – is used unsparingly. The expression of adversity written over their faces, emphasized by subtle but expert use of make-up, paves the way for the play's climactic description of the execution of a family friend. The monologue revolving around the guillotine happening, new for the theatre, sent shock waves throughout the audience.

[. . .] Dumas predicted failure as soon as Antoine announced his decision to produce Tolstoy's *The Power of Darkness* (1886). First and foremost, it was far too melancholy a play for French audiences to digest; second, not one of the characters was sympathetic. Although a cruel truth and real beauty are implicit in Tolstoy's drama, Sardou remarked, he felt that this kind of work should be read and not staged. Augier considered it less a play than a novel in dialogue form; its length alone made it impossible for a French stage (Antoine 1964: 61).

[. . .] That Tolstoy's play had been banned from the stage in Russia might also have whetted Antoine's appetite: he reacted powerfully to such a challenge. There were difficulties involved in staging *The Power of Darkness*. In certain scenes, twenty-two characters would be on stage at the same time; their movements had to be handled both dramatically and with clarity of purpose; an ambience of Russian peasantry had to be created on stage, otherwise the play would surely fail. The first problem was resolved by his talent as director; the second, by a strange quirk of fate. Russian political refugees had recently arrived in France and were willing to give him their native costumes for the occasion. The colorful fabrics on stage lent just the perfect note to the dramatic event.

The Power of Darkness is an example of *direct theatre*. It attempts to communicate with all types of audiences, both untutored and educated. Tolstoy, who wanted brutal moujiks to be moved and purified by stage happenings in general, and by his play in particular, considered theatre a moralizing agent – an edifying experience. In 'What is art?' (1897), a study on aesthetics, he stated that since theatre is a human activity, it must have some *value* and, therefore, serve people. Art 'is a means of union among men, joining them together in the same well-being of individuals and of humanity' (in Simmons 1946: 538). [. . .]

Tolstoy's play was based on a grim incident which had taken place near his estate in 1880. A peasant told the guests assembled at his stepdaughter's marriage that he had killed the child he had by her and then tried to kill the six-year-old daughter he had had with his wife. Tolstoy, whose goal was to underscore the dark and hidden areas of the human soul and psyche, succeeded in his adaptation of the incident to suit his needs.

In Act I we learn that the thirty-seven-year-old peasant, Nikita, has seduced the young Marina. After abandoning her, he became the lover of Anissia, the wife of Petr Ignatitch, his master. When Nikita's mother, Metrena, learns of the illicit relationship and realizes that Anissia cannot get along without Nikita, she tries to make the most of the situation. She suggests that Anissia poison her husband Petr and marry Nikita.

The crime takes place in Act II. Anissia is calm and collected as she blends some poison with her insomniac husband's sleeping medicine, and then watches him writhe in pain. With complacency, she steals Petr's money before he dies and gives it to Nikita to put in a safe place. They marry and pay for the wedding feast with the stolen money. Soon Nikita becomes Akoulina's lover, Petr's young daughter from a first marriage. Anissia cannot bear such a situation and decides to find the now-pregnant Akoulina a husband. They hide her condition from her peasant fiancé and a large dowry makes the relationship acceptable.

In succeeding acts, Anissia and Metrena, her mother-in-law, convince Nikita, the guilty and adulterous father, to kill his newborn infant. He will do so in a barn and simultaneously with the wedding ceremony. Fearful lest he be discovered, he quickly digs a hole in the cellar of the building. Meanwhile Anissia brings him the baby. When she notices his hesitation, she resorts to threats. It is then that he decides to go through with the murder: he throws the crying infant on the ground, places a wooden beam over him, sits on it and crushes him to death. The scene was so realistic that audiences could actually hear the bones of the dead baby cracking. Nikita, terrified by his deed, rushes out, leaving his wife and mother to bury the infant. He interrupts the wedding ceremony, confesses his crime, begs Akoulina and others he had deceived for their forgiveness and accepts his punishment of forced labor as expiation.

Antoine, whose goal was not to give audiences lessons in morality, but rather to perform fine plays, cut sections of Tolstoy's work which he thought French audiences might find tedious: the lengthy confessions which slowed down the pace. Like Greek tragedy, *The Power of Darkness* bore within its plot and characterizations mythic and mystic qualities. For great theatre to be born, Antoine believed, truth alone – and not idealism – must live on stage.

Melodramatic as well as mystical elements abound in *The Power of Darkness*. Unlike French thrillers, where crimes are multiple and extreme, and endings climactic and most usually positive, the sequences and tenor in Tolstoy's work are grave. The graphic nature of the happenings – the drunken scenes, the poisoning, and the infanticide – was devastating in power and horror and portentous in intent. Its spiritual message – the protagonist's redemption or ascension toward light after his crime – lends a supernatural aura to the entire work.

Although Sarcey had reservations about the play, he not only admired Antoine's production of *The Power of Darkness*, but was also moved by the verisimilitude of the atmosphere created on stage and by the acting. He suggested, however, that unlike Aeschylus and Sophocles, whose poetic flights were masterful, Tolstoy's language was repetitious, even whiny and bathetic at times. The Russian writer does not succeed in evoking the terror and pity, which are Aristotle's parameters for tragedy. Because Tolstoy's creatures are inferior, living as they do on an instinctual and animal level, they cannot evoke the sympathy of cultured spectators (Prunier 1958: 30).

Zola approved of Antoine's production. It inspired him to write some of the grueling scenes in his novel *La Terre*. Adolphe Brisson was astounded by Tolstoy's understanding of the psychological factors and motivations involved. He was also impressed by the fact that *The Power of Darkness* transcended the usual theatrical clichés. It disoriented viewers, creating a kind of malaise among the spectators – a positive comment on Brisson's part since he felt it forced the people watching the play to think about their own bestial ways and perhaps do something to remedy them.

The consensus as to the acting? Never had a play been better served. Mevisto as Nikita was the paradigm of the moujik: savage and ferocious, boorish and churlish. When drunk, he was scurrilous and obscene, his foulness reaching unheard-of proportions. Mevisto's incredible portrait was the outcome of his own natural gifts and intelligence. He had allowed his imagination free rein; it had not been repressed or spoiled, Antoine remarked, by traditional theatrical training. On the contrary, the performers at the Théâtre Libre were taught a new view of acting based on reality and naturalness – and *experience*.

Antoine as Akim, the devout, addle-pated, besotted, old fool of a father, was commended for his fine performance. Enclosed as he is in his narrow religiosity, he stutters along throughout the play, broaching only two subjects: God and cesspools. It is he who stands for consciousness and morality and encourages Nikita to confess at the end.

The sets were rustic with the usual fireplace at the far end of the stage, benches on the side, tables, and chairs. What did upset some critics, however, was Méténier's translation. Rather than trying to render the flavor of Russian peasantry, he used slang of the *faubourgs* of Paris. A corruption of the refined language used in city life, it in no way conveyed the primitive language of the moujik and, they argued, on this level, lost the real flavor of Tolstoy's Russian play.

Aurélien Lugné, known to the theatre as Lugné-Pöe, the last name having been added ostensibly out of admiration for the American writer, was as indefatigable, as zealous, and as innovative as Antoine, in whose company he performed. Like Antoine, Lugné-Pöe was drawn to the avant-garde; unlike him, he was taken with symbolist and impressionist *mise-en-scènes*. His vision of the theatre went beyond the visible world, directly into the occult, sometimes nightmarish, transcendental domains. His goal, he wrote, was to bring the work of art to the theatre and to stir ideas. As founder and director of the Théâtre de l'Oeuvre, his productions included works of Maeterlinck, Rachilde, Bataille, Shakespeare, Jarry, Ibsen, Gogol, and Sanskrit dramatists.

A look at three of Lugné-Pöe's productions would be instructive: Henri de Régnier's *La Gardienne*, Maurice Maeterlinck's *Intérieur*, and Shudraka's *The Little Toy Cart*.

A symbolist in Mallarmé's entourage, Régnier wrote verses in *La Gardienne* (1894) that were virtually unintelligible. Audiences neither heard nor understood the modulations of the sonorities, rhythms, or multiple nuances of meanings inherent in the images. The evanescent beauty and charm, the fleeting sensations of Régnier's lines were lost to all those unfamiliar with the poet's work.

The green gauze curtain and the greenish lunar hues for *La Gardienne* created the desired eerie and mysterious mood. They also triggered vague and evanescent qualities in the spectator's unconscious, paving the way through suggestion for the dream world to come into being. Jules Lemaître was taken with Vuillard's painted backdrop: a dreamy landscape, with blue trees, a violet palace, a Puvis de Chavannes-like fresco (Lugné-Pöe 1894).

The *mise-en-scène* was innovative. The stage area had been divided into two separate parts: the reciters were hidden in the orchestra pit while the actors, remaining silent, stood on stage behind a green gauze veil. As the latter replicated the feelings enunciated below in slow pantomimic language, such vocal and visual dichotomies increased the already intense sense of remoteness and mystery inherent in the play. By severing tone from the optical image in his *mise-en-scène*, Lugné-Pöe accentuated a malaise already present in Régnier's poetry. Because the voices and pantomime were not synchronized, the technical aspect of the production was faulty. The words frequently preceded or trailed behind the gestures, inviting waves of laughter to ripple forth at the wrong times, disconcerting both performers and those in the audience who were familiar with Régnier's poems.

Although *La Gardienne* was considered one of Lugné-Pöe's 'follies,' the techniques used in his *mise-en-scène* would be copied by many a twentieth-century writer, such as Apollinaire, Cocteau, Strindberg, O'Neill, and Anouilh.

Maeterlinck's *Intérieur* (1895) is a meditation on death. The play's action takes place in a house, visible through three ground-floor windows, and in a garden in front of the mansion. The family inside the house consists of a father, a mother holding a baby in her lap, and two young girls dressed in white. These characters do not speak; they merely rise, walk, gesticulate in 'grave slow, sparse' ways, as though they had been 'spiritualized by distance.' In the garden are an Old Man, his two daughters, and a Stranger. They are talking, trying to determine the best way of breaking the terrible news (death by drowning of a daughter) to the seemingly peaceful family within.

The emphasis Lugné-Pöe placed on the mimetic art was unsettling. The dialogue in the garden, consisting almost exclusively of a series of comments and conversations concerning the family in the house, creates a close rapport between those outside and the emotions expressed through bodily movements of the people within. The dissociation of speech and action, novel for the period though it had been tried in *La Gardienne*, breaks to a certain extent the conventional empathy usually existing between actor and audience. Although distance separates those inside and outside the house as well as the house and the stage, and though speech is dissociated from action, the thoughts articulated by the Old Man and the Stranger are for some inexplicable reason sensed by those in the house and mirrored in their pantomime, in a kind of active silence. One wonders if 'in the house' might have suggested audience as well. When, for example the Old Man and the Stranger speak of the corpse that was found in the lake the two sisters in the house turn their heads toward the window as though aware of some mysterious feelings, some excruciating anticipation. [. . .]

L'Intérieur is an extraordinary and excoriating work. The inevitability of death is made so powerful by both the stage happenings and the pace of the drama as to become unbearable. The contrast between the peaceful family scene visible through the window, and the sorrowful news that must invade this atmosphere accelerates in intensity as the drama unfolds, reaching its apogee at the end. As in classical drama, all unessential material has been eradicated, leaving only the play's theme (the obligation of informing the family of death) as essential.

[. . .] Lugné-Pöe's production of the Sanskrit play, *The Toy Cart* (1895), revealed his proclivity for both the esoteric and the eclectic. Written by the mythical king Shudraka, supposedly between the first century BC and the first century AD, *The Toy Cart* as produced by Lugné-Pöe at the Théâtre de l'Oeuvre fulfilled a need in Parisian audiences for the different and the remote. Critics such as Rappel responded for the most part favorably to the 'exquisitely sentimental and lyrical sequences' – particularly those which emphasized the purity of the child and the beauty of altruistic love.

Many in the audience – particularly the symbolists and Parnassians who had been students of Indian culture and philosophy – were familiar with the mysteries and marvels of this ancient land. Edouard Schure published his syncretistic work, *Great Initiates*, in 1889, in which he pointed up parallels between Hindu beliefs and contemporary spiritual views. So, too, had Leconte de Lisle, Michelet, Maeterlinck, and countless other creative spirits gone back in time probing long-forgotten eras, so as to broaden and deepen their views. What intrigued theatre people most intensely were the complex rules and conventions involved in Indian performing arts. These had been laid down by the legendary sage Bharata (first century BC to AD 2) in a thirty-chapter work, *Natyasastra* (*The Art of the Theatre*). For the Hindu, theatre is a rite of passage which takes an individual from one state of being to another. The spectacle, therefore, is not to be considered merely a work of art, entertainment, or an object to be admired for its fine craftsmanship and expert character delineation, but rather as an experience to be absorbed and assimilated, one which gives its participants spiritual nourishment.

Partly historical and partly fictional, like other Sanskrit theatrical works, *The Toy Cart* fuses word, music, song, dance, action, and iconography. Unlike Western theatre, the aim of Sanskrit theatrical performance is to create in the spectator a feeling of aesthetic delight (*rasa*) expressed not through words exclusively but via suggestion and the combination of art forms. *Rasa* means 'flavor' or 'relish' and refers to aesthetic or sensual taste and emotional sensitivity. An abstract transpersonal perception, *rasa* comes into being via symbols and auditory sensation. What is crucial, then, in Sanskrit theatre is the sensual evocation of emotions and not the story-line or the characters. The protagonists are not considered real. They are prototypes, idealizations, portraying certain basic human feelings (*bhava*) as concretized in specific situations.

Symbolists, mystics, avant-gardistes, elitists, and literati of all schools were fascinated by *The Toy Cart*, for reasons of aesthetic and philosophical interest, for political reasons through identification of its theme with anarchical values, or for snob appeal. After all, how many had seen Sanskrit theatre before?

Certain episodes were singled out for praise. In the third act, a child is seen crying because he only has a clay cart with which to play while another has one made of gold. When a beautiful young courtesan, Vasantasena, sees him so sad, she takes off her magnificent jewel and places it in his little chariot, transforming the vulgar object into a precious entity. So, too, may all things in the world of contingencies be elevated in value: destiny divests some in order to enrich others. The gentility and tenderness of the courtesan, as Lugné-Pöe had her make her way most unobtrusively to the child, and the child's amazement as he sees the miracle occurring before his eyes, found favor with the great majority of critics.

[. . .] Toulouse-Lautrec designed the much admired program cover and the backdrop for the play. Unfortunately, its pastel colorations and luxurious tones were barely visible from the orchestra because of the extreme subdued lighting on stage. In keeping with Hindu tradition, the decors were so sparse as to be virtually nonexistent. Since Hindu drama is suggestive it needs only a few symbolic items to carry out the meaning and philosophical impact of the work. The toy cart, sculpted by Henry Cros, therefore stood out.

Reactions to Lugné-Pöe's production were mixed. Erik Satie, formerly a Rosicrucian who had severed his relations with this group in 1892 to found his own church, the Metropolitan Church of Art of Jesus the Leader (the purpose of which was to foster art, beauty, and morality), was offended by the production. He wrote Lugné-Pöe a scathing letter in which he condemned him for having sinned against the higher values of art. The nudity he had seen on stage was unacceptable. The author of an article in *La Plume* (1893), seeking to quell such remonstrances, labeled the composer '*Erik Sottise*.' Others, such as Romain Coolus, dramatic critic for *La Revue Blanche*, conveyed his gratitude to Lugné-Pöe for the extraordinary beauty of the work produced, which proved once again the '*jeunesse infléchissable*' of this ancient drama. Jules Lemaître's critique was positive: a masterpiece, he declared, and 'nothing in Greek, English and French theatre appeared to him superior to this Indian comedy' (Lemaître 1891: 27). Although the ramifications of the subtleties of Sanskrit theatre and culture escaped him, and he erroneously confused Dumas's and Hugo's depictions of the redeemed courtesan with Hindu metaphysics on the subject, he was impressed by the aesthetic message of the play. Silvain Lévi, the author of *Le Théâtre indien* (1890), was disturbed by the distortions made by Victor Barrucand, the play's adapter. Not sufficient stress was placed on the Hindu's disdain for the real world, considered an illusion; nor would Vasantasena, he suggested, ever feel intimately connected or related to society's untouchables, as she was purported to be in the French adaptation. Others, like Mallarmé and Gustave Kahn, commented on the beauty of the adaptation: its language was able to convey finesse and graciousness and also to express so well the essential paradox of the courtesan, who not only humbles but impoverishes herself so as to become worthy of her lover, while still remaining a paradigm of sensuality. [. . .]

The talents, energies, and drive of Antoine and Lugné-Pöe brought fresh and vital works to the stage, while also injecting new life into classical texts. Plays by foreign authors – Ibsen, Strindberg, Tolstoy, Hauptmann, Gogol, Wilde, Poe, and more – were accepted for production by Antoine, Lugné-Pöe, and Copeau, lending an international flavor to their endeavors. Painters, such as Vuillard, Bonnard, Toulouse-Lautrec, Forain, Signac, and Munch, were invited to create backdrops and sets, bringing greater artistry to their productions.

Prior to the advent of Antoine and Lugné-Pöe few had been given the opportunity to imprint their stamp on productions. The choice of plays to be performed became their responsibility, as did the casting, costuming, lighting, decors, and *mise-en-scène*. Directing, as they practiced this art, became a stunning outlet for their talents. [. . .]

NOTE

1 Indeed in 1888 when Antoine staged Icres's *Les Bouchers* (*The Butchers*), he hung real carcasses of mutton, impaled on hooks, on stage – an aesthetic gesture of naturalism that struck many viewers as excessive. (Editors' note.)

WORKS CITED

Antoine, André (1964) *André Antoine's 'Memories of the Théâtre Libre'*, trans. Marvin A. Carlson. Coral Gable, FL: University of Miami Press.

La Plume, 6 August 1893.

Lemaître, Jules (1891–6) *Impressions de théâtre*. Paris: Sociéte d'imprimerie et de librairie.

Lugné-Pöe, Aurélien (1894) *Journal des Débats*. 24 June.

Prunier, Francis (1958) *Le Théâtre Libre d'Antoine*: *(1) le répertoire étranger; (2) les luttes d'Antoine*. Paris: Minard.

Roussou, Matei (1954) *André Antoine*. Paris: L'Arche.

Simmons, Ernest (1946) *J. Leo Tolstoy*. Boston: Little, Brown.

3

STANISLAVSKY
Uncensored and unabridged

Sharon Marie Carnicke

T137, 1993[1]

Pronounce the name of Stanislavsky and you invoke mythic images: a grand-fatherly teacher in a *pince-nez* who reveals the secrets of great acting to insecure young students; a strict disciplinarian who demands total commitment to art; a great realistic director who harnesses the truths embedded in plays and in actors' souls. The force of these myths in the United States is discharged not only in theatrical circles but also in popular culture. Audiences do not need to study theatre to get the central joke in *Outrageous Fortune*, a film in which Shelley Long and Bette Midler vie for places in an acting class taught by a man with a mysterious East European accent and a name suspiciously like Stanislavsky's (Dixon 1987). This is our image of the *ur* acting teacher. Nor are the references to the Method in *Tootsie* lost on the wider public. In this film Dustin Hoffman, himself a member of the Actors Studio, plays an actor who has been fired for conscientiously but inappropriately applying the Method in his work (Gelbard and Schisgal 1982).[2]

While nurtured by a dissimilar cultural context, remarkably similar images of the great realistic director and acting teacher developed in the Soviet Union. By the 1930s Soviet newspaper headlines heralded Stanislavsky with mythic praise. He was 'Our Pride' (Yura 1938: 412), 'The Genius of Theatre' (Derman 1938), 'The Creator of Realistic Theatre' (Khailov 1938), on the front lines of 'The Battle for Realism' (Gus 1938) as a 'Tribune of Scenic Truth' (Grigor'ev 1938).

The commercial, political, and social circumstances which so successfully nurtured these myths have also made it difficult to find the man behind the image. Theoretically, one might expect Stanislavsky's books to serve as corrective to mythic distortions. Couldn't we simply test our common knowledge of him against his written word? While this approach might be normal and scholarly in most cases, in Stanislavsky's case his books raise a new set of questions. To date, his writings have been published in modified versions that present at best partial and at worst distorted views of his ideas. The same circumstances that proved fertile ground for mythmaking stifled access to written information.

In the Soviet Union, censorship and suppression of writings that ran counter to the official Party rule encouraged a modified and retouched portrait of the artist. Stanislavsky courageously fought against these incursions into his books, and in great measure won significant victories. Thus the standard edition of his *Collected Works* (1954–61), while satisfying the Party line in some measure, still represented the best source of written information. This edition never found its way into English.

In the United States, commercial publishers rejected subtle and complicated explanations of the experiential nature of acting in favor of more widely marketable books, insuring that his writings appear in highly abridged and modified versions. For example, *An Actor Prepares* was accepted for publication only upon condition that it be shortened and that all Russian references too obscure for an American readership be cut. In the United States, Stanislavsky acceded to commercial demands in part because he desperately needed money and in part because he could not read English. Thus, in most cases the standard English versions of his texts vary significantly from the Russian books.

In addition to pressures of publication, Stanislavsky himself complicated the situation. He was constantly evolving his theories, never satisfied with answers he had found to even the most essential questions. He agonized over every word, repeatedly revising and revamping every page. He thought of everything he wrote as 'working notes for the actor.'[3] He left behind largely unfinished drafts, alternate passages, and endless revisions, every page of his manuscripts and typescripts revealing his tortured and obsessive work. Desperate to meet publishing deadlines, he relied upon a series of editors to finish his books, including a Russian émigré, Aleksandr Koiransky; a close friend, Lyubov Gurevich; two U.S. citizens whom he had befriended on his tours, Norman and Elizabeth Reynolds Hapgood; and his student, Grigory Kristi. These editors played their roles in refashioning and in part constructing the theories of Stanislavsky. Their work must be disentangled in order better to understand what constitutes authoritative texts by Stanislavsky. In short, while we thought we knew Stanislavsky, we have not actually seen what he wrote in uncensored and unabridged forms.

We now enter a new era of Stanislavsky studies, which questions the strong mythic images that developed during the 1930s. During the past few years, in international meetings at Moscow, Paris, Cambridge, MA, and Louisville, KY,[4] scholars and theatre practitioners alike began examining long-held assumptions about who Stanislavsky was and what he taught. Much of this extraordinary activity has begun to demythologize the man and the artist, resuming him once again to the active and imperfect world of theatre practice. This project, however, needs new sources of information in order to proceed. In Moscow, while debating the needs of the International Center for Stanislavsky Studies, representatives from every corner of the world stressed the urgency for accurate information.

As if in answer new uncensored and unabridged editions of *The Collected Works of Konstantin Stanislavsky* are now being published in Russian (by Moscow's leading performing arts publisher, Iskusstvo).[5] The Russian volumes not only republish Stanislavsky's already canonical works but also show variants that reveal the work of the editors in relation to the process-oriented drafts of the author. Drawing upon long-hidden archives in the Moscow Art Theatre, the Russian edition also includes manuscripts and letters never intended for publication, untouched by factors that modified his published books. The main strength of the Russian edition is the publication of new materials that will change not only our understanding of the biographical facts of Stanislavsky's life during the Stalin years, but also give us new glimpses into the thought processes by which the famous Stanislavsky System developed.

To understand how revolutionary these new sources are and how much they will help clarify those aspects of Stanislavsky's work that run counter to our common myths, we must first examine the 'given circumstances'[6] that created flawed primary sources about Stanislavsky in the first place.

The circumstances which created Stanislavsky's portrait as a theatrical god of realism in the U.S.S.R. trace a single but tragic trajectory. In the Soviet Union, censorship and growing governmental control over the arts culminated in the establishment of Socialist Realism. In 1934, four years before Stanislavsky's death, all writers were united into a single union and were forced to adopt a single style. Socialist Realism was intended to make the arts widely accessible to a largely uneducated populace and to depict an idealized reality that viewed the establishment of communism as the logical and teleological goal of history. The same newspaper writer who hailed Stanislavsky in his 'battle' for realism also reminded his readers that 'Realism cannot be genuine, profound, or logical if it attempts to promote a false idea, if it attempts to go against the historical tendencies of social development' (Gus 1938: 3–4). This interpretation of what is real caused particular grief for playwrights. By the 1940s *bezkonfliktnost* (conflictlessness) was advanced as a necessary formula for drama. In direct opposition to the most deeply ingrained dramatic traditions, writers were told that conflict was not good for the drama. After all, if one lives in the best of all possible worlds, the only real conflicts that exist are those between 'better' and 'best.' Such ideas deadened Soviet drama. Theatres, experiencing a crisis in their repertoires, sought desperately for interesting new plays, but found mediocre 'potboilers' as Stanislavsky himself labeled them (in Benedetti 1990a: 322).

Stalin's policies on the arts needed a model for Socialist Realism in the theatre. By virtue of the realistic productions of his youth that opened the Moscow Art Theatre in 1898, by virtue of his international renown as well as his venerable age, Stanislavsky, willy nilly, was transformed into Stalin's theatrical prototype. That he himself differed from the created image mattered little. By the time of his death, his theatre had become the legal pattern for all theatres in the Soviet Union, and his System the exclusive curriculum for all theatrical institutes. His more experimental ideas were stifled; any spiritual and psychological techniques that challenged Marxist materialism were either downplayed or suppressed; his early realism and his Method of Physical Actions were exalted. Correspondence between Stalin and Stanislavsky, recently unearthed in the Moscow Art Theatre Archives, suggests that indeed Stalin manipulated Stanislavsky's image in the world, imposing a virtual internal exile on him during the last four years of his life. During these years, Stanislavsky did not leave his home except for short visits to a nursing facility for medical examinations. [. . .]

Stanislavsky's writings, too, were appropriated for the cause. In 1932, when the government decided to create a model acting school as adjunct to the Moscow Art Theatre, *An Actor Works on Himself*,[7] over which Stanislavsky was then agonizing, became less a private endeavor. The government saw the book as setting forth the model curriculum for this school and therefore as its primary textbook. A commission was appointed specifically to vet the book and bring it into line with dialectical materialism, which, as Stanislavsky himself put it, had become the philosophy 'required of all' under communism.[8] As expressed in communist Russia, this Marxist philosophy saw all aspects of the world as materially, economically, and socially caused. All other explanations were pejoratively rejected as 'idealistic.'

In 1930 and 1931, when she read the manuscript of *An Actor Works on Himself*, Stanislavsky's longtime friend and editor, Lyubov Gurevich, warned him of the 'dangers' of his work which 'frighten her.' She tells him that he is living 'locked away in the world of your art.'[9] [. . .]

Two aspects of Stanislavsky's drafts rankled with the powers-that-be. On the one hand, many of his examples and exercises were throwbacks to a bygone era of capitalism and bourgeois values. As such, they were perceived as offensive to Soviet youth. On the other hand, his System itself – based upon the premise that there is an indissoluble link between mind and body, spirit and flesh – violated the required philosophy. Russian dialectical materialism rejected all schools of psychology in favor of behaviorism, which seeks physical causes for mental phenomena. Only the physical half of Stanislavsky's equation was therefore acceptable; the other half was considered dangerously 'idealistic,' a criticism which dogged Stanislavsky during his post-revolutionary career.

The first of these criticisms makes sense when seen in light of the realities of a country torn apart by revolution and civil war, suffering widespread economic depression and material deprivation. In an acting exercise, Stanislavsky's fictional persona, Tortsov, asks his student Maloletkova to search for a valuable brooch. He tells her that by finding this brooch, lost somewhere in her apartment, she can insure her continued study at school. Its value will pay for her classes. In another exercise, Stanislavsky uses a scene from a play in which a character inherits a fortune. In the reality of Soviet Russia, such examples that depend upon owning jewels and capital were offensive. In the recurrent exercise – the étude of the 'burned money' – a clerk has brought a large amount of cash home from his office to count; he finds that his retarded brother-in-law has playfully burned it.[10] The physical reality of handling, counting, and burning money strikes a particularly disturbing note in view of the poverty of the times. These examples are especially striking when one considers that Stanislavsky himself suffered from the economic realities of his day. He had lost the family thread-manufacturing business and the family fortune during the revolution. He wore threadbare clothes while on tour in the United States, and struggled to find enough hard currency to pay for his son's tubercular condition. Suggesting self-censorship, Gurevich urges him to find other examples. He answers that he can think of no others, and resists the pressure to contemporize his ideas. He wants to write about universal truths, he says, calling his system a 'psychotechnique for all times.'[11] His original examples remain in the published text.

The other primary area of censorship, and the most pernicious, involves terminology. In letters from 1928 and 1929, Gurevich warns her friend about terms such as 'affective memory' which do not conform to predominant trends in Soviet behaviorist psychology. She repeatedly asks him to seek out scientists to gain a better understanding of current Soviet thought. In 1931, she warns that terms like 'the life of the human spirit,' 'the soul,' and the 'magic if' (for which she suggests substituting 'creative if') invite 'Marxist scissors,' because they invoke non-material ideas that dialectical materialism strongly rejects. And indeed in 1936, the government calls such dubious terms 'hazy' (*tumannye*), and adds 'intuition' and 'subconscious' to the list.[12]

Stanislavsky may have compromised his theatre to Stalin, but he defended his book, *An Actor Works on Himself*. All the concepts attacked by dialectical materialism go to the heart of his System. Stanislavsky saw them as essential components of artistic creativity and defended all suspect words like 'soul' and 'subconscious' in a letter to the Central Committee of the Communist Party (see Benedetti 1990a: 346–7). To maintain the terms, the Party in turn asked Stanislavsky 'concretely' to uncover their 'realistic' content in his texts (Ancharov in Dybovskii 1992). Compromises were made on both sides. [. . .] Similarly, whenever Stanislavsky mentions the mind and emotions, he reiterates their connections with the body. By making such concessions to materialism, Stanislavsky retained 'idealistic' aspects of his System within the texts; even with deletions and changes made during the first printings, he successfully sidestepped the censor. These Russian books still serve as one of the best keys to his actual concerns about art. [. . .]

With so much of the soul and subconscious left in the book, it remained for Soviet critics to make the content more acceptable to Marxism than the text itself. Soviet interpretations of the System emphasized its physical aspects, privileging the Method of Physical Actions over other experimental techniques for the actor. Such interpretations further insured that Stanislavsky's books remained acceptable. For example, by judiciously overlooking the more spiritual aspects of Stanislavsky's work, Soviet critic Pavel Simonov subjects the System to a strictly behaviorist analysis (1962). In this project, Simonov relies almost exclusively upon one half of Stanislavsky's psychological understanding, but in so doing, he leaves the less acceptable half alone.[13] This interpretive dynamic protected the sources themselves, leaving elements for revisionist readings intact.

Stanislavsky's mythic portrait in the West developed in much more complicated and convoluted ways than in the Soviet Union. The Moscow Art Theatre's tours to the U.S. in 1923 and 1924, the indirect transmission of information about his System to American actors, and the English publication of his books all contributed.

Stanislavsky brought his oldest and most realistic productions with him when he toured the United States. While these tours certainly 'encouraged us to revise our ordinary scale of dramatic and theatrical values,' as reviewer R. A. Parker put it (in Emeljanow 1981: 242), they also fixed our image of him at the earliest phase of the Moscow Art Theatre's history. [. . .] The repertory did not reflect Stanislavsky's current interests. Clearly, the Moscow Art Theatre had chosen this repertory because it was least controversial at home, where political wars over the arts were beginning. However, U.S. theatre professionals, such as Lee Strasberg, saw virtue even in the age of the productions. 'We were fortunate,' Strasberg told members of the Actors Studio, 'in seeing not productions but works of art, [. . .] not just the successes of that year; they brought to us the successes of their entire career. [. . . .] We were privileged' (Strasberg 1956–69: 4/23/68). This choice of repertory – in short, the tours themselves – helped establish Stanislavsky in the United States as an exclusively realistic director and actor *par excellence*.

A creative dynamic emerged in the classrooms of émigré teachers that slowly but surely transformed the System into the American Method. While interest in Stanislavsky grew throughout the 1920s and 1930s in the United States, little written information could be found. Actors may have watched the results of Stanis-lavsky's rehearsals on stage, but they could infer little about the creative process from the productions themselves. Written information was scarce. They had no better texts than *My Life in Art* (1924), a memoir written in part to support the publicity surrounding Stanislavsky's U.S. tours. *An Actor Prepares* appeared in 1936, fully five years after the founding of the Group Theatre in New York, which had already adapted many of Stanislavsky's techniques for their own use. Of the Group, only Stella Adler studied with Stanislavsky directly, and then only for a brief time. Therefore, those who sought to study the System turned to émigré teachers who transmitted their experience of the System in classes rather than in texts. [. . .]

This mode of transmission, however, involves a number of stumbling blocks. Émigré teachers were indeed the best source of information, but they were imperfect sources. They spoke in an acquired language, sometimes struggling to explain concepts clear in Russian but transformed into something a bit different in the new cultural milieu. Indeed, for Polish-born Boleslavsky, English was a third language. On the simplest level, the 'bits' of the play, strung together like the 'beads' of a necklace, became the 'beats' of the scene, and 'affective' memory became 'effective' when pronounced in a Russian accent. On a more subtle level, Russian understanding of 'emotional memory' became confused with Freudian psychology, popular in the U.S. but not adopted in Russia. Of course, the very nature of acting classes which necessarily filters the System through the individual creativity of teachers and students alike, like a game of telephone, slowly but surely transforms the source ideas. Finally, most of the émigré teachers, like Richard Boleslavsky, had worked with the System in its earliest stages, at the Moscow Art Theatre's First Studio which had been founded in 1911. Here the first experiments on the System were conducted. Therefore, like the tours themselves, these teachers exposed U.S. actors to Stanislavsky's earliest thinking (see Carnicke 1992). In short, the classroom exerted its own mythmaking pressure.

Both these forces – the tours and the teachers – operated too subtly to do more than suggest their dynamics in this article (see Carnicke 1998). Yet, even this min-imal outline sets the scene for the crucial story of Stanislavsky's publication history in the West, which dramatically argues for new and more accurate primary sources in English. Within this context of indirect and oral information, Stanislavsky's books would seem to fill a special need for written sources. However, publication history itself also played the role of mythmaker.

Stanislavsky chose to publish his first two books in English, a language which he did not speak or read, before he published them in Russian. He was in desperate need of hard currency. His personal wealth was completely lost with the national-ization of all property after the revolution, and his son was seriously ill with tuber-culosis. While the Moscow Art Theatre had found one of their most enthusiastic audiences in the U.S., Stanislavsky himself had reached a deep level of despair [. . . that] extended to the future of his theatre. As he wrote to his codirector, Vladimir Nemirovich-Danchenko, in 1923 from New York:

> We must get used to the thought there is no longer an Art Theatre. [. . .] All these years
> I flattered myself with hope and salvaged the moldering remains. During the time of
> our travels, it has become clearer and clearer, most precisely and definitely. No one has

any thought, idea, no great goal. And without that, an enterprise based on ideas can not survive.

(SS 1961: 7. 41)

The U.S. seemed to offer the only relief to Stanislavsky's despair. The tours unquestionably represented a strategy for financial survival. Stanislavsky took half of the Moscow Art Theatre company abroad in an effort to save the theatre from financial ruin after the revolution. As he wrote in a letter to Nemirovich-Danchenko dated 12 February 1924, 'America is the sole audience, the sole source of money for subsidy, on which we can count' (<i>SS</i> 1961: 8. 84). Despite the enthusiasm of audiences, profits sadly continued to elude the theatre.

Similarly, publishing in the West offered Stanislavsky a personal financial strategy. United States copyright law, along with international copyright law, would insure that he earn immediate money on all translations of his books and that future earnings would continue to go to his family. [. . .] He thus wrote <i>My Life in Art</i> hastily, so that it could be published in 1924 during the second American tour. As he himself put it, he worked 'like a convict with only a few days left to live' (<i>SS</i> 1961: 8. 87).[14] He was unhappy with the results. When he returned to Moscow, he completely revised the book; the Russian revision, which he considered definitive, has not yet been translated into English.

Similarly, the manuscript of <i>An Actor Prepares</i> was deemed uncommercial. Initially, Yale University Press rejected it; Stanislavsky had missed several deadlines and the book was expanding to excessive length. Theatre Arts Books agreed to publish it, but only on condition that the translator, Elizabeth Reynolds Hapgood, make significant cuts and modify Russian references, deemed too obscure for its readership. Editor Edith Isaacs explained to Hapgood that the book appeared to her 'practically useless to publish in this form,' because it would not be accessible to an 'Anglo-Saxon' readership (in Hobgood 1986: 159). On the most superficial level, the resultant highly abridged English versions (half as long as the Russian) disrupt much of Stanislavsky's careful logic and exacting descriptions of the experiential process of acting, doing away with his Socratic style and much of his wit in the process.[15]

While Stanislavsky had tested the waters of Western publication in 1924 with <i>My Life in Art</i>, he formalized arrangements for all his future books in 1930. While in France recuperating from a heart attack, he signed a legal agreement with Hapgood giving her publication and translation rights to all his current and future books in all languages, including Russian. (He also included recording and movie rights.)[16] They had first met and become friends in 1924; she had served as interpreter for him and his company when they were presented to Calvin Coolidge at the White House. This extraordinary agreement was designed to secure U.S. and international copyright protection for all his writings.

After the 1930 agreement until her death in 1974, Hapgood functioned as 'attorney-in-fact' of the Stanislavsky estate, controlling all his books in the West. In her capacity as agent for Stanislavsky, she negotiated with Western translators and publishers, protected his financial and legal interests, and publicized his importance throughout the United States and in other countries throughout the world. Without her efforts, Stanislavsky's writings would certainly have taken much longer to be known outside Russia. After her death, the Hapgood estate took over as Stanislavsky's 'attorney-in-fact.'

While protecting Stanislavsky's financial interests, this agreement also promoted the abridged and problematic English versions of his books as the sole authoritative texts. Once in print, the English versions became the legal original protected by copyright. Any competing translation from the Russian books would threaten this copyright. Consequently, Hapgood staunchly defended her published versions of the books, even though she herself had protested some of the cuts requested by Theatre Arts Books.[17] When arrangements were made to translate Stanislavsky into other languages, Hapgood naturally insisted that all translations follow her versions, not the later Russian editions. Her right to do so was upheld by the Italian courts, when Theatre Arts Books challenged a 1956 translation made directly from Russian (Bari: Editori Laterza). [. . .]

As stipulated by her agreement with Stanislavsky, her control extended beyond those books she herself translated to include all of his writings. Thus, in 1948 she acquired the rights to J. J. Robbins' 1924 translation of *My Life in Art*. She also negotiated permissions for the publication of other materials and quotations in scholarly studies, which she herself did not translate.

In sum, because the English books were, legally speaking, the original language sources for Stanislavsky's writings, Hapgood and her publisher, Theatre Arts Books, guarded against rival translations, successfully defending the 1930 agreement in international courts. Moreover, since the copyrights insured that all translations of Stanislavsky be made from English not Russian, the commercial pressure that modified Stanislavsky's books in the United States extended throughout most of the West and even into Japan. This publication and translation history means that Hapgood's choices in terminology and style together with Theatre Arts Books' editorial decisions became the dominant form for Stanislavsky's ideas outside Russia. As U.S. scholar Burnet Hobgood so succinctly put it, we have suffered from an 'English language curtain' (1973: 158).

That differences exist between the English and Russian published editions of Stanislavsky's oeuvre is not news. Not only are the books significantly shorter in English, but terminology is also inconsistently and sometimes inaccurately translated. Joshua Logan, one of the few American directors who traveled to the Soviet Union to study Stanislavsky's methods directly, testified unwittingly to these differences when he wrote: 'The books Stanislavsky wrote himself are difficult to understand in English translations. His writing is nowhere as vivid as his speech' (in Senelick 1981: 209). In fact, Stanislavsky as a writer is much more dynamic than his English-language guise.

As early as 1954, Henry Schnitzler, assistant professor of theatre at the University of California-Los Angeles, analyzed the discrepancies between the English and the Russian Stanislavsky, after reading an alternative but unpublished English-language translation. Although he could not read Russian, he sought out the unauthorized German translation, in order to confirm his initial feeling that *An Actor Prepares* is not the complete System, and that *Building a Character* shows 'a surprising lack of editorial care' (1954: 13). Theatre Arts Books saw his article as an attack. Hapgood asked her friend, Varvara Bulgakova, to write a reply. Bulgakova had been an actress with the Moscow Art Theatre; she toured with the theatre to the United States and had remained there after Stanislavsky left. She vouched for Hapgood's accurate representation of Stanislavsky's System.[18] [. . .]

Nonetheless, word about the discrepancies percolated from the scholarly community into the professional theatre world. In 1969 during a tape-recorded session at the Actors Studio in New York, Lee Strasberg said that '[Stanislavsky's] books give a wrong impression, that the books are partially wrongly translated into English, [. . .] that the American editions are edited editions, edited not by Stanislavsky, but by the translator, who has made herself responsible, so to say, for the presentation of the Stanislavsky material in a form that she considers to be suitable' (Strasberg 1956–69: 1/15/61). He, like Schnitzler, had read the unauthorized German versions of Stanislavsky. [. . .]

Eric Bentley also consulted the German: 'Some of us who may not be up to reading all of Stanislavsky in Russian have read quite a lot of him in the admirably complete German translations.' He noticed that all references to Théodule Ribot, the psychologist from whom Stanislavsky took the term 'emotional memory,' were deleted from the English-language editions. 'Mystery is created,' he complained, 'only when a translator decides to leave out so much that is of interest [. . .].' He felt that such deletions, especially in light of the importance of emotional memory in the American Method, was dangerous for theatre scholars (Bentley 1962: 128).

One final word of caution must be added concerning the variations which exist between the U.S. and Russian editions of the acting manuals. As discussed earlier, Stanislavsky's texts are all works in progress. His constant revisions produced scores of variant texts. The pages which Hapgood translated, edited, and abridged were not exactly the same texts which were adjusted to Soviet needs. Concerning *An Actor Prepares*, Jean Benedetti rightly notes that we are 'faced with two versions of the same work based on two separate sets of editorial decisions both of which appear at one time or another to have had Stanislavski's [*sic*] approval' (1982: 79). Without access to these variants, major questions have remained unanswered: What typescripts did Hapgood actually use? Did Stanislavsky make changes specifically directed at foreign audiences, as he did for his Russian audience when he revised *My Life in Art*? Are there indeed versions which represent 'pure Stanislavsky,' untouched by other hands?

For one volume at least, questions such as these may now be answered. In 1935, Stanislavsky sent Hapgood a version of his *magnum opus*, *An Actor Works on Himself, Part 1*. He labeled this version 'definitive for America,' and he initialed every page. Hapgood translated and edited this version, which has become known as *An Actor Prepares*. This typescript has been released by the Hapgood and Stanislavsky estates, and variants from it can now be compared (Carnicke 1998).

The history of Stanislavsky's books both in the U.S.S.R. and in the United States sets the scene for the new publications that are now emerging.

The Russian publisher, Iskusstvo, is reissuing all materials previously printed in the former eight-volume Soviet edition from 1954 to 1961, expanded from new research in the Moscow Art Theatre Archives. Thus, *My Life in Art* and the acting manuals now appear in complete versions with copious notes containing variant drafts. More radical is the inclusion of newly found materials, published for the first time. For example, the 'Artistic Notebooks,' which Stanislavsky composed over many decades, appear as he himself configured them – montages composed of random thoughts about acting, directing ideas and plans for plays, critical reviews of what he saw on stage and read, letters from famous people, which he carefully preserved and pasted onto the pages of his notebooks. Because they were private they escaped the censorship that his formal books endured. In a previous edition, only bits from these private writings were selected and neatly arranged by editors for publication, disrupting the flow of Stanislavsky's thought (Stanislavskii 1986). Other volumes will include correspondence with major figures in twentieth-century art and politics, and with those to whom Stanislavsky himself was closest. Letters to Stalin and other government officials reveal little known facts about Stanislavsky's later life and about the history of the Moscow Art Theatre during the 1930s; letters to his codirector, Nemirovich-Danchenko, expose a long-lived but ambivalent love–hate relationship; his writings to Hapgood and letters to his wife, only recently released by his family, show personal concerns. As Smelyansky writes: 'This time, we will publish Stanislavsky as he is in his totality, with all the contradictions in thought that distinguish a living artist from those counterfeits, which often issue forth from the image of a great person. The reader will have the opportunity to enter into the very laboratory of his ideas, and understand the path which his experimentation took. And surely this is now most important!' (Smelianskii 1992). [. . .]

Recently, Anatoly Smelyansky wrote that the goal of the new Russian edition must be 'to discover the artist anew. Stanislavsky needs this, perhaps more than others. He has suffered more from Stalin's mythology, which tried to appropriate his ideas. He has also suffered in these new times, when new mythologies are proclaimed in place of others' (Smelianskii 1992). [. . . The West, too, suffers from similar mythologies created about Stanislavsky as early as the 1930s, and we, like the Russians, need to reassess his legacy anew.]

NOTES

1 This essay is the only one in the collection which the author updated. Minor changes have been made throughout to update the essay. (Editors' note.)

2 Russian names have been anglicized in the text. Bibliographical citations in the endnotes are transliterated according to the Library of Congress system. All translations from Russian sources are mine unless otherwise noted.

3 From a discussion with Inna Solovyova, Professor at the Moscow Art Theatre's Studio-School and the Russian Academy of Theatrical Arts (formerly GITIS); see also Benedetti (1990: 317).

4 'Stanislavsky in a Changing World,' The International Center for Stanislavsky Studies, Moscow, 1989; 'Symposium on the Translation of Stanislavsky,' The Moscow Art Theatre, Moscow, 1990; 'Le Siècle Stanislavski,' Centre Georges Pompidou, Paris, 1988; 'Colloquium on Stanislavsky,' Palais de Chaillot, Paris, 1988; 'Russian Émigré Drama,' Harvard University, Cambridge, MA, 1991; 'Russian Classics in Context,' Actors Theatre of Louisville, Louisville, KY, 1989.

5 The new Russian edition, *Sobranie sochinenii*, began appearing in 1988. By 1995 several volumes had been published, including a two-volume set of Stanislavsky's artistic notebooks.

6 I borrow this use of 'given circumstances' from Vladimir Dybovskii's documentary history of the creation of *Rabota aktera nad soboi* (*The Actor: Work on Oneself*), 'V Plenu predlagaemyx obstoiatel'stv,' which he shared with me in typescript.

7 This translation of the Russian title (*Rabota aktera nad soboi*) is more literal than the familiar English, *An Actor Prepares*.

8 From a letter to Elizabeth Reynolds Hapgood, 7 April 1932, the Konstantin Stanislavskii archive (in Dybovskii 1992).

9 From a letter by Gurevich to Stanislavsky, 7 April 1931, the Konstantin Stanislavskii Archive, no. 8064 (in Dybovskii 1992); Gurevich to Stanislavsky, April 1929, Konstantin Stanislavskii Archive, no. 8058; and 17 December 1930, no. 8062 (in Dybovskii 1992).

10 For examples of such exercises see *SS* 1989: 11. 89, 11. 46.

11 Letter to Gurevich 23–24 December 1930 (in *SS* 1961: 8. 271).

12 Gurevich to Stanislavsky, April 1929, and 7 April 1931, the Konstantin Stanislavskii Archive, no. 8064 (in Dybovskii 1929); A. I. Ancharov of the Central Committee of the Communist Party to Stanislavsky, 22 November 1936, the Konstantin Stanislavskii Archive, no. 12019 (in Dybovskii 1992).

13 U.S. critic Burnet Hobgood in his article 'Stalinslavski's books: an untold story' (1986) warns of this peculiarly Soviet interpretative dynamic, questioning the Russian editions.

14 In a letter from Stanislavsky to Z. S. Sokolova and V. S. Alekseev, April 1924. For a full and excellent account of the creation of *My Life in Art*, see Laurence Senelick's article 'Stanislavsky's double life in art.' (1981: 201–11).

15 For a fuller treatment and in-depth analysis of how the term 'objective' was distorted through the translation, see Carnicke 1984.

16 A copy of this agreement is in the Theatre Arts Books Archives, at Routledge's New York offices.

17 In fact, to protect the Stanislavsky agreement further, she and her husband registered with the Library of Congress as coauthors of *An Actor Prepares*; they had spent nearly a year with Stanislavsky in Europe helping him with his seemingly endless revisions on the book. For fuller details see Hobgood 1986.

18 From letters by Robgert MacGregor, 6/29/54 and 8/2/54, the Elizabeth Reynolds Hapgood Archive, Performing Arts Research Collections, New York: New York Public Library; see also MacGregor (1966: 181).

WORKS CITED

Benedetti, Jean (1982) *Stanislavski: An Introduction*. New York: Theatre Arts Books

—— (1990a) *Stanislavski: A Biography*. New York: Routledge.

—— (1990b) 'A history of Stanislavski in translation.' *New Theatre Quarterly*, 23 (August): 266–78.

Bentley, Eric (1962) 'Who was Ribot? Or did Stanislavsky know any psychology?' *Tulane Drama Review* 7, 2 (T19): 127–9.

Boleslavsky, Richard (1923) 'Stanislavsky: the man and his methods.' *Theatre Arts Magazine*, 37 (April): 27, 74, 80.

—— (1933) *Acting: The First Six Lessons*. New York: Theatre Arts Books.

Carnicke, Sharon M. (1984) '*An Actor Prepares/ Rabota aktera nad soboi*: a comparison of the English with the Russian Stanislavski.' *Theatre Journal* 36, 4 (December): 481–94.

—— (1992a) 'Boleslavsky in America.' In *Wandering Stars*, ed. Laurence Senelick. Iowa City: University of Iowa Press.

—— (1992b) 'Stanislavski: Stanislavsky's last years.' *Theatre Three* 10/11: 152–65.

—— (1998) *Stanislavsky in Focus*. Australia: Harwood Academic Publishers, Gordon and Breach International.

Derman, A. (1938) *Literaturnaya gazeta* 15: VIII, no. 45: 5.

Dixon, Leslie (1987) *Outrageous Fortune*. Directed by Arthur Hiller. Touchstone Pictures.

Dybovskii, Vladimir (1992) 'V Plenu predlagaemyx obstoiatel'stv.' *Minuvshee* 10. Paris: Atheneum.

Emeljanow, Victor, ed. (1981) *Chekhov: The Critical Heritage*. Boston: Routledge and Kegan Paul.

Gelbard, Larry, and Murray Schisgal (1982) *Tootsie*. Directed by Sydney Pollack. Columbia Pictures.

Grigor'ev, A. (1938) *Trud* 10: VIII, no. 183: 3–4.

Gus, M. (1938) *Sovetskoe iskussivo* 6, 412: 3–4.

Hobgood, Burnet (1973) 'Central conceptions in Stanislavski's system.' *Educational Theatre Journal* 25, 2: 147–59.

—— (1986) 'Stanislavski's books: an untold story.' *Theatre Survey* 27, 1 and 2.

Hoover, Marjorie (1982) 'Review of *Meyerhold at Work*, ed. Paul Schmidt.' *The Slavic Review* 41, no. 1 (Spring): 194.

Khailov, L. (1938) *Sovetskaya Belorussiya* 9: VIII, no. 138: 2.

MacGregor, Robert (1966) 'Further entries for a chronology.' In *Stanislavsky and America*, ed. Erica Munk, 178–81. New York: Hill and Wang.

Schnitzler, Henry (1954) 'Truth and consequences of Stanislavsky misinterpreted.' *Quarterly Journal of Speech* 40, 2 (April): 3–15.

Senelick, Laurence (1981) 'Stanislavsky's double life in art.' *Theatre Survey* 22, 2: 201–11.

Simonov, Pavel Vasilievich (1962) *Metod K. S. Stanislavskogo I fiziologiia emocii*. Moscow: Akademiia nauk.

Smelianskii, Anatolii Mironovich (1988) 'Stanislavski et le Stainisme.' Paper presented at 'Le Siècle Stanislavski,' a colloquium on Stanislavsky, Centre Georges Pompidou, Paris, 2–6 November.

—— (1989) *Mikhail Bulgakov v Khudozhestvennom teatre*. Moscow: Iskusstvo.

—— (1990) Unpublished paper presented at 'Stanislavsky in a Changing World,' International Centre for Stanislavsky Studies, Moscow.

—— (1992) 'The experimental path.' Unpublished manuscript.

Stanislavskii, K. S. (1924) *My Life in Art*, trans. J. J. Robbins. Boston: Little, Brown, & Co.

—— (1954–61) *Sobranie sochinenii*, 8 vols. Moscow: Iskusstvo.

—— (1986) *Iz zapisnyx knizhek*, vols 1 and 2. Moscow: VTO.

Strasberg, Lee (1956–69) *The Actors Studio (Sound Recording No. 339A)*. Madison: Wisconsin Center for Film and Theatre Research at the State Historical Society of Wisconsin.

—— (1957) 'Acting.' *Encycopaedia Britannica* 1: 58–64.

—— (1966) Letter to the editor. *Tulane Drama Review* 12, 1 (T33): 234–9.

Yura, G. P. (1938) *Sovetskoe iskusttva* 6, 412: 3.

4

THREE SISTERS AT THE MAT

M. N. Stroyeva

T15, 1964

'After the success of *The Seagull* and *Uncle Vanya* the theatre felt that it could not do without a new play by Chekhov,' wrote Stanislavski.[1] 'The fate of the theatre was in his hands: if he gave us a play we would have another season; if he didn't the theatre would lose all its prestige.'

Three Sisters was the first play Chekhov wrote especially for the [Moscow] Art Theatre [MAT]; actually, on order from it. After a preliminary discussion, Nemirovich-Danchenko went abroad, so that the rehearsals were conducted by Stanislavski alone. His production plan (now in the MAT archives) clearly includes rehearsal changes, since Stanislavski finished it on 8 January 1901, and the first full run-through took place at the end of December 1900.

What strikes one on examining it is Stanislavski's handling of the play as an integral unit, as a completely developed harmonious symphonic work. In *The Seagull* the emphasis seemed to be on the external behavior of individual actors. In *Uncle Vanya* some actors were given characteristics not entirely consonant with the general mood of the play. In *Three Sisters*, however, all elements were logically integrated, woven into the very texture of the production, and closely bound up with the director's central concern – to reveal the ruling idea of the play, which could be defined as man's inner struggle against the power of triviality. This conflict between character and environment had been tried on earlier occasions by Stanislavski, but it had never emerged so sharply. In the earlier productions of *The Seagull* and *Uncle Vanya*, the characters' way of life had played rather a passive part, being used merely to illustrate or explain the reasons for actions or moods. In *Three Sisters* this living background becomes fully consonant with the author's thought; active, aggressive, a much more dangerous force. It seems to corrode people's lives, it gradually traps them in its toils, it invades the most intimate sides of their lives, it clings to them whenever they move. With cold indifference and scorn, it dulls their inner desires and dreams. But a Chekhov character, a person of lively, sensitive, delicate feelings, richly gifted, will not remain static. In this play [as Stanislavski directed it], inner activity no longer requires an external solution, however strongly it exists and seeks its objective. [. . .]

The clash between two hostile forces provides the dramatic core for the entire production plan. This clash begins in the second act. The first act, as in all Chekhov plays, is bright: a happy prelude to 'a party, springtime, gaiety, birds singing, sunshine . . . The branches with their buds just turning green look in at the window, only just opened now after the winter. Irina is preparing food for the birds, you can hear them chirping outside, beyond the bay window . . . In a mood of springtime, Andrei offstage is playing some melodious sonata on his violin.' Thus the first act in Stanislavski's production plan begins. There are lots of flowers on the stage, you hear music, loud laughter, happy exclamations. Any wistfulness is quickly interrupted; a smile chases all tears away. Stanislavski put in whole scenes of laughter, amusing banter, unexpected outbursts of gaiety, in order to underscore the atmosphere of a buoyant love of life. Dreams of going to Moscow easily still any nostalgic memories of the past. The struggle between the two motifs and the quick victory of a springtime hope for the future provide the basis for the opening scenes.

But, as in *The Seagull* and *Uncle Vanya*, the trivialities of life take over in the second act and engulf the leading characters. Later, in the third act, these two elements clash and result in an explosion which completely annihilates every hope of a real existence corresponding to their dreams. All that remains to them is a most unselfish faith in a better future for humanity.

Appropriately, Stanislavski's plan for the second act calls for a beginning which is almost dark. Here the director, by use of light and sound, at once produces a sense of the uneasiness which has stolen into the house:

> To begin with: It is dark in the living room, the fire is almost out, there is only a streak of light falling from the open door leading into Andrei's room. Now and then Andrei's shadow cuts across the band of light as he walks up and down in his room, thinking aloud back over his lectures. You hear Andrei's steps and his low monotonous voice, an occasional cough, sigh, his blowing his nose, and the creak of chairs being moved about. Silence. He has stood still by the table and is leafing through some blank notebooks. Rustle of papers. There is a sound suggestive of weeping, then again he blows his nose, you hear his steps, his low voice, and see his shadow move. In the dining room, the lamp is almost out; it flickers, then dies down. The windows are frozen tight. There is snow on the roofs . . . outside it is snowing. A blizzard . . . The piano has been moved so that it now obstructs the bay window.

Then, as if to explain the reason for the changes in the house, the director points out that 'the furnishing of the room has been done over in the taste of Natasha.' Immediately it is clear that she has filled the premises with herself and her Bobbik. 'A child's blanket is strewn over the divan: toys, a tiny harmonica, a clown who claps two cymbals together. On the floor, near the piano, a large rug, on which lie the cushions from the divan, more toys, a child's accordion, a top, a tiny cart, etc. On top of the piano: pieces of material, scissors, a towel.' One feels that the room does not contain a square inch free of Natasha's petty concerns. All light and air have been banished. In the dim light all one hears is 'The monotonous tick of two clocks . . . The wind howls in the chimney.' And a heavy snowstorm 'lashes at the window panes.' And then, as if to underscore the heavy atmosphere of hopeless melancholy, there are sounds from out of doors, 'the music of an accordion, the bells of a troika driving by in the street, drunken shouts and . . . faraway the drunken song of a passing reveller.' [. . .]

It should be noted that in his plan for *Three Sisters* Stanislavski meticulously and coherently sticks to the principle of introducing only important and necessary details of background life. The [added] 'sounds of the drunken voices' and 'singing to an accordion' are not only closely knit with the local life (it is Carnival time) but also in their impact they emphasize, if one follows the director's thought, the triviality and vulgarity of the surroundings.

This, for example, is how Stanislavski builds the scene between Masha and Vershinin: when they enter, 'it grows light in the room.' But the excited, imaginative conversation, the confession of the two who are in love, is based on interruptions. During one pause, the 'extremely mournful wail of a violin' comes from Andrei's room, then there is 'the sound of someone sawing – apparently Andrei turns from one thing to another out of a sense of hopeless yearning, but everything drops from his hands.'

Stanislavski explains that against this background Vershinin's bitter question is inevitable and unanswerable: 'Why do Russians, who have such a great inborn capacity for elevated thought, fall so low in their aims in real life? Why?' This chasm between dreams and reality is graphically emphasized at every point. Now it is Irina who expresses her disillusion: 'Work is without poetry in it or thought behind it.' Irina again begins to dream of going to Moscow, and at this moment Vershinin picks up a toy lying on the table – the cymbal-playing clown. He holds the toy in his hands and from time to time makes the clown clap the cymbals, providing a kind of ironic accompaniment to Irina's words. But she doggedly goes on, 'We shall move back there in June . . .' and again you hear the mocking 'sound of the clown's cymbals.' Here Stanislavski is following exactly the pattern used by Chekhov in the last act of the play, when Olga says, 'I want so passionately to go back to Moscow,' and Chebutykin says, apparently quite by accident but obviously with mockery, 'Not on your life!'

This pattern of contrasting details is used even more clearly by Stanislavski in the 'philosophizing' scene that follows. Vershinin suggests, 'At least we might philosophize a bit,' and Tusenbach picks up a little music box, plays a tune, then says, 'About what?' Vershinin replies, 'We might dream a little . . . about what life will be like in two or three hundred years after we are gone.' There is a pause. Tusenbach turns the handle of the music box two or three times; it emits vague sounds. 'And in a thousand years man will still be sighing in just the same way and saying: "Oh, how hard it is to live!"' says Tusenbach as he holds the music box in his hands, from time to time turning the handle so it gives off mournful little sounds. But Vershinin retorts warmly: 'In two or three hundred years, or even a thousand, a new and happier life will begin. We shall not be part of it, of course, but it is for its sake that we are living, working, suffering now – we are creating it and that is the sole purpose of our existence, or, if you like, that is our sole happiness.' Stanislavski notes, 'It is very important to arouse the audience here, to be buoyant, lift the tone.' And opposite Vershinin's words he writes, 'The distant sounds of an accordion and drunken voices purposely recall the fact that all that Vershinin is talking about is far away in the future.' He underscores and initials these words. One can only be impressed by Stanislavski's penetration into the thoughts of the author, into the deep drama of these scenes. [. . .]

The whole second act is worked out along these lines. There is the constant contrast between the inner state of people, with their aspirations and desires, and a life which in every instance seems to say: 'No!' However, Stanislavski found it important to show that people do not give up, that on the contrary their thirst for life is intensified rather than stilled. This is brought out in the meeting between Natasha and the guests who have come to see the Prozorovs. Stanislavski puts in a 'laughing scene' after Natasha affects a few French phrases: 'some laugh scornfully, others rock with laughter and roll on the sofa.' Tusenbach, to show relief after Natasha has gone out, 'begins to sing, to dance a little waltz downstage . . . laughs, dashes around gaily, and ambles over to the piano,' saying, 'I am going to play.' When Masha hears the notes of a waltz she 'jumps up, begins to dance – alone, singing to herself, but she dances in a rather desperate way. Róde puts his arm around her and then they dance together.' Later, when Natasha rather rudely ushers the guests out of the house, Stanislavski underlines this by making it a 'comic, happy departure.'

It is the same when the Carnival masqueraders come into the vestibule. Stanislavski builds a whole scene out of this, as if his intention were to introduce a fresh, happy-go-lucky atmosphere into the half-light of the empty house. 'You see them, you hear their joyous voices, there is a sound of bells.' But, on Natasha's orders, they are not allowed to enter. 'Silence falls. All the jollity evaporates. Someone whistles. The laughing spirits of the crowd are dampened. In fact they are rather embarrassed.' The whole end of the act is dominated by Natasha and Protopopov. The sound of voices is drowned out by the bells on Protopopov's troika: 'During the scene with Kulygin, Irina, Olga, and Vershinin one can hear the troika outside the house; the horses are shaking their heads and their bells tinkle and tinkle.' This is the preparation and basis for Irina's wistful despair: 'Irina has been motionless . . . now she sadly moves towards the piano. Natasha walks through. The troika drives away. Pause. The lamp in the dining room burns low, flickers; the gnawing of a mouse is heard. Irina sighs, as though she were in pain; to Moscow, to Moscow! She puts her head down on the piano. The pendulum of the clock ticks.'

In the third act the clash of hostile forces is heightened. The whole atmosphere becomes highly charged. Stanislavski states it expressly:

> Wherever possible in this act the tempo should be nervous. Pauses must not be overdone. The crosses, all movement, should be nervous and quick. Now it is no longer a question of a gnawing mouse, the squeaking sounds of a music box, or the distant sounds of drunken revelers to create the 'mood.' All during the act one hears with increasing frequency the insistent sound of a fire alarm . . . the engines roar by the house carrying the firemen, there is a red glow from the windows which falls in streaks across the floor.

In this moment of confusion and disturbance the forces of triviality take the offensive. An embattled Natasha defends her rights as the all-powerful lady of the house. In the second act she was still able to handle Andrei or Irina 'with tenderness,' indeed 'almost with affection.' Now in the scene with Anfisa she speaks 'quietly but with great emphasis and boldness and dismisses her with a single gesture.' Later, with Olga, she begins to speak again, 'quietly but firmly, and when Olga makes the slightest move she becomes increasingly irritated. She finally winds up with a squeaky hysterical shriek. She squeaks with tears in her voice.' Then, having established herself in this manner as the head of the household, Natasha stalks across the whole room with a candle, not looking at anyone, and angrily slams the door. It should be pointed out that this was very close to the author's intent. Chekhov wrote to Stanislavski, 'It is better if Natasha crosses the stage in a straight line, without looking at anybody or anything, with a candle in her hand, à la Lady Macbeth – this would be shorter and more awe-inspiring.' Originally, as Stanislavski had written Chekhov, the plan was to have 'Natasha go through the house at night, putting out lights and looking for burglars under the furniture.'

In these circumstances, the feeling of frustration in the lives of Chekhov's leading women works up to the point of unbearable suffering. Irina groans with yearning, shakes her head, throws herself restlessly around, rolls on the bed, sobs, 'I can't, I can't bear any more! . . . I can't, I can't.' She hasn't the strength to tear herself away and as if she were appealing to others to do this for her, to help her, 'she almost screams "throw me out, throw me out, I can't bear any more!" After this she goes off into real hysterics (behind a screen) in rising crescendo . . .' But 'not out of control, for Heaven's sake,' Stanislavski added.

The third act consists of the sisters making an intensified effort to find a way out through action. Masha, the strongest and most daring, would seem to have found her solution and is determined to break with the cheerless triviality of her life. This is how Stanislavski staged her confession to her two sisters.

> Masha stands up quickly, she is excited, she has made her decision, she is nervously wrought up, she nervously stretches out her arms, she gets down on her knees, as does Olga, by the head of Irina's bed; she puts one arm around Irina, the other around Olga. She speaks in a low voice ('I love this man . . . I love Vershinin') as she draws their two heads closer to her own. The heads of the three sisters are close to one another . . . Masha looks up at the ceiling dreamily and with a glow on her face, recalls her whole romance.

After Olga's words, 'Do stop. I'm not listening to you anyhow,' Masha 'gets up with disappointment, brushes off her knees, then goes over lightly to Olga; her tone is desperate, she has decided to throw discretion to the winds.'

Stanislavski points out that Olga, at heart, understands and sympathizes with Masha (which is something Chekhov does not bring out in this scene). 'Olga caresses her, the sinner, as she does innocent Irina. Olga kisses Masha tenderly, pats her.' Stanislavski finds it important to show that their common aspirations unite the sisters. In this regard we have his interesting note: 'Masha goes out of her way to comfort Irina although this is not part of her character.'

The shared hopes of the three sisters, all struggling to find a way out of their impasse, are especially clear in the scene where Masha is going out: 'As Masha leaves she is nervous and upset; she hugs Olga, and speaks as she moves towards the door. At the door, Olga, in a tender, motherly way, kisses her. She really understands Masha, and realizes deep down that she would do the same thing in her place. Now she no longer criticizes her but pities her. Therefore she kisses her tenderly as a mother would.' Then, to underline the importance of this moment as a turning point in Masha's destiny, the fire engines are heard again in the street. 'They rumble past the house, there is a big racket, bells ring, the empty water barrels they carry resound, two voices yell at one another against the background of all this noise.'

The fourth act brings the death blow to all their hopes; they must surrender all dreams of possible happiness. 'There is no happiness for us; it cannot, it will not be

. . . We must work – and happiness, that will be for our far-off descendants.' That is the leitmotif of the last act. To make a contrast with the first act, which was laid in spring, Stanislavski gives these directions: 'They all wear coats – light overcoats. All during the act yellow leaves drift down to fall here and there. As the curtain rises there is the sound of bells ringing at a nearby church (after mass has been said for the departing troops).'

There is a lot of movement to and fro by people of all sorts, a yardman, an orderly, a cook, a maid, etc., seeing the military off. Baggage is being hauled away, the garden gate is slammed and slammed. Each one of the leading characters is immersed in his own sorrow, his grief at the parting. Tusenbach 'keeps looking about anxiously; he frequently glances at his watch, he keeps clearing his throat nervously. Irina notices the state he is in and anxiously watches him.' He knows that the duel is unavoidable, and he foresees the tragic outcome for himself. Yet in saying goodbye to Irina he tries to suppress his own grief and makes every effort to appear light-hearted. This is how Stanislavski builds up the scene of the farewells:

> The music comes closer . . . Tusenbach caresses Irina, smoothes her hair, wraps her shawl more snugly around her, kisses every finger on her hand. Irina concentrates completely on Tusenbach. She never takes her eyes off him. He pats her on the head. She clings closely to him . . . Tusenbach says: 'I feel so happy.' He is much more spirited, livelier . . . Then 'Now I must go, it's time.' He quickly kisses her hand, goes to the garden gate, and takes hold of the latch to open it. Irina rushes after him with an anxious look, grabs his arm and holds him back. Tusenbach forces himself to smile. Irina embraces him and lays her head on his shoulder. Tusenbach looks wistfully in the direction of the garden.

Masha is in the same state of unhappy premonition. 'Some cranes fly by. Masha hurriedly stands up. She is distraught, she bursts into tears . . . The music recedes into the distance. Masha wipes her forehead, gives a deep sigh, shakes her head . . . She looks at her watch, she is very nervous, and sunk in thought.'

Meanwhile, as the atmosphere of restlessness and sadness outside the house gets heavier and heavier, inside a life quite alien to that of the suffering people in the garden goes on in its own special way. Natasha and Protopopov, now inseparable, hold sway. Echoes of this life are carried out from time to time into the garden, in noisy, indifferent dissonances. In order entirely to shut out what is going on in the garden, Natasha 'yanks' a curtain over the balcony and inside one hears loud laughter, 'especially the deep bass laughter of Protopopov.'

Out on the stage there is the gentle lyricism of sadness, punctured now and again by the heartless gaiety coming from within the house, 'voices, the tinkling of a musical top, the sound of a large ball being bounced on the floor, the noise of a wooden ball rolling across the floor. Now and then a burst of loud laughter (notice-ably the bass voice of Protopopov).' Stanislavski, wishing to show that this atmos-phere intruded into the garden, notes: 'At one point a ball bounces out through the balcony; the nurse comes out to pick it up in the garden and carry it back indoors.'

But when the grief, the human suffering, reaches its climax, Stanislavski removes all traces of triviality from the stage:

> Up to the point of the farewell scene (between Masha and Vershinin) the sounds of playing with toys and balls have not interfered with the action on the stage; but now

they die away to nothing . . . Masha, distraught, comes rapidly along the garden patio. Vershinin says: 'I have come to say good-bye.' Masha replies 'Good-bye!' and throws herself into Vershinin's arms and sobs. He can scarcely hold back his tears. Olga wants to take hold of Masha but Irina advises her nor to interfere, to let her cry herself out.

The surmounting of the sorrow at the end of this play is the most important task of all for a director. He sees the 'affirmative thought of the author' as Chekhov's characters, even in times of deepest personal grief, find the strength to raise themselves to the level of dreams about the future happiness of humanity. Stanislavski directed that Olga's final words be spoken 'as buoyantly as possible.'

In the first version of *Three Sisters*, Chekhov had made a note after Olga's words 'if only we could know': 'the music gradually fades; upstage there is a noise, a crowd of people watching Tusenbach (who has been killed in the duel) being carried away. Kulygin is jovial, he smiles as he carries Masha's hat and cape; Andrei pushes a go-cart in which Bobbik is sitting.'

When Stanislavski finished his plan for the play he came to the conclusion that Tusenbach's body should not be carried across the stage. He gave detailed reasons why he felt it was important to alter Chekhov's stage directions:

> It must be pointed out to Chekhov that according to his version it would be necessary to insert a crowd scene, the noise of the people carrying Tusenbach's body; otherwise it would be a ballet. In carrying his body through such a narrow stage-space all the scenery would rock. The crowd would make a noise with their feet. All this would cause an irritating, dampening pause. As for the sisters, how can they take no part in the removal of Tusenbach? One would have to add something for them to do. I am afraid that if we go gunning after so much game we shall miss our main quarry, which is to present the author's final and optimistic summing up, which compensates for the many sad parts of the play. The carrying away of the body will either be a bore, or a nuisance, or, if we manage to overcome all the obstacles, terribly depressing, which would intensify the overall sadness of the play.

Stanislavski's desire to avoid emphasizing the play's sadness stemmed primarily from his effort to underscore the affirmative sentiments expressed in the beginning. This coincided completely with the wishes of Chekhov, who, as is well known, said at the first reading of *Three Sisters* that the play was 'not a painful drama of Russian life,' and kept assuring people that he had written a 'comedy.' Therefore he gladly consented to eliminating the procession with Tusenbach's body. [. . .] This episode demonstrates that in the course of their common labors the director and the playwright succeeded in probing greater depths and in putting a more polished finish on the play. It also established a deeper relationship between them.

Stanislavski's production plan for *Three Sisters* shows how profoundly he entered into the lives of the Chekhov characters. Here one senses his fusion with the playwright; his composition is based concretely on Chekhov's creative intentions.

He saw in Chekhov's plays a confrontation of two mutually hostile forces set among the so-called 'intelligentsia' of those times. The social implication of this confrontation is that although the forces of bourgeois triviality triumph, the moral victory goes to the anti-bourgeois characters; in this case the three sisters who inwardly free themselves from the power of the narrow confines of their existence.

At the same time, in his production plan, Stanislavski clearly emphasized an affirmation of life in the beginning of the play – the dreams of Chekhov's leading characters and their resistance to the horrors of reality. [. . .]

But even while revealing the playwright's intentions, Stanislavski did not hesitate at times to ignore some of Chekhov's own stage directions. He was so absorbed in keeping the central idea in high relief that he was ready to suppress other ideas which he felt were purely subsidiary. In order to underline the breaking down, the growing shallowness of the sisters' lives, he deliberately 'demoted' them in 'rank.' Nothing in their home suggests that they are the daughters of a general. On the contrary, the house is 'most ordinary, with cheap furnishings.' (Simov recalls that Stanislavski asked him to design the house as if they were the daughters of a captain.)

Stanislavski made every effort to envelop the main characters in a stuffy, oppressive atmosphere, planning it down to the last detail so that one would sense at once that to continue such an existence would be unthinkable – thus he made their conflict with reality inevitable. Yet this conflict could only become the active pivot-point of the play if the people involved reacted with sufficient force against it.

According to Stanislavski, the right solution occurred because of something 'unexpected' that happened at one of the rehearsals, and it was only then that 'The Chekhov characters came to life . . . It turned out that they were not dragging around their burden of sorrow but were really looking for gaiety, laughter, animation; they want to live and not just vegetate. I sensed the truth in this attitude, it encouraged me, and I intuitively realized then how I must proceed.'

It is typical that the production only got into full swing when its super-objective was pinpointed and set forth by the director in the phrase quoted above: 'they want to live and not just vegetate.' Only an active, vital super-objective like this could have helped the actors 'live' on the stage and not just 'act,' for true living in the theatre depends on finding true action. [. . .]

This definitely destroys the prevalent false notion that 'mood' was the principal concern of the MAT's production of Chekhov's plays. What Stanislavski and Nemirovich-Danchenko understood by 'mood' was the realistic atmosphere of the production, the realistic creation on stage of the truths of life as seen through the prism of Chekhov's vision. 'The difference between the stage and life is essentially the author's vision,' wrote Nemirovich-Danchenko to Chekhov in reporting on the rehearsals of *Three Sisters*, 'all the life portrayed in this production has been filtered through the world outlook, the emotions, the temperament of the author. It takes on a special coloring called poetry.' [. . .]

One week before the play opened Stanislavski replaced Sudbinin in the role of Vershinin, because he was able to give a lighter tone to the first part of the play. This reasoning was also confirmed by the stubborn insistence by both the directors that Tusenbach (played by Meyerhold) should convey a greater feeling of *joie de vivre*. 'Meyerhold is not liked,' Olga Knipper wrote to Chekhov on 7 January 1901. 'He lacks buoyancy, strength, life – he's dry!' On 12 January Vishnevski wrote the same thing to Chekhov:

> Nemirovich-Danchenko has returned and is taking a great part in the rehearsals. The play will be splendidly produced with one minor exception. (I can tell you in confidence): Meyerhold is very somber . . . the play and his own role require that he be full

of high spirits. Stanislavski and Nemirovich-Danchenko did everything in their power to get the tone right for this part, yet, as everyone knows, they were unable to achieve this until the role was taken over by Kachalov, who, according to his own words, played 'an optimist, in love with life.'

The main idea – that the social structure was a failure and robbed a man of the joy of intelligent occupation, reached the public but provoked varying opinions. The reactionary press sharply rejected it, but the success of the production with the broad public increased day by day and made itself felt especially in St. Petersburg during the MAT's subsequent tour.

Olga Knipper wrote to Chekhov on 21 February 1901: 'Despite the panning in the press it is a success with audiences.' How solid this success was in St. Petersburg was conveyed to Chekhov by Vishnevski: 'We must be very, very happy about St. Petersburg in every respect – and if the Kugels and the Suvorins rail at us, that is something we foresaw, because they were, are, and will be a bunch of villains and scoundrels!!! The public takes no stock in them, indeed reviles them, and the evidence for that is that our run in St. Petersburg has long been completely sold out.'

The obvious social implications of the play during those years when the tide of revolution was rising made it a favorite among a whole generation of the most democratically minded intelligentsia. Gorki wrote to Chekhov in March 1901: '*Three Sisters* is going marvelously! It is better than *Uncle Vanya*. This is music – not acting.' Chekhov himself agreed. *Three Sisters* was probably the only production of his plays that he accepted wholeheartedly. The strict and demanding author was, according to Stanislavski, very satisfied with the performance. Chekhov wrote to one of his friends: 'It's well worth going to this theatre . . . My *Three Sisters* is wonderfully produced.'

NOTE

1 The spellings of Russian names are reprinted here as published in the original. (Editors' note.)

5

MY RUSSIAN NOTEBOOK, 1934

Lee Strasberg

T57, 1973

Editors' note: This material was published in *TDR* as 'Lee Strasberg's Russian Notebook (I934).' The introduction below was edited from a recorded interview with Paul Ryder Ryan on 28 December 1972. Following the introduction are notes that were excerpted from a workbook/diary that Lee Strasberg kept during his visit to Russia in 1934. Russian spellings are from the original publication.

My trip to Moscow in 1934 was a present from Sidney Kingsley, whose play, *Men in White*, I directed. He wanted to give me something because the play was such a success, and he asked my wife of that time, Paula Miller, what would be the best thing to give me. She said a trip to Russia.

For me it was an unusual opportunity. I had seen the Moscow Art Theatre in New York in 1923 and 1924. This was the beginning of my engagement with the practical problem of creative acting. I'd read a great deal, but until I met the people of the Moscow Art Theatre, some of whom remained in New York to open a laboratory theatre, I had little actual awareness of the training methods used at the Moscow Art Theatre. These methods, for me, were and still are the most total sense of acting contribution that I've ever seen. I had seen great individual actors before, but I had never imagined that what they were individually capable of doing could be achieved by an entire company, which included people of diverse talent and of much lesser talent. These people in the Moscow Art Theatre created an intensity of conviction and reality on the stage that was really unbelievable. So my trip to Moscow in 1934 was an occasion to verify these initial reactions. It also was a chance to compare the work that we had already done in the Group Theatre, which had led to successful conclusions. In addition, the Russian theatre at that time was probably the most exhilarating in the world. Directors like Meyerhold, Stanislavsky, Tairov, and Okhlopkov were achieving results that we had all heard about but that we had very little occasion to see unless we went to Russia. So the Moscow trip was a voyage of remembrance and discovery for me.

We all went separately. I went first, followed by Mr. Kingsley. And then Miss [Stella] Adler came, and then Miss [Cheryl] Crawford and Harold Clurman. The directors of the Group Theatre at that time were among the most poorly paid in the theatre. I would not have been able to do it on my own without the present from Mr. Kingsley. The trip was not only of value to me personally but to whatever it is that I may have contributed to the theatre. To me it was a very important experience. The only others to compare with it were my later experiences with the Brecht theatre and the Chinese theatre.

The results of the trip to Moscow can be divided into two areas. First, the Moscow Art Theatre was in a deplorable state in 1934. Stanislavsky, I think, was not actively engaged in the work of the Theatre anymore. He was doing more experimentation on his own with actors who came to him; he was also sick by that time. Stanislavsky's last production, Beaumarchais' *The Marriage of Figaro*, retained a certain flair and aliveness, but most of the other Moscow Art Theatre productions were rather tired. Because of my feeling about the state of performance at the Moscow Art Theatre, I did not go to see Stanislavsky because I felt I would be critical instead of sympathetic, and frankly, I did not want to confront him in that mood. I also felt that our group in America had correctly understood and utilized the procedures that Stanislavsky supposedly stood for, that we had nothing to learn in that respect, that, in fact, we had gone further in our own work. We were somewhat more theatrical, closer to the ideas of Vakhtangov in the sense of theatre, without quite accepting the total idea of theatricality because I am personally more of a realist.

For me, therefore, the great experience in the Moscow theatre was the discovery of Meyerhold despite the fact that I did not share any of his ideas about acting and especially about what biomechanics could do for the actor. The acting on the stage at the Meyerhold theatre was not satisfactory, and Meyerhold himself was the first one to recognize it. When I confronted him with it (which I never would have had the courage to do with Stanislavsky), asking whether he didn't want his actors to feel, to experience on the stage, he looked at me with annoyance and said he did. I then asked him: 'Well, why don't they?' And he very abruptly said: 'Because they are bad actors.'

Visiting with Meyerhold, I not only spoke to him, but also to the people who were in charge of the work in biomechanics. I saw their work. I was frankly not too impressed by it from the acting point of view. They seemed interesting exercises physically, but I couldn't foresee, either on the stage or in theory, what they could actually accomplish for the actor from an acting point of view or from a creative point of view. The teacher of the biomechanic exercises gave me the photographs of the exercises.

The directing work of Meyerhold, for me, however, was an illustration of the possibilities of the theatre, which is still unparalleled. The other great director, of course, is [Max] Reinhardt, but he was not as original in his approach to a play as Meyerhold was.

Meyerhold is the basis of an understanding of the director's possibilities in the theatre. He exhausted almost every theatrical device and phase of theatre that could possibly be imagined. Meyerhold was somehow able to conceive events that would clarify what [an] author was trying to get at, yet in a way the author himself had never imagined. Vakhtangov has said, 'Every one of Meyerhold's productions created an entire period.' In other words, when Meyerhold did a production he set a new style. His next production was totally different. Certainly no one would ever come up with the kind of thing that he came up with in his production of [Fernand Crommelynck's] *The Magnificent Cuckold*, which was nothing more than a bedroom farce. Meyerhold turned this into a satire by workers, not only a satire on what was taking place within the play, but he turned it into a poem of joy for the worker's own sense of achievement, for his dexterity, his love of the physical, and so on. I certainly could not recognize the original play.

The sketches for Okhlopkov's production of [Gorky's] *The Mother* were given to me by Tsetnerovich, who I think designed or was in artistic charge of the production. [. . .] During a talk with Tsetnerovich, he presented me with some drawings that he had made to show the possibilities of theatre-in-the-round, as it might be called. During this discussion, he tried to define the basic approach of the Realistic Theatre, stressing that it was not limited to one particular spatial relationship but that a spatial relationship was found for each particular play.

I think others have already observed that there is a relationship between the vision of the Okhlopkov–Tsetnerovich theatre and that of Grotowski. The difference, to me, would seem to be that, whereas in the Realistic Theatre the spatial relationships always somehow brought you closer to the play, making it possible for the play to move with greater logic and conviction than it might have on a confined stage, in the case of Grotowski the spatial relationships are arrived at as a result of an image of the play. They are not related to how the play should take place; they are related to almost a pictorial image that Grotowski would like to leave you with. In the work of the Realistic Theatre, no matter what the style of the production, you are always brought closer to the event, not just to the sense of style or theatricality.

Editors' note: The following are excerpts from Strasberg's workbook/diary. The 11 May entry followed the 25 May entry in the notebook.

25 MAY

Am writing this now simply to record our experience of the 23rd when Stella, Jay and I went to visit Mme. Vakhtangova in the apartment lived in by Vakhtangov – his study now being a museum containing material on him. It was one of the most thrilling experiences I have ever had – when Mme. Vakhtangova's secretary translated the two letters Stanislavsky had written to E.V., one in 1914 on finishing the school, the other in 1922 after the first performance of *Turandot*. I had difficulty to keep from crying. As Stella remarked afterward – 'It was so thrilling because it was important to see that we had not just read things into our idea of Vakhtangov, but that we had been able correctly to estimate his value and significance' far away in America with very little to go on. In fact, my feeling is that we more correctly understand his work than they do here in Russia. It was important to see that Stanislavsky looked upon him as his only 'heir' – which shows that Stanislavsky, too, understood his work.[1]

Vakhtangov's value lay in dissociating the Stanislavsky System as a technique for the actor from the Stanislavsky method of production, thus, of course, the 'System' was enriched and improved. His own way certainly proved that the 'Method' in the proper hands did not produce only realistic acting, but that the process of 'inner justification' was a necessary technique in a creative process regardless of the style desired. His second achievement was his sense of perfection – which I have not seen equaled (Meyerhold has it – but is unable to convey it to or thru the actor) – his ability to penetrate with every gesture, intonation, etc., into the spirit of the play. This example which he set seems not to be sufficiently appreciated [in Russia] – perhaps in words, yes, but not in deeds.

Meyerhold uncovers the social content of the play – Vakhtangov displays the play in all its manifestations. Thus, Vakhtangov's production (of *The Dybbuk*, e.g., which I have seen) was complete – Meyerhold's [productions] all appear like fragments, episodes (his technique is episodic, too). Thus, Meyerhold's production seems to be against the content of the original text, while Vakhtangov's somehow simply lays bare the undiscovered content of the text and seems to remain true to the author.

After seeing *Comédie Humaine* at the Vakhtangov [theatre] on the evening of the 23rd, it became clear that without a deep understanding of the text – without some real idea – there can be no solution to a problem. I was thinking today how much my own sense of interpretation was trained by my early works in history – finding causes, tracing origins, analyzing traditions into their component parts (biblical criticism, etc.) and how much any new work I will do now depends upon understanding dialectic materialism, etc.

11 MAY

Editors' note: The following are Strasberg's notes from a lecture on biomechanics by Nikolai Kustov, actor and teacher of Meyerhold's biomechanical exercises – physical attitudes and actions for training and production to be used by actors individually or in ensemble.

Chief characteristic of Meyerhold's school – subordinated to mathematics and mechanics –

In order that the actor be the most expressive means in the theatre – necessary to know everything connected with it – actor must be very vivid, lively and possess many means of expression –

Since we demand as much from the actor it was necessary to create some theory for his training – and Meyerhold took Pavlov's reflex system – [. . .]

Taylorism is taken as a basis for work. In this school we try to find the mechanical movements which should educate the actor –

We try to find out and reveal and build the laws of scenic time and space –

Insofar as this is our aim it is necessary that the body is able to find its place in rhythmic time and space –

1. the first rule is finding the center of balance.
2. the second task is to keep (have) the body in a certain expressive position within a space.

Taking as a basis these correct movements we begin to teach the actor how to think correctly. After the actor has learned the movements we ask him to direct his mind toward the theme of the étude –

Besides the above-mentioned it is necessary that the artist also has temperament –

In connection with the reflexes he begins to feel the experience. So the correct and natural movement already opens the way for emotion [. . .]

The basic rules for his emotion and general acting are coordinations of his movements of hands, head, stage, etc. –

The basis for mastership of coordination is polyphasing and counterpoint –

sound & movement
sound & movement & thought

The main feature of the actor's work is exactness – not more, not less than necessary –

If we speak in the language of architecture, we can call it a construction – a house that must include emotion and that this construction must be worked out very well because upon it depends the contents –

N = mastership of actor
$N = a^1 + a^2$ (a^1 = body ; a^2 = control)

Control of actor is connected with thoughts, beliefs, ideas –

Pantomime is the last element of actor's mastership – and this we call social mechanics –

Still looking for forms to complete the actor's education – to see achieved by social life – shock work, acting in factories, etc. –

An artist who does not live in the social sphere that surrounds him will not feel the pulse of life –

On the cultural front our actors must become the educators of this audience –

Since movement must find its correct place in space we take the principle of *rakurz* (position-pose) –

The situation of the body in space defines the style and national character (Japanese dagger, Egyptian . . .)

(This last thing seems very interesting and important – he explained and illustrated that in *Camille* they used the movement of the *commedia dell'arte* – movement of the shoulders, rounded movements – it seemed to me as much as I could tell from the performance that it was very interesting and gave the scenes a certain distinct style and character – as differentiated from the characterizations in the MAT *Figaro*, which were mostly hand movements in the usually adopted French style and posture of body – but not really in movement – it struck me that at times the Meyerhold production achieved results that approximated pictures of French eighteenth-century acting – but not in a satiric way – but rather grand fashion – and effectively. [. . .])

Kustov also explained that there were elements of Kabuki, *commedia dell'arte*, Shakespearean theatre in biomechanics. The main difference between classic movement and bio-m is that the latter uses knees as base (as in Japanese theatre).

[After Kustov's lecture], at 1 o'clock, Jay and I met Tsetnerovich at the Realistic Theatre. Showed us sketches for *Mother*, [*Pierre*] *Patelin* and a new production of a Labiche comedy –

It was very interesting to see the different forms created for each play though the same principle of playing in the midst and around the audience was used in all three. Short fragments from his talk:

Two main lines historically in the theatre –

Bourgeois Renaissance stage (picture stage – aims at illusion, machinery, actors as pictures, two-dimensional, the audience sits back in its chairs and watches) –

People's theatre (uses a platform stage) – surrounded by the audience – the actor is master and shows off sculpturally – three-dimensionally – this theatre makes an active effect on audience –

[Tsetnerovich's] theatre obviously derives from the latter, though he always felt it to be right – it was only after a number of productions that he was able to analyze why this kind of theatre had a different effect on the audience. The audience seated around the stage looks across at the other audience – as an actual reflex action it reacts not to a background but to an atmosphere – whereas in a theatre with a backdrop it meets just material – no matter how blue it is painted. The audience physically reacts differently. [. . .]

At 3 [o'clock] to Meyerhold to watch rehearsal of *Camille*. The rehearsal was interesting because both Stella and I remarked on how much more relaxed the actors were and how much better they seemed. Jay thought it might be the difference in the costumes, which are a difficult burden – but it seemed that besides that there was an actual psychological ease and therefore spontaneity that was lost the moment they knew they were acting. [. . .] They rehearsed the second scene, Act 1, the party scene – they were shortening it and tightening it up. As they went through the same section a number of times I was able to make an abstract scene [below] – one of the best productions where Meyerhold by simple means and a continuity of action succeeds in building a 'wild' party scene.

From Armand's dialogue (where he comes from) enter crowd stage R go into a quick valse – 4 couples – ending Marguerite chair C and Prudence R front stage – Prudence's partner runs across to piano – Marguerite's partner to Prudence – go into music-hall song by Prudence – and since bunched around piano 3 on floor front of piano – Prudence stage R – on second verse two men and girl exit – at end of song without breaking rhythm 2 men masked enter very military – followed by confetti and balloons. Scene other side (R) stage – people rest exhausted – dialogue stage RC Marguerite and man – followed by entrance girl – boy – declamation – 4 people on stage back to audience – shielding person declaiming – for scene with fan other side Marguerite back of piano – music – at finish, girl declaiming carried off someone's shoulder – stage clear – for scene Armand, Marguerite, De Verville – two men dash on – take 3 chairs from table downstage – around declamation – Valse started by Marguerite – followed by St. Gauden dance with mask and dress on a stick – continued by Prudence dialogue with man – high-keyed – music all through the scene – drinking to Marguerite – cluster going into group around piano – into first part cancan – feet held – kicks – going into second part with St. Gauden – 6 people music-hall line – stopped by Marguerite song on piano – cluster around piano – floor –

(Note: the variety of listening positions – which emit [sounds] composed separately – adds to feeling of movement-party-gayness – built up. Note: How the scene swings from slow-declamatory to fast party – until the end when it continues on one rhythm – till Marguerite's song breaks it – and her breakdown.)

28 MAY

The one impression you do carry away from Russia is that despite its excellence – technically – the Moscow Art Theatre has nothing to give. Even if it were inspired simply by its old motto of search for the Truth – it would be more vital and inspiring – for real perfection. Without that – without the straining of the soul of which we've been accused – one would much rather see something more crude – more active – more vigorous – something of today. One begins to get a feeling [about] what the critics and others mean when they cry out against the 'psychologism' and 'detailization' as reactionary [. . .] it occurred to me that the conditional stage (of Meyerhold) is first of all misunderstood when it is thought of as being theatrical, that it derives from the desire NOT to be limited by the stage – or rather the set – and secondly, that the only way of bringing a play alive lies along that road. Thus, for instance, in [Ostrovsky's] *The Forest* Meyerhold can have the girl ironing, hanging clothes, chasing pigeons, people on a road, fishing, love scene on the road marvelous in its effect of throb and pulse – the swings, the seesaw, where in a realistic set he would be tremendously limited. The same thing is true of the [Ruben] Simonov production of [Ostrovsky's] *Talents and Admirers* where the act is broken up with a number of episodes and permitted to take place where it will be most effective. Its use here is, of course, not as imaginative [as with Meyerhold] but the principle holds true. [. . .] It is not a striving towards theatricality – it is a desire to mirror and explore life more fully – though its total effect is one of showing off the art of the theatre. Look at all the life-activity which Meyerhold is able to put into the forest which a seemingly realistic set makes impossible. The realistic set is a stage – the Meyerhold, etc., stage is a probing of life – theatrically. How this stage is used varies –

31 MAY

Saw *Turandot* at the Vakhtangov twice 29th and 30th; also last two acts of *Camille* at Meyerhold. 29th was 12th anniversary Vakhtangov's death. Was a little disappointed by *Turandot*. It is not as significant as *Dybbuk*, which is [Vakhtangov's] best work, but helped to clarify Vakhtangov's image especially in relation to Meyerhold. It becomes clear after seeing *Turandot* why V. wrote that 'Meyerhold is a genius.' M. is. Neither in *Turandot* nor *Dybbuk* are any flights of the *regisseur* to compare with Meyerhold's inventive business. What there is is a careful, painstaking and brilliant creation of the play conceived in a new spirit. No individual things stand out – even when there are episodes (as in *Dybbuk* rabbi and pupil) it is not episodic whereas in Meyerhold there is a pervading design. The images for each scene are so striking that the impression becomes episodic. Vakhtangov's are finished perfect jewels, Meyerhold's magnificent boulders. Meyerhold actually makes the impression of some phenomena of nature – each thing seems a new piece of nature torn from a mountain, i.e., it has an entire life of its own, crude and harsh, rough-hewn. If only he understood the actor better. Spoke with Held, the German member of Meyerhold's brigade of *regisseurs*. He said that Meyerhold worked absolutely alone. It was difficult to make suggestions to him. And the personality of each actor counted for nothing with him. He insisted on each move, gesture, etc., as he – Meyerhold – did it and wanted it. [. . .]

Coming back to [Vakhtangov's] *Turandot* – it certainly was clear that the whole thing had grown from the spirit of improvisation, each detail of costume, makeup, music, movement, and had also grown from each actor – that it was really a collective work [. . .] – and yet [music, props, business] lacked the character of being the most significant [thing] or the activity most needed to bring the scene alive, or interpret the scene (as swings in Meyerhold *Forest* or seesaw, etc.) And yet it is interesting to remember that both *Dybbuk* and *Turandot* had revolutionary significance when they were produced. Was it the new theatrical means used?

Stella asked the actors whether performance had changed. They said 'yes.' The 'youth' had gone out of it, though the form remained. It used to be like 'champagne.' It was easy to see that they were right.

NOTE

1 When Stanislavsky died, four years after Strasberg's visit, Yury Bakhrushin recalls him saying shortly before he passed away: 'Take care of Meyerhold; he is my sole heir in the theatre – here or anywhere else' (cited in Edward Braun, *The Theatre of Meyerhold: Revolution on the Modern Stage*. London: Methuen, 1986: 167). (Editors' note.)

6

AN INTERVIEW WITH OKHLOPKOV

Lee Strasberg and Sidney Kingsley (8 May 1934)

Translated by Molly Hasbell and Jay Leda

T57, 1973

Editors' note: Before attending Meyerhold's training, Okhlopkov directed two published plays in Irkutsk. His first production was a spectacle before 30,000 spectators, *The Struggle of Labor and Capital*, May Day 1921. On May Day 1922 he directed Mayakovsky's *Mystery-Bouffe*, again as a large spectacle. After training with Meyerhold, Okhlopkov became the director of the Realistic Theatre, which changed its name to 'Krasnaya Presnaya Theatre.' His first play, produced there in 1932, was called *Running Start*. The second play, which he refers to here as his second production, was Gorky's *The Mother*, produced in 1933. Strasberg and Kingsley interviewed him during a 1934 visit to Moscow (see Chapter 5).

Strasberg: Could you tell us what your methods of work are?

Okhlopkov: Our methods of work are based on a critical approach to two basic systems – that of Stanislavsky and that of Meyerhold. We maintain the positive elements of both and add new elements that we have uncovered within the process of our own creative work. In some respects, we depart completely from both the Stanislavsky and Meyerhold methods.

Strasberg: Which elements do you take over from Stanislavsky and which do you discard from Meyerhold?

Okhlopkov: We took from Stanislavsky his sincerity and his realism. But we don't believe in intuition, as Stanislavsky does. He builds his work on his belief that the moment when emotion arrives for the actor – when he begins to experience creatively, completing the theatre image – is a *sudden* moment. We don't think so. We believe that you cannot *invent* life. We prepare a theme and its structure, we make a plan for it, we make an ideological-political analysis of the plan, and only then do we begin our work. We give our work a broad, sound, class viewpoint, and the details come later. Stanislavsky also has a plan, but his is more that of a trusting priest, while our plan, with its base firmly set upon class-consciousness, is the plan of an engineer.

From Meyerhold we take his deep love for the body of the actor, but we avoid the sole attention he sometimes gives the body at the risk of neglecting the actor's mind and feelings. Our aims differ from Meyerhold's in the same respects that his theatre differs from the Greek theatre and the Japanese theatre. In the Meyerhold production of *Earth on End* [by Sergei Tretyakov, also translated as *The Restive Earth, The Earth in Turmoil, Earth on its Hind Legs*], he sent a funeral procession, corpse and all, through the audience. Meyerhold never repeated this maneuver, because for him this was only an occasional element in the production. While in the Japanese theatre you will still find flower paths [*hanamichi*] between the stage and the audience, as you would have ages ago, because this is a tradition as necessary as life. We must consider and determine more seriously how the relationship between stage and audience is going to change, what forms it will take in the future, but certainly *not* as an occasional element. Meyerhold actually cut the continually developing line of revolutionary theatre architecture. He threatened to do away with the stage; he even removed the curtains forever from his stage; but his Constructivism not only retained the stage but the elaboration of the stage as an element that Constructivism required. Meyerhold sanctioned the existence of the stage.

We believe that with his means, Meyerhold will never come close to his audience. His methods are too cold. We are trying to create an intimacy with the audience, and this requires different means. We want to create the kind of intimacy that a soldier marching to the battlefield feels toward the soldier marching beside him. Our ambition is to achieve a 'fraternization' between the audience and the image on the stage. And with this in mind, we surround the audience from all sides – we are in front of the spectator, at his side, above him, and even under him. The audience of our theatre must become an active part of the performance. By 'active' we don't mean necessarily that the audience should physically participate in the play. We believe that when suited to a state in which the audience does not move, that then it actively participates in the play. Here we depend upon the audience, because they are the core of our creative work. We want our theatre to become a theatre in which, instead of the audience applauding the actors, the actors applaud the audience. We want to create actors who will forget the limits of the playing space, who will even forget how to act – so perfect will be the harmony between spectators and actors.

This is one of the means we used to draw the audience into our last production – *The Iron Flood* – when the spectator comes into the theatre, he finds all the actors already playing – he walks into *life*. On trucks, carts, boxes, tree-stumps, everywhere people are doing their everyday work – washing clothes, cleaning guns, feeding babies – or quarreling, talking, laughing, crying, fighting – a picture of a revolutionary camp. Out of this scene grows a picture of a revolutionary camp. Out of this scene grows the opening of the play proper. If we had more space, we would have the audience also sitting on boxes, tree-stumps, etc., with only a few chairs for those who do not want to drop the conventional view of theatre. The smallness of our theatre is the only thing that prevented us from doing this.

Before we go on to another subject, I want to say that we have no theory that says that physical closeness to the audience creates intimacy with them. In a larger theatre, the means of achieving this goal may take another form. [. . .]

Strasberg: Don't you think that you could and should take more from the emotional means that the Stanislavsky method can give you? It seems as though your actors can express emotions when they have to express it through action, but when they stand still, they just stand still.

Okhlopkov: You're right. But don't forget that *Mother* is only our second production. What would you have said if you had only seen Stanislavsky's second production?

Strasberg: Let's consider it this way: a violinist prepares himself for his concert all the day before the concert, no one disturbs him –

Okhlopkov: – If a violinist has to prepare himself for the evening, he is a bad violinist. We don't want our actor to occupy his mind with his future work. Our actor must be healthy, his mind must be absolutely free.

Strasberg: How do you work with the author? Does he participate in the actual production? Do you revise scenes with the consent of the author? Does he indicate where music is to be used or is that exclusively in the theatre's hands?

Okhlopkov: This depends upon the character of the author. If he is good-natured, we consult him on every point. As a rule we carefully examine every word of the author and keep the manuscript as intact as possible. But if the author, for instance, has written a conversation between two friends in a room, and we think that that conversation can have more power and meaning if it takes place in a public bath, then we persuade the author to let us make the change. Pantomime also gives us results that the author did not at first consider possible. But on the whole, we change scenes only after thorough investigation and only in cases of absolute necessity. We showed our play *The Iron Flood* to the author only when it was completely ready. Comrade Serafimovich believed that a production of a dramatization of his novel faced almost insuperable technical difficulties. Therefore he had to wait until we had solved them ourselves.

Every playwright must be a director to some degree. How else can he write his plays? The ideal playwright works side-by-side with the director, attending every rehearsal, not only allowing changes to be made but suggesting changes himself.

As to music, the author rarely indicates music-points in his manuscript. This is a fault. We are working to effect a working collaboration between playwright and composer. This would be the ideal form of playwriting.

7

Meyerhold's production of *The Magnanimous Cuckold*

Nick Worrall

T57, 1973

On 20 April 1922, having rehearsed with a scratch cast of actors for less than a week, Meyerhold mounted a production (his fifth version) of Ibsen's 'Nora' (*A Doll's House*). The performance took place at the Actors' Theatre in Moscow (formerly the 'Nezlobin') and the set consisted of old Nezlobin flats with their painted surfaces reversed, arranged in a fairly indiscriminate manner against the back and side walls of the stage.

A few days after this, on 25 April, this time with a fully trained cast of actors from his own Workshop, Meyerhold staged a production of the Belgian dramatist Fernand Crommelynck's lyric farce in three acts, *The Magnanimous Cuckold* (*Le Cocu Magnifique*)[1] with Constructivist décor by Liubov Popova. The importance of these events may not seem clear unless the course of Meyerhold's development as a director can be seen in relation to other movements in the arts which serve to explain, at least partially, what he was trying to do and how the dominant influences of the period found expression in his work.

MEYERHOLD AND RUSSIAN FUTURISM

The breakdown of Naturalism, of the artistic principle of 'truth to external appearances,' which was followed by the reorganization of the fractured elements of appearances as a structure of lines, planes, and surfaces (for example, in Cubism), together with the fracturing of reality as a continuum brought about by, among other things, the technical principles of film editing; these developments may be said to have been paralleled in the literary field by the fracturing of the conventional poetic flow in Futurist verse structure.

The breaking down of the structure of poetic language, as this had been transmitted as part of a continuity of meanings and habits of expression, which stemmed from the nineteenth century and earlier, had obvious parallels with the breaking down of the patterns of stage Naturalism, toward the destruction of which Meyerhold had been working from about 1905 onwards. The breaking down of linguistic structures featured as part of a whole historical process which was bound up with disintegration, revaluation, and reassembly. The atomic nucleus, which lay at the furthest point of the breakdown of matter, had been discovered in 1910. The Quantum Theory was published in 1901. In 1905, the whole basis of received patterns of thought and habitual meanings was unsettled by the publication of Einstein's 'Theory of Relativity.' The founding of many major movements in the arts dates from this period, as does the creation of the Russian Futurist movement, by Mayakovsky and others, in 1912.

When these major theoretical and artistic innovations are seen within the context of the technological revolution, which was simultaneously taking place, some sense of a need to revalue the older historical pattern, as well as a need to accommodate the new, can be seen to have formed an intrinsic part of the philosophical scope as well as of the literary and artistic practice of contemporary movements in the arts.

The invention of the internal combustion engine and the mass production of motor cars, for example, can be seen to have affected Futurist verse production, as well as Futurist stage forms, in the directest of ways. In reflecting a revolt against the passive, contemplative world of the Symbolists, the Futurists aimed at a dynamic reconstitution of reality. In terms of versification this meant the resubstitution within the poetic structure of that which had been absent from Symbolist verse – namely the verb. The verb is nothing less than a motor. The restoration of the verb meant the introduction of the engine into what had become an etiolated form.

As this affected Meyerhold's theatrical practice, it can best be seen as a movement away from the static, hieratic stage forms of his Symbolist period, with their slightly mystical overtones, toward a more dynamic theatre of movement within a stage area which had been opened out for action. His experiments with new techniques of acting, which were to be called 'biomechanics,' can be seen to relate to the Futurist emphasis on a technology of artistic 'production' harnessed to the verb as 'engine.' Meyerhold's attitude toward the actor's creativity was one based on physiology rather than on inspiration. The 'engine' analogy can be traced through the theories of 'motor' reflexology in William James and Pavlov. The placing of emotional response in a secondary position within a chain reaction where instinctual response precedes it became incorporated into biomechanical stage movement, where the motor-reactor of the performer was sparked into a state of 'emotional excitation' by purely physiological means. The classes which Meyerhold held in biomechanics were directly prior to his production of *The Magnanimous Cuckold*. The production became, among other things, a proving ground for his theories.

Just as the attack on Naturalism carried with it an attack on nineteenth-century 'individualistic' concepts of character, so biomechanics became orientated toward collective, integrated, and nonindividualistic stage action. In this sense, *The Magnanimous Cuckold* was a manifestation of collective performance where the living out of intense personal emotion in the Naturalist habit became the object of ironic parody.

Certain technical devices that were used by the Futurists could be traced in Meyerhold's production of *The Magnanimous Cuckold*. For example, the verbal device of reverse homonymy – something which can be read backwards and forwards with the same meanings – could be seen in the extended physical patterns of stage movement and in the groupings. The fact that meanings no longer necessarily constituted part of a single-directional, ongoing pattern, was reflected in the stage images which became equal in importance to the recovery, in the stage architecture of structural patterns belonging to the history of simultaneous forms of staging.

The Futurist tendency to play with traditional imagery, to deform it and present it in a new manner in the form of a 'shifted image' for purposes either of caricature, or to give traditional forms a new dimension, was also a feature of *The Magnanimous Cuckold* in the way Meyerhold converted the predominantly farcical ethos of a play from a Western European culture into one purified and galvanized by the energy of a Russian Futurist dynamic.

The Futurist theme of the rebellion of objects (*vosstaniye veshchey*) against their environment and their fixed meanings could be seen directly in the 'liberated' stage objects and in the fluctuating meanings of the stage construction. This emerged as a composite of two factors; first, as an aspect of theatre as 'conjuring,' where objects acted in a manner which rebelled against logic but, more importantly in this [second] instance, as a means whereby the fixed identity of objects on the Naturalistic stage began to take on life, in their new context, halfway between function and symbol, between the literal and the diffuse. The place which they could be seen to occupy was that of a semiological 'second-order' language, dependent on verbal language, but whose meanings as objects 'underlie' language.

Part of this process has been realized in the metonymy of the Futurist verse of V. Khlebnikov where, for example, in his poem 'Demon,' the individual existence of a girl is representatively replaced by her boots, the boots themselves being 'black-eyed,' i.e., an aspect of the owner which is transferred to the object. An interesting comparison arose from the way Meyerhold used Maria Babanova in the part of Stella in *The Magnanimous Cuckold*.

With regard to the question of a semiological language, among the most important theories to come into being when Russian Futurism was at its height was that put forward by Ferdinand de Saussure in 1916. His postulation of the existence of a general science of signs, or semiology, of which linguistics would form a part, was important in going beyond language to incorporate any system of signs which form the content of ritual, convention or public entertainment. In so doing, the theory pointed to areas where the union of language and images, as in the theatre, opened up vast possibilities, a number of which Meyerhold (albeit unconsciously) was to begin to exploit in his production of *The Magnanimous Cuckold*.

MEYERHOLD AND RUSSIAN CUBO-FUTURISM

Meyerhold learned from the comparative failure of Russian Cubo-Futurism in seeming instinctively to sense the logic of the application of its 'painterly' content within a theatrical form – in sensing the possibilities, less for illustrating the movement of single persons (which the film could do perfectly) than in abstracting elements from a tendency to schematize form as part of an effort to illustrate what is most interesting about man: his active, rather than his contemplative nature.

Looking at typical paintings of the Cubo-Futurist genre, like Kasimir Malevich's *The Knife Grinder* (1912) or Natalya Goncharova's *The Cyclist* (1912/13), the element which strikes is the typical Futurist fascination with speed and movement (see fig. 7.1). What the artists each appear to have done is taken separate consecutive images of movement (as these might be seen on a strip of film), simplified the form in order to give an 'impression,' and then transposed these images, one over the

Fig. 7.1 Kasimir Malevich's *The Knife Grinder*, 1912. (Photo courtesy of Yale University Gallery.)

other, at graduated intervals. Both attempts appear as 'deficient attempts of art to accommodate the pervasion of reality by the apparatus' (Benjamin 1970: 252), the apparatus in this instance being the film camera.

Yuri Olesha's description of Mayakovsky walking in the street as looking like 'a man with ten legs . . . which flashed like the spokes of a bicycle' (in Woroszylski 1972: 349) would seem to indicate how deeply ingrained the Futurist vision had become. Similarly, Meyerhold's utilization of Cubo-Futurist elements may be said to have been equally instinctive. What he can be seen to have done was to separate out the layers of the schematic image in the Cubo-Futurist work so that these became several distinct units. He retained a sense of the simultaneity of action which related to the depiction of the movement of single persons, while distributing aspects of each particular stage of the action among the general, separated units of the actors. The static frame of the Cubo-Futurist painting was broken by the inclusion of its contents within the liberated area of the opened-out stage space and by the 'destruction' of the proscenium arch. By these means, Meyerhold transformed the circular, self-reinforcing impression of painted activity into the dynamic, extended reality of theatrical action.

MEYERHOLD AND RUSSIAN FORMALISM

The theoretical formulations of Russian Formalist critics are also of interest for the light they throw on Meyerhold's work. Early Formalist writings, in common with the Futurist, were linguistically orientated. Roman Jakobson, for example, talked of the 'verbal device' as being 'the only hero of literature' (in Pomorska 1968: 22). These remarks, and others, were directed against a nineteenth-century psychological conception of character considered as a real, separate entity. In Formalist theory, ontological fictions came to be replaced by verbal fictions, and the concept of character was replaced by a concept of character typology. One can clearly see the connection with Meyerhold's selection of a character typology, based on popular theatrical forms, which he opposed to the ontological existence of Naturalist dramatic character.

The key word in Formalist critical language is 'structure.' Part of this interest in structure can be seen to relate to Constructivism and, in particular, to Constructivist stage architecture. The relatedness of all organic matter was scientifically and artistically posited by the discovery of the electron and by the structural discoveries of Cubism. Just as verse structure was the most important area for Formalist critics, so body structure was among the most important elements in the formulation of a biomechanical science of the actor.

Formalist uninterest, at first, in semantics led to their emphasizing the rhythmical structure as dominating the syntactical, logical one of meaning. The main emphasis which came out of this was on the 'deformation' of metrical variations. When allied to the Futurist interest in 'the word as such,' where deformation of the individual word led to an interest in its susceptibility to phonemic patterning as sound and to the use of the word as a pictorial element, the deformation and restructuring of the word in architectural terms can be seen to have formed the essence of early stage Constructivism which, like Cubism, also exploited the materials of mass production. To take a basic 'literary' word like TEXT (see fig. 7.2) and rob it of its semantic attachment, to deform it and restructure it architecturally, is to arrive at a pattern which first appears on the stage in Meyerhold's production of *The Magnanimous Cuckold* in 1922.

Popova's set for *The Magnanimous Cuckold* was the first example of a pure Constructivist setting in the history of the theatre (see fig. 7.3). Basically, the construction consisted of two platforms placed parallel to the front of the stage, one slightly higher than the other, each of which could be reached by sets of stairs at either end of the construction. The platforms were connected at the top by a sloping ramp and the lower platform was connected to the stage floor by another, more steeply inclined ramp. Incorporated in the structure of the higher of the two platforms was a revolving door with, downstage of it, a curving, slightly sloped structure, rather like a children's slide but low enough to clamber or jump onto at

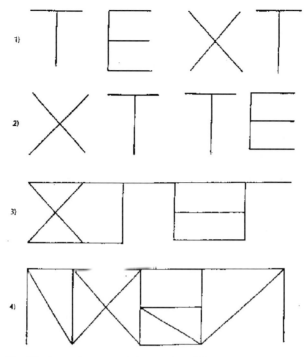

Fig. 7.2 Computer-generated examples of Meyerhold's exploration of the materials of mass production. 'To take a basic "literary" word like **TEXT** and rob it of its semantic attachment, to deform it and restructure it architecturally.' (Courtesy Sarah Mertz, 2001.)

Fig. 7.3 Rendering of L. F. Popova's set for *The Magnanimous Cuckold*. (Edition Albert Levy, Paris.)

its higher end. Set on, and to the rear of the higher platform was another revolving door which gave on to a small platform behind it. In the same position on the lower platform was a tall, latticed construction like a slatted fence but with the cross-beaming irregularly patterned. Behind the construction were three wheels, the largest colored black, the higher of the other two colored red, and the lower the color of plain wood. The surface of the largest wheel was enclosed and on it, at irregular intervals, were printed the letters CR ML NCK. Slightly overlapping each other and part of the bottom section of the black wheel were the other, open-framed wheels, like spinning wheels, the lower of which was larger than the upper. The highest point of the structure, the tip of which was about 27 feet above the floor of the stage, consisted of a set of wooden sails reminiscent of a windmill. The doors, wheels and sail were all moving parts of an otherwise static construction.

Its originality and its skeletal quality are immediately striking. Quite apart from the signs it contains of a particular location (the action of the play is set in a mill), what is striking about the basic elements of the construction is their relation to the disordered, skeletal framework of the setting for 'Nora,' here stripped of that which is no longer functional and reset in a firm, rhythmically structured pattern. The first noticeable absence is canvas. What formerly contributed to an illusion of three dimensions has been torn away to reveal an open, three-dimensional structure, predominantly nonrepresentational, standing in space. It is something which can be passed through, walked round, climbed on, swung on and slid down (see fig. 7.4). The world as illusion has metamorphosed into the world as tangible reality. The construction is solid. If the actor walks into it, it hurts. To live with it, to operate in it, demands new and specific skills. This world requires the kind of fearless agility with which children naturally approach the constructed world of a playground, or that awareness which the average man living in the twentieth century needs to bring to bear on crossing a busy street in safety, or what the average worker in, say, a steel plant brings to work with him in terms of ever-present alertness to the potentially dangerous solidity of the world which surrounds him.

Fig. 7.4 State Theatre set, Moscow 1922. Popova's 'mechanized' set for *The Magnanimous Cuckold*. (Photo by A. Temerky, courtesy of Editions Albert Levy, Paris.)

In being stripped of its outer cover and in having the skeletal frame revealed, the world of the construction has been divested of its Naturalistic trappings in the shape of perspective scenery, the illusion of place – those equivalents in the inanimate stage world to the psychological conception of character, particular people in particular closed places and truth to the minutiae of individual circumstances. The Constructivist figure mirrors, not external truth, but the internal skeletal patterns of the human frame. In shedding its canvas, the device asks that its dynamic configuration be registered in the patterns of human action. How is this best realized? By a pattern of action which reveals the body structure underlying the outer 'canvas' of the human frame.

It is a *general* pattern that the construction calls forth, not particular, individual factors. Thus, a general pattern of costume is called for, which will serve as a sign of a general condition and a collective function. The '*prozodezhda*' pattern which Popova designed for Meyerhold's actors has a direct correspondence to a working man's overall. Its pattern converts the stage into a workshop and the structure into a working implement, like a lathe, incorporating at the same time the sense of a total workplace, like a gantry in a foundry. Yet these are not industrial workers but actors and the *prozodezhda* is not an overall, but a conventionalized costume.

In the first place it is simply an adaptation of other costumes in previous Meyerhold productions. It is similar to the overalls worn by the 'Unclean' in *Mystery-Bouffe* (1918 and 1921), but its pattern is closest to the military-style uniforms of *The Dawn* (1920). The First World War pattern of puttee and breeches has been retained in a modified form. The strips of material have gone from the lower part of the leg but the upper, flared pattern has been retained. This has been done so that the flow of the human frame, which a conventional stage costume serves to enhance, becomes irregularly structured. It can be seen as an attempt to impart to the human frame, through the way the material of the loose-fitting overall has been cut, the structural patterning of human figure depiction in Cubist painting. This fractured, fragmented quality in Cubist figure painting is then enhanced by the nonnaturalistic movement and placement of the arms and legs. But whereas the dynamism in Cubist painting is a factor of extension – the pattern which only coheres if it logically extends in imagination beyond the borders of the frame (see Berger 1971: 153) – in the action of *The Magnanimous Cuckold* the dynamism is a feature of structure and connectedness revealed through movement which breaks down the artificial barrier created by the proscenium arch.

The *prozodezhda* of *The Magnanimous Cuckold* also retains aspects of the costume of the clown or Pierrot, familiar in earlier Meyerhold productions and most particularly associated with his own portrayal of Pierrot in Alexander Blok's *The Show Booth* (*Balaganchik*) in 1906 and 1914. With this kind of costume, detail of gesture cannot get beyond the masking of movement which its shapelessness inhibits. Its very style appears designed so that the underlying structure of the human frame needs to be projected through it. In other words, what is projected is not feeling in the Naturalistic habit, not the precise and particular detail of idiosyncratic, personal action but epitomizing, general elements of skeletal movement. The body, in movement, is shown to be made up of working parts in much the same sense as the working parts of the stage construction. Indeed, during the course of the action, these are made into the signs of what had previously passed for the projection of human suffering, now transformed into kinetic signals through stylized gesture and the operation of the stage mechanism. [. . .]

The dynamic impetus of Meyerhold's production of *The Magnanimous Cuckold*, while an aspect of a liberated, revolutionary spirit, was a direct result of the collective synchronization of movement, the revelation of the individual pattern only in so far as it contributed to the organized pattern of the whole. Particular movement was structurally supported and reinforced, integrated with the physical structure of the stage architecture.

[. . .] An extended arm or leg is never a gesture in isolation but is a gesture which repeats a pattern in the stage architecture. The rigidity of the structure imparts a rigidity to the gesture. A stance with the feet placed stably apart tends to be a repetition of an inverted 'V' pattern in the wooden frame. The individual figure fits into the literal framework like an organic part of it. Just as the Cubist painting dissolves human structure in the surrounding world of inanimate objects, so the actor's place within and against the construction either coheres or is at variance with it. Thus the 'sufferer' in terms of the conventional action of the play – Bruno – can be made to seem caught in the structure as in a trap, as in a world in which he has not found his place.

The simple story of Crommelynck's farce (which although written in 1920 is very much within a nineteenth-century tradition) – of a jealous young husband (Bruno) who suspects his wife (Stella) of infidelity and, to prove her guilt, invites every male in the village to pass through her bed, convinced that he who refuses the invitation will be the guilty one – was the perfect vehicle for a parody of self-induced suffering. Igor Il'insky, who played Bruno, exemplified the duality of the new actor's function in embodying both the idea of suffering and his own parody of it, demonstrating suffering rather than living it out realistically. Wearing the sign of a clown in the form of red pom-poms round his neck, he exemplified the grotesqueness of the character's jealous madness by extending and enlarging naturalistic gesture to the scale of biomechanical semaphore. His jealous ravings were accompanied by an exaggerated rolling of the eyes, excessive sighing and moaning. In counterpoint to these melodramatic excesses were the wheels on the construction which spun in coordination with, alternately, Bruno's jealousy or his melancholy. In this fashion, states of feeling were kinetically signaled – a stable, external registration of human feeling by an inanimate world, which was the essence of stability and symmetry; the inanimate equivalent of reason in the human world.

The independent existence of the environment against which the actors' incongruity or adaptability was measured was reinforced in such a way as to attribute to a mere structure an almost rational degree of sensibility which, by the contrast it afforded, exposed the over-sensitized, inane behavior of the protagonist. For example, while singing the praises of his wife and showing her off in front of her cousin, Bruno notices a flame of desire spark in the eyes of the latter and, despite having started the fire himself, fetches the cousin a resounding thwack in the face. As if in comment on the inanity of this, but also as a metaphorical registration of the effect of the blow (a kind of 'seeing stars'), Meyerhold had the smack trigger off all three wheels on the construction at once, which, in revolving, seemed themselves to be laughing in comment on the action.

At another point, Meyerhold staged a piece of slapstick that might have come straight from the world of Buster Keaton's *Neighbors*, where the inanimate world takes over and does violence to those who are badly adapted. In the act of leaving the stage, the town mayor struck the left-hand side of the revolving door with his backside, whereupon the right-hand side came forward and sent Pierre (the cousin) flying forward along the sloping slide. Turning to say, 'Sorry!', the mayor unwittingly pressed against the right side of the door, turned, and met the left side full in the face. Then the door swung back in the opposite direction, caught up with the mayor as he passed through, and sent him flying (see Rudnitsky 1969: 269).

A point about the largest of the three wheels, on which the letters CR ML NCK were painted, is analogously suggested by some remarks which the critic A. Gvozdev made about the acting of the three principal characters, played by Il'insky, Boris Zaichikov, and Maria Babanova. In the article, entitled 'Il'-Ba-Zai,' Gvozdev marveled at the sympathetic unity of the collective movement of the three actors, which was completely synchronized. Each, while retaining individual characteristics of movement, was permanently conscious of his place in a group context, to the general pattern of which he was subordinate. It was as if, separately, each character constituted merely the sign of his identity, 'Il',' 'Ba' or 'Zai,' and it was only as part of a whole, in action and in movement, that their individual presences were fleshed out and given meaning and coherence. If this idea is then related to the letters on the wheel, it becomes apparent that, over and above their Futuristic associations, their deformation, it is only in movement that the separated letters of Crommelynck's name come together to form a whole on the spinning wheel. At rest, the separated letters form three different 'typological' groupings made up of three different letter-types and different sizes of lettering. They are not placed in a sequential order but are displaced 'individualistically.' As seen at rest they constitute disconnected, almost random, signs. In movement, although no longer individually distinguishable as particular letters in the Roman alphabet, they combine in a blur of movement in which all three parts obliterate their particular selves and become a unified whole.

The pattern of interrelatedness, which was built up in this way, informed everything on the stage. [. . .] No single action can be seen to take place in isolation from another. At no time is anyone at rest on the stage. Even when stationary, the state of reflex excitability, of sprung tension, is never relinquished. Every level of the stage and construction is used and every possible combination of physical position is permutated, from a kind of contortionist acrobatics at floor level to kneeling, climbing, and hanging from the gantry. The action of climbing the four steps is accompanied by arm and leg movements which are a mimetic replaying of the activity of the legs and a plastic imaging of the pattern of the steps. The zig-zag-step pattern, and the pattern which it forces the body to adopt, can be emphasized by taking two steps at a time, so that the gap between each leg becomes a perfect oblong. The arms, held in a square, muscle-flexing stance, repeat the shapes of the steps and become echoed in the angles of the cross-beams. A simple pace forward, which establishes an inverted 'V' shape, can be balanced in the upper half of the body by an extension of one arm in front and upwards, while the other is held downwards and back. In this position, the body is a precise reflection of the three possible patterns in the framework. The arms are reinforced by the cross-beams, the body by the upright sections and the legs by the V-shaped crosses on the revolving doors. Everything becomes a question of balance and harmonic integration. Imbalance, in the psychological world of the farce becomes, in the physical action of the production, a literal matter of being unable to maintain a sense of physical equilibrium.

It became clear from this production that the ambiguity, emptiness or fullness of otherwise neutrally defined objects and locations derived their meaning not from being faithfully depicted according to existing models, but by being defined through a process of use, by being acted on and in during the course of the action. The meaning of a place, or an object, became intrinsically linked with human activity, with the creation of meanings in a theatrical landscape whose meaning was, otherwise, only potential or latent. The meanings which arose may be said to have belonged to both the local world of the play's action and, more broadly, to a historical context from which other sets of meanings arose.

To take the locally created meanings in the first instance, there is an obvious sense in which the sign which denotes a set of mill sails, given that the action takes place in a mill, could mean little other than 'a pair of mill sails.' In the action, however, the way in which they functioned threw a whole historical order into question. In a conventional mill the action of the sails, driven by the wind, moves the wheels which operate the machinery which grinds the corn which produces the flour. It is a 'natural' flow with a linear bias toward the kind of history which produced this kind of mill – harnessing nature for man's particular ends, but ultimately dependent on the vagaries of nature. The order is experienced as irreversible. The stage mill, on the other hand, reversed the order at will, or made the process subject to those laws which were created in the course of an action. In the liberated world of *The Magnanimous Cuckold* the turning of the wheels could occur in an order in which man, rather than nature, was the prime mover. For the actors to spin the wheels in any direction they chose, either separately or simultaneously, was to reveal the power of active choice in reversing a previously immutable order. When the laws were taken into one's own hands the sense of release converted the making of choices, the making of new laws into, literally, a matter of 'child's play.'

It is the factor of child's play which affects the way parts of the structure can now be regarded. In a 'natural' world, the inclined planes have fixed meanings as chutes for sacks of flour. In this world of linear historical development and single-dimensional meanings, objects can only have one possible set of meanings which are seen to be 'externally' imposed by their appearance, and which cannot be transgressed. Their law is the truth of external appearances and is associated with stage Naturalism. Once released from this sense of the dominance of single meaning through the power of arbitrary choice (child's play), the chutes, for example, take on other meanings. They become slides in a children's playground. The platforms become climbing frames. The wheels, whose function was formerly governed by a scheme in which Nature was the prime mover, can now be spun either mechanically or by hand in a combination of different directions. What was formerly a closed, linear world determined by a consciousness dating back to the sixteenth century and culminating, as far as the theatre was concerned, in the forms of stage Naturalism, has become the world of *The Magnanimous Cuckold*, an open-ended one in which meanings are created in the process of producing oneself and a condition. The signaling of these meanings through what was called the 'semaphore' of a new kind of stage acting was not, in the terms of someone like Artaud, a signaling through the flames of a destructive universe, but a communication of basics now that the inessentials, the accumulation of centuries, had been cleared from the stage, together with the canvas and the costumes, the scenery, the drapery, the masking, the footlights, the cyclorama, the borders, the whole paraphernalia that had served to frame the flow of history as it passed in steady sequence across the enclosed proscenium arch stage during the previous 300 years or so. What was being signaled was a basic-ness about a human condition and a setting as starting points from which meanings could be jointly created by actors and audience through means which acknowledged the creative powers of each.

[. . .]

Using a similar kind of analytical model, it can also be seen that the construction offers itself for consideration as a model of a period of history, as a machine by which elements of time past are regained.

In order to do this it becomes necessary to condense a longer argument and to invite a consideration of the 'flow stage' of Naturalism as being related to a concept of history seen as progressing linearly, on an analogy with a steam-engine; and a regarding of the construction of *The Magnanimous Cuckold* as a recovery of a sixteenth-century pattern of simultaneity; of history sensed as something both moving and eternally present, on an analogy with a clock (see Lévi-Strauss 1969).

To think of a clock is to think, automatically, of its face which registers time as something constantly moving onward. The tendency is not to think of the clock as a machine repeating sequences of twelve hours' duration. Neither is there a tendency to think of a clock as being, basically, the structure of its internal workings. To talk of an historical model in terms of a clock analogy is to mean the organic, inner workings considered as a structure, not to consider the face which registers the passage of time in another, linearly historical dimension. That this preoccupation with the face of the clock and with history as linear flow is a comparatively recent one is testified to, in another context, by what Marshall McLuhan has defined as the encroaching predominance of the single sense of vision during the sixteenth century (1962). In becoming a slave to appearances (the face of the clock) man became a slave to the linear concept of history as well as to the notion of cause and effect.

There would seem to be a clear connection between this new concept of time, which entered European consciousness during the sixteenth century, and the emphasis on vision, with the development of flow staging, movable scenery and their culmination in the forms of stage Naturalism. If it is suggested that what Meyerhold did with the 'face' of stage Naturalism in 'Nora' was to reverse it, in doing so he reversed a whole historical pattern. In reversing the face he rediscovered the workings.

To reexamine the stage structure of *The Magnanimous Cuckold* in this light is to see the open workings of an almost clock-like mechanism. It is as if the actors on the stage have got out of one historical phase – the flow of which the clock – face registered – and have, as it were, come round the back to see how it works. In these terms it is not too fanciful to imagine the numbers and the hands to be on that side of the large enclosed wheel which faces away from the audience, so that the CR ML NCK are like the maker's initials engraved on the back of the dial. This rediscovery of the mechanism that has been controlling history involved a recovery of that which was lost or which had atrophied as a consequence of the overemphasis on a single sense. If the disassociation between clock-face and workings can be seen as a split in consciousness, as a form of alienation, between social classes, between mind and body, between word and action, the consequent historical emphasis on intellectual and literary factors can be understood as here being answered by a counteremphasis on the body and on activity. If the fundamental split can be understood as one between classes, then the rediscovery of the workings becomes the conscious exploration of society by that element which has been excluded from participation in its making – a metaphor for the entry into this world of a new class. In rediscovering the potentialities of this world, through action, the actors acquaint the audience, dulled by its apparent familiarity, stifled by the narrowness of its perspectives, with a sense of its fresh potential as a place to be acted in; as a place for the creation of new meanings; as a place where neutral, meaningless substance is rendered meaningful through the exercising of a common creative energy.

NOTE

1 *Author's update*: This essay was originally published in *TDR* with the translation of Fernand Crommelynck's play as *The Magnificent Cuckold*. In the 1970s I was using the 1966 translation by Marnix Gijsen in *Two Great Belgian Plays about Love* (New York: James H. Heineman) where the title appears as *The Magnificent Cuckold*. Since then, it appears to have become more common among Russian theatre experts to refer to the play, and the production, as *The Magnanimous Cuckold*. This essay has been altered throughout to reflect that trend.

WORKS CITED

Benjamin, Walter (1970) 'The work of art in the age of mechanical reproduction.' *In Illuminations*. London: Jonathan Cape.

Berger, John (1971) 'The moment of Cubism.' In *Selected Essays and Articles*. New York: Penguin Books.

Gvozdev, A. (1924) 'Il'-Ba-Zay.' *Zhizn'Isskustva*, 27.

Lévi-Strauss, Claude (1969) 'Clocks and steam-engines.' In *Conversations with Claude Lévi-Strauss*, ed. G. Charbonnier. London: Jonathan Cape.

McLuhan, Marshall (1962) *The Gutenberg Galaxy*. London: Routledge and Kegan Paul.

Pomorska, Krystyna (1968) *Russian Formalist Theory and its Poetic Ambience*. Mouton.

Rudnitsky, K. (1969) *Rezhissyor Meyerkhol'd*. Moscow: Izd. 'Nauka.'

Woroszylski, W. (1972) *The Life of Mayakovsky*. London: Gollancz.

8

REALITY IS NOT ENOUGH
An interview with Alan Schneider

Richard Schechner

T27, 1965

Schechner:　First, a little bit about your directing background and training.

Schneider:　Well, the fact is I haven't had much training, precious little background. I got into theatre by accident, and never had any formal training, except a fast master's degree at Cornell. [. . .] My training has come largely from a variety of experience with a variety of actors and directors. I did take a ten-week course at the Theatre Wing with Lee Strasberg in 1948 just after I came to New York. [. . .] Lee gave me my first concrete training or discipline in the Stanislavski Method, although I'd been on the periphery of it for a long time prior to that. [. . .]

Schechner:　Was it a class in acting or directing?

Schneider:　Directing. Once a week for ten weeks. It was very stimulating and very frustrating, because one only got to do two scenes – I made myself do two instead of one – most people did one in ten weeks. Lee's criticism was very severe, and indeed at one point I was ready to cut my throat. [. . .]

Lee was very valuable to me in opening up the whole area, of exploring the subtext, of the off-stage life, the life in the other rooms of the house – and the whole idea of working with actors creatively. I hadn't had anybody talk to me like that before. My training came from the people I happened to work with. [. . .]

Chronologically, without real detail, [my background is] very simple. I graduated from college with the idea of being a newspaperman. I got into radio because all the newspapermen were unemployed. I couldn't stand radio, and in order to make myself stand it, I went into community theatre work. The director of the group, Day Tuttle, suggested that I stop dodging theatre, get a master's degree, and go into university theatre. I got out of Cornell and got a job teaching and directing at Catholic University at a time when the department was just starting – there were only four or five of us: Walter Kerr, Father Hartke, Dr. Josephine Callan, designer Ralph Brown, and myself. I learned a lot from Kerr. Kerr was a theatricalist director. My greatest sources of influence at Cornell – before that I'd never read a book on the theatre – were the theatrical directors: Meyerhold, Vakhtangov, Reinhardt, Tairov . . .

Schechner:　You read Russian?

Schneider: Yes. I was born there . . . I did my master's thesis on Nicholas Evreinov, the 'theatre in life' guy. My whole orientation was theatricalist. On the other hand, my interest in the theatre had come from my having gone to the Group Theatre as a kid in Baltimore and seeing *Awake and Sing* and *Men in White*. I was very interested and stimulated by their work. But I didn't know anybody who acted or directed this way, so that when I started directing, I was not aware of any influences directly from the Group. The thing I started to say – this is, perhaps, indicative of my whole position, philosophical or aesthetic, if I have any – is that, to the theatricalist guys, I tend to be a realistic director, a Stanislavski-oriented director; to the Stanislavski guys, I'm a theatricalist director.

Schechner: Who are you to you?

Schneider: I think I'm in the middle. I think that's a weakness and a virtue. I have great difficulty in confining myself to any particular point of view exclusively. There's no question in my mind that my influences are in two directions. The two strongest influences have been Stanislavski as interpreted by Lee Strasberg on the one hand, and Brecht and Beckett on the other. I will use any and all methods to achieve whatever I feel necessary; and, indeed, if I tried to confine myself, I'd simply fail. I wouldn't know how to operate. I have no dogma. Maybe I'm overly pragmatic in my approach. Very often I find it difficult to verbalize, to talk about concept. To me a production is an exploration. And increasingly over the years, I know less and less of how I'm going to achieve what I vaguely sense or feel.

Schechner: What productions have been most important or best achieved by you?

Schneider: All productions are relative failures, in my opinion, and one accepts that. Which ones achieved most what I set out to achieve?

The first time I felt that anything had happened to my work was when I went back to Catholic University. After my course with Lee, I went back there in '49 and stayed for three years. I directed mostly classical productions – *Oedipus*, *Othello*, *Macbeth*, *The Cherry Orchard* – which benefited by my newly aroused Stanislavski orientation. I tried to make *Oedipus* 'real.' The setting was 'tribal,' primitive, the tone very much like the Scofield–Brook *Lear* – not as good, of course – the chorus was an actual chorus of townspeople. And in *Macbeth* I tried to make the psychology terribly, specifically, believable in the most contemporary terms. I remember that after Lady Macbeth died, they brought her body out and Macbeth actually closed her eyes at some moment that related to the text. I thought it was very clever of me to use the text for some realistic behavior, and that was my whole attempt. But in spite of that, I felt, for the first time, that the quality of my work had changed appreciably. The second stage of my development came when I went to the Arena in Washington [in 1951] and suddenly discovered the open stage.

Schechner: And that was your first professional directing?

Schneider: With professional actors. I did *The Glass Menagerie*. I felt that it came off better than any production I had previously done, or maybe than any I've ever done.

Schechner: Let's linger on *The Glass Menagerie* because you've just finished it at the Guthrie. First, a very general question: How did your changing techniques of directing and your changing vision change your interpretation of the way you did the play the two times?

Schneider: At the Arena in 1951, I tried to make it real, detailed, and atmospheric in a small arena theatre. Thirteen years later, in a much larger theatre, my intention was to make the play larger, more theatrical, bolder, more vigorous, accessible to a larger audience. [. . .] I always saw the play as occurring in the mind of Tom – you know, it's a memory play – and the particular device I chose to start it with, while the details differed – the way he came back to the room and uncovered the elements in the room – was the same concept, and the way of working with the actors was the same. My way of working hadn't changed as much between 1951 and 1964 as it had between 1941 and 1951.

At first I used to start purely physically and visually. I made nice geometrical patterns on my floorplan, and I was interested in visual composition and pictorial effect. Lee made me realize that the basic thing the director does is to create the life from which the lines spring. I hope that's what I do now. The only reason I cannot consider myself one hundred percent Stanislavski is that *any* method or *any* approach or *any* point of view or *any* way of achieving the semblance of reality is, to me, legitimate. I'm no longer as concerned with the reality of the actor as I am with creating some sort of reality for the audience – and this may come out of something the actor feels is artificial or complicated. I cannot confine myself. [. . .]

The only real problem that I have with realistically trained actors is that, over the years, I've come to believe that there is no such thing as an abstract, rigid 'reality'; every play, every scene and every moment demands for its presentation a great selection of reality. The selection is partly a result of the director's inclination, the style of the production, the casting, the theatre you're in, accident, costuming, and so on. The actor tends to believe that there is somewhere an ideal or arbitrary 'reality' which will work in any production. I do not believe that's so. 'Reality' depends on the texture of the play or the production, and that is selected by somebody and must be worked for. [. . .]

Schechner: Let's take one or two of the plays you were most satisfied with.

Schneider: I hadn't finished that list. I started with *Menagerie* because I thought that in terms of atmospheric detail and some of the devices that I chose to achieve that detail, it worked. For instance, I used an actor as the father – I had an actor carrying a picture frame down the aisle – and everybody said no, it was ridiculous, but we had a big company and were using only four actors, and I had a good actor with a rubber face, and I didn't know where to put the picture in the arena. Where do you put the picture? You need three pictures, which is what we did in Minneapolis. Anyhow, in Washington an actor came down the aisle, and when we got to the picture, a pin spot hit him – you could barely see anything but his face and the picture frame he held in his hands – and his face really lit up. Theatrically, it was bold enough, and yet authentic enough, to achieve the result. I think anything, within the author's intention, that works – that the audience will accept – is all you're after. I'm not interested in being a teacher of actors while I'm directing – as a matter of fact, I'm bloody annoyed at it. 'If you can't do something right away in rehearsal, please do some homework. You're a talented actor and I know you can do it.' I had an actor, Gerry Hiken, whom I admire tremendously, who, when I put him in as Clov in *Endgame* – he was a replacement [. . .] and I had to put him in in five days – and the first day, he wanted to explore Clov's behavior. He didn't think Clov would go up that ladder, but here's Beckett, who says Clov 'gets up on it [the ladder], draws back curtain . . .' and so on, almost a page of very specific stage directions. And here's this very talented actor who's been in a company with me for four seasons and to whom I am devoted, and he wants to 'explore' the behavior of Clov. So I gave him twenty minutes to explore the behavior of Clov, then I said, 'Look, I think what you have to explore is why he goes up the ladder, not why he doesn't go up.' [. . .]

I felt one of the most happy productions, most successful in the sense that I accomplished what I wanted to accomplish, was *Chalk Circle* at Arena. It opened the new Arena. I had always wanted to do Brecht; I liked this play; it seemed ideal for the open stage. I set myself a very simple task, scenically; somehow to achieve the equivalent of the Berliner Ensemble production in arena form, obviously with different actors and scene designer. I took the exact elements of the Berliner Ensemble production, which, in my opinion, could not be excelled. I think if something is excellent, to imitate it is not, in itself, bad. [. . .]

Schechner: You say you tried to duplicate the Berliner Ensemble production, but you must have had a central image or central idea?

Schneider: That's the hardest thing to say. I thought of it as a kind of fairy tale for adults. There are elements of enchantment, of fantasy, of legend, of fun telling a story. I tried to make the movement from one of Azdak's trial scenes to another almost like a carnival, a dance, or frolic. But the element was a story that was fun to tell and that was somehow embroidered with fantastic or beautiful or bizarre or strange elements. The style was a kind of free fantasy, but based exactly on what I had seen the Brecht people do.

Schechner: That play requires an acting foreign to us, especially the aristocrats.

Schneider: Just as I put masks on the aristocrats, I tried to get them to overdo certain elements of behavior. The Adjutant in Berlin hopped around as though he were on a horse all the time. I didn't impose on the actor that specific a piece of business; what I said to him was that I wanted him to be always trying to interfere with everything, to be everywhere. So the guy wound up with his own particular behavior pattern – he played it as though he were on a bicycle.

Schechner: Did you work closely from the text, or did you have improvisations?

Schneider: I worked closely from the text. I'm not as adept at improvisation as I'd like to be, and I very rarely use it, except where I feel that the actor is absolutely stymied. Then I'll throw everybody out and I'll fool around with trying to free him of this block, whatever it happens to be.

Schechner: To get the style, did you rely heavily on rehearsals in costume and the early use of props?

Schneider: I always do. I talked a great deal about the style, showed them pictures of the people. The costumes, masks and props did impose certain things, particularly on guys like the four soldiers, because the heaviness and ponderousness of their costumes required them to walk in a certain way. When we had chases, we'd try to do pantomimic walking – the kind of thing Marceau does – because we didn't have a turntable. I've done four Brecht plays now, and I cannot really talk very clearly about alienation as a totally different style of acting. When I was doing *Threepenny Opera* at Arena, I said one thing to the actors, 'I want you to play this whole thing as though you absolutely hate every member of the audience – total contempt – and I want you to play it as though you don't give a damn for anyone or anything.' Is that alienation? But it got me a great deal of what I wanted. In the case of *Chalk Circle* I didn't do anything of that kind.

Schechner: Alienation as Brecht talks about it is not simply distance between the actor and the audience, but a kind of distance between the actor and the role. [. . .]

Schneider: [. . .] I didn't make use of the third person [exercize] at all. Maybe I should have. Seeing a Brecht company do *Mother Courage* about twenty-five times, my observation must be deaf, dumb, and blind, because I did not find anything in that production different from what I would call a good, marvelously acted, and tremendously theatrical realistic production.

Schechner: Let's talk about *Play.* I thought it was a brilliant production. The problem I'm raising is a director's problem. The *mise-en-scène* here is –

Schneider: – Samuel Beckett. In all the Beckett plays I get credit for following Beckett's intentions. Rightly or wrongly, I consider that to be my responsibility; if the intention is specifically stated, I try to follow it as specifically as it's stated. Obviously, the actors interpose something, and my faulty interpretation of the author's intent interposes something.

Schechner: In the Brecht you've suggested that there is, indeed, an inner life to the characters, and when they're well acted, they're well acted. In a play like *Play*, what is there?

Schneider: To start off, I chose actors whom I knew, who had worked with me at Arena, because I felt that the specific formal demands – the tonelessness, the particular rapidity, the physical confinement to which they were subjected (it wasn't only that they were in urns; they couldn't move their heads) – would require very cooperative actors. But once I'd given them the limits of their task, then we tried to justify it as we'd try to justify anything. In other words, I said, 'These people are in some kind of limbo, or they're trying to find a source of light, or they're trying to make the light go away.' We talked about being in the electric chair, being confined to a dungeon, and being tortured.

Schechner: Were there other rooms to this house?

Schneider: No, there were no other rooms to this house; this was the condition of their existence, and in that sense it was a house that had no other rooms.

Schechner: In that sense, this play was a play whose environment was determined by the play itself.

Schneider: You mean there was no outside reality? No, the nature of the reality was that there was nothing but this room, nothing but this place and nothing but this time. For example, they all wanted to know how they'd gotten here. We discovered they were dead – we worked it out almost like a detective story – who was killed first, who was killed how – I'm not sure the audience knew they were all dead.

Schechner: Did they have bodies?

Schneider: No; that was the justification for not being able to move anything.

Schechner: And did they react to the light as if it was light, or was the light something else?

Schneider: Sure it was a light. Although you might say that the light was like a bell; it was 'something' that made them respond. Whenever the light wasn't on, I tried to get them to be utterly without consciousness. (We called the light Sam, by the way.)

[. . .]

Schechner: Since you're the only person in the country who's directed all the Beckett plays, what do you think of Beckett and what's your relationship to him?

Schneider: What do I think of Beckett? I am absolutely devoted to him. I have tremendous admiration for him, both as a person, and as an artist. I consider him primarily a poet, a man whose tools relate ultimately – in the theatre – to the use of language, and who is all the time posing himself the task of eliminating all the means at his disposal and still creating some kind of valid metaphor. Whenever we do a Beckett play, I say, 'Fellas we're not gonna get into the philosophical aspects – what the meaning is – until we're open. In the meantime, I'm going to deal with the local situations.'

Schechner: Let's go through some of these local situations. Let's start with *Godot*.

Schneider: Two guys – tramps – who live out in some desolate place are waiting for somebody. The local situation is that they're waiting. While they're waiting, they're killing time with various activities. One of them is intelligent about it and the other is not. My own feeling is that Vladimir might be considered to be the mind, or the intellectual faculties, and Estragon to be the body, or the physical faculties. I can't say that I didn't mention that to the actors, but I don't think I did. Beckett does it for me – Estragon is physical, he's dealing with his shoe, and he's sitting and crouching and eating, and he's hungry. Everything with him we make physical in terms of tasting, smelling, seeing, hearing, anything to do with his senses or animal instincts. In the case of Vladimir I tried to emphasize all his intellectual and sensitive and imaginative qualities.

[. .]

Schechner: What about *Endgame*?

Schneider: *Endgame* is more local than anything else, because there is some kind of place, very well defined – he calls it 'the shelter,' the refuge – so you're in the cellar of some old building. One of my big contributions to *Endgame* was to convince the set designer, David Hays (who is very talented), to reject his original sketch and wind up with the bare walls of the Cherry Lane Theatre. Clov's den was just the downstairs of the Cherry Lane. I felt that the Cherry Lane was the refuge. They weren't the last people in the world after an atomic holocaust or anything of that kind; for the actor it was a basement in which these four people had been somehow left.

Schechner: And you built, with the actors, an inner life? Now I'm an actor and I say, 'Why am I in an ashcan?'

Schneider: The script says you lost your legs in a bicycle accident, and he dumps you in there because he doesn't want to take care of you. In other words, he doesn't have the responsibility of seeing you fall off a cliff somewhere – he can control you.

Schechner: And I'm Clov and I say, 'Why don't I leave?'

Schneider: Because you're scared. There's nothing to eat out there. At least you've got something to eat here. Also, you can't walk; your legs hurt. And, after all, you've been here a long time.

Schechner: You discuss the roles with the actors in terms of physical, palpable ideas which they can relate to their own experience. The play is not necessarily – especially a Beckett play – going to have that kind of an effect on the audience, or is it? Do you want the audience to believe that this is a basement and he is afraid to go out – do you want the motivation of the actor to get across to the audience?

Schneider: The playwright provides a text. If the actor plays that he is cold in the basement, the audience may get from that that he is cold, lonely, lost, and there's no heat, and that's the end of fires in the world, and so on. That's not the actor's responsibility. If the text serves the playwright's purpose properly, it may be sufficient for the actor to play 'I'm cold' for the playwright's purpose to be 'this is the end of all human warmth' or 'the fires have gone out.' I see no contradiction between that and the author's intentions. I try to avoid implications, but I don't try to avoid carrying out the author's intention.

Now we're on the movie: Here's Buster Keaton, who is one of the greatest performers I've ever seen – and I use the word advisedly rather than 'actor' – who has projected a certain personality in the films of a certain era, and indeed, he has retained that personality. One of the things I worried about in casting him was whether it would be possible to take that personality and make it fit into Beckett's purpose – not to change it into Beckett's purpose, because that was very clear to me; you can't change Buster Keaton after forty years. There were lots of discussions about that before we cast Buster. [. . .] Buster wanted to wear his own hat – though he would have worn any hat we wanted. The original idea was for a hat which would hide his face from the world because the character was trying not to be observed. Buster was willing to do that, but he wasn't too happy about it. One day Sam looked at Buster's hat and said, 'O.K., go ahead,' and he put a handkerchief on under the hat to hide Buster's face, which is a typically Beckett solution to the problem. Buster was happy and Sam was not unhappy and it worked. [. . .] He is stylistically comedic and tender and eloquent and expressive in pantomime, so every motion counts. This may seem cynical of me, but I could have contributed nothing more to Buster Keaton's performance by enlightening him on the philosophy of perception, or talking about Bishop Berkeley. Indeed why the hell should I?

Schechner: You might have detracted from the performance. I agree with you absolutely. I want to talk about the movie a little more. Is that the only time you worked directly with Beckett in rehearsal?

Schneider: It's the only one where he was there during production. I've talked to him about all the others, so I felt I at least knew what he wanted. But he never saw any of them.

Schechner: What did he say when you talked to him about the plays?

Schneider: He would only answer specific questions. For example, the actors in *Endgame* always wanted to know why Clov's and Hamm's faces are red and Nell's and Nag's white. And he said, 'Why is Werther's coat green?'

Schechner: Is that typical of the kind of answer you'd get to a specific question?

Schneider: No, a lot of the answers were more helpful. I wrote to him about *Godot* and said I couldn't understand about this 'Let's do the tree for fun' business while they're doing exercises, and in almost every production the actor playing Estragon simply stands on one leg and holds his arms out like the branches of a tree. He wrote back and said that's exercise fifty-two in the yogi series of exercises, and he drew me a little diagram – the 'tree' is when you stand on one leg with the other leg propped up, and with the arms in the position of prayer (a balancing exercise). The next line is 'Do you think God is watching me?' If he is accidentally in a position of prayer, then becomes aware of the position into which he has strayed, and wonders whether, by accident, that position of prayer has had some impact on God, then that transition becomes a logical and organic thing. To Beckett it was crystal clear. He doesn't avoid answering if he has an answer, but I always ask him specific questions, never thematic questions.

Schechner: Now the movie. What's the thing called?

Schneider: It's called *Film*.

Schechner: Like *Play* is called *Play* . . . Could you describe the four-way relationship – Beckett to you to the cameraman to the actor – especially because that was the one where Beckett was there.[1]

Schneider: I'm not sure it's that unusual. I read the script almost two years ago, and I happened to be in Paris on another deal with him, but we talked a little bit about the script. There were a lot of things I didn't understand – what he meant about the 'angle of perception.' There's a man pursued by someone else, and that someone else is the person represented by the subjective camera. Whenever the camera exceeds a certain angle in relation to this man, the man becomes aware of it; when the camera withdraws, the man ceases to be aware of it. I would ask a question like, 'What does he think happened to the other guy?' He doesn't exist; he exists only when he exceeds the angle, and when he withdraws from the angle, as far as this guy's concerned, the other fellow doesn't exist. That's the premise. So I have to accept and go on from there. [. . .] Then he came, and it was that weekend that we went over the script shot by shot. That was the revealing time, because a lot of things were unclear in terms of how or why certain things happen to this guy in the room.

On the other hand, certain things were clarified for Sam, like 'Why don't we add this shot?' or 'Yes, we'll try it.' There was a constant attempt on the part of the professional movie people involved to 'free' the script. [. . .] I wanted Sam on the set, although I had my qualms about it – the director's in command – he had to look at what we were doing. So we brought him on the set, and the sequence was very simple. Sam would look at the scene, then I would insist that he look at it through the cameras, and then we would shoot the scene.

[. . .]

Schechner: You've been doing Beckett's plays for eight or nine years; what sort of development do you see in him?

Schneider: I think, again, he works in more and more specific metaphors. He is searching for the ultimate stripping down of his medium – he is trying to reduce the whole theatrical spectrum to a toneless voice in a disembodied head, and I see nothing wrong with that. It's theatrical as hell.

Schechner: You think it's theatrical?

Schneider: I think as long as it's theatrical, it's valid – how much farther can he go? There are lots of jokes – I've been told that his next play is going to be a two-act play where the first act starts with the house lights going down and then the curtain doesn't go up at all. Then there's an intermission, and the second act, which is the same except it's only half as long as the first act. I laugh at that, too, but I think when Sam has stripped the medium as clean as he can, he will go off and start completely from another direction.

Schechner: What is Beckett's theatricalism?

Schneider: Well, I'm not a theatre critic. But you might say that Beckett is a Mozart; there's a precise, elegant, graceful, formal, but small-scale pattern of rhythm and tone in his work. [. . .] If you're asking me to compare Beckett, Brecht, Pinter, and Albee: Beckett is Mozart – a string quartet – and Brecht becomes somebody like Stravinsky, where everything is going in all directions in some kaleidoscopic manner – highly romantic, or maybe that's the wrong word, in the sense of a sprawling, seeming disorder, but very rigidly controlled by his thematic material. It's like a great big bunch of varicolored scarves that you throw around, instead of one very small embroidered handkerchief – I don't think that's too profound an image. Pinter has been called a disciple, or at least a follower, of Beckett, and I think Pinter couldn't have existed as a playwright had he not read Beckett. But then he goes into his own field – a rhythmical, contrapuntal use of language and repetition of words, playing on words so that his plays are colloquial in a funny way and formal in another way – making some mystical thing out of the absolutely ordinary. Albee builds with words and emotions, too. Albee is highly theatrical – in *Zoo Story* he depends on a certain flair and sensationalism.

Schechner: I want to talk about [Edward Albee's] *Who's Afraid of Virginia Woolf* – about putting the production together. [. . .]

Schneider: There was one great advantage we had, apart from the luck in casting – that is, we got the right actors for all four roles – but, on top of that, we were sort of united against the universe. Also, there were only four, and they were almost always on stage. It was a concerted effort so, in a sense, the lack of time and the lack of having worked together previously was made up for by being all together, even offstage and outside rehearsal hours. [. . .] Usually, Broadway rehearsals are just one agony after another.

I had some idea when I read it of the texture that it had to have – it was not a literal view of life in 1961 on a particular campus; it was some kind of witch's Sabbath. [. . .] We read the play for three days because we didn't have Arthur [Hill, playing George], and Uta [Hagen, playing Martha] had eight million questions – some of which Edward [Albee] answered, some of which none of us answered. We changed some lines around, did some cuts. Then Arthur came, and we read the play for a couple more days while he asked questions. We tried to get a basic tempo, a basic texture, just vocally, so that the lines would be easier. Edward was terribly concerned with tempo – the beats, the basic rhythm of a scene. Uta wanted to get it on its feet as soon as possible; in this way she was following my strongest inclination, because I normally want to stage things fairly rapidly.

Schechner: With the script in hand?

Schneider: It depends. I haven't for years said, 'You've got to learn the third act by Friday.' I used to, but usually they learn the third act when they feel like it. I wanted it staged as fast as I could, but I had a terrible time trying to plan the staging ahead of time. Usually I know the key scenes, but here I couldn't do even those; there were too many imponderables. So we worked on the staging, and it's a long play. We did it in about nine days, working fairly freely, basically working out what the logical relationships would be in the staging. It was about the hardest work I've ever done, because there was no indication of it in the script, and where or how they talked was not clear.

Schechner: Did you block it, or, with a small cast, did they block it with you?

Schneider: They blocked it with me; I never just block a show, except in the cases like 'Clov goes up the ladder.'

Schechner: You don't prepare a book for it beforehand?

Schneider: I normally do for the key scenes – I have some idea, but I try not to let anybody know I have the idea. But in this, I couldn't do it – I tried, I gave up. We worked it out very cooperatively and very little was changed.

Schechner: What I'm driving at also is that an actress like Uta Hagen, with her Stanislavski training –

Schneider: – I gave her a great deal of leeway. But Uta – and I must make this clear – was very pragmatic about the whole thing, Stanislavski or not. She'd say, 'Look, shall I cross here because I've been over by the sofa too long' – she's very good at that, and I appreciated it. [. . .] Uta came prepared much more than I did; she had a notebook with a floorplan of the part of the room we didn't see.

Schechner: How did you blend them all together? [. . .] I'm driving for the technical, tiny bits of craft which define a director's style – of specific things you did.

Schneider: Well, that's hard to pin down. For example: everyone thought the opening scene of the second act with the two men was too long and should have been cut. I thought it of it as a kind of chess game – all the scenes between them where chess games in which the two men who had contempt for each other would win a pawn and lose a pawn, and we actually structured the scene around winning pawns. In their first scene, George says, 'What made you decide to be a teacher?' and Nick says, 'Oh, the same things that motivated you, I imagine,' and he thinks he's off the hook. Then George says, 'What were they?' and Nick says, 'Pardon?' 'What were they?' repeats George, and Nick can only say, 'I don't know.' He's lost a point. Then George says, 'You just finished saying that the things that motivated you were the same things that motivated me.' He thinks he's got Nick pinned down, but the kid says, 'I said I *imagined* they were.' He slips out of it, a minor victor, but skillful skirting around the edge of conflict. So now he's won a pawn. That was the way we approached the whole thing. There's a kind of parry and thrust on a very subtle level, but each one's aware of it. Similarly, we built the second act scene of drunkenness on the sofa in terms of the two men. It's harder for me to talk about Uta and Arthur although, in effect, we worked the same way.

Schechner: This is such an exhausting play for the actors –

Schneider: – It's exhausting in one way and invigorating in another. Uta always said that when she played it right, she was never tired – not as tired as when she didn't play it right.

Schechner: Did the life of the play ever carry offstage?

Schneider: No, I don't think so. I think this is an affectation that, honestly, I don't go along with. Uta was always backstage playing solitaire or kidding around, and she'd hear a cue and go onstage, and have a tremendous capacity for picking up the scene.

Schechner: In terms of the overall conception of the play, you said you saw it as a phantasmagoria. Do you have anything to add?

Schneider: It's also, in a funny way, very formal, very musical in structure, with rhythmical repetitions of elements and themes to be more stressed and less stressed, growing and fluctuating in intensity. I find it hard to go beyond that because, again, concept and execution rarely jibe. I started by saying that directing was an exploration. I felt this with *Virginia Woolf* – and I'm not talking about the success of the play or the audience reception, but what the production would end up as. Once we had those four actors, and once I had some sense of Edward's intention and his concern for formal structure – it was a symphonic score – we just had to be a little more intense here, a little simpler there.

[. . .]

Schechner: I've got one last question on the difference between the challenge of the proscenium and the open stage, since you've worked on both.

Schneider: You're talking about two very different sensory experiences? It's easy enough to say the proscenium is a visual form and the open stage is plastic or three-dimensional. I think what the open stage allows is more freedom, more opportunities for different relationships, more interesting choreography and more meaningful and less conventional physical relationships. I always think of the proscenium as the shuttle from Times Square to Grand Central – all you can do is move left or right. The two forms have advantages and disadvantages, and I see no reason why one should have to be better than the other. I like not to work in one exclusively. I find it invigorating not to go back and do the same thing over and over again; you repeat yourself at best, but when you go back and forth, you repeat yourself less.

Schechner: Back to *Virginia Woolf:* how did you turn some of these actors on to the characters?

Schneider: You cast them right. If you cast them right, you don't turn them on; if you don't cast them right, you're not a Svengali. I've got a kid playing in the road company of *Virginia Woolf* now, and I think we cast him right, but he's inexperienced. Everything has to be spelled out. He's willing and we have a little time, so it's not so bad, but it's a pain in the neck. I'll do anything – I'll show him if I have to, I tell him, I talk to him, I take him out for drinks, I ask him to play a record.

Schechner: Do you prefer, in any sense, to work with actors who have Method training rather than other actors?

Schneider: I prefer to work with actors of any kind who are talented and willing.

Schechner: Do you think there's any problem of actor training in this country?

Schneider: Yes, there's a terrible problem, because our actors have been trained for a certain basic playwriting which we have gone away from – that is, the playwrights have stopped writing realistic plays and the theatre is now concerned with more formal and intensified material, whereas the actor has, for thirty years, been concentrating on the creation of simple reality. Now the actor who has learned to be 'real' on stage has got to find a way to make the reality larger, not room-size.

Schechner: [. . .] My question is one of how to make the internal life large enough to fill a Hamlet or a Lear.

Schneider: But also not to be content with the selection of internal life without regard for the specific demands of the production and the play. [. . .] There's no such thing as an emotional demand apart from a technical demand.

Schechner: Do you think that our training fits many of our actors for the emotional demands of a Lear?

Schneider: In general, no, it's not enough. Lee Grant opened *Electra* a while ago – you wind up with her emotional demands met, but according to all reports she wasn't able to play Electra.

Schechner: We add to Method training the training of the externals. Is that what you're suggesting, or do we also change the kind of internal training to a certain degree – modify it?

Schneider: You have to modify it toward making the actor aware that internal training is a means to an end and not an end in itself and that his concern for it is a relative and not an absolute concern. I do not think that the attainment of reality, in itself, can be made a goal. The end is the production of a play.

NOTE

1   Buster Keaton was the only actor in *Film* (1964). It was directed by Schneider with Beckett's supervision and produced by Barney Rosset and the Evergreen Theater. (Editors' note.)

9

BRECHT AS DIRECTOR

Carl Weber

T37, 1967

[. . .] Brecht had worked for the theatre nearly all his life, as a critic first, then as a playwright and director, [but] it was not until 1949 that he found a permanent place for his experiments, a company, and later a building, which he could form into the ideal instrument for his ideas, a theatre which was a laboratory, a place for investigation, analysis, and construction of models.

When Brecht returned to Europe after his wartime stay in the United States, the East German authorities offered to let him direct a production of *Mother Courage* with his wife, Helene Weigel, in the lead. [. . .] The production opened in 1949, at the Deutsches Theatre, Berlin, and was the turning point of German theatre history, perhaps in this century – surely at least since Max Reinhardt. The critics – who had almost unanimously condemned Brecht's work in the years before 1933 – did a somersault, and the production was a great success. I went to see it as a young man coming from the university at Heidelberg; it remains the greatest theatre experience of my life. It is hard now to describe exactly what was so unique, since I since have come to know the production so well, from acting in it and restaging it in 1954. One thing: it was the first time I had ever seen people on the stage behave like real human beings; there was not a trace of 'acting' in that performance, though the technical brilliance and perfection of every moment were stunning. The economy of the set, of every prop used, was absolutely overwhelming to one who had seen until then only run-of-the-mill – and sometimes the best – German theatre. And it was astonishing how the idea of the play was brought across without pushing, without hammering it into the audience. All this was above and beyond the superb individual performances of Weigel and the rest of the company.

I decided that I had to work with Brecht, but it was not until 1952 that the Ensemble had a vacant position for an assistant director. I went to a dramaturg of the company, Peter Palitzsch, and asked how to apply to Brecht. He answered that Brecht didn't like to interview people and the best thing was to submit a piece about one of the Ensemble's productions – not a review, just a description of what the actors did, why, and whether it worked. I went to see *Puntila* several times, wrote about two of its scenes, and sent it to Brecht. [. . .] Then three weeks went by [till] Brecht had read the piece and wanted to see me.

The next morning, there he was in his cap. I was very embarrassed and shy, and right away he became even more shy than I. He said, 'Yes, you are . . . Yes, I have read . . . ' There was a long pause. I didn't know what to say and he just looked at me. Then finally he said, 'I have to go to rehearsal. Why don't you go to our business office and talk to Weigel about your contract?' And off he went.

I asked at the office if I could watch a rehearsal, and they told me that anyone who had a legitimate interest could watch rehearsals unless Brecht, as happened rarely, thought an actor was extremely nervous – even then he would work with that actor separately, but the rest of the rehearsal would be kept open. He wanted actors to get used to spectators, to get laughs, to be in contact with the people down there as early in the process as possible, to work *with* an audience.

At that time they were rehearsing the *Urfaust*. [. . .] I walked into the rehearsal and it was obvious that they were taking a break. Brecht was sitting in a chair smoking a cigar, the director of the production, Egon Monk,[1] and two or three assistants were sitting with him, some of the actors were on stage and some were standing around Brecht, joking, making funny movements and laughing about them. Then one actor went up on the stage and tried about thirty ways of falling from a table. They talked a little about the scene '*Im Auerbach's Keller*' (Mephisto brings Faust into an inn where drunken students enjoy themselves with dirty jokes and silly songs). Another actor tried the table, the results were compared, with a lot of laughing and a lot more horseplay. This went on and on, and someone ate a sandwich, and I thought, my God this is a long break. So I sat naively and waited, and just before Monk said, 'Well, now we are finished, let's go home,' I realized that this was rehearsal. And it was typical of the loose way Brecht often worked, of his experimental approach and of the teamwork the Ensemble was used to. Whatever ideas he brought to rehearsal he tried out, threw away, tried something else; sometimes forty versions of one scene were tried, once in a while only two. Even when a production had opened, and been reviewed, he reworked parts of it, rerehearsed it, changed the blocking. The actors also took an experimental attitude. They would suggest a way of doing something, and if they started to explain it, Brecht would say that he wanted no discussions in rehearsal – it would have to be tried. Of course, his whole view of the world was that it was changeable and the people in it were changing; every solution was only a starting point for a new, better, different solution.

All this was – of course – not just for love of experiment. Brecht was mainly concerned with the play as the telling of a story to an audience, clearly, beautifully, and entertainingly. If he found that in an almost completed production one certain part was opaque or boring, he cut it. I have never seen anyone cut a script as mercilessly as Brecht cut his own. Brecht had another important ability: if he had worked at a scene, and then dropped it for a week, he could come back and look at it as if he had never seen it before. I remember a scene from the third act of *Caucasian Chalk Circle*, when Grusha, with her adopted child and her brother Lawrentij, arrives at the house of the dying peasant whom she is forced to marry. The scene hadn't been done for about three weeks (the play was rehearsed for eight months); he came back to it, and we all thought it was going rather well when suddenly Brecht yelled, 'Stop!' He asked what the actor playing Lawrentij, who was walking across the room, was doing. Well, we answered, there's a good reason; he has to be over there for his next line, you blocked it this way. Brecht denied this angrily, saying there was no reason for such a move. 'But his next line asks for it.' 'What line?' he barked. The actor said the line. 'But that's impossible, I couldn't have written that!' We had to show him in the book that he had indeed written it, and he was furious – at us. But he rewrote the scene. He had looked at it as if it were by someone else, from a play he'd never heard of before, which he was judging as a spectator, and it failed.

The initial preparation of a play usually took about half a year, while it was discussed and adapted (if it was a translation). The set was developed on paper and as a model during that period, as were the costumes. Then, when Brecht went into rehearsal, it could take three to four months to block the play. This blocking involved the working out of a considerable number of details. To Brecht, blocking was the backbone of the production: ideally, he thought, the blocking should be able to tell the main story of the play – and its contradictions – by itself, so that a person watching through a glass wall unable to hear what was being said would be able to understand the main elements and conflicts of the story. To work out blocking this clear takes an enormous amount of time; he would try out every thinkable possibility – and if a scene didn't seem to work in dress rehearsal, the first thing reworked would be the blocking.

After the basic blocking was finished, we started to work on the acting detail; by this time the actors knew their lines completely, and could play around with them freely. The most meticulous attention was paid to the smallest gesture. Sometimes it took an hour to work out whether an actor should pick up a tool one way or another. Particular attention was devoted to all details of physical labor. A man's work forms his habits, his attitudes, his physical behavior down to the smallest movement, a fact usually neglected by the stage. Brecht spent hours in rehearsal exploring how Galileo would handle a telescope and an apple, how the kitchenmaid Grusha would pick up a waterbottle or a baby, how the young soldier Eilif would drink at his general's table, etc. Often paintings or other pictorial documents of the play's period were brought into rehearsal for the study of movements and gestures. Brecht's favorite painters were Breughel and Bosch: their paintings told 'stories' (not in the sense of the veristic nineteenth-century school, of course), their people were stamped by their lives and occupations, their vices and beliefs. The influence of pictures he had seen often could be felt in Brecht's work; certain moments of the blocking, as well as character-images, were derived from paintings or photos.

Each moment had to be examined: for the characters' situation, for the story's situation, for the actions going on around the character. When all these details had been brought to a certain point, not of completion, but of diminished possibilities, Brecht would have the first run-through. This might be six months after the actors started work on the play, six months of working on blocking, single beats, and small units of scenes. The first run-through was usually a disaster – it was impossible for the actors to pull things together so fast. But this was just what Brecht was waiting for; in the second and third run-throughs, a rhythm began to appear, and all the mistakes made so far emerged clearly. So then Brecht broke the whole thing down again into short beats and small units, and reworked every part that had been unsuccessful. After the second break-down of the play, the final period of rehearsal usually came. This included run-throughs – but interrupted by frequent reworking of scenes and details. A week or more was given to the technical rehearsals. Lighting a show sometimes took five days alone, and extras were used to walking through all the motions, so the actors wouldn't waste their time and energy. During dress rehearsals, details were constantly changed or developed further, including the blocking and quite often even the text. I remember first nights, when actors would find a little note from Brecht on their dressing-room tables, wishing them good luck and asking them to say a new line in scene X instead of one Brecht had decided to cut, because audience reactions in dress rehearsals had indicated that the former line didn't work the way Brecht intended it.

After the last dress rehearsal Brecht always did an exercise, which he called the 'marking' or 'indicating' rehearsal: the actors, not in costumes, but on the set, had to walk quickly through all the actions of the show, quoting the text very rapidly, without any effort at acting, but keeping the rhythm, the pauses, etc., intact. The effect – if you were sitting far back in the house – was very much like an early silent movie: you saw people moving and gesturing very quickly, but you couldn't hear the words or get any kind of emotions, except the most obvious ones. This proved to be an extremely helpful device; it made the actors relax, helped them to memorize every physical detail and gave them a keen sense for the show's rhythmic pattern.

Finally first night came, which in fact was a preview with audience, after which rehearsals were used to change the production according to audience reactions. After five to eight previews, the official 'opening' with press and invited guests took place. Brecht introduced these previews to Germany, probably drawing on his American and English experiences. In the beginning, the German critics strongly rejected this procedure; now other theatres have followed Brecht's example. After the opening, work on the production didn't stop. The director – or one of his assistants – watched every performance, and whenever changes or a reworking were felt necessary, rehearsals were scheduled.

This sounds like a monumentally laborious process, and to some extent it was. But it took place in an atmosphere of humor, ease with experimentation, relaxation. Actors (and directors) new at the Ensemble were usually very tense, and tried to get results right away – as they must when they have only a few weeks' rehearsal time. Brecht would tell them, 'Fast results are always to be regarded with suspicion. The first solution is usually not a good solution. Not enough thinking goes into it. Instinct is a very dubious guide, especially for directors.'

Brecht regarded design as of the highest importance, and had worked out his methods of handling it with his friend Caspar Neher. When Neher designed a play for him, he started with little sketches depicting the important story situations – sometimes he arrived at a kind of comic strip of the entire play. He began with people, sketching the characters in relation to a given situation, and thus visualizing the blocking. When he and Brecht were satisfied with the sketches, they started to develop a set. For Brecht, for Neher when he worked with Brecht, for Otto and von Appen, who worked with Brecht in the 1950s, the set was primarily a space where actors tell a certain story to the audience. The first step was to give the actor the space and architectural elements he needed; the next was to work out the set so it by itself would tell the audience enough about the play's story and conflicts, its period, social relations, etc.; the last step was to make it beautiful.

Whatever is called the 'style' of Brechtian productions was always something arrived at during the last phase of production. Brecht never began with a pre-conceived stylistic idea, even something so 'basic' as whether the production should be 'period,' 'naturalistic,' or whatever silly labels theatre convention usually pins on plays. He began with a long exploration of the intricate social relationships of the characters and the behavior resulting from them. Their psychology was not left out, but was developed from the social relations. The designer watched, working out his ideas as Brecht rehearsed. Twice I saw about 75 percent of a completed set – and the finished costumes that went with it – thrown away after the first dress rehearsal, because although it was beautiful it did not tell the audience what Brecht and von Appen wanted. An enormous amount of money was poured into these experiments, but certainly not wasted. One of Brecht's favorite proverbs – 'The proof of the pudding is in the eating' – was always applied to his theatre work.

From the time Brecht began directing in Munich in the 1920s, until the end, he liked to have people around him when he directed. He asked everyone he trusted to come to rehearsal and constantly asked their opinions; he controlled his work through their reactions. In the 1950s, his productions were always teamwork, and he constantly used all the people connected with a production – assistants, designer, musicians (Eisler was at many rehearsals). Brecht asked the Ensemble's technicians to attend dress rehearsals, and afterwards sought their opinions. I remember the last rehearsals of *Katzgraben* (a play by the contemporary East German novelist and playwright Erwin Strittmatter, which Brecht produced in 1953), to which Brecht had invited a group of children between 10 and 14. He spent two hours with them after rehearsal to find out what they understood and what not, trying to pin down the reasons. The discussion's result was a reworking of many scenes to achieve more clarity, a higher quality of 'telling the story.' [. . .]

In the Ensemble, Brecht decided that the young directors should co-direct – two or even three of them as directors of the same standing. This worked well. The directors would arrive at a basic concept on which they could agree before going into rehearsal. But in actual rehearsal, beautiful things would come out of the tension between different minds working on the same problems – better solutions than any one of the directors could have arrived at on his own. In fact, many productions before and most productions after his death were directed in this way. [. . .]

Brecht never cared how his actors worked. He didn't tell them to go home and do this or that, or to go behind the set and concentrate. He didn't give a damn about the mechanics they used, he just cared about results. Brecht respected actors and was extremely patient with them; he often used their suggestions. During breaks, he would listen sometimes to rather obvious nonsense from the actors, wanting them not to feel uncomfortable with him, wanting to gain their confidence in all matters. He himself could probably have become a great actor. He could be a marvelous clown: sometimes the actors would provoke him to demonstrate something, for the sheer joy of watching him. He did not prod the actors to ape what he had demonstrated, but rather would exaggerate enough so that while they saw exactly what he wanted, they were never tempted to copy him.

It is interesting to compare the way in which I saw Brecht direct actors with what's reported by Leon Feuchtwanger's wife (who was there) about his first directing. When Brecht was 24, and his play *Drums in the Night* was being rehearsed in Munich, the director found to his surprise that the young author was coming to rehearsals, interrupting him, yelling at the actors, and demonstrating how they should do things. Pretty soon Brecht had almost taken over the entire production, and the director – a mature man – was practically his assistant. As usual in the German theatre of that time, the rehearsal period was short, somewhat under three weeks, but by the last week the actors, some of whom were quite prominent, were trying very hard to do what Brecht wanted them to. Basically, he was attempting to wean them from the pompous, over-ambitious typical German manner of the time, to bring them back to a realistic treatment of the lines. Mrs. Feuchtwanger's report is of great interest: that very young man, who came to attend rehearsals for his first play, kept yelling at the actors that what they offered was shit. When I met him in his fifties, mellowed perhaps, but not the least weakened in his determination, he was still busy cleaning the stage (and all art) of 'sweet lies.' [. . .]

Brecht tried to present in his theatre a real view of the world, no gold-plated images, no false heroes, no 'revealing' photos of rabbits, busy nibbling cabbage and humping their mates, of whatever sex. Doubt in manmade gods, doubt in man-made rules, doubt in whatever man is told to accept were proclaimed on his stage. And a profound insight into man's weakness and longing to conform – an insight, by the way, which was not without understanding and compassion.

Edited by Erika Munk from a lecture given at Tullane University, February 1967

NOTE

1 Egon Monk was Brecht's assistant and collaborator on the earliest Berliner Ensemble productions. Later he directed under Brecht's supervision. He would not have been on board for the 1949 production of *Mother Courage*. For the 1951 Berliner Ensemble production of *Mother Courage* the *Regie* is Egon Monk alone. The 1954 production was a restaging of Brecht's 1949 production. (Editors' note.)

10

THE REVOLUTIONARY MOMENT

Lee Baxandall

T42, 1968

1. [. . .] Naturalism is far from dead. In America, Europe, and Russia, the virtually unsurpassed mode of dramatic expression, strenuously and yet unfortunately, is still Naturalism. Its greatest living practitioner is Samuel Beckett. To the extent he has any expressed politics, Beckett is a man of the left. He verbally supported the Spanish Republic in its civil war; he was somehow involved with the French Partisans during World War II. His left sympathies, however, are not of a piece with his dramatic imagination. His enthusiasm, if that is the word, is for victimization and helplessness. In this compulsion lies another – implicit – politics; it is not the kind of implicit politics we need in drama, not the kind we increasingly are able to move towards. For Naturalism, though far from dead, is not quite living.

2. These remarks are by way of preface to a discussion of naturalistic drama in conjunction with Socialist consciousness, politics, and drama. It is at this conjuncture – frequent, as Beckett's case suggests, and for theoretical purposes crucial – that we find the basis for regarding Naturalism as a more capacious and enduring category than often is supposed. [. . .]

3. Naturalism is far from dead; its decisive quality lies not in a style or subject matter, but in a social philosophy. Beckett does, in fact, continue the 'low,' 'sordid,' 'shocking' subject matter of Zola, Ibsen, or Hauptmann, if he does not quite discover 'a new slice of reality.' [. . .] His style, rather than assuming the presumably naturalistic 'clinical,' 'detailed,' and 'documentary' approach, is 'poetic,' 'inventive' and 'theatrical.' This trend within Naturalism [bears] the implicit conviction or attitude or outlook (however inarticulate) which treats man as incapable of free will. [. . .] The social philosophy brings forth characters whose ineffectual deeds are determined by the overwhelming forces of the social system (and sometimes, in some part, by heredity).

  [. . .] Beckett's creations do demonstrate blood kinship, *mutatis mutandis*, with Zola's Thérèse Raquin, Ibsen's Mrs. Alving or Johannes Rosmer, and the peasants in Tolstoy or Hauptmann. Occasional cries of outrage, even of revolt (as in Megan

Terry's *Viet Rock*) cannot violate an overriding despondency; O'Neill wrote his *Hairy Ape*, Ibsen had his Dr. Stockmann. *The Wild Duck*, *The Iceman Cometh*, or *Waiting for Godot* come back with the fundamental ice-water reply inherent to the Naturalist outlook: man has no freedom but he requires illusory hope for ephemeral happiness. The political implication pervading the diversity of Naturalism comes clear, then, precisely at the point Pozzo or Rosmer accepts – after some blather and fuss – his own *a priori* futility. It had been better not to strive, for the Rat-Wife is in waiting for every such *naif*. The politics through almost a hundred years have been *quietistic* – not saying Yes, but not doing No to the Way Things Are.

Ruminative, Didi and Gogo are seated – or walking or talking or eating or pissing, it doesn't matter – somewhere on the grounds of the Rosmersholm property. A social philosophy was their time machine.

4. The trouble is: we have had little else for nearly one hundred years but naturalistic social outlook in our ambitious theatre. The period of modern drama was indeed opened by Naturalism. Its outlook was at one time a bold revelation; it stood nearly at the pinnacle of social-scientific awareness. No longer. Each year's collection of naturalistic truths becomes a little less compelling or interesting. And the dramaturgical instrument itself becomes, in all but the greatest hands, like Beckett's, an almost-unexamined, almost-enervating cliché. We go to the theatre – if we still go – not knowing the story we are to hear but perfectly anticipating its punch line. Somehow all the stories turn out to be a sick joke at the playwright's and his listener's expense. Why should audiences not, as they do, turn towards the cinema, where far more *reality* gets caught willy-nilly in the camera within a comparable lapse of real time, irrespective of whether the movie story is naturalistic, even 'escapist'? True, Naturalism is a realism, and theatre can create confrontations with reality, which the cinematic medium cannot duplicate. But the public is not merely reality-hungry. It craves reality captured by means of a philosophy which is adequate to a view of the present-as-history and life as perhaps more than a somber sick joke. [. . .]

The task of playwrights and theatres is evidently to move on. Not so much in style or subject matter as in outlook. This is not simple. Playwrights and directors do continue to sense their situation within the bounds of a social philosophy given dramatic memorableness almost a century ago. And our novel and renowned dramatic structures generally turn out to have dank naturalistic basements, because other foundations are not readily to hand. Our lives have not the cast of freedom. The customs and institutions of conformity appear to loom more omnipotently and without alternative – despite business-academic social science, bohemian outlets and Socialist politics – than ever previously. The reprehensible cliché abides upon a profound social fact. Those seeking to go 'beyond' the naturalistic drama more easily fall 'beneath' its achievement.

5. With this estimate of the major question of our theatre, we can seek at once to elaborate it, and to discover the basis for a 'going beyond' if any now exists, if we bring to bear upon Naturalism, in an experimental spirit, the outlook and dramaturgy of Socialism. Through most of Naturalism's existence, Marxists of major stature have to do with its *ménage*.

6. Brecht can properly be termed a Naturalist – in his early plays. With *Baal*, he hymned the natural forces, urging complicity with their obscene fecundity and with one's own inevitable attrition and death. The returned soldier of *Drums in the Night* is an animal; the animal's instinct chooses sex and security over revolutionary highjinks. Darwinian fisticuffs dominate *In the Jungle of Cities*. Here Brecht flaunts his spunk, his fierce will to impose the greatest sport upon the human organism's social growth and competitive bouts and solitary decay. His discovery and assimilation of Marxism in the late 1920s set Brecht severely against the social philosophy which he, with his brains and sportiveness, never quite believed.

'The word Naturalism itself,' Brecht now wrote, 'is criminal. To present the relations we find among men as natural, and man as a particle of nature, incapable therefore of changing the relationships, is precisely a crime.' The gaining of mastery over social competition and chaos could be the most exacting and rewarding and freest sport of men. With *The Mother* (1930–1) and *The Measures Taken* (1930) he achieved two of the outstanding Bolshevik revolutionary dramas. It was a breakthrough he and other major Marxist playwrights of the time could not sustain. We shall have more to say of this genre.

In the course of the 1930s Brecht returned to a drama of the individual who fights without much assistance for survival. The collective mastery of social fate was no longer (*Mother Courage, Galileo*) represented directly. It had faded from a present reality to a savaged, convalescent ideal, and a chastened Brecht looked back from the perspective of 1953 to declare:

> I was never a Naturalist, never loved Naturalism, but for all its defects I see in it the breakthrough of realism into modern literature and modern theatre. Admitting that it is a fatalistic realism, the inessential elements of a developing case history overwhelm, the image which it renders of reality cannot be utilized, the poetic side is crippled, etc., etc., yet it does bring reality into the light, even granting that some of it remains crude and not permeated by thought. A great epoch in literature and theatre, despite everything, which only socialist realism can surpass.

7. That a latent politics resides within the 'objectivity' of Naturalism was at one time widely recognized. Mistakenly, the politics were often held to be Socialist. Spokesmen for Socialism in certain naturalistic plays (Hauptmann's *Before Sunrise*) fostered the impression. So did muckraking protest works like Ibsen's *Pillars of Society* or Herman Heijermans' *The Good Hope*, both dealing with corrupt shipping barons who risk their sailors' lives. The growth of the Socialist labor movement concurrently with the appearance of Naturalism's great beginners has been presented more than once, too, as evidence of political 'influence.' The influence, however, was almost wholly upon subject matter and language. We may characterize the naturalistic drama politically as, at best, a theatre of despairing 'protest,' which scarcely hopes for an audience capable and audacious enough actually to put society to rights. [. . .]

The naturalistic drama attracted many non-Marxian Socialists and also Marxists in the late years of the nineteenth century. They felt gratitude and satisfaction even for a one-sided breakthrough which knew only of a dreadful determinism and neglected socially combined struggle. Naturalistic drama had the prestige and honor due the one serious theatre movement in decades. On the other hand, organized Marxism, with Marx dead, was itself slipping towards an overly deterministic stress. Many who might *know* better – if theory counted as intellectuals prefer to hope it counts – could thus be persuaded that Ibsen, Hauptmann, and the early Gorky of *The Lower Depths* were indeed Socialist playwrights. Evidence of these confusions within and about Naturalism and Socialism was provided by the first theatre organization for the workers, the Freie Volksbühne, the Free Stage of the People, in Berlin.

8. In 1887 an amateur theatre enthusiast, the Paris gas company employee Antoine, first dedicated a theatre primarily to the furtherance of Naturalism. His Théâtre Libre, which initiated the free stage or little arts theatre movement, was followed in 1889 by the Berlin Freie Bühne guided by Otto Brahm. A learned and gritty literary critic and editor, Brahm borrowed from Paris his ideas for repertory and the organizing of a subscription public. Thus, for theatre dedicated to the new in art, free of police censorship and commercial compromise, Brahm's systematic skill in getting naturalistic drama on the Berlin stage, despite resistance from established theatres, was admired by Dr. Bruno Wille, a Social-Democrat devoted to the education of the working class. However, the high price of subscriptions served to restrict the Freie Bühne performances to middle-class culture lovers and intelligentsia. Dr. Wille held that Naturalism was the rightful drama of the proletariat and not of an elite; he opened the Freie Volksbühne in 1890, offering substantially lower prices. Unlike Brahm's autocratic operation, this theatre was ultimately under the artistic and organizational control of the entire membership, which reserved the right even to oust its leaders (this was to be the fate of Dr. Wille). Brahm was a great collaborator with Wille, sitting on his board, lending a stage director, suggesting plays, even proposing a merger of the two enterprises.

Naturalism, then, was initially the backbone of the Freie Volksbühne repertoire. How did it fare? Not very well: of the naturalistic repertoire, only *The Weavers* scored palpably with this public. The felt need for a Socialist labor-oriented drama had been misinterpreted by Dr. Wille. The Social-Democratic leaders had sensed this from the start of the venture. They distrusted Wille personally, deeming him a dilettante in politics and art, a bourgeois anarchist with condescending and class-distorted ideas of the proletarian's need to be given an appreciation of the newest art of the middle class. [. . .]

9. [. . .] Still and all, Naturalism was the only serious theatre around. [. . .] Moreover, even Marxists who went beyond the naturalistic outlook in theory might find that it corresponded to the reality of their lives. Thus the youngest daughter of Karl Marx, Eleanor Marx Aveling, became important to the breakthrough of Naturalism in the English-speaking world. Her personal tragedy, as distinguished from her political work, shows the ambiguous attractiveness of Naturalism.

Immersed as a girl in the family's Shakespeare cult (she on occasion played Hamlet to Karl Marx's Ghost), Eleanor had tried to become a professional actress. When this dream was relinquished, she directed much of her enthusiasm into the cause of Ibsen. Trying to win him his first London production, she organized a dramatized reading of *A Doll's House* in January 1886. Bernard Shaw took the part of Krogstadt. Eleanor played Nora. Havelock Ellis' collection of three plays (1888), which broke the English ice for Ibsen, contained Eleanor's version of *An*

Enemy of the People, later printed in the William Archer standard edition. She was also the first to translate *The Wild Duck* and *Lady From the Sea* into English (1890). Like Shaw, Eleanor Marx mightily lectured and agitated for Ibsen.

The efforts of both Marx and Shaw (in the opinion of Shaw's biographer, Archibald Henderson) were acknowledged in a letter of 28 August 1890 from Ibsen to the *Daily Chronicle*. Ibsen confessed to 'satisfaction' that he 'should without conscious or direct intention, have arrived in several matters at the same conclusions the social-democratic moral philosophers had arrived at by scientific processes.' That Ibsen noted the overlap of his own and Socialist thought was, for Eleanor Marx, only part of the basis for attraction. She stared into his plays and saw her image. After her father's death in 1883, she became locked into an emotional relationship with the charming and unscrupulous Edward Aveling which she felt powerless to change. Aveling eventually drove Eleanor Marx to suicide: her advocacy of Naturalism should not be separated from her sense of this unhappy fatality.

As to Bernard Shaw, one might argue that he managed to go beyond Naturalism as his friend Eleanor Marx did not. Certainly Shaw made her the prototype of a tragic character in *The Doctor's Dilemma*. Despite that, despite his verbal wit and brilliance, Shaw's entire Fabian optimism culminates in less than full-scale confrontation with modern social questions and processes. [. . .]

10. Karl Marx died too early to have formed an opinion of the naturalistic development. It is not difficult to decipher what it might have been. In March of 1861, while visiting Berlin, he was invited to a 'comedy, full of Prussian self-glorification . . . altogether a disgusting affair,' he noted. Most men of high cultural standards had this reaction to plays written in the decades preceding Naturalism. [. . .] The night following the Prussian comedy, a ballet at the Imperial Opera proved deadly dull but Marx found solace in the painted scenery, 'everything being represented with photographical truth.' Early Naturalism's appeal was in part due precisely to visual veracity.

Marx would have welcomed Naturalism as a vast improvement of the modern theatre, yet a remark from 1842 presages the combined attraction and reservation of Marxists towards Naturalism. 'In the frightening dramas of the royal houses of Mycenae and Thebes the greatest Greek poets *rightly represented ignorance as tragic fate.*' Marx would only have had to add that whereas in Greek drama the *characters* went to their tragic fates through individual ignorance, in Naturalism the *playwrights* – through individual ignorance of combinational struggle if not social science – created a world of foredoomed characters. In a way they never intended, the Naturalist authors would demonstrate for modern audiences the social tragedy of ignorance. [. . .]

11. Engels died in 1895, having seen, as Marx did not, the winning-through of Naturalism to stage prominence. Thus he mentions in a letter of 5 December 1892 that his personal secretary, Louis Kautsky, is 'at a meeting of actors and dramatists for the foundation of a *freie Bühne* or *théâtre libre* or what not.' According to his old friend Friedrich Lessner, Engels began to 'study Norwegian when he was over 70 years old in order to be able to read Ibsen and Kielland in the original.' [. . .]

Engels commented in a letter of 15 July 1887 upon Conrad Schmidt, a young man he had met who 'admires Zola in whom he has discovered the "materialist connection of history."' Engels judged Schmidt a 'decent fellow' but 'the greenest fellow I ever saw.' Writing to the novelist Margaret Harkness the next year, Engels reaffirmed a view long held by himself and Marx: that more than any other modern literature the novels of Balzac portrayed with supreme organic artistry the concrete *detail*, the authentic *typicality*, and the dynamic historical *tendency* of contemporary life. Thus Balzac remained the master over 'all the Zolas *passés, présents et à venir*.' However, Ibsen did gain Engels' admiring respect. He wrote on 5 June 1890 to Paul Ernst, a young critic of Ibsen, declaring there had been in Norway a 'literary renaissance' during the previous twenty years 'unlike that of any other country of this period, except Russia.' 'These people are creating more than anywhere else, and stamping their imprint upon the literature of other countries, including Germany.' Engels believed this was so precisely because the characters in Ibsen's dramas had 'character and initiative and the capacity for independent action' exceeding that portrayed in the dramas from nations where 'the petty and the middle bourgeoisie,' as in Germany, were historically more divested of such qualities. Undoubtedly Ibsen as well reflected that same class sphere of consciousness, Engels added. [. . .]

12. The signal for a decisive leap in Socialist dramatic practice was given by the Bolsehvik Revolution of 1917. In this transition, especially as it casts light upon Naturalism, the most revealing figure is George Lukacs, the great Hungarian theorist and critic. Lukacs is today noted for his vehement opposition to literary fatalism and despair. As he traces it in *Realism in Our Time*, this attitude comes from an absence of perspective upon historical decay and resurgence – a perspective to be gained only by accepting if not committing oneself to Socialism. His fervor can perhaps only be explained if we are aware to what extent Lukacs was himself, as a young man, implicated by the naturalistic outlook.

Lukacs co-founded the first Budapest little arts theatre, the Thalia (1904–7), which contributed to the Naturalist impression on social consciousness. Concurrently he wrote and revised his *Sociology of Modern Drama* between the ages of 19 and 29, a work which to this date provides the most profound analysis of Naturalism's antecedents and social and aesthetic features. The study was written 'from within' the naturalistic drama; Lukacs acceded to its implicit claim to be the inevitable portrayal of man within capitalist society. The bald thesis of *The Sociology of Modern Drama* is this: one can no longer 'easily distinguish between man and his environment' nor locate 'the relation of a man to his action, to the extent that his action is really still his,' for modern man has become 'merely the intersection point of great forces, and his deeds not even his own. Instead something independent of him mixes in, a hostile system which he senses as forever indifferent to him, thus shattering his will.' Though vitality in life is considered lost, Lukacs nonetheless sought for a means to vivify the drama. 'Man grows dramatic by virtue of the intensity of his will, by the outpouring of his essence in his deeds, by becoming wholly identical with them.' 'Pathology,' he declared, 'is a technical necessity' of the present-day drama.

Bolshevism triumphant changed Lukacs' convention. He saw *that with collective political action, angry men could achieve their willed desire* to overturn a social system weighing upon them. (The distance between 'pathology' and a radical political audacity may not be as great as might appear: 'You have to be a little crazy to make a revolution,' the trained psychiatrist Che Guevara has reported. Though smiling when he said it, he was serious.) Lukacs reacted to the astounding events in Russia by entering the Communist Party of Hungary. During its revolutionary regime in 1919 he headed the Education Ministry and was also a commissar at the fighting front. Lukacs had shaken from his mind the acquiescent viewpoint expressed in his *Sociology of Modern Drama*. A steady stream of books and articles since then put his case for social and literary struggle against any capitulation to his passivity. *History and Class Consciousness* (1923) was the political summation of his changed outlook.

13. In the United States John Reed became the prism through which the naturalistic drama was to appear insufficient at the time of transition to a Bolshevik optimism. Remembered best for *Ten Days that Shook the World*, Reed was an eyewitness to the Russian events of 1917. He became, moreover, an actor in the revolutionary drama: he was a courier for the Bolsheviks. Back in America he addressed numerous meetings and even faced a Congressional committee, defending the Bolsheviks; he was a founder of Communism in America, and stood trial for war resistance. There is no doubt John Reed found his proper dramaturgical outlet in revolutionary deeds. In 1913 he had taken 2,000 working men, women, and children participating in a Paterson, New Jersey, textile strike and moved them in a body to Madison Square Garden where, under Reed's direction and before an audience of 15,000, they recreated the songs and suffering and hope of their strike. It was an audacious effort to educate the public about a slurringly reported, hard-fought struggle. The theatre reviewers came and wrote excitedly of a new art form: and it was.

Reed encountered Naturalism between his pageant of Paterson and 1917. Reed's one-act *Moondown* was performed in 1915 by the Washington Square Players. In summer 1916 his satire *Freedom* was acted by the Provincetown Players. Eugene O'Neill was actually introduced by his friend Reed to this little theatre company. There O'Neill had his first play performed; it was *Bound East for Cardiff*, and John Reed appeared in the cast. Late in the same summer of 1916, O'Neill acted in one of Reed's plays.

Reed's full-length, unproduced proletarian comedy, *Enter Dibble*, is imbued with vitality and is more Shavian than naturalistic. But his plays were not Reed's major effort or enduring achievement. During their Provincetown summer O'Neill and Reed shared common theatrical interests and a single girlfriend between them, afterwards parting in directions so distinct and characteristic for the time that they became exemplary: O'Neill lived seemingly in order to turn his traumatic experiences into drama; John Reed brought drama into his own life. In Lukacs' phrase, Reed grew dramatic 'by virtue of the intensity of his will, by the outpouring of his essence in his deeds.' While O'Neill won acknowledgment as America's great naturalistic dramatist, John Reed, before his death in 1921 of typhus, played an indispensable political role. And it was Reed who got the girl.

14. The prototype Bolshevik was of course Lenin. An entire generation of Marxists sought to emulate his thought processes, policies, and even mannerisms and gestures; and Lukacs wrote a book-length study of him. It is therefore curious, and

revealing for the purpose of our inquiry that Lenin felt abiding affection for one Naturalist play. Hauptmann's *The Weavers* was first performed at the Freie Bühne in early 1893; Lenin saw it some time thereafter, one May Day in a theatre of the workers' district in Geneva. His sister Anna made a Russian translation in 1895 which Lenin edited, and got the People's Will publishing house to print despite its scant financial means and the great political demands on its press.

It is certain Lenin had taken *The Weavers* to be revolutionary drama, although Hauptmann testified subsequently before the Imperial courts to the innocence of his play. But had not Hauptmann worked, after all, from an on-the-spot account of the weavers' uprising written by a lifelong friend of Karl Marx? And were not the events themselves revolutionary in import? *The Weavers* must be said to tread the narrowest of lines between fatalistic determinism and radical hope, but doubtless it falls toward the former. Hauptmann couched the story more in terms of its tragedy than the continuing potential of its radical defiance. And not only had this revolt occurred fifty years before, but its cottage-industry basis was anachronistically distant from the conditions of modern industrial struggle. Contemporary Russia more resembled Germany of the 1840s than did modern-day Germany, however, and Lenin knew it. Precious few plays even skirted the question of revolutionary action. Lenin had second thoughts about *The Weavers* after 1917, when one no longer went to a free stage to get a notion of revolutionary endeavor but direct to revolutionary Russia. His friend Bonch-Bruevich reports that Lenin wanted a preface written for the text, 'in order to give the proper perspective to the conditions of the weavers among us before the revolution and after.'

15. Lenin would probably have agreed with Napoleon. On 2 October 1808, speaking to Goethe at Erfurt, Bonaparte expressed his 'disapproval of the drama of fate,' saying that it belonged to a darker age. 'What do people want with fate nowadays?' he said. '*Politics are Fate.*' He was referring to the French classical drama, but the remark bears equally on the Naturalist philosophy. The practical difficulty with this prospect was that the political groundwork for a new dramaturgy existed well before its realization. Thus the audience of the Berlin Freie Volksbühne, more or less repelled by naturalistic fare and at the same time offered no serious, vigorous, dynamic drama of a Socialist stamp, turned to imaginative and heroic plays of an earlier day. [. . .] The effect of the Bolshevik Revolution was to transform this situation decisively. The establishment and survival of the Soviet system in Russia, the irrefutable example set by the Bolsheviks, liberated the dramatists' imagination as Marxist theory alone had not, any more than had the painful gains of organized labor or the checkmated revolutions and uprisings of 1789, 1830, 1848, 1871, and 1905. [. . .]

Melancholy hindsight must not seduce us into undervaluing the authenticity and liberating impact of this Bolshevik moment upon social and dramatic consciousness. We need no further reminder that the cold-water *douche* of Stalinism smothered the example of the Leninist flame. We perhaps do not fully recall or comprehend that Leninism had its emancipating day, which promised to become a new mode of social being, or that for some brief years, say 1920–35, a renaissance of dramatic perspectives occurred. Early Bolshevik thought and activity took full account of (Naturalist) determinism-by-milieu and took the *next step* (Brecht's *The Mother* as a luminous example) of correcting the former acquiescence, even in

Socialist circles, to circumstances. The heavy continuance of Naturalist drama thus asks aloud for our understanding. In part the Naturalist revival and survival is surely due to the Bolshevik failure to establish itself in permanence, for reasons we cannot take up here but which should not be considered a final argument against revolutionary efforts. To that we must add that the present make-up of our drama is even more due, *horribile dictu!*, to our own and *present* failure to go beyond the present circumstances, which of course include the checking of the Bolshevik impulse. The Leninist model proving not suitable, we can invent our own.

16. It will not do to neglect what is perhaps the strongest, most lucid and moving play created on the Bolshevik model in Russia itself. The more so because *The Optimistic Tragedy* (1932) by Vsevelod Vishnevsky is profoundly and directly a challenge to the Naturalist outlook – and because of the fate this play suffered, which offers solid confirmation of the Stalinist degeneration of drama to a point well 'below' that of Naturalism.

Vishnevsky's plot embodies his outlook. A tough crew of Russian sailors in the Baltic fleet have reacted to the news of the Tsar's overthrow by erupting in anarchical revolt. The Bolsheviks send a representative to be their guide in politics. This commissar is an intellectual and a girl [*sic*]. Much of the play is concerned with the way she wins the sailors' respect for her politics and person, and establishes a new order. The sailors thus come ashore to battle the White armies of reaction. One of the crew shouts during the conflict, 'Don't you think for an optimistic tragedy we've got too many dead?' and another replies: 'No more than Shakespeare!' The play is highly sophisticated, aggressive, ironical, theatrical. The girl lies mortally wounded in the final scene. As the sailors woefully gather she bids one who has an accordion to play. The crew at first are shocked. They then get her idea. Personal death is tragedy unmitigated; yet if suffered while contributing to social gains which transform the meaning of future human existence, the amalgamate sensation is *not only* pity, nor only tragic. Thus, accepting the girl's lead, the sailors take up the tune, defiantly they start to laugh, they banter and dance as the girl dies. 'For us there is no death,' remarks one; another: 'The revolution is immortal.' The sailors have at the last accepted the girl's philosophy and politics; the sense of her personal death is transformed. [. . .]

I saw *The Optimistic Tragedy* performed in rehearsal with great verve and energy at the Berlin Ensemble in 1961. But one must add that the Berlin Ensemble had reverted to the author's preferred first version of his play. In the Stalinist degeneration of the Soviet stage, this work too was affected. [. . .] It seems that Vishnevsky, urged to conform to the just-minted official formula for Socialist Realism, finally complied with a partially sentimentalized reworking. This revised version of 1933 is translated in *Soviet Literature*, no. 11 (1965). In this form, the death-defying laughter of the sailors is out. Instead the play ends with only an accordion 'softly' taking up 'an old and beloved tune from the revolution of 1905 . . . the melody gradually fading away.' In a sense, the State takes responsibility for shoving the optimism in tragedy away from Vishnevsky and his very human sailors; in this version, one is treated to a final grandiose spectacle with hordes of men marching towards battle amid musical and lighting effects. The sailors are silent and bypassed. It is at this point precisely that the tragic impasse for the Bolshevik moment of revolutionary drama became apparent.

What of Stalinist drama, which eradicated the Bolshevik moment? To say that it is Naturalist is to miss the essence of Naturalism, and to degrade it. As Herbert Marcuse wrote in his *Soviet Marxism*, the Socialist Realist genre is 'cut off from its historical base. Socialized without a socialist reality, art reverts to its ancient prehistorical function: it assumes magical character.' [. . .]

17. Are new, effective tactics and models for radical social change emerging? And will our drama again take fire from them? Shall even our lives take on, in the splendid tradition of John Reed, the aesthetic impulse, beat, grace, and realization of a radical dramaturgy? This is possible.

[. . .] Almost always, the choice of Naturalism spreads involuntarily into mind from an accumulative experience, and is not a true choice. But as the choice evolved out of the distinctiveness of the playwright's background, so do today's naturalistic outlooks offer differing potentialities for going beyond Naturalism. We have reason to discriminate further among our Naturalisms.

Take the new Black drama. The playwright's recognition of ineffectuality is still central in such plays as Jones' *Dutchman* or Buhns' *The Electronic Nigger*. Naturalism will flow without paradox – angry remarks notwithstanding – from a relatively bourgeois Black home and school training, should not all the ensuing illusions and assumptions have been pinned against the author's wall for total scrutiny. Black drama is often the expressive output of conflicted intellectuals who increasingly regard themselves not as individuals only but as black cadres speaking for and guiding their increasingly anti-bourgeois and militant community. The obviously naturalistic, middle-class values accepted by Lorraine Hansberry are in eclipse. And 'tell it like it is' becomes a weak and sullen catch-phrase when everybody *knows* how well everybody knows how it *is*. Now T.C.B. ('take care of business') begins to head the agenda in street talk. If this attitude can make the leap in theatre, the drama could be carried 'beyond' Naturalism. The grave question is whether Black drama shall instead begin to fall short of the naturalistic truths themselves, by careening toward a messianic theatre for the exorcizing of devils. LeRoi Jones appears bent upon developing a Black-nationalist version of Socialist Realism. His recent plays, *Experimental Death Unit, No. 1* and *A Black Mass* – violently militant without an organizationally militant reality – now revert openly to nihilist ritual and demagogic magic. This chiliastic regression is so unrealistic, in the context of America's sophisticated repression, as to suggest an utter (bourgeois-intellectual) sense of powerlessness. Radical Black leadership must seek a politics – and all that goes with radical politics – such as Jones does not imagine. Keen-eyed, steady-nerved Ed Bullins, a naturalistic playwright to watch, is *also* an officer of the Black Panther Party. Black drama which 'goes beyond' Naturalism will do so hand-in-hand with the development of an adequate Black structure for radical politics.

The problem for White drama is similar. Living examples give rise to life-enhancing plays. The Bolshevik model became as sterile for the inspiration of post-Naturalist drama as had the very short-lived revolutions of 1871 or 1905 for earlier playwrights. To gloat over this disgrace of revolutionary theatre would seem to me a case of downright masochistic *Schadenfreude*. The very presence of so much helplessness and anguish upon our stage points to the need for a dramaturgy to shatter our bondage to the established social and theatrical system. Naturalistic drama does reassure us that we are not totally lost since we can at least *recognize* our rote behavior and the system which initiates it, even if we can't *do* anything.

But perhaps we can, Julian Beck and Judith Malina concluded in the 1950s – the least propitious period for finding any meritorious example of anything whatsoever – that one had perhaps to make one's own start, not waiting around for examples. In the Living Theatre they sought to achieve and maintain *within their own structure of organization* the nucleus of an exemplary lifestyle. For years the result onstage was naturalistic protest theatre (through *Frankenstein* and *Antigone*), more sharply focused, contemporary, and risk-taking than most. Finding itself last May in the thick of the uprising of French students and workers, the Living Theatre took advantage of its experience and courage. The explosive political events confirmed and reinforced the coiled-spring value of the Becks' patiently developed perspectives. They boldly stepped beyond Naturalism and the first result is *Paradise Now!*

Paradise Now! as revolutionary theatre does not exactly follow or resemble its Bolshevik forebear. The international activism of a new left has novel perspectives, and the Becks are at one with the evoking, positive social model in advanced countries of the West, which will not now be Leninist. The 'anticipatory democracy' of SDS is more like it. Brecht in *The Measures Taken* wrote a Bolshevik poetry: 'The Party has a thousand eyes' and can know best how to take care of business. That aspect of Brecht and the Bolshevik moment is quite alien to young American radicals who are proud of (perhaps) a million eyes in 500,000 heads which act autonomously but with a growing coordination of the whole. We seem to be discovering the basis for a diverse, widespread, relatively autonomous kind of shared initiative for social change and a new form of community. Automation, affluence, instant communications, improved education enable those forms to evolve. No miracles yet – everyone still understands what Ibsen and Beckett are all about – but a beginning.

To the extent this novelty requires substantiality, the naturalistic drama can only survive as a function of habit and antiquarianism. Living examples do feed a living drama. The Becks were more than ready, Richard Schechner's *Dionysus in 69* may prove a milestone on the way. We are beginning to get a revolutionary theatre, deriving from the historical urgency, sensed especially among the young, of a grassroots initiative which is voluntarily coordinated into social compacts. The authority principle – permitting the most basic and precious decisions of one's life to be made by decision-makers beyond one's effective influence – is coming under an attack which should prove fatal. The most vital theatre collectives work on the 'participatory' principle, and our plays and a dramaturgy of radical politics should be increasingly invigorated.

Taking the longest view, perhaps the Naturalist sense of abandonment to crushing forces was the inevitable result of a particular societal form not only designed for class advantage, but also capable of killing the metaphysic of hope. But if that is so, have we not learned to live in our godless world, and to eliminate elitist combinations through the combination of all our forces and resources? After one hundred years of Naturalist anguish it's the moment for change!

11

PARADISE NOW!
Notes

The Living Theatre

T43, 1969

During the course of the rehearsals for *Paradise Now!*, Judith and I and many other members of the company kept notebooks recording more or less what was said and tracing the development of the ideas of and for the play. The notebooks then served as a gathering place for these ideas, a storeroom which we visited repeatedly and from which we drew supplies in constructing the play. The following eight entries record the first three pre-rehearsal discussions between Judith and me, and the first five general discussions, what we call the first five rehearsals, with the entire company. The first five of about one hundred. Discussions such as these have become an integral part of our working method, and were the source material out of which *Mysteries*, *Frankenstein*, *Paradise Now!*, and the *mise-en-scène* for *Antigone* were created.

Julian Beck

JB	Julian Beck	JH	Jenny Hecht
JM	Judith Malina	ST	Steve Thompson
NH	Nona Howard	RH	Roy Harris
HH	Henry Howard	CB	Cal Barber
RC	Rufus Collins	GG	Gene Gordon
CE	Carl Einhorn	LT	Luke Theodore
WS	William Shari	DS	Dorothy Shari
SBI	Steven Ben Israel	DVT	Diana Van Tosh

27 JANUARY 1968: ARTH-AM-SEE, SWITZERLAND

JB: What do we have to say – i.e., what do we know – that gives us the right to make this play? I think the form could be anything. [. . .] Glimpses of the post-revolutionary world. Does that include glimpses of how to get there?

JM: It would seem very unimportant to me if it didn't contain some suggestions of how to get there. For me it can't be political enough.

JB: It has to. Because *Paradise Now!* is How To Get There. Paradisial Events apart from the transitionary period. What is the object of the striving? Depiction of the state of being we imagine as desirable.

JM: We can't map out how to get there because we don't have the map. But we have to make a map. This is the paradox.

JB: Simplest answer: we don't have the map but we have some clues, hints, foretastes, intimations. [. . .]

JM: I would like to see the whole thing as one big game with rules.

JB: Maybe. A free theatre form. Chance?

JM: Something between chance and free theatre. I think of a free theatre piece with chance-type rules. But rules chosen for their appropriateness and not at random. [. . .] Rules as the Principles. The discovery of the principle of gravity teaches you how to fly (to the degree that flying defies the rules of gravity). You can defy the law by understanding the principle. What the actors are doing shall always be paradisial. That is, it would always be a pleasure to do. [. . .]

28 JANUARY 1968: VICINITY OF LUGANO

JB: Practical time. When to rehearse: what and how many hours? How to divide the time then: discussion, physical world, exercise, staging.

What we know. Investigations of what we do not know.
How to divide the time most usefully, the disposition of the company.
The predilection for false leads into the Mysteries, the mysterious.
What are we searching for? To get the apples to the city.
Anything else? What else?
How much time is there to ask questions?

JM: The method of The Living Theatre is to find something, an idea, so true that when you do it with your body, it gets expressed. [. . .]

29 JANUARY 1968: ROME

JB: *Paradise Now!* has to be, is, my, our message to the world. It has to be. *The Mysteries* are Warnings and Promises (Harold Norse). *Frankenstein* is the Empirical study of the Historical Conditions. *Antigone* is the profound enactment of the moral and political predicament. The achievement of the *mise-en-scène* of *Antigone* is the profundity of devices.

It is time for something else.

Program
Practical functions
Time and place
The children: who cares for the babies while the work is being done? Who cooks? Who washes the dishes? Who buys? Who cleans? How does the community function?
And the psycho-sexual problems.
And the quotidian psychological problems.
And our own community. [. . .]

11 JANUARY 1968: ROME

Rehearsal No. 1

NH: Is not a play but a state of being
   comes out of a state of being
   this will result in freedom
   freedom is honesty
   the means and ends are the same
   the means and ends are honesty
   will result in new forms of human behavior unknown to the present eye
   a new – a fully realized – self can realize a new world
   anything else is merely politicking
   in this being lies a source of being on the earth
   none of the 'à bas l'état' can happen without the change in the individual
   each person on this trip will discover things about himself
   to have a play *about* something is some form of masturbation
   looking down the wrong end of the tunnel
   my burning desire to see people burning to achieve this
   there is no need to talk about discipline when everyone is burning
   I would like to see this form of behavior given form
   there is a difference between the path to pleasure and the one leading to joy
   if beauty is truth what is beautiful
   it is a state of being and not a play about a play
   every moment is a play
   the level is your choice
   I think it is time to do it

SBI: Step No. 1, to create ritual that redeems the earth, done with a perfection
   that makes man aware that there is a divine process on earth that he can dance
   with. [. . .]

GG: I see people now that Greece has taken on a fascist regime.
   I see people as I walk through Italy, Switzerland, Germany.
   I see them raise their hands in a fascist salute:
   I see the rise of fascism again.
   I find it difficult to work on a play about Paradise Now without working on
   the real problems of fascism – money war wages.
   Paradise Now means a complete change in the world.
   If we don't see what's happening in every country, even in the USSR –

HH: – May I interrupt . . . *Mysteries* and *Antigone* treat this. We are planning
   a play that transcends it, to create a play that will change, pop the bag, the
   outlook.

GG: We have to be sure of what we do if we want to change the world and live
   for centuries: why do we still smoke cigarettes?

WS: I want the right to feed myself poison.

SBI: At this point in the theatre, we have to give the alternative. To give people
   the things they can do to transcend, to exist.

NH: Means to be able to include everything, not to exclude.

GG: The people in Germany were kept away from what was happening.

JH: To do a play called *Paradise Now!*

in a world which is doing a play called *Hell*
is a revolutionary act.
To find an anarchy (of a sort) in our community
An example for loving the world
That may be the next exemplary step in getting the world to change [. . .]

GG: To change the world we have to get rid of money and governments but to get there we have to listen in the streets and to the sound of our own voices shouting in anger at the waiter and the garage mechanic. It takes an understanding and if we don't get that understanding we are in grave difficulty.

JM: But I think it very important to realize that we are not there and that we find out how to get there. The moral issues: 'I didn't teach my son to live a longer and less happy life.'

HH: What is the behavior in Paradise? This is the question. The theatre is a laboratory. *Man Is Man – Brig – Mysteries – Frankenstein.* . . The next play is called *Paradise.* What puts us there, how do we get there? Those scenes are going down, and this is what we can do about it –

The theatre is unsatisfactory.

JH: I think this behavior must be a happening between people.

HH: Someone is grooving and someone shatters him. We do that all the time.

LT: Paradise forms come out of suppressed areas – jazz out of a suppressed people – they took instruments, they found a way in which imitation was unnecessary and they learned to play, and then the jazz musicians came together.

JB: If what you say is true about jazz then the problem is how to use that method to get the apples to the city.

JH: To establish a state of being 24 hours per day.

HH: The theatre is a place of magic and the unknown. This is the highest unknown. [. . .]

(The remaining time went again to the baby problem.)

1 FEBRUARY 1968: FILMSTUDIO, ROME

RH: That the physical work and the performance be therapeutic for the actor and the spectator. Changing colors: without lights. The actors changing colors. Perhaps we can do our own light show without lights. Change the temperature of the playing area, whatever was the human being can affect his environment – singing, dancing, chanting – building structures with our bodies: our architecture for the age of Paradise. A geometry onstage, using the body in a different way of new sounds: thirty-five people moving new. This can change every performance.

GG: The natural realities that are hidden by our society, hidden by those who use the suppression to exploit and maneuver.

[. . .]

RC: The whole thing, the whole hippie thing is a search for –

JB: A concern with primitive and mystic rituals.

SBI: To make good more interesting than evil.

CB: Are we doing this play for people who are sitting in their seats or does the audience have the possibility of participation?

SBI: The recurring process: take it and put it on the stage and call it *Paradise Now!*

ST: *Paradise Now!* would create an open atmosphere and clean air so that the audience can rise up and fill the space in the theatre, the temple.

CB: There must be the possibility of liberation in the space.

SBI: What do we want the audience to do?

RC: To drop out.

JB: To change. To start the Revolution.

HH: Where do we begin? We have to presuppose that the war is stopped. Not how to stop the war or feed the people in India. Getting back to the source [. . .]. The inability to experience each other. This is a point we must clarify now: is this play about stop-the-war or something else? Revolutions come and give the same bad answers.

CE: We have to be ready to answer the questions of the public. In the rigid structure of the theatre – rigid seats, tickets, money, time – what are the alternatives?

JH: Our experiencing it on the stage is the statement.

CE: Not to shy away from the word political. Sitting on a mountain is political.

GG: This *Paradise Now!* has to be free. The people in Italy are not free. But neither do we show them everything of ourselves. I'm not playing a game, I'm giving my life. I'm ashamed we have to live in an economic system.

JB: Yes, ashamed of my world. [. . .] The work is to make everyone artists, into their rightful state as creative beings.

Creative eating working sleeping being. As we, not only in our work but in our lives.

LT: To change the audience. I have experienced this with our audiences.

HH: When jazz musicians play today, they play until it happens. 1 – 2 – 3 hours until we make it.

CB: How do we want to affect the Audience? How do we initiate the Audience? [. . .]

RC: The audience must change because the play makes them take the trip. The forms differ from city to city.

JH: We have to stop thinking of the audience as Argives, as people beneath us to be taught. They are with us, are us.

CB: If this play is the vehicle, we have to find out what the behavior of the vehicle is.

ST: Maybe we can't take them. Maybe we can only go ourselves.

RC: But we can assume that we can't go without oneness, not until we are together.

HH: I want the audience to see a new HH onstage. Tuning into another's trip: a knack, an experience.

GFM: I find it very difficult to talk about something without experiencing it. How can I drink boiling water? I am interested in that.

[. . .]

HH: In 1968, images are hocus pocus. But states of being, of nature, are interesting. I can be this Tantric cross (pendant) or this . . . or you can be that white screen: that's a point at which we begin theatre. [. . .]

JB: I think we have to think about the efficacy of our Paradise Now. We have to judge the Paradise that we create.

RC: Unification is Paradise.

JB: What is Paradise? (CE's question) Is it the mystical experience or is it making a shoe?

CE: The moment is always passing. Our visions of Paradise are only fleeting. You don't lose the vision but it isn't always available.

ST: I think it's always available.

CE: We're talking about changing the availability, maintaining the experience.

JH: Digging the scenery.

[. . .]

2 FEBRUARY 1968: FILMSTUDIO, ROME

[. . .]

RC: We are feeling the vibrations of those who are pushing us to look to Paradise.

CE: The spiritually highest developed society is the cruelest in terms of starvation.

HH: The Attributes of Paradise – perception changes. First stage: every object assumes a double; I begin to see people's auras. In the final moment: the unity between subject and object – nothing has a double.

JM: In Paradise, nobody dies. Paradise is unnatural. Nature is not paradisial.

[. . .]

CB: Ecstatic wonder. Ecstatic accurate movement. Ecstatic intuition.

CE: Unity of language.

HH: The absence of mundane time.

JB: The process of turning the wheel, the work of the world, is invested with constant enlightenment. Tasks are performed so that they are perpetually revelatory (revealing?). In which cleaning the sewers is a gas because we dig the smell. Where breaking rocks is ecstatic because of our perception of our muscles. In which weariness is an incantation to vision. In Paradise you fall in love with the world instead of looking for something else. [. . .]

JH: Paradise does not have to do with miracles and with a different natural environment. When I think of Paradise, I think of practical possibilities, of what we are capable of now.

CB: A synthesis of the internal and external universe; living and being in accord with the infinite universe; the tree of life with the tree of knowledge.

CE: A fulfillment of his own evolution. A growing up into the uses of his own self. The other 90 percent of the brain. Not the impossible but the possible. The transitional – that way calls for reorientation for many people.

RC: When we have this glimpse of Paradise, we can only experience it, not observe it. [. . .]

3 FEBRUARY 1968: ROME

No rehearsal (no place to rehearse).

4 FEBRUARY 1968: CASA DI CULTURA, ROME

[. . .]

JB: Is there theatre in Paradise? Is it cold? Is there physical love? Is there food? Is it edible? Is there work? Is there reading? Are there bridges? What comes after air flight? What is unparadisial about walking on the earth or crossing bridges?

Are there furs? Are there only chemical foods? Are there meats? What's the nutrition? What's the sleep program? Is there Paradise only in the theatre? Is there privacy? How many people are there? Are there ships? Who makes them? Is there excrement? Is there plumbing? What do we mean by Paradise Now? All the physical miracles we talk of? Is grief compatible with Paradise?

[. . .]

WS: There's a roomful of people that believe in Paradise. We are together to find the source of the experience.

JB: That is, we have all had some evidence of it.

JM: We are unhurt; we are fortunate people. There is enough potential in the world to solve the food and housing problems, with some strong effort at the beginning. We then go on to the next change.

DS: The notion of the perpetual challenge is a cop out. Using tasks as a game to avoid facing the self.

CB: Is there conflict in Paradise?

RC: The concept of reward after labor has to go.

CE: High tide and low tide are not in conflict with each other.

JM: Are we all agreed that we are talking about the real world?

RC: In Paradise, I wouldn't have to eat and shit so much.

JM: In Paradise, reality changes.

[. . .] Whatever we are doing should be an inspiration to the revolutionary spirit. Don't despair. Maybe there's a possibility and maybe this is the direction in which to look for it.

[. . .]

5 FEBRUARY 1968: CASA DI CULTURA, ROME

(More baby-care problems)

[. . .]

JH: Most of what we do onstage is the result of our dreams and visions – creative intuition.

JM: Contradiction – my moments of inspiration are founded on concrete discussion.

SBI: What we want to do in this piece is give the message to dig the room you're in.

[. . .]

JM: Not to get hung by your own barriers. We talked of making the rehearsal period as paradisial as we can. Each of us has a strong individual conscience.

JB: The individual conscience lives naturally in Paradise. Can we talk about laughter. Nothing positive, laughter on poppers, on mj, on LSD, on merc. The horrors.

JM: When I laugh, it's to translate the horrors into the bearable.

JH: Is there laughter which is not vicious, that is the opposite of tears?

SBI: Expanded reality produces laughter.

RC: We're talking about laughter in Paradise.

SBI: Not an in-joke but mother-laughter.

JB: Child-laughter.

LT: On grand occasions, after a bust, at reunions.

JH: When you find out things aren't over or rolling down a grassy hill. Paradise is not a fake place where the body doesn't feel pain but a place where there are more ways of releasing it.

DVT: On acid: an ecstatic state of laughter, a state of being that produces laughter.

JM: Yes, but it gives me the horrors.

DVT: It's pure for me.

RC: If you walk around and laugh, they'll bust you.

[. . .]

JM: Biochemistry – I'm stuck, hung-up that certain things occur in scientific conditions but are not theatrical events. We are all saying we want to do something but we continue the discussion because we are looking for the spark that is so new that it is going to change all the old. This is what I mean by the miracle, by biochemistry, by changing physics. I don't think we can make a study of biochemistry. We can't learn enough between now and Avignon. The scientists have this. We can do experiments but not rational experiments. To search for a principle. When we have the principle, we have something to give.

JB: Paradise, Paradise Now, implies a state of higher consciousness, higher awareness. Because in the domain of lower consciousness, there is no Paradise.

JM: Apokatastasis: the turning of the force of evil to the force of good. We should do experiments in positive/negative forces – in turning the negative energy in us into the positive.

JB: It's a changing-the-world experiment.

JM: It's the physical-present-learning experiment.

[. . .]

JM: Experiment with anger.

SBI: Five stages that make the sixth. The individual destroys all the space that he has occupied. The individual enters the space with the natural fear of revealing himself.

1. With short sounds and movements, destroys space, like a Samurai who fights with arm cut off.
2. He comments on what he has done with the absurd comical attitude.
3. Man, did I really do that?

4. Sorrow: O Universe, I am sorry.
5. Thank you, Universe, for redeeming me.

WS: These first four things are done by any actor in *John Loves Mary*.

RC (angry):   We can reduce anything to the banal. The problem is to go in the opposite direction!

12

FROM *ART IN EVERYDAY LIFE*

Linda Montano

Art in Everyday Life, 1981

THE MONTANO-PAYNE VICTORIAN MUSEUM
(115 Shotwell Street, San Francisco, 1975)

Art: I declared our house a museum and gave tours as different people, chosen
by the person viewing the house.
   Notices were sent to papers advertising the tours.

Life: The house had become overwhelming and I felt trapped by its demands.
I tried to become friends with the house by declaring it a museum.

LIVING ART: A COMPLEX THEORY WHICH STATES THAT LIFE CAN BE ART
(Living with Pauline Oliveros in the desert for ten days, December 1975)

Art: Pauline Oliveros and I lived in the desert for ten days and agreed that
everything we did would be considered art.
   We documented the event.

Life: Living art was incredibly exhilarating . . . I thought that the life/art transference was finally made because I began interacting more truthfully and
spontaneously. I called each day art and not life.
   I was happy and making art at the same time.

LISTENING TO THE 1980S: INSIDE/OUTSIDE
Dedicated to Pauline Oliveros and Magda Proskauer

(San Francisco Museum of Modern Art, 3 January 1980)

Participants: George Coates, Steven Collins, Vincent De Luna, John Duykers,
William Farley, Linda Montano, Pauline Oliveros, A Sensual Nun.
Costumes, Jackie Humbert.
Sound, Roger Jans.

Art:　A twelve-hour event consisting of three actions repeated once every hour by the participants.

Each action:　Sitting – 30 minutes
　　　　　　　　Walking – 15 minutes
　　　　　　　　Singing Past Guilts – 15 minutes

These were performed in unison.

The first two actions, sitting and walking, took place in the Green Room.
The third action, singing, was performed on the museum balcony.

Bells rang throughout the day to indicate the death of guilt.

Life:　This was my first large-scale ensemble – a truly magnificent event with nuns and priests in reversed roles, sitting and walking in stoic, dedicated silence and asceticism, while being taunted by a flirtatious nun.

The piece was grand – mainly because of:

1. The costumes which were impeccable and uniform.
2. John Duykers's operatic arias, supported by our disguised recitation of guilt, filling a city block.
3. Time, which was measured exactly and carefully by the bell ringer and as a result left us free to experience changes.
4. The scale of the Green Room and balcony – colossal, ecclesiastical and filled with medieval associations.

Everything worked perfectly on every level and after twelve hours I could not remember any more guilt.

Plus I did not have to do it alone.

13

INVISIBLE THEATRE

Augusto Boal

Translated from the French by Susana Epstein

T127, 1990

[. . .] I began doing 'Invisible Theatre' in Argentina in 1971. And until today, after so many years and all the countries I've been to, I have never participated in such a rich experience as the one in Liège, Belgium, in October l978.

I will start at the beginning.

Anne Martynow and Bruno Ducoli invited me to do one of my 'Theatre of the Oppressed' workshops first in Brussels and then at Liège. There were about forty participants, men and women ranging in ages from 18 to 50 years old, from

Fig. 13.1 Augusto Boal conducting a workshop at NYU. (Photo by NYU/Jon Roemer, courtesy of Princeton University Library.)

Belgium, Morocco, Tunisia, Italy, France, and other countries. What we usually do in these workshops for the first three days are in-house group exercises, games, and discussions about the different forms of the 'Theatre of the Oppressed.' On the fourth day, we normally do Invisible Theatre pieces in public places, such as restaurants, supermarkets, trains, and streets, depending upon the chosen subjects. Finally, the workshop finishes with a public performance called 'theatre forum' which includes spectator participation.

We spent the first three days in Brussels, then we went to Liège and prepared only one Invisible Theatre performance.

It took place in the following way:

1st action: About a dozen actors go into a supermarket and start buying things.

2nd action: François, the protagonist, gets in line with his shopping cart. He has bread, milk, margarine, and eggs. Nothing extra, only indispensable items. Nine other actors get in the neighboring lines waiting for their turn to get to the cash register.

3rd action: François gets to the cash register. Before the cashier starts checking the prices out, François warns her that he needs everything he's got in his cart but that he doesn't have enough money to pay for it. He explains that he is unemployed and that he has spent several hours trying to get a job, but since there are approximately 600,000 unemployed people in Belgium it is very difficult to find one. The cashier says that his story is none of her business and that her job is to charge for the merchandise that people buy. François insists that he would like to pay. He adds that after all he could have tried to steal what he's got in his cart but he would rather pay . . .

> 'How come? You've just said you don't have the money.'
> 'Let's do it this way: you tell me how much what I have in my cart costs and
>   I'll work in this supermarket as many hours as necessary to pay for the
>   whole thing. It's simple: I offer to pay with work instead of money . . .'

The cashier, becoming angry, explains that she cannot exchange goods for labor. She can only accept the ordinary way of buying and paying.

4th action: Participation of the other actors, each of them in her/his own role. One among them, Anne, accuses François of being a bum.

> 'Those who really want to get a job always find one . . . It's only those who
>   don't want to work who can't get a job!'
> 'What's your job, Miss?'
> 'I work at home. My husband is the manager of a corporation . . .'
> 'Ah . . .'

Another actor announces that he is unemployed too and that he admires François's courage to admit that he has no money. He blames the Belgian economic system for the situation. Obviously it is not their fault since they are willing to work but can't get jobs. Another actor tells François to try and find a job in another city. At this point, a discussion about the different Belgian 'nationalities' and the current economic problems takes place. (Many industries have moved to the cheaper northern part of Belgium, bringing wealth to the Flemish region while impoverishing the southern French-speaking 'Walloon.')

The cashier threatens to call the manager. Another actor says that François is right since he doesn't want to steal, he only wants to do the same thing everybody else does but in reverse . . .

> '*You, Miss, for instance, what do you do? You work at this cash register 8 hours a day and by the end of the week, after having worked for 40 or 45 hours, are paid. Then, with the same money, you do your own shopping in this same supermarket. It's perfect. Him, he wants to do the same thing but the other way around . . .*'

The cashier does not know what to do and she calls the manager. By now all the customers are talking about unemployment, prices, and salaries, possible solutions, etc. In so doing, they are helped by the actors–jokers who 'warm-up' the public by bringing up new subjects of discussion and posing questions to feed the debate.

5th action: Arrival of the manager who in the meantime has already called the police. The manager tries to convince François to leave the line. François continues to be extremely polite, never raising his voice while trying to sound sincere and persuasive since he is defending a valuable principle. The other customers insist that François be allowed to express himself. One of the actors suggests collecting money to solve François's problem, but acknowledges that this is not a good way to solve the problems of 600,000 unemployed Belgians. They do very well and in only a few minutes they gather around BF 600, which is close to FF 150. François pays his bill but to his surprise, the supermarket's manager and some security guards stop him from leaving. They even block him with a whole line of shopping carts. They want the police to arrive before François leaves the store. François attempts to leave one more time but he can't. At this point, all the actors, including those who, according to the script, are supposed to be against François, take on his defense helped by an overwhelming majority of real customers.

6th action: The police arrive. Making use of their proverbial politeness, they push around those people who bother them, maul those who are the slowest to follow their instructions, and even manage to immobilize François. They want to arrest him but everybody protests loudly. People are on François's side. The police officers cannot believe what they see.

The officer in charge asks the manager, '*Is this a thief, yes or no?*' Everybody says no and offers to be a witness. The manager, getting angrier by the minute, insists that François be taken to the police station.

> '*Well, how do you want me to arrest this man when he hasn't stolen anything and when there are all these witnesses ready to declare in his favor? They are all saying that not only he hasn't taken anything but he hasn't even tried to steal a thing!*'

The manager, however, is a stubborn woman:

> '*I want this man arrested for having caused a public disturbance!*'

Her argument is that the normal functioning of her store has been hurt by this incident since she has lost time and money during the disturbance, and the incident is going to prevent many customers from coming back.

The police officer in charge has few choices. François is taken to the police station to verify his identity and answer the accusations. [. . .]

At this point, I must tell you something important. Annie Declerck from Flemish TV had asked to film an Invisible Theatre piece for a program she was preparing on me and the Theatre of the Oppressed. Both my group and I had agreed to the project and so everything in the supermarket had been filmed. François had a microphone inside his shirt. The sound technician had hidden his equipment among the fruit he was carrying in his shopping cart. The camera operator had hidden the camera inside a plastic bag which had a small hole the exact size of the lens. Being very experienced, he had no difficulty filming everything with his camera under his arm: close-ups, long shots . . . absolutely everything! Annie was at my side with the script person who was putting everything down in writing. Besides which, there was a privileged spectator, the theatre director, actor and playwright Fernando Peixoto, who had just arrived from Cologne, Germany, where he was then working in radio.

The fact that television was documenting this event added a new dimension to this story.

This is what happened: Annie and François arrived at the police station and continued in their roles. Being such good actors, they could keep up their Invisible Theatre personas without being suspected. Eventually, however, the police discovered the truth. Besides discovering François's microphone, they found out that he had a job and earned a regular salary. As the investigation proceeded, François finally confessed that he was just doing Invisible Theatre.

The police officer in charge could not believe what he was hearing. He became extremely upset because he felt that his authority was being mocked. In a threatening tone he said:

> 'What do you mean that you were just doing theatre? You have created this
>   major disturbance only because you were playing around? You have
>   disturbed the public order at the supermarket where people do their
>   shopping without problems, you have taken up everybody's time, and this
>   was simply a show? Fine. The manager accuses you of incitement to
>   disorder and we, the police, accuse you of having a public performance
>   without permission from the corresponding authority! You have two
>   charges.'

The interrogation lasted for six hours. After they were released, Annie and François returned to the theatre where we were waiting for them. We were all actually very worried by now. Especially me, because any problems with the police immediately remind me of the arbitrariness of Latin American police.

Once they were back, they told us what happened and we discussed the goals of what we had just been through. Somebody proposed a third charge: we should accuse the police, because there is no artistic censorship in Belgium. Therefore, the police have no right to censor a theatre piece. To demand a permit for an Invisible Theatre event was equivalent to making it visible, that is, destroying its very theatrical form. In order to continue as such, the Invisible Theatre has to be a clandestine theatre. If it becomes 'visible,' the spectator takes a passive role rather than her/his much more productive one as a true protagonist of the event. In short, the Invisible

Theatre cannot be subject to the same rules which limit conventional theatre. To demand authorization means stopping aesthetic research. Since there is no censorship in Belgium, and a permit would be a form of it, we are entitled to accuse the police of harassment.

The situation was already complicated enough. Now it was becoming an absolute mess! But that Saturday we decided to rest while getting very excited at the three legal issues coming up.

According to Belgian law, it is up to the king's prosecutor to decide whether charges will go to court or not. I wanted very much to go to court because it would have offered theatre the occasion of being defined 'legally' as opposed to 'aesthetically,' as it always has been. For every artist the theatre is something different. What about the judges? Each artist can have her own style, her own view, and her own definition of the theatre. [. . .] Can a judge prosecute an artist using the same criteria used to prosecute an artisan? Can he impose limits? [. . .] Can the law establish the boundaries for aesthetic creation?

Although I usually don't know the answers, I pose many questions. But I would sincerely like to see an open debate on this passionate subject. In court, if possible.

Anyway, on Saturday we rested. On Sunday we prepared for the theatre forum, but not for the unexpected – so we had a few surprises in front of us.

[. . .] We were all happy. In the morning the French-speaking television had announced our performance in a supportive tone. The theatre was full. There were many foreigners. Most of them had their papers in order, but there were also many African and Latin American political exiles whose papers were not in order.

Our group had prepared three theatre forum scenes on racism, unemployment, and women's liberation. I remember that I was standing talking to an actor, Raulf, a Tunisian who had already worked with me in an Invisible Theatre project on the Paris subway the previous year. Brigitte, from the group Cirque Divers, joined our conversation. She had assisted me in a workshop I had conducted in Italy and wanted me to work with her group. We were all three discussing this possibility when somebody approached me and asked:

'Mr. Augusto Boal?'
'Yes.'
'Police!'

He showed me his ID. I was a bit shocked because I would have never thought that the Belgian police could come in like that. I asked him what he wanted, and he said that I had to accompany him for an identification procedure. Another plainclothes policeman joined the first officer along with a third in uniform who had a furiously barking dog.

I searched through my pockets for as many pieces of ID as I could find. I had my two passports (Portuguese and Brazilian), my ID as a professor at La Sorbonne, my birth certificate, and even my orange card. . . but the police did not accept any of them. They insisted:

'You must come with us to the police station!'

I started to walk, but Raulf seized me by the arm and cried out that I was being arrested. There was confusion. Everybody was shouting and pushing while the dog kept on barking. The two plainclothes police officers grabbed me, while Raulf, helped by six or seven people, pushed me into a room marked 'Private.' In Belgium, the police cannot enter private spaces without authorization. As Raulf and the others were pushing me into this room they were also pushing the three policemen out of the theatre.

The first police officer, who was the most unpleasant of the three, left yelling that he was going to get reinforcement. However, he left with the others. The doors were closed and we quickly divided into several groups to decide what to do. One of the groups, who had helped organize the workshop, was in charge of protecting me. I must say that I felt very well protected. This group took me through corridors and rooms to an apartment (private property where the police could not come in). Once we were there, my friends got on the phone and informed the media, the local authorities, and even a lawyer about the incident.

The lawyer arrived and considered my predicament: I was in Belgium legally. Consequently, the police behavior was completely abusive. It was decided that we should protest. The lawyer called the police. The officer who answered his call was perplexed.

> 'We have not ordered the arrest of anyone. It must have been the "gendarmerie".'

The lawyer called the gendarmerie.

> 'No one from the gendarmerie has left our headquarters to arrest anybody. It must have been the "antigang brigade".'

In fact, we looked through the window and saw three cars from the antigang brigade driving around the theatre. The lawyer called the brigade headquarters:

> 'No, Miss. It must be a mistake. No order of arrest has been issued by us.'
> 'Excuse me, but I'm looking at three brigade cars going around our building right now . . .'
> 'It's true. There are many of our cars in that vicinity because it is an area of illegal foreigners. This is the only reason. But I repeat: we have not issued any orders of arrest . . .'

We were confused: how come all three local forces of repression – the police, the gendarmerie, and the antigang brigade – denied any participation? However, the facts remained: two police officers dressed as civilians plus another one in his uniform had harassed us, in addition to that bloody dog which never stopped barking!

The lawyer asked me whether I had read the police officer's ID carefully. Slightly embarrassed, I admitted that I hadn't: I am shortsighted. Then we started to doubt the authenticity of the police officers, because there were three policemen when the rule in Belgium is for only two to cover routine procedures. Also, only one of them was in a proper uniform. As we were thinking about details, something else appeared suspicious: police dogs are usually trained to intimidate people. Instead, the one they brought with them seemed to be scared of us. Conclusion: it wasn't a police dog. Second conclusion: the police officers were fictitious. Third conclusion (which later proved to be wrong): it was evidently a rightist group who wanted to put pressure on us.

We decided that there was only one solution: if the police had not taken part in these events, what we had to do was to call the police! In fact, given that the police were not responsible for what had happened, we wanted them to be responsible for what could have happened. The lawyer immediately called all three police units and, in less than ten minutes, the entire neighborhood was overflowing with uniforms.

Meanwhile, there was great excitement in the theatre. People were discussing, proposing solutions, and inventing interpretations. It was normal for them to be nervous. Brigitte was probably the most nervous of all. She was so nervous that Raulf was somewhat concerned about her and started to ask her questions. Finally, Brigitte confessed that the actors from the Cirque Divers had decided to mount an Invisible Theatre piece. A piece against us! All three policemen and the dog belonged to the group. There were another two members of the group in the auditorium who confirmed Brigitte's story. Moreover, one of them had videotaped the incident.

It wasn't easy to explain what had happened to the audience. But, before explaining anything, we decided to protect the three actors from Cirque Divers. We took them to a different room. The public was indeed furious which was very understandable. This scene had been going on for an hour and a half, after all. During this time, lots of immigrants and refugees who were present had been put through hell. And all for what?

These are the three main answers we obtained from the Cirque Divers actors when we questioned them:

> '*We do not trust people any longer!*'
> '*We wanted to experiment with Invisible Theatre techniques.*'
> '*We wanted to demonstrate that people act according to Pavlovian reflexes, that is, conditioned reflexes in any given circumstance!*'

They also asked for help:

> '*You must help us get out of the theatre because the audience is furious and we need your protection.*'

We did help them to get out of the theatre. Afterwards, Emile Copferman criticized us for having used such paternalism. In his opinion, this was a mistake on our part: '*If they wanted to experiment, it was up to them to run all the risks inherent in their adventure.*'

Copferman also came up with an interesting explanation of the experience: the Cirque Divers actors wanted to use the Theatre of the Oppressed, which actually threatened them, against me. They were feeling at stake as artists, or as people somehow overloaded with an 'exceptional' role in society. The Theatre of the Oppressed proves exactly the opposite: **artistic creation is inherent to all human beings**. All people are capable of doing what one person is capable of doing. If a person is able to sing, paint, swim, or perform, all people can do the same. [. . .]

I have spent a great deal of my life teaching and applying these ideas. The Cirque Divers actors had simply used them against me to protect themselves.

Another member of the group added a supplementary hypothesis: jealousy. In fact, the Cirque Divers had also invited me to run a workshop but I had refused and accepted an invitation to conduct a workshop with their rivals. What did the Cirque

Divers people do then? They became overnight stars by destroying the theatre forum performance that we had prepared. They took over our event.

But in addition to becoming overnight stars and using Invisible Theatre techniques against me, they prevented a large audience from getting acquainted with other Theatre of the Oppressed techniques. [. . .]

It is useful to remember a few things regarding the theory of Invisible Theatre. I did not invent Invisible Theatre. I did not wake up one morning with a good idea. Rudimentary forms of Invisible Theatre, or partial Invisible Theatre techniques have always existed. In espionage for instance, spies use techniques such as camouflage, interpretation of roles, and simulated realities – which are all Invisible Theatre techniques. Even in the supermarkets, where we regularly play Invisible Theatre, there are 'invisible police,' that is, women and men who complement the closed-circuit TV's function of discouraging and detecting shoplifting. In the Liège case, we tried to use the principal action (François) and the parallel dialogs (actors–jokers) to explain the relationship between unemployment and the exploitation to which employees submit themselves (if nobody accepted exploitation, there would be enough jobs for everybody.)

THE INVISIBLE THEATRE never places itself in an illegal position, because it does not intend to violate the law. It intends to question the legitimacy of the law, which is a very different matter altogether.

I'll explain myself: if we wanted to break the law, it would have been very easy for us to plan a scene that would have distracted people in the supermarket so we could steal anything we wanted. Quite frankly, this happens every day, which is why many stores add a 'shoplifting' premium to the cost of their goods to cover their losses.

As I said, we wanted to question the legitimacy of the law. Because laws can be written by anybody, I can make my own laws too. Laws are only promulgated, however, by those who have the power to make them. Every dictatorship is eager to legalize the illegal act that brought them to power. Therefore, a law promulgated by the military has no validity. No law is valid unless it has the support of the people to which it will apply.

This is precisely the importance of the Invisible Theatre (and of other Theatre of the Oppressed techniques): the difference between the concepts of legality and legitimacy.

Most oppression exists legally. In many countries women cannot vote yet. In many countries, they are underpaid. In other places, they do not have access to certain positions. In most cases, women are still subject to male authority either openly or subtly, psychologically or socially. And everything is being done in the name of the law. However, a law which is imposed on half of humankind cannot be legitimate since it does not have the consensus of its victims, that is, women.

The same way one can question laws and customs that oppress women, one can dispute all oppressive laws and customs, regardless of their victims: workers, peasants, immigrants, blacks, etc.

I want to clarify once and for all that the **Theatre of the Oppressed techniques are meant to help the oppressed; they are actually their weapons of liberation.**

Going back to the Liège case, the Cirque Divers actors, apart from doubling the already existing oppression, committed an illegal act by wearing police uniforms which made them subject to a new charge, the fourth one in this crazy story.

An actor dressed in a policeman's uniform! One can wonder: but isn't this what always happens in the theatre? Isn't it true that one person simulates another? One can also argue that, if the spectator knows that the actor is playing a role, it's fine, but if the spectator does not know that she is dealing with an actor and believes herself to be in the presence of a 'real person' is this correct? Is it ethically right to borrow somebody else's identity and use it abusively?

I want readers to allow me to make a leap in time and space. It was January or March 1978 in Bari, a southern Italian city. We made an Invisible Theatre scene. It went like this: a young actor (clearly Brazilian) sat down in a public garden and started to talk into his minicassette recorder. He said lots of upsetting things:

'I am by myself!' (The cassette repeated: *'I am by myself!'*)
'I don't have any friends.' (The cassette repeated: *'I don't have any friends.'*)
*'Nobody wants to talk to me because I am a foreigner and in this country and
    in this city there is discrimination.'*

Again, he listened to his own voice in the recorder. The casual passers-by could hear the recording. Some of them even stopped to listen.

'I am unemployed.'
'I am unemployed.'
*'I tried to kill myself yesterday, but I did not have enough courage. I put the
    bottle away, but I still have all the pills. Maybe today I'll do it. Maybe
    today I'll kill myself . . .'*

The tape recorder repeated everything he was saying. People were approaching him without knowing what to say. Some of them offered comfort, help, their sympathy, friendship, support, understanding, etc.

It was a scene of rare tenderness, almost an intimate scene despite its public setting with crowds, cars, and noise.

The group was shattered and somebody brought up the question: Is it morally correct what we have done? Because quite frankly, what the actor was saying wasn't true. Our Brazilian had a good job, was married . . . the opposite of the character he was impersonating. Consequently, it wasn't true.

It wasn't true? I kept on asking myself this question. Why wasn't it true? Which truth? The fact that the actor who plays Othello does not 'really' strangle Desdemona does not make it less true that Othello kills his defenseless wife. What truth are we referring to?

The truth was that the Brazilian actor was not suffering any of the tortures that he was describing. But it was true that those tortures existed. If it wasn't true that he himself had attempted suicide, it was certainly true that another émigré a few months earlier had actually killed himself.

So although the Brazilian actor's story wasn't strictly true, it was truth.

Although it was not a **synchronic truth**, it was still a truth. It was in fact a **diachronic truth**. This was not happening here and now, but it was happening elsewhere at a different time.

We had not lied at Liège, in spite of having been accused by the police after they discovered that François had a good job and was not unemployed or hungry. It was not true that the actor was the character but it was true that they both existed! And their problems were indeed real problems. There is unemployment in Belgium, the way the actor described it, and the causes we aired in our piece are the real causes of unemployment in Belgium. Consequently, **everything was true.**

For me, the 'invisible meetings' at Liège were very important. They touched on the ethics and aesthetic of a practice that had been very intense for all of us during the 1970s. We had the opportunity to reflect upon certain aspects of this practice thanks to the Liège events, and these reflections confirmed to us that we were right, that we were doing what we had to do. As artists, by abdicating our being 'exceptional' and helping the oppressed spectators free themselves from at least their first oppression: that of being spectators. By becoming protagonists, they will be qualified to use the Theatre of the Oppressed tools in order to make it what it should be, a theatre of liberation.

Part II

AUTEUR THEATRE

14

INTRODUCTION TO PART II

Gabrielle Cody

Auteurism is, in a sense, at the root of ancient and classical theatre; Sophocles is said to have performed solo his own choreography. Molière – in the tradition of *commedia* managers – wrote himself into his productions as protagonist. Yet auteurism is often regarded today in distinction to normative directing practice in the theatre. How and why did auteurship make a return in the contemporary theatrical landscape? Why is it some auteurs privilege the body and others privilege visual spectacle over literary text? When, how, and why did the director move from an interpreter of (generally) another's text, to the primary, if not sole originator of the theatrical *mise-en-scène*? Why is auteurism associated more with the symbolic than the naturalistic, and what are the historical bases and social implications of that association?

Antonin Artaud, who starts off this section, is perhaps most famous for his insistence on 'No More Masterpieces' and his zeal to end the Western thrall to text as the primary determining property of theatrical experience. However, many of the auteurs who come after Artaud, such as Kantor, Monk, Wilson, Foreman, Bausch, and Abdoh can be said to be creating 'masterpieces' even if textuality is not the baseline factor. But masterpieces with a self-conscious twist. These artists, many of whom where not trained in the theatre,[1] manipulate their *mise-en-scènes* with a high degree of reflexivity. At times the 'individual' artist even appears to be at odds with his creation – as when Kantor and Foreman, present on their sets, manipulate objects or sound loud buzzers as if the unruly stage picture were constantly threatening to come undone. Wilson often slows the pace of his actions down to a such a degree that time seems to be going backward in space that has liquified and lost its definition. These are, then, masterpieces on an edge of self-destruction where, if there is a 'play' at all, it is a broken text strewn about the stage amid other theatrical debris.

We might read these self-conscious masterpieces relative to the trauma caused by two World Wars which generated a deep distrust in the reliability or truth-value of textual remains. In abandoning the 'play' as the thing, these auteurs can be interpreted as responding to the unspeakability of twentieth-century trauma through phenomenological means. Each has developed a theatricality that in Herbert Blau's words dramatizes 'perception, reflecting on itself' (in Carlson 1984: 514), a kind of echo-chamber of cultural and historical consciousness. Of necessity, this impulse to explore a post-apocalyptic ontology deflects normal linear development and instead relies heavily on the sign (see Foreman's program notes to *Pearls for Pigs*, Chapter 20). This orientation toward a theatre of images can be traced back to early symbolism's distrust of rationalism. Auteurism then, often embraces the subjectivity of symbolic theatre languages and favors the plurivocal fragmentation of image–text–sound over realism's seamless, unified, and outwardly 'intelligible' staging of experience.

Documents such as Artaud's letters to Gide, Jouvet, and Paulhan regarding his upcoming production of *The Cenci*, included here, are expressions of a belief in theatre's shamanistic healing potential, its therapeutic power. Similarly, Wilson's formative years were steeped in theatre as a form of therapy. As Bill Simmer points out, Wilson's early work was irrevocably influenced by his fascination with the interior lives of subjects such as Raymond Andrews, who is deaf and mute, and Christopher Knowles, who is mentally disabled. Kantor, Wilson, Bausch, Foreman, Abdoh, and Oguri dramatize surrealism's logic of dreams and the obsessional dimensions of historicized memory to create images that verbal language cannot reach, or amplify sounds which return words to an inexorable materiality. Thus auteurism presents itself as a form of sometimes quite literal self-centeredness, the artist's insistence that he/she will witness the unnarratable narrative of history. These auteurs have seemingly accepted as a site of creativity the paradoxical notion that the medium of theatre reifies presence, while also asking 'what *is* present?' (Carlson 1984: 515).

Most interesting, however, are the numerous distinctions between Kantor, Foreman, Monk, Wilson, Abdoh, Bausch, and Oguri, evident in this section. While Monk, Wilson, and Foreman might be termed formalists, Bausch and Abdoh have boldly broken with high postmodernist theatre and introduced strong points of view into their aesthetic arsenals (see Chapters 21 and 22). Wilson uses technology in ways that Foreman refutes, and Kantor and Abdoh utilize the dead body of this century's cataclysmic history as their primary locus of dramatic action. Monk sets the body in intimate settings that contest the space between tangible and pre-discursive reality. Bausch works with distantiation to dramatize the cultural history of the body. Oguri, as Meiling Cheng argues, uses 'an active stance of passivity' as a means toward his critique. Cheng suggests here that Oguri 'stands to disrupt the pedigree of Western auteur-directors in the twentieth-century theatre' by his company's:

[. . .] ability to empty out their human wills and to become continuous with their surroundings, existing unintrusively as a blade of grass in a meadow or a sand painting in a desert. Without the benefit of an external force like the atomic flash, these performers seem to be able to turn that violence inward, letting it implode like a breath-holding tranquility: they endure their own progressive fossilization with patience and intensity.

As Marvin Carlson suggests, such extreme aesthetic postures are also responses to the growing field of performance and cultural theory over the past three decades: 'The complex and always evolving play of incompleteness, substitution, repetition, and deferring that this generation of critics has brought into theatre theory promises to open this theory to the same range of new perspectives already opened by recent critical work in other genres' (1984: 515). Thus we find that auteurism is a term which accommodates a plurality of intentions, performance strategies, and reflections on culture, but which has as its overarching impulse the will to fuse historical events and narratives into a diorama of synthesized images, sounds and non-linear temporalities.

NOTE

1   Kantor was trained as a painter, Wilson as an architect, Bausch as a dancer.

WORKS CITED

Carlson, Marvin (1984) *Theories of the Theatre*. Ithaca, NY: Cornell University Press.

15

ARTAUD'S *LES CENCI*

An account by Roger Blin, Artaud's letters, and critical reviews

Translated by Charles Marowitz

T54, 1972

Editors' note: *Les Cenci*, adapted from Stendhal and Shelley and directed by Antonin Artaud, opened in Paris on 6 May 1935. The following statements by Roger Blin about the production are taken from an interview with Blin by Charles Marowitz.

I had known Artaud since 1928. We met quite frequently. I'd gone to see the productions of his Alfred Jarry Theatre, and he made me his friend.

One day he turned to me and said: 'Would you like to be my assistant? I want to put on *Les Cenci*. I've written an adaptation based on Stendhal and Shelley, would you like to work on it with me?' And so, we set out in search of a theatre. It was difficult. We had very little money, but we kept at it. Eventually, we found a theatre we didn't much care for, a former music hall in the Avenue de Wagram, and began rehearsals in a small adjoining room.

Artaud always held a large notebook and some colored crayons – one color for each of the cast – and he said to me: 'Make a note of everything I say,' and opposite the text, I would draw diagrams of the movements he indicated for each character. And then, one day, he said to me: 'Not only make notes on what I say, but even on what I don't say. You must act as a medium and be able to divine what I think and what I am going to say.'

He wanted the actors in the Banquet Scene of *Les Cenci* to act in a stylized manner. He wanted each of the princes to resemble an animal. But it was extremely difficult because none of the actors had any idea about this kind of acting. They hadn't been trained for that sort of thing. They came from the Conservatoire or the Boulevard Theatre where all that was asked of them was good diction and here Artaud was asking them to play animals and make certain throaty noises. One day, after we had searched in vain for two or three actors to play the deaf-mute assassins, he asked me to go up on the stage – something which had never occurred to me – and he found that I wasn't too bad, and that's how I came to act for the first time in my life: in *Les Cenci*.

Most of the actors understood his ideas, but they couldn't carry them out – but then Artaud hadn't taken the trouble to explain himself. He was so completely inside his subject and tended to have faith, perhaps too much faith, in their abilities to comprehend him. He needed more time for rehearsal, and especially to find parallels, to find simple images to help the actors understand. It was rather abstract, but then it had to be, for it was the true, the great theatre that Artaud wanted to show them.

Les Cenci was for him only a means toward making the public aware of some of his ideas concerning Theatre of Cruelty, concerning the word, gesture, certain little-known musical traditions. That's why, with Roger Désormière, his conductor, he made experiments with the seven-beat rhythms of Inca music. And, incidentally, it was the first time stereophonic sound was used in the theatre, with the sound of bells on tape and speakers placed in different points of the auditorium. That had never been done before.

Artaud hoped that the success or the half success of *Les Cenci* (for him it was only a half-way point toward his real goal) would enable him to raise enough money to present his next production, the one he dreamt of, his scenario of *The Conquest of Mexico*.

When Artaud was looking for a composer for *Les Cenci*, his friend Pierre Souvtchinsky introduced him to Désormière. Artaud worked closely with Désormière and was quite explicit about the music and effects that he wanted. He hoped to use real bells and to include other actual sounds, but, for the most part, he had to settle for recorded noises. Fortunately, Désormière had a good deal of experience working with microphones and recording techniques. Typical of their experimentation was the attempt to create music for the last scene by using anvils, screw nuts, files, and other metal objects.

The audience was surrounded and constantly bombarded by sound. The tolling bell resounded from the four corners of the auditorium before the curtain was raised. Désormière underlined the actors' movements with sound. At moments the performers' steps were echoed by recorded footsteps at full volume. Rhythmic stamping was backed by the sound, broadcast at different volumes, of a metronome oscillating at various speeds. In the assassination scene a tempest rages: Désormière used the loud, resounding tones of the Martenot and recorded voices that shouted and whispered Cenci's name in a contrapuntal composition; the words crossed one another and were at first separated in time but came closer, rising in a crescendo that was immediately silenced.

LETTERS

Antonin Artaud, to André Gide
Paris, 10 February 1935

Dear Sir and Friend,

I have finished a tragedy *with text*; although the dialogues are condensed, they are fully set down.

This tragedy will be playing at the Comédie des Champs-Elysées at the beginning of next April – and the rehearsals will begin any day now.

But before this I propose to give a lecture to some friends. All the actors will be present at this lecture.

I would like to ask you to give me the honor and your friendship by being present at this lecture [. . .], and here is why.

The dialogue of this tragedy is, I dare to say, of extreme violence. And *there isn't anything* that won't be attacked among the antique notions of Society, Order, Justice, Religion, Family and Country.

I therefore expect very violent reactions on the part of spectators. This is why I would like to prepare opinion in advance.

There must be no misunderstanding.

Everything that is attacked is much less on a social level than on a metaphysical level.

It is not pure anarchy. – And this is what must be understood.

Even those who ideologically think most freely, in the most detached manner, in the most evolved way, secretly remain attached to a certain number of notions that I attack in one fell swoop in this play.

This play doesn't have to be a roaring or continual protest.

There is no anarchist who has ideologically decided to throw the idea of family to the winds who still does not have a profoundly rooted human attachment to his father, his mother, his sisters, his brothers, etc.

But in this play, nothing is treated with respect. I want to make everyone understand that I attack the social superstition of the family without asking that one take up arms against such and such an individual. The same for order, the same for justice. [. . .]

I seek, therefore, to keep the public from confusing ideas with men and, more than that, from confusing them with forms.

So I destroy the idea from fear that respect for the idea will only result in creating a form, which in its turn, favors the continuance of bad ideas.

Here is why I depend on your presence and why I also ask you to fix a date or rather an evening after dinner.

I will wait for your response before calling my friends and my troupe together.

While waiting for your reply, I remain your faithful and sincerely devoted friend.

Antonin Artaud
Hôtel des États-Unis, 135 Blvd. Montparnasse, Paris

P.S. The place of the lecture will be at M. Jean-Marie Conty's house, 12 rue Victor Considerant (Place Denfert-Rochereau).

Antonin Artaud, to Louis Jouvet (Director of the Athénée Theatre in Paris)
Around 1 March 1935

. . . It is now completely finished, and it is an original play. It is not what one would call an adaptation. I insist on this point. . . .

I am presently in negotiations with many theatres. But I persist in telling you again that I am ready to incur expenses for this play from all points of view, publicity included.

Nothing is decided with anyone. And I can undertake to show it in three weeks, if I have a theatre at my disposal.

I have some sensational musical and sonorous elements.

And concerning the play, you can either get the opinion of André Gide, or Charles Dulin, or read it.

The décor and costumes of Balthus are also ready.

I point out to you, in closing, that there are elements of terrible actuality in this play.

Faithfully Yours,
Antonin Artaud

Antonin Artaud, to Louis Jouvet

Dear Friend,
I ask you not to keep me waiting. I want to try to perform the play at the end of the month, and it is still possible if we begin to rehearse immediately: It needs at least three weeks to get the sound machinery ready. And it seems to me that one can be immediately for or against this text but that hesitation one way or another is impossible.

I am faithfully yours,
Antonin Artaud

Antonin Artaud, to Louis Jouvet
7 March 1935

Dear Friend
[. . .] Bearing in mind now the objections that you have given me, I think that there is no longer time to retrench behind a reproach of insufficient clarity with a text like this one where it is only the dynamism that counts and exists above all.

Some of the most important intellects of the period have sensed and have spoken to me about dynamism. And I think that they would be ready to bear witness.

I can also tell you about the impression that this play had on the actors and all the gatherings of people to whom I have read it and who compose the active part of your public and that of the Atelier.

There has been unguarded enthusiasm for the text alone. [. . .] Reading it over again I have found in it, moreover, the simple elements that you demand; good, evil and treachery. And I will say to you, moreover, that for me theatre has never been that.

I believe that it is time to finish with routines and with these conventions at the moment when all values are collapsing, when no one has the right to make any conjecture any longer. When the public thinks they understand something, it isn't what they understand that acts on them, but precisely the rest, the forbidden zone of rational intelligence where the unconscious intervenes.

And it seems to me that all the audiences in the world have an unconsciousness that, in a period like this, is ready to burst out of its membrane. The clever calculations and healthy prudence that are thought to evaluate forces but evaluate only the results will persevere as long as the world does. But the world turns by itself and shows us its terrible other side.

You, yourself, have sided with ingenious, balanced plays because an era that clings to its remains can still preserve its appearance. Now it can no longer save face.

Moreover, I prove with this play that when I read it to the public everyone trembles and is excited. Only certain theatre directors resist, even though it would be in their interest to surrender.

Moreover, when have we truly given this discredited public an opportunity to be deeply moved? The unconscious is the same everywhere, one need only reveal its powers. Count on arousing the masses by energies, by pure forces with which this play has been proven to be abundantly provided, and don't count on reasonable calculations anymore.

I am anxious to point out, in conclusion, that until now, everything has been miraculous in this play and in this affair. And we are, it seems to me, in an epoch when miracles have become the law.

Yours faithfully,
Antonin Artaud

P.S. You must give me an appointment very soon to speak at length on this project, at noon or in the afternoon.

PREVIEWS

Le Petit Parisien, 14 April 1935
'The Theatre of Cruelty'

On 6 May the Theatre of Cruelty will perform Les Cenci *and, as if for a great celebration, the bells will ring at the Folies-Wagram, where we will hear . . . the great bell of Chartres Cathedral.*[1]

'I could not hope to use direct sound,' *Antonin Artaud told us,* 'and, as it was done in Russia, have bells thirty feet high installed in the theatre, which would have enveloped the spectator and brought him to our mercy in a network of vibrations. I had to use recordings: a microphone was put under the bell of the cathedral, and this very morning Désormière, who is of invaluable help to me, recorded, from machines in a suburban factory, those noises that would be at home in a medieval torture chamber.

'The Tibetan *Book of the Dead* emphasizes the power of sound caught by the human ear; I do not think anyone will question this power, and everyone knows that repetitious sounds have a hypnotic effect. I did not hesitate to use the Martenot: It is the first time that sound of such volume and kind will be heard.'[2]

And the lighting?

'The function of the lights is not to illuminate. We are interested in distributing and diffusing the color and density of light but, above all, let's not talk about falsely naturalistic lighting!

'Text, gesture, sound, lighting – each is equally important to me: the play lives off this whole, and whoever neglects one of these elements is depriving this body of an essential organ . . . There is no true language in the theatre except action. It alone counts.'

What is being prepared in this establishment, which has had such a varied history, is none other than the conclusion to this 'Manifesto of the Theatre of Cruelty' published under the name of Artaud by La Nouvelle Revue Française . . .

'I want to return to that idea of a universal life beyond good and evil, which used to give the Mysteries of Eleusis such strength. Let us not be mistaken, Cruelty for me has nothing to do with blood or duty . . . It means doing everything the director can to the sensibilities of actor and spectator.

'I believe in the necessity of using physical means to bring the spectator to submission, to compel him to participate in the action. Inevitably groping, I am looking for the principles of a science that inspired certain painters: Vinci, El Greco, Tintoretto and even Veronese.

'Balthus, the costume designer, is well acquainted with the symbolism of colors. He also designed the sets, which are conceived in a spirit of true grandeur and are made only of real elements. In *Les Cenci* you will see a palace built like an actual ruin, with its scaffoldings and draped nets instead of friezes.'

And the actors?

'I tried not to use professional actors. In Russia there are workers who do *King Lear* miraculously well. I do not believe in a professional career and loathe everything this word stands for, but I do believe in temperament and work.

'Professional actors who have kept themselves "pure" are rare.

'The alchemists of old realized that in each human being there are three elements to be reached: the body, the soul, and the mind. With harmonic combinations, we hope to awaken a sensibility that has not been lost but is, as it were, isolated by an infinite number of obstacles. It should be made clear that what we are attempting is not in imitation of any country's work and that our only aim is to return dignity to the theatre.

'*Les Cenci*. A subject that is barbaric, out of time – a performance that I want to leave the actor and the public exhausted. All I took from Shelley was the subject matter, replacing his lyricism with action . . .

'Iya Abdy will be Beatrice and, suspended on the wheel of torture by her hair, she will receive the punishment reserved for parricides.'[3]

Iya Abdy is a tragedienne with a beautiful face . . .

'I admire Baty,' *she confided to us.* 'After a performance of *Crime and Punishment*, which had stirred confusing echoes deep inside of me (petty Russian blood runs in my veins), I went to see him. It was he who encouraged me. I worked with Dullin for three years.'

Lady Abdy wanted us to forget her rank . . .

'There is no reason why,' *she protested*, 'we should be completely deprived of talent for having lived in high society. The obstacles are more numerous and there are potholes hidden under the flowers in the road . . .'

'Do you think people will like me?' *she worried with charming modesty, all the more unexpected from this young woman blessed with every gift . . .*

'Because I want to please the "inexpensive places," the "seats for 40 francs."' '

Artaud, from *La Bête Noire* no. 2, 1 May 1935
'Les Cenci'

Les Cenci, that will be performed at the Folies-Wagram as of the 6th of May, is not Theatre of Cruelty yet but is a preparation for it.

I drew my play from Shelley and Stendhal, which does not mean that I either adapted Shelley or imitated Stendhal.

From both I took the subject, which is, moreover, true and far more beautiful in reality than on stage or in manuscripts.

Shelley embellished nature with his style and language, which is like a summer's night that is bombarded by meteors, but I prefer the starkness of nature.

While writing *Les Cenci*, I did not try to copy nature any more than I tried to imitate Shelley, but I imposed the movement of nature on my tragedy, that general gravitation that moves plants and beings like plants and which we also find in a static form in the volcanic eruptions of the earth.

All of the staging of *Les Cenci* is based on this movement of gravitation.

The gestures and movements are as important as the text; and the latter was established only to serve as a catalyst for the rest of the play. And I think this will be the first time, at least here in France, that we will be involved with a dramatic text written in terms of a production whose modalities left the author's imagination concrete and alive.

The difference between the Theatre of Cruelty and *Les Cenci* will be the same as that between the din of a waterfall or the outburst of a natural storm and the violence that remains once their image is registered.

For this reason it was impossible in *Les Cenci* to use direct sound. To equal the vibrations of a cathedral bell, I had to record the bell of Amiens Cathedral with a microphone.

As in the Theatre of Cruelty, the spectator at *Les Cenci* will find himself in the center of a network of vibrations of sound; but instead of the sound issuing from four bells each 30 feet high and placed at the four cardinal points of the theatre, it will be diffused by loudspeakers situated at similar points.

Dummies will intervene in *Les Cenci*. And in this way, too, I will return to the Theatre of Cruelty by circuitous and symbolic ways.

First of all in *Les Cenci* there will be what the characters say: and they say roughly everything they think; but in addition, one will hear things that nobody could say no matter how great his natural sincerity and the degree of his self-knowledge. The dummies in *Les Cenci* will be there to make the heroes of the play say what is disturbing them and what is impossible in ordinary speech.

The dummies will be there to formulate the reproaches, bitterness, regrets, anguish and demands, and from the beginning to the end of the play, one will perceive a language of gestures and signs that concentrates the anxieties of the time into a kind of violent expression.

Les Cenci is a tragedy in the sense that, for the first time in a long while, I have tried to make beings speak instead of men; beings, each of whom are like great forces incarnate and retain enough of rational man to be plausible from a psychological point of view.

And it seems that we hear these beings groan and turn, brandish their instincts or vices, and pass like great storms vibrating with a kind of majestic fatality.

We are not with the Gods yet, but we are almost with heroes as they were understood by the Ancients. And in any case, there is that exalted and legendary aspect; that atmosphere, created by heads that have lost their reason and radiate in the clouds, which belongs to the heroes of great stories and marvelous epics.

It seems to me that with *Les Cenci* theatre is and recovers this almost human dignity without which it is not necessary to trouble the spectator.

Artaud, from *Le Figaro*, 5 May 1935
'What the Tragedy of *Les Cenci* will be'

The father in *Les Cenci* is a destroyer. And it is in such a way that this subject revives the Great Myths.

The tragedy, *Les Cenci*, is a Myth that brings some truths to light.

And because *Les Cenci* is a Myth, it became a tragedy when it was adapted to the theatre.

I clearly mean a tragedy and not a domestic tragedy; for men are more than men in this play, if they are not yet gods.

Neither innocent nor guilty, they are subjected to the same essential amorality of those gods of the Ancient Oracles, the sources of all tragedy.

[. . .] I thought it was a good idea in a time like ours, when nature speaks louder than men, to revive an ancient Myth that touches contemporary problems to the quick.

[. . .] I then had to make this Myth palpable and put it in words: For if nature speaks louder than men, it seemed to me that, with a few rare exceptions, the general tendency of the times was to forget to wake oneself up.

I tried to shake off this hypnotic sleep in direct and physical ways. And this is why everything in my play rotates and why each character has his turn to speak.

I wrote the tragedy of *Les Cenci* because I had met a tragedienne who could yell without swooning, – and whose strength grew in proportion to her developing frenzy.

Iya Abdy will start to live her own life in the role of Beatrice. –

One will find in the staging a whole attempt at symbolic gesture, where gesture is equal to a written word.

This means that gesture is as important to me as what we call language, for gesture is a language of its own.

The lights, like the gesture, will also be equal to a language, and in this effort toward a unique theatrical language, at every moment, light will verge on joining sound. [. . .]

Gestures, sounds, noises, sets, text, lights – we have tried to present the Parisian public with an experiment that can rival those that are now being done in European countries where theatre has become a religion once again.

Pierre Barlatier, from *Comoedia*, 6 May 1935
'Regarding *Les Cenci*, M. Artaud tells us why a Theatre of Cruelty'

[. . .] Beginning this evening, the Folies-Wagram Theatre offers hospitality to an experiment of a completely new and most unexpected order regarding the means employed for the *mise-en-scène*. [. . .]

Shelley and Artaud have taken their subject from history, but the play by Artaud does not resemble Shelley's *Cenci* any more than Racine's *Andromache*, for example, resembles Euripides' *Hecuba*, although the issues of each obviously spring from the same essence.

With *Les Cenci*, M. Antonin Artaud entrusts the public with his first work that illustrates his conception of the 'Theatre of Cruelty,' and this work will be followed by many others, among them a *Macbeth* and *The Torture of Tantalus*.

'My heroes,' M. Artaud tells us, 'place themselves in the domain of cruelty and must be judged outside good and bad. They are incestuous, sacrilegious persons, adulterers, rebels, insurgents, blasphemers. And this cruelty in which the entire work is bathed does not come only from the story of the Cenci family. It is not a purely corporal cruelty but a moral one. It goes to the limits of instinct and forces the actor to plunge in up to the roots of his being so completely that he leaves the stage exhausted. Cruelty also acts against the spectator, and it must not permit him to leave the theatre intact, but he also must be exhausted, involved, transformed perhaps!

'Also I have sought, by all available means, to place the audience in the middle of the action.

'Not only the sound of the great bell of a cathedral but noises of a tempest will be diffused during the presentation. Not only has M. Désormière succeeded in creating unexpected, shrill and flat timbres with the Martenot, but I also wanted to play with light since I think it is certainly capable of direct activity on the spectators' nerves as well as decorative effects.

'Finally, in this play, one will find an experiment with symbolic gesture, because a gesture can be as symbolic as a word and can carry a hieroglyphic meaning.

'And the young painter, Balthus, one of the strongest personalities of his generation, who admirably knows the symbolism of forms as well as of colors (green for death, yellow for evil death), makes use of this symbolism in his choice of costumes and in designing the magnificent decor, built by an artisan who is above all an artist: M. Guillaudin. The ultra-real decor is ultra-constructed but, like ruins, it creates an impression of an extraordinary dream.'

REVIEWS

Raymonde Latour, from *Paris-Midi*, 7 May 1935
'Before all of Paris, the Theatre of Cruelty was born last evening'

Every now and then, the imagination, the brilliance, the luck and the genius of Paris combine to create something bizarre and a little miraculous. Last evening at the Folies-Wagram was an example. The play had begun as early as nine o'clock on the sidewalks of Avenue Wagram. Fervent followers of *Solidarité Française*, meeting next door, stopped, stupefied, before the white rose bushes and sheaves of arums that attentive and excited friends had sent the new star. And Antonin Artaud's guests, as they were stopped at the theatre door, seemed visibly upset when they were obliged to slip through fifty or so policemen to go and applaud *Les Cenci*.

Inside the theatre, there was complete contrast. For they had picked the ugliest theatre in Paris for this sumptuous tragedy, full of brilliance and mystery, beauty and revolt. One expected evening dress, diadems, and a delightfully snobbish atmosphere . . . there were jackets and berets, but alas! few reactions.

One of the characters says something like: 'Myself, the Church, the family and honor, I put all that in the same basket!' With that he slaps his thigh and exits.

Nobody flinches. Anyway, no more so than at other lines, which obviously had been inserted to 'bait' the public and finally to provoke 'varied' reactions. 'Antonin Artaud won't have his battle of *Hernani* tonight!' remarked one critic.

Alas, sometimes with the waves, the bells, and the sound of the wind in the Roman countryside, audacity was lost for a pleasing image. But then, Antonin Artaud's impeccable diction, impetuosity, brutality, or ardor compensated for this, hitting us in the face with the most searing words and passionate phrases, like slaps or battle cries.

I do not know what the reviews will be like, but what struck me most during the intermissions was the absence of animated discussion. One can either love or detest this unusual play, but one should not remain indifferent to the courage and audacity of the effort. [. . .]

F.D., from *Le Temps*, 8 May 1935
'*Les Cenci*: a theatrical evening'

A tragedy of ancient inspiration? It was sought after so eagerly that the mob beat down the doors and quarreled with the ticket collectors. With the first words of the wild Cenci, a knavish, cruel, and, ere long, incestuous nobleman, we recognized the sonorous and dissolvable language of melodrama . . . M. Antonin Artaud, author–actor, displayed sunken and swarthy cheeks and feverish eyes; the viperine ways of the old Taillade. He had a muffled voice.[4] He sneered, he defied heaven and virtue; and mumbled his words that were poisoned by *crime*, *vice* and *arrogance* . . . Next to him, Mme. Iya Abdy cried no less. She was Beatrice, the 'beautiful parricide.' Her marvelous face, tormented by horror, made one shudder with astonishment. She wrung her hands, beat on the walls, turned on herself, shook her head of golden hair; she became mad even before the incest. What would she do after she clearly told us about the crime!

Some young people giggled. Sentences like: 'The worst is yet to come . . . You see what a jam . . . It has misfired . . .' ricocheted in the hall, stirring up small, joyous ripples. Nevertheless, the play had some beauty. The blasé liked its daring décor of inexplicable architecture; their passion for theatre was revived by these naive and untamed efforts, which were not at all faint-hearted, certainly, nor mediocre, nor sluggish.

Alarming noises filled the auditorium. Recorded on records, amplified by giant microphones [*sic*], the great bell of Chartres rang at full peal over our heads, and we cringed under the vibrations of the tolling, while remembering the bell of the *Jardin des Supplices* . . . Then the tempest raged. A symbolic and real tempest of horror as the Martenot spun the guests of François Cenci, who were already frightened by his cynicism, his eloquence and his grimaces, upon the stage like tops . . . The glimmering greens and reds of the lanterns signified wickedness and spilt blood. When Cenci died, two daggers in his breast, and Pope Clement VIII, invisible and present, sent Beatrice to the torture chamber – the executioner binds her wrists to a chariot wheel . . . is this torture? – a formidable death procession was heard. Pieces of wood were knocked together, as if planks of the stage, the handles of the axes and the headsman's block were following the condemned, limping.

Voila! The 'Theatre of Cruelty!' Cruel and amusing. More passionate, unquestionably, than our little capricious love affairs . . . and deserving, if not respect at least goodwill.

Colette, from *Le Journal*, 12 May 1935

'*Les Cenci* at the Folies-Wagram'

Because of the conviction and the passion that animates him, we will pardon M. Artaud the presumption of his profession of faith. He wishes, he declares, to raise a type of votive edifice to Cruelty – a theatre. It is more easily said than done. He tried to do it with all his soul, and so he certainly deserves not to be discouraged. But what difficulties raise themselves before him! Not limited to merely charnel entertainments, the domain of cruelty has boundaries where the trusting and short-sighted spirit grievously bruises itself because it believed these limits to be far away.

I fear even murder, rape, and scalping, considered as fine arts, have only deceived M. Artaud. From the point of view of theatre, I do not put my trust in punishment itself. As for the stake, I only know that, in former times, a hippodrome has presented it as a family spectacle. The audacious men who burned Jeanne d'Arc before the placid audience of children still endure in diminishing numbers. When the repertory of M. Artaud has examined a zodiac of torments, toward what cruelty will it turn? There are not thirty-six ways to eat a heart, or to cut up a child. Thus, M. Artaud will have to exploit the torments and illnesses of the spirit – which is equivalent to reinstating ordinary theatre.

It is too early to show too much anxiety. It is sufficient enough that the protagonists of *Les Cenci*, united for the first time and animated by the same ardor, give the impression of a coherent troupe. The music, which stays within the confines of a shriek and a railroad disaster, the costumes, the décor, the acting and mime of the actors stem from the same aesthetic. I will not say that they come together 'in a melancholy and profound unity.' Where M. Artaud fails is in the result that he flatters himself he has obtained. Until now, his theatre is the theatre of vehemence and not of cruelty or of terror. Judging from what he is doing, M. Artaud does not know how to change the nature of ill-fated phenomena that act upon us. Our anguish arises from shadow, silence, the unexplained. M. Artaud screams in vain that he is a demon, that he is nourished by perjuries, various crimes, incest, and twenty modes of rape, he even drinks an imitation of his children's blood in a skull of molded cardboard. We watch him do it, we listen to him with the same interest that we would a goblin. We accord more credit to a cruel person if he is calm, even jovial, and if he is charming and reserved. We will believe him to be all the more unrelenting – look at Richard III.

Les Cenci of Artaud drive a train from hell that does not affect us. As soon as they are silent, they recover an interior life and fragments of power. One of the scenes that has received the most attention and success is that in which Beatrice Cenci, the angel of parricide, arms two hideous mutes and directs them toward the sleeping Cenci. This moment, which depends on pantomime and on choreography, makes an impression and, at the same time, gives a precise stage direction to Beatrice's interpreter, who is still not ripe for long speeches. [. . .]

Antonin Artaud, from *La Bête Noire*, 1 June 1935

[. . .] From the partisan dishonesty and the total prejudice of certain people who only came to see *Cenci* with the intention of seeing it fail and to destroy the play, and who were finally muzzled by the fourth and last act, from this medley of reviews, restrictions, eulogies, excitement, reservations, honesty and dishonesty, I get the impression that the French public is not mature enough for a feast of the gods; there proved to be more than one spectator who recognized the unprecedented atmosphere of the *Cenci* as being dangerous. [The following letter] extracted from my abundant mail, [is] proof.

13 May 1935

My Dear Friend,

I am disgusted by your rudeness and impertinence.

I have come from the Abbey of Ligugé where Huysmans used to live and shall return. In the interim, I had the opportunity to see your play and have an impression to give you, or at least an opinion to share with you.

You don't seem to give a damn. Continue.

But don't think that you are launching such diabolical vibrations and spells over Paris with impunity.

You are playing with fire . . . Around me spectators were laughing like lunatics, trembling with hysterical laughter.

Nevertheless, there was an uneasy doctor who wanted an explanation, a resolution, a solution to this demonic tale.

He wanted peace.

My poor Artaud, there is nothing more to be done for you.

Cordially.

Eugène Gengenbach
Hôtel du Théâtre des Champs-Elysées, 10 Avenue Montaigne, Paris

NOTES

1 In *La Bête Noire*, 1 May 1935, Artaud wrote that the bell recorded was that of the Cathedral of Amiens. (Translator's note.)

2 The Martenot is an electric keyboard instrument that sounds only one note at a time. Invented by Maurice Martenot, it was introduced in 1928. (Translator's note.)

3 Lady Abdy contributed financially to the play. (Translator's note.)

4 Roger Blin reported that Artaud was nearly voiceless during the first few performances because he had shouted so much during the last rehearsals. (Translator's note.)

16

TADEUSZ KANTOR'S JOURNEY

Jan Klossowicz

T111, 1986

It's not easy to explain who Tadeusz Kantor really is or to say clearly what is more prominent in his artistic life – his work as a visual artist or his theatre. He has been involved simultaneously in both since the mid-1930s when he was a student at the Academy of Fine Arts in Krakow. The international success of Kantor's Cricot 2, founded in 1955, was heaped on top of the recognition he had already earned as a visual artist. Moreover, Kantor's artistic development is not linear. His creativity is a compilation of contradictions and antinomies; he was susceptible to transient and lasting trends in modern art, while remaining firmly rooted in his own theoretical writings. [. . .]

From 1934 to 1939, Kantor attended the Academy of Fine Arts in Krakow. Since the partition of Poland in the nineteenth century, this Gothic and Renaissance city had become its cultural center. There were two important aspects of Krakow's art world: Cricot, the theatre of avant-garde visual artists; and the memory of the turn-of-the-century neo-romantics and symbolists. While at the Academy, Kantor studied under Karol Frycz, a famous stage designer and a scholar of European and, what was rare at that time, Oriental theatre.

> Before World War II, I was interested in constructivism and Bauhaus, which I took to be at the roots of the Polish avant-garde led by Wladyslaw Strzemínski and Katarzyna Kobro. But my inner voice made me question the aesthetics of this movement. I had been brought up on and lived among the works of the symbolists.
>
> (Kantor in Borowski 1982: 20)

This conflict of artistic styles was reflected in Kantor's first experimental theatre – the Euphemeric Theatre, a puppet theatre he founded in 1938. There he presented Maurice Maeterlinck's *Death of Tintagiles*. This production was heavily influenced by the Bauhaus style of Oskar Schlemmer and Laszlo Moholy-Nagy. At the same time, Kantor was fascinated by the Polish symbolists Jacek Malczewski and Witold Wojtkiewicz and neo-romantic painter-poets such as Stanislaw Wyspianski. He was also very interested in Leon Schiller's productions of the plays of Polish romantics.[1]

Then came the war. And:

[. . .] complete isolation. The information concerning the other European cultures was blocked. The artistic past, its fascinations, manifestos, and credos suddenly seemed so far away as to acquire the status of myths. Reality was condensed to such a degree that it erased all previous aesthetic models and demanded new definitions. All forms of artistic life were prohibited [by the Germans] under penalty of death. An absolute, unspeakable terror swept our world. It was in those conditions that a group of young people, mainly painters, gathered [. . .] and conducted inflammatory radical discussions. This was the atmosphere in which I organized my Underground Theatre.

(Kantor in Borowski 1982: 20–1)

Underground Theatre's most important production was Wyspianski's symbolist drama, *The Return of Odysseus* (1944). Kantor dreamt of an Odysseus who returned to Krakow by train: the mythological hero appears at a dirty, overcrowded station; he steps into the waiting room which is under constant Nazi surveillance. The play was staged in a room partly blown apart by the war. Kantor did not alter his aesthetic principles, but applied them in a new way. Chunks of reality were thrown into the domain of art – decrepit and repugnant chunks: an old decayed wooden board, a cart wheel smeared with mud, parcels covered with dust, a soldier's uniform . . .

All the members of the group contributed whatever they had or could find. There was no prior concept of how that room should look. [. . .] When the room was filled with objects, the text of the play lost its importance. What was important was constructing that environment, and the action of finding, choosing, bringing those objects in. At that time we did not label those activities 'anti-art' nor did we use the term 'ready-made' to describe the objects. Our action was an outburst reflecting the growing aversion towards Constructivist forms with their particular baggage of aesthetic values. We were not yet familiar with the works of Duchamp.

(Kantor in Borowski 1982: 23)

In 1945, after the war, Kantor, together with other visual artists, reestablished the Krakow Group which was active before the war. In 1947 he went to Paris where he was exposed to surrealism and abstract expressionism – trends still little known at that time in Poland. Upon his return to Krakow, he and his friends in the Krakow Group organized an exposition of modern Polish art. Kantor was appointed professor at the Academy of Fine Arts but when the stringent rules of socialist realism[2] were imposed, he publicly refused to participate in official cultural life. His professorship was revoked in 1949. From 1949 to 1956, Kantor's paintings could only be exhibited underground, and he earned his living as a stage designer.

After 1956, during the period of de-Stalinization – the 'thaw' – Kantor traveled abroad again. On his return he was able to participate in mainstream cultural activities in Krakow. [. . .] Kantor's theatrical work during this period was an attempt to break with socialist realism and its rules and to introduce his aesthetic principles to the professional theatre. In the early 1960s when this attempt had failed, Kantor left the state-controlled theatre. But since 1955 he had already been organizing Cricot 2, in an 'accidental rather than official place' – in the basement of a Krakow palace. Cricot 2 drew on the tradition of Cricot, the prewar theatre group of painters. Except for Kantor, none of Cricot 2's members had much professional theatre experience.

Cricot 2's first production, Stanislaw Witkiewicz's *The Cuttlefish* (1956), marked the first stage in the theatre's development, implementing Kantor's theory of the Autonomous Theatre (see Kantor 1986: 115). [. . .] While preparing a project, Kantor writes essays, notes, and manifestos.

> This keeping of records is indispensable, since every committed artist who undergoes a process of development constantly experiences its various stages for which he has to provide different names. That is, new ideas erupt, old concepts become obsolete or require reshaping and modification. Even though the concepts change, one's principles and way of thinking remain the same, especially in the case of theatre.
>
> (Kantor in Borowski 1982: 102)

In 1961, with Kantor's staging of Witkiewicz's *In a Small Country House*, the second stage of Cricot 2's development began. Kantor called this stage the Informel Theatre from the French *informe* – meaning formless, misshapen (see Kantor 1986: 123). He wanted to make art from the 'reality of the lowest rank' – which meant spontaneity, chance destruction.

> The auditorium is full of stools, parcels, desks, which are chaotically scattered around. [. . .] In the wall there is an old, decaying closet. [. . .] From behind this closet's doors come the barking and howling of dogs. Suddenly the closet doors open and an incredible number of big bags fall out. One could not clearly distinguish between the bags and the actors who also fell out from behind the closet doors. From that moment on, the action of the performance takes place in a space filled with bags, stools, and actors constituting together the 'matter' of the performance.
>
> (Kantor in Borowski 1982: 59)

Soon Kantor divorced himself from the 'informel' and focused on concrete objects – his favorite being an umbrella. Next he became a minimalist. His new paintings were 'announcements,' thus no art object actually existed in a physical sense. In 1963 he organized an exhibition in Krakow made only from his notes, pieces of paintings, and found objects. This concept was fully explained in Kantor's manifesto, *The Zero Theatre*, or *The Theatre of Nullification* (1963) (see Kantor 1986: 125).

In his 1963 production of Witkiewicz's *The Madman and the Nun*, the actors were pushed aside as the whole stage was filled up with folding chairs. Kantor wanted to destroy any possibility of stage action; he wanted to cancel 'art' in general. During this period his works were dominated by the wrapping up of objects and people. His paintings were replaced by parcels, bags, suitcases, and wrapped humans. He exhibited these in Warsaw in 1965 as *Living Emballages*.

That same year Kantor came to the United States, where he met people who made happenings. He later said he had been staging happenings since World War II, without benefit of the name. When he returned from the U.S. he organized many happenings in and out of Poland. [. . .] Audience participation figured strongly in *Panoramic Sea Happening* [on the Baltic coast of Poland, 1967], which was a concert 'conducted' by Kantor. At the end of the happening dead fish were thrown at the audience which was sitting in an 'auditorium' flooded by the sea.

Happenings as such were not the final stage of Kantor's quest for 'reality.' In 1967 he staged yet another Witkiewicz play, *The Water-Hen*. He called this piece a 'theatre-happening'; it was closer to a theatrical interpretation of the play than to a 'happening' as it is commonly conceived. Kantor ceased to be interested in the nature of a happening. It burdened him with its 'physicality,' and he was more interested in the experience of approaching rather than passing the borderline of art.

In *The Water-Hen*, Kantor gave his actors complete freedom of action, while rejecting audience participation. The central motif of the production was a journey. The actors were eternal wanderers – bums packing and unpacking, always on the move carrying all their earthly possessions. [. . .]

Kantor's prolific activities as a visual artist from the late 1960s to the mid-1970s was dominated by his idea of enlarging or multiplying objects even as he was trying to get beyond them. *His Mother's Portrait* (1975), for example, was a psychological or 'spiritual' rather than visual work. It was during this period that he began working on *The Dead Class* which premiered in Krakow in 1975. Simultaneously he published his well-known manifesto, *The Theatre of Death* (Kantor 1986: 137). *The Dead Class* and the writing associated with it reveal a metaphysical aspect of Kantor's theatre, while underlining his ongoing struggle against illusion in the name of reality, in the name of the performance as an autonomous composition.

Even though it contains fragments of Witkiewicz's *Tumor Brainowicz*, *The Dead Class* was mainly Kantor's own creation inspired by Bruno Schulz's short story, 'The Pensioner.' Schulz focuses on an old man who at the end of his life decides to return to school – starting with the first grade. Kantor remodeled this story by making his old men return to school from the realm of death. It was also Schulz who gave Kantor the idea of using dummies. In the story the old man carried a copy of himself from the past: a wax figure of a child in a school uniform. For both Schulz and Kantor, the dummy is a symbol of artistic creation, of debased reality, of an awkward, cheap imitation of life. Wax figures 'imitating' humans had already been used in *The Water-Hen*, but they acquired new meaning in *The Dead Class* and *Wielopole, Wielopole* where they embodied past events, or life after death. Kantor called *The Dead Class* not a play but a 'seance.'

Wielopole, Wielopole (1980; see fig. 16.1) was not based on a literary text. In it, Kantor – like the old men of *The Dead Class* – returns to his childhood, to the death of his mother's uncle. *Wielopole* also refers to events from Polish history between the two World Wars. While working on *Wielopole, Wielopole* he stressed, in an essay only in manuscript, that he wanted the production to 'bring tears' to the audience's eyes. This thought materialized in his principle of the 'architectonics of affection' or 'emotional construct' which means a conscious manipulation of the audience's reactions. The performance of *Wielopole, Wielopole*, during which spectators are torn apart by experiencing extreme emotions, can be treated as a musical composition based not on harmony but on contrast.

Let the Artists Die (1985) which premiered in an abandoned factory in Nuremberg, connects the tragic wanderings between Nuremberg and Krakow of an artist, Veit Stoss,[3] with the history of Poland as personified by General Józef Pilsudski.[4] Kantor's own story manifested itself in a new way. He did not use dummies as actors' doubles but presented himself as three different character: a 6-year-old boy: I when I was 6; the author of the performance: I – the Prime Mover; and himself in the future: I – Dying. What fascinates Kantor is the lack of chronological continuity in life, making it possible to split a man – Kantor himself in *Let the Artists Die* – into different figures from different periods of life.

Fig. 16.1 The 1980 production of *Wielopole, Wielopole*. (The Cricoteka Achives. Photo by Maurizio Buscarino, courtesy of Princeton University Library.)

Balancing this existential, psychological, and metaphysical theatre is Kantor's black humor. He believes that humor is the only dignified human response to the unpredictable turns of the wheel of fortune, suffering and death. The grotesque has long been a favorite tool of the Polish avant-garde. Kantor's productions bear a resemblance to the tragi-farces of the crude market square booth stages in which historical events are interjected in *commedia dell'arte* acts and metaphysics are presented with a dadaist sense of humor.

The last item to be mentioned here is Kantor's presence during performances – a presence that has become a source of numerous contradictory interpretations. Kantor has actively participated in his productions since *The Water-Hen*. He appears on stage wearing his own clothes – but the color of his garments always corresponds to his visual compositions. He moves around the stage reacting in different ways but never saying anything. Often he does nothing but observe his actors and the audience.

Who is this person? What is his role? The actors know he may interfere in their acting, change the order of scenes, alter their rhythms, or regulate the volume of the music. Spectators are at a loss to discover whether or not Kantor is really conducting his performances as an orchestra leader conducts the musicians. Kantor does not conduct so much as he plays the role of the conductor. He does not create new actions in front of the audience as does the creator of a happening. He says that the reason for his presence on stage is his need to see whether or not the principles of his aesthetic, which are imbedded in the piece, come across clearly. A sensible interpretation of his role is given by Kantor himself. He says that he is on

Fig. 16.2 The 1988 production of *I Shall Never Return*. (The Cricoteka Achives. Photo by Jerzy Borowski, courtesy of Princeton University Library.)

stage to control the interaction between illusion and reality taking place during a performance. His presence plays with reality in order to crush whatever illusion still exists.

> When an actor gets rid of illusion – that means when a spectator believes that an actor turns into a spectator – this is the time when illusion is automatically reborn. When I see that an actor 'overacts' that means when he leaves the plane of concrete reality [. . .] I come up and stay by him. It is enough [to crush illusion] because I am a spectator and not an actor.[5]

Kantor sees himself as a spectator because his presence in the performance is 'illegal' from the point of view of orthodox theatrical convention.

> I am a private person, I am the author. But what brings me happiness is this role of a provocateur, i.e., the director should be hidden, he is not needed on stage. But I stand there [. . .] because this illegality fascinates me [. . .] because I destroy illusion, since I appear on stage as if to say: I do not like that.[6]

However, this statement does not fully explain Kantor's presence.

In calling himself 'I–the Prime Mover' in *Let the Artists Die* he reveals [. . . that he] wants to create theatre that is his alone – the same way a painter is the sole author of her/his paintings. [. . .] He is not part of any group (though he uses the same actors in production after production); he is not interested in training the actors; nor is he interested in the anthropology of theatre, its ritual character, or its social function. He is only interested in theatre as a spectacle or a mirror of an artist's – his, Kantor's – inner process. Theatre is his own 'journey' – in which he participates both as a man and as an artist – leading through different stages of life and artistic development to the borders of the unknown and the impossible. But, as Kantor maintains, the actuality of this journey, which he tried in 1985 to visualize as a series of drawings, has not yet materialized in his theatre.

NOTES

1 Leon Schiller (1887–1954) is described by Jerzy Tymicki as 'the Polish disciple and follower of Edward Gordon Craig. Schiller was the best Polish director between the two World Wars. For years he was head of the directing department at the National School of Drama in Warsaw with many students, followers and imitators. His impact was still great in the 1960s and 1970s' (Tymicki 1986: 13). [. . .] Schiller was imprisoned at Auschwitz during the war, but from 1945 to 1949 he regained his preeminent position among Polish directors. But when socialist realism became the only accepted mode of theatrical presentation, Schiller fell from favor.

2 Socialist realism was established in 1934 'when the Union of Soviet Writers proclaimed "socialist realism" the appropriate style for all writing: "socialist realism" requires from artists truthful, historically concrete representation of reality in its revolutionary development. Moreover, truth and historical completeness of artistic representation must be combined with the task of ideological transformation and education of the working man in the spirit of socialism' (Brockett and Findlay 1973: 341–2). In the theatre, socialist realism meant strict censorship of both plays and productions and a heavy naturalist production style.

3 Veit Stoss (1445–1533) was a German sculptor who spent almost his whole creative life in Krakow before returning to his native Nuremberg as an old man where he was imprisoned and tortured. His most important works are the altarpiece of St. Mary's Church in Krakow and the great wreath of carved roses in St. Lorenz Church in Nuremberg.

4 Józef Pilsudski (1867–1935) was the general who ruled Poland from 1918 until his death. As early as 1905, Pilsudski organized the military branch of the Polish Socialist Party and he demanded independence for Poland from Czarist Russia. After the Russian Revolution, when Poland attained its independence, Pilsudski ruled. Sometimes he was premier, sometimes military dictator. Pilsudski was fiercely anti-Russian, and he used force to restore Poland's eastern frontiers to the borders of 1772. Under the Treaty of 1921, Pilsudski was able to incorporate millions of Ukrainians and White Russians into Poland. Polish independence ended with the invasions by Germany and the U.S.S.R. in 1939.

5 and **6** These quotes are from Klossowicz's unpublished translation of Kantor's speech, 'My Way towards the Theatre of Death.' A different English translation was published in *International Theatre Yearbook*. Warsaw: Theatre Critics Association. 1977.

WORKS CITED

Borowski, Wieslaw (1982) *Tadeusz Kantor*. Warsaw: Wydawnictwo Art. i Filmowe.

Bridgewater, William, and Elizabeth J. Sherwood, eds. (1950) *The Columbia Encyclopedia*. 2nd edn. New York: Columbia University Press.

Brockett, Oscar G., and Robert R. Findlay (1973) *Century of Innovation*. Englewood Cliff, NJ: Prentice-Hall.

Kantor, Tadeusz (1986) 'The writings of Tadeusz Kantor: 1956–1985,' trans. Michal Kobialka. *TDR* 30, 3: 115–76.

Tymicki, Jerzy (1986) 'New Dignity: the Polish theatre 1970-1985.' *TDR* 30, 3: 13–46.

17

THEATRE AND THERAPY: ROBERT WILSON

Bill Simmer

T69, 1976

As Robert Wilson's theatre is more widely publicized, he is inadvertently develop-ing a reputation as an experimental 'therapist.' Several newspaper articles have pointed to his work with brain-damaged[1] children in Texas, his early involve-ment with Headstart programs and his work with the aged and terminally ill at Goldwater Memorial Hospital. Although this work was done many years ago, his reputation as a 'therapist' continues to grow because of his continuing collabor-ation with Christopher Knowles, a brain-damaged youth (see fig. 17.1), and, earlier, his work with Raymond Andrews, a deaf-mute. However, Wilson is not a therapist and does not consider himself one.

According to Webster, therapy is 'a remedial treatment of bodily disorder' or 'an agency (as treatment) designed or serving to bring about social adjustment.' If we accept this definition, then what Wilson has done is very different; in fact, almost the opposite. Instead of trying to help Knowles and Andrews adjust to society, Wilson tried to, in effect, adjust to them. He recognized that Knowles' and Andrews' perceptions of the world were different from other people's; Raymond because of deafness; Christopher because of severe brain damage. Wilson tried to discover the way they structured their perceptions in order to understand what their world was like. Then, with their help, he created theatre pieces that attempted to deal with reality in similar ways. In both cases, this involved learning their particu-lar languages to communicate with them on their own levels. Instead of trying to change their modes of perception, he recognized how valuable their modes were and encouraged them to share their vision of the world. [. . .]

RAYMOND ANDREWS

Wilson met Andrews in 1968 while conducting workshops in Summit, New Jersey. The deaf-mute boy was then 11 years old. Wilson spoke in an interview about his reactions: 'The thing that interested me about Raymond was the fact that he did not know any words . . . You know, he did not think in words, so that it was curious to know how he thought. I sort of think, well, I think in words; or I thought I did.'

Fig. 17.1 Robert Wilson, left, performing with Christopher Knowles, far right, at Shiraz in Iran during the Eighth Festival of the Arts in 1974. (Princeton University Library.)

Wilson watched Andrews very closely, trying to understand what he knew must be thought processes very different from his own.

He felt certain that Andrews was smart. 'Just a feeling I had, that he was a bright man,' he said, 'and perhaps even highly intelligent.' He also realized that Andrews was often attuned to things that he himself was not aware of. The youth always seemed to understand the social situations he was involved in. If someone told a funny story in a workshop, for example, Andrews would invariably laugh before the story was over, while everyone else waited for the punch line. He was able to understand the situation and how to respond to it even though he did not know what the story was about. Wilson maintained that it was clear that 'he was tuned into another language, and because of that, he frequently understood things that we did not necessarily get, because we were primarily concerned with words and he was not.'

Wilson, fascinated by Andrews' perceptions, began searching for better ways to communicate with him. Gradually, he discovered that Andrews could, in some sense, 'hear' sounds. He tells about banging on a piano one night in the loft at the Byrd Hoffman School of Byrds on Spring Street in New York City.[2] Andrews was standing at the other end of the room and responded to the music by putting his hands on various parts of his body. [. . .]

[Wilson] also discovered that he could stand behind Andrews and shout his name very loudly and that the youth would not respond; but if he imitated the sounds that Andrews himself made, the youth would turn around as if he had heard them.

'It seemed that because he was familiar with those sound vibrations . . . his body was familiar with those sounds. They were in his body and he could pick them up. So, in a sense, it was a language.'

Wilson began to think about this in more general terms – in terms of society's responsibility to the deaf. Society puts a great deal of time and money into the study of languages and the nature of language itself. Most of our major cities have large centers devoted to the study of language. He wondered if it was not possible to learn the 'deaf language.'

> All the work that I've seen or heard about with the deaf had never considered that idea of learning the language. All the work was imposing a hearing world's language on a non-hearing person . . . And in some ways that will never happen. It is impossible, because they will never hear what we hear. And they will never be able to say what we say because they do not hear what we hear. But through imitating what we do there is some understanding, and in turn, society could assume the responsibility in reverse, and imitate what they do.

One of the things Wilson and members of the Byrd Hoffman School of Byrds attempted to do in their workshops, therefore, was to learn Andrews' language by imitating him. They learned his gestures and the way he moved, as well as the sounds he made. [. . .]

Once members of the Byrds, as they refer to themselves, had learned [a set of Andrews' movements], it became a part of their vocabulary, appearing several times in plays. In *The Life and Times of Joseph Stalin* [1973], for example, it was performed by a whole row of soldiers (see Deak 1974).

In the course of Wilson's thinking about the nature of Andrews' perceptions, it occurred to him that everyone sees and hears on two different levels. On the one hand, we experience sensations of the world around us on what he calls an 'exterior screen.' This is the basis for most of our visual and audial impressions of the people and situations we encounter. On the other hand, we also see and hear on an 'interior screen'; but we usually are not aware of it, except, for instance, when we are asleep and dreaming. But Wilson maintains that the interior screens are operating all the time, even when we are only paying attention to the exterior screens. Blind people, however, see things only on an interior visual screen, and the deaf hear things almost entirely on an interior audial screen. As a result, their interior screens are often much more highly developed than other people's. [. . .] Wilson found that in his longer plays – the twelve-hour *The Life and Times of Joseph Stalin* (see Deak 1974) and seven-day *KA MOUNTAIN AND GUARDenia TERRACE* (see Trilling 1973) where the audience tended to blink more (and more slowly), the interior and exterior screens became intertwined. In speaking with people who had been in the audience, he noticed that they would often mention seeing things onstage that had not actually been there. But people would insist they had really seen them. He attributes this to a blending of the two types of screens:

> There's a point, I think, where the interior–exterior audial–visual screens become one . . . Through these long durations of time, you get a more homogeneous balance . . . And actually people sleep. And going to sleep, these interior images mingle with the exterior images until it all becomes one thing. There is no separation . . . I was interested through *Stalin* and the seven-day play [*KA MOUNTAIN*] I did in Iran, with

what happened when you get a more homogeneous balance . . . between exterior and interior audial and visual screens.

By imitating Andrews in the workshops, as well as by performing in the long, almost wordless plays, Wilson and the Byrds found they were becoming more attuned to their interior screens. [. . .]

Deafman Glance [1970] (and most of *Stalin* as well) did not have many words; it dealt almost entirely in images and in deaf sounds like the ones Andrews made (see fig. 17.2). The youth contributed much of the specific material for the play. Wilson recalled: 'I said to him, "Why don't we make a play together?"' After that, Andrews began showing him movements and gestures and giving him drawings. From these he developed a great deal of the play's imagery.

Andrews left the group in 1973. He is now attending a school for the deaf in New Jersey (he had never gone to school before joining the Byrds). Last year, he gave a concert at the Byrd loft in which he sang and played an electric guitar that Wilson had given to him.

MOVEMENT WORKSHOPS

Imitating Andrews was only one of many things Wilson and the Byrds learned to do in the workshops that were held regularly at the Byrd loft. These were essentially [two- to six-hour] movement workshops, which provided a framework within which Wilson could work out his ideas, as well as rehearse the actual productions. [. . .] It would be difficult to overestimate the connections between these workshops and

Fig. 17.2 Raymond Andrews in *Deafman Glance*. (Photo by Edward Grazda, Princeton University Library.)

Wilson's performances, since they were the proving ground for his experiments. Almost everything that appeared onstage had been developed beforehand in the workshops.

The main purpose [of the workshops] was to allow the participants to discover their own unique vocabulary of movement. [. . .] The approach to movement explored in the workshops had begun to develop as early as 1962, when Wilson worked privately with a small group in Texas, researching body movement with brain-damaged children. It involved going back and 'relearning' very simple movements that had become distorted in the course of day-to-day living by various anxieties and inhibitions. The emphasis was on the personal growth of the people involved. Wilson wanted them to be able to present themselves naturally onstage, without self-consciousness. What he was interested in, theatrically as well as personally, was each person's unique way of moving and behaving. Even imitation served to underline the natural differences in the individual ways different people performed the same movements. [. . .]

There was never a consistent formula for conducting the workshops. They grew and developed along with Wilson's ideas and varied according to the particular production he was preparing [. . . and to] the particular needs of the individual members. [. . .] Nonetheless, some aspects of the workshops remained consistent over long periods of time. Usually, everyone moved in unison for at least part of each session. Sometimes they would all run around the room, or jump up and down, or sit back-to-back in pairs, rocking back and forth. Sometimes they would simply lie on the floor and breathe, or close their eyes and listen for a while. They tried to build and then sustain higher levels of energy: Wilson referred to this as 'raising your energy and sitting on it.' Often there was a single, simple activity that was repeated over and over again. Cindy Lubar recalled a workshop that was held in Iowa when they were rehearsing *Deafman Glance*:

> We walked back and forth across the room for the entire workshop, just walking in parallel lines. We walked in tracks back and forth across the room for maybe two or three hours, and there was a tape of someone talking in the background.

Another common activity was to do simple body movements very slowly, in an effort to get in touch with some of the subtler physical ways in which the body is able to communicate. Like many of the other workshop activities, this was an attempt to approach non-verbal methods of communication and perception similar to Andrews'.

Sometimes, the workshops were divided between group movements and individual activities. One at a time, the participants would be asked to perform for the rest of the group. The particular activity was chosen specifically for the person who had to do it. It would be very simple at first: a newcomer might be asked simply to walk over to a chair and sit on it, or stand facing the back wall and walk from one side of the room to the other. As he became more comfortable performing in front of the others, the activities would become more difficult. This was a gradual process. It might be months, for instance, before someone was asked to speak in front of the rest of the group. This became one of the most effective ways of getting over anxieties about performing, because nobody was ever asked to do anything difficult until he was comfortable performing the simpler tasks. [. . .]

The activities often involved imitation, and again, this was done both individually and in groups. Lubar discussed this:

> Sometimes doing a movement that somebody else has developed himself . . . helps other people to find their own vocabulary of movement . . . Doing Raymond's movement and sound with him – I did not do it exactly the same way he did – but just trying to do that myself really was a breakthrough of some kind for me, in terms of getting in touch with my own vocabulary of movement.

After Christopher Knowles [. . .] joined the Byrds, imitation became a regular feature of the workshops. Knowles was often asked to lead the group activities. Usually, he would stand at the front of a long line and the others would follow, doing whatever he did and repeating everything he said.

Because of the orientation toward the individuals involved, the dynamics of the workshops depended upon Wilson's sensitivity to the individual members' daily development. He was always searching for activities that would help spur them forward; consequently, the activities were constantly changing. Wilson says that he works intuitively, and many of the people who have worked closely with him attest to the sensitivity of his intuitions. [. . .]

CHRISTOPHER KNOWLES

Knowles was born with serious brain damage after his mother contracted toxoplasmosis (a microscopic parasite) during pregnancy. In the early years of his life, he had problems with speaking and reading. His parents enrolled him in a Philadelphia-based program called the Institute for the Achievement of Human Potential. His father described this program:

> These are the people who have kids creeping and crawling and kids are manipulated, made to move in infantile patterns, which, according to the theory, would reestablish whatever neurological pathways had been damaged. And this went on for about eight years. Very intensive work – eight hours a day, seven days a week, no time off. [. . .]

When he finished with that program, Knowles attended the O. D. Heck School in Schenectady, New York, which is a part of the State System of Mental Hygiene. He had a tape recorder while he was there, and it broke one day. He was so upset that his parents bought him another tape recorder while the first one was being fixed. So, before long, Knowles had two tape recorders. His father described what he did with them:

> He started taping words on the tape recorder and then feeding it back over to the other tape recorder, stopping and starting it, so he was able to break the rhythm of the spoken word by this transposition from one receiver to the other. He apparently secreted himself in his room for about a week and then suddenly came out with this fantastic tape, which was 'Emily Likes the TV.' The total number of words was relatively few – about twenty minutes, one full side – using words as musical notations.

Mr. and Mrs. Knowles played the tape for some of their friends and one of them suggested they show it to Wilson, whom they had known since the time he was studying architecture at Pratt. After he heard the tape, Wilson asked the Knowles if they would consider having their son join the Byrds. They were dubious at first, but after consulting with Dr. Hugh Lafave, Knowles' supervisor at O. D. Heck, and several other professional advisers, they agreed.

The first time most of the Byrds saw Knowles was the opening night of *The Life and Times of Joseph Stalin*. The youth appeared in the production without any rehearsal, performing a variation of 'Emily Likes the TV.' Soon after that, Knowles moved into the Byrd loft. [. . .]

Much as he had done with Andrews, Wilson tried to understand Knowles' unique vision. To do this, he began trying to learn Knowles' language and to communicate with him on his own level. [. . .] As soon as Knowles joined the group, therefore, Wilson asked him to lead some of the workshops. By imitating him, Wilson was eventually able to approach some understanding of his thought processes. 'I saw that he had very similar concerns as I had . . .' said Wilson, 'in terms of language – in terms of his patterning words and thoughts. Once I learned . . . his patterns, then we had this exchange through his way of structuring thoughts.'

As was the case with Andrews, Wilson realized that Knowles dealt with the world more on interior than exterior screens. 'He was a dreamer,' said Wilson,

> . . . a daydreamer. Sometimes when you spoke to him, there was no apparent register of him hearing you. He would just stand and look out the window for five hours . . . preoccupied with his own mental process, and did not necessarily – the way we do – pick up and relate to the exterior things happening . . . so maybe he was hearing more on an interior audial screen. Even his vision – well, even now, Christopher does not look at you very much. He looks down at the floor, or he is looking somewhere else . . . so that, even his visual screens are interior screens. But they are very highly developed interior audial and visual screens.

[. . .] Of course, learning Knowles' patterns was a gradual process. Dr. Hugh Lafave, who has tried all along to keep in touch with Knowles' development, noticed several general 'stages' in the youth's relationship with Wilson. They did not talk to each other much at first. 'I think the novel thing,' said Dr. Lafave,

> is that Bob and Christopher developed a relationship on terms other than verbal terms – the way they looked at each other, the way they moved, the way they sized each other up. They were getting along very well in a non-verbal way before they ever talked to each other much. There was some kind of a spark that sort of jumped the gap between those two from the moment they met, but there was very little dialog.

As Knowles began leading the workshops, Wilson became interested in the patterns of his movements. This, according to Dr. Lafave, was the next 'stage' of their interaction. 'The thing that impressed me,' he said, 'was how much was being communicated through movement and dance . . . It seemed to me there was a lot of body language going on between them.'

After that, there was a period when the most dynamic form of intercourse between the two seemed to Dr. Lafave to be through drawings and pictures. Both Wilson and Knowles were keeping notebooks, which for a time seemed to be a major source of their exchange. Knowles showed his notebook to Dr. Lafave. 'What impressed me most were the drawings and graphics,' he said. 'There were words, but initially there were more pictures.'

It was only after that 'stage' that speaking became their most important means of exchange. During this period, Dr. Lafave recalled that they used tape recorders a great deal, which they played back and forth for each other. Later, Knowles became more interested in written language. He began composing poetry on a typewriter, arranging the words in graphic patterns on the page. He was a perfectionist – Lubar recalled that he once spent three days working on a single page. [. . .]

In the end, it was Knowles' unique use of language that fascinated Wilson the most, and contributed most profoundly to his theatre. The youth seemed to see words in visual patterns, not only in his writing, but in his speech as well. 'His word constructs are probably graphic,' said Ed Knowles:

> He sees thoughts, rather than thinking abstractions . . . It is his visual awareness which he translates. Like with the 'Emily Likes the TV' thing, if that were ever to be spelled out, you would see that it has a definite pattern, a visual pattern as far as the spoken pattern is concerned.

Often, before one could understand something Knowles said, one would have to see him write it out: then it would be obvious that it was the graphic pattern of the words that mattered, rather than the meaning. Wilson [. . .] used the word Kathmandu (which he happened to see on an envelope sitting on his desk) to illustrate what Knowles did with words:

> I was particularly interested in Christopher's use of the language. Words were like molecules . . . This was the word Kathmandu. Later, it would be Cat; then Cat-man-ru. Later, it would be fat-man-ru, and then it would be fat man, and then it would be fat, and then it would be man or something. He would just be breaking off parts. And every time he used it, he was not afraid to destroy the word. The language was really alive, the words were really alive. They were always growing and changing. He would take anything on the radio – he would hear an announcement, or anything – and he just started to see the words distributed on the page. The way we use language, we are not allowed to do that. It is very rigid in terms of the laws and the grammar. And I respect that. But this was also another way . . . like molecules bursting apart into all directions all the time. It really was three-dimensional, like in space or something.

In both *A Letter for Queen Victoria* [1974] and *The $ Value of Man* [1975] (see fig. 17.3), Wilson tried to use language in this way. Knowles wrote much of the dialog of both plays. [. . .] Knowles also took an actual part in devising the physical structure of the play and he directed half of the rehearsals himself.

WILSON AND THERAPY

Wilson does not consider his relationships with Knowles and Andrews in terms of therapy. He was at least as much interested in learning from them as he was in helping them. He did plays that explored their unique ways of perceiving the world. That was his main interest – theatre, not therapy. He does not want to be thought of as a therapist. Nonetheless, both Andrews' and Knowles' close contact with Wilson had what might be called a 'therapeutic effect.' To note only the most obvious manifestations of this, Andrews was attending school (which he had never done before meeting Wilson) and Knowles was living independently and producing a large body of poetry as this article was being prepared.[3] [. . .]

Wilson's approach to both Knowles and Andrews, his attempts to learn their languages and to meet them on their own terms – does not relate to the typical way

Fig. 17.3 Christopher Knowles in the 1975 production of _The $ Value of Man_. (Photo by Carl Paler, courtesy of Princeton University Library.)

therapists approach people with similar problems. Ed Knowles described what he considers a more typical therapeutic approach:

> Most of them are real rough academicians who know all of the neurological tests and they go around with a little rubber hammer hitting you in the knee and making great judgments about you. As far as trying to work with the kids as people, there is a tendency to . . . depersonalize the cases. They are so anxious to arrive at an IQ number. 'OK, let's do the IQ thing!' and then they feel very pleased and they say, 'OK, you have an IQ of seventy-two and a half.' Now, what the hell does that mean? So here is a kid who has got problems in one area and he is a genius in the other area. How do you cope with that if you are a professional with a thing hanging on the wall?

But at least one professional therapist, Dr. Lafave, has begun to adopt some aspects of Wilson's approach. 'I've come to borrow some of the things I've watched Bob do,' he said. 'And I find now that I know if I'm relating to people who have trouble with language, not to push that aspect in our first meetings.' It does not seem impossible that as Wilson's work becomes better known, other therapists will do the same.

NOTES ADDED BY EDITORS

1 It has been pointed out to us that the words 'brain-damaged' and 'deaf-mute' may, today, no longer be appropriate to describe disability. Had the essay been written today, perhaps Simmer would have chosen the phrases 'mentally challenged' or 'physically disabled.' Interestingly, it was acting work like Andrews' and Knowles' and directing work like Wilson's that contributed to drawing attention to the socio-cultural dismissal of different (dis)abilities. Though the issue of whether or not Wilson was 'using' Andrews and Knowles was a point of contention at the time of production, Simmer argued for the perspective that such collaborative work emphasized the gift versus the 'damage' in physical and mental disability.

2 Wilson's performance group, founded in 1968, lived communally and operated out of Wilson's Spring Street loft. The group went by the name the Byrd Hoffman School of Byrds. At that point Wilson was calling himself Byrd Hoffman, after a dance instructor he had studied with in Waco, Texas. Byrd Hoffman, in her seventies, helped the teenage Wilson with his speech impediment. See Laurence Shyer, *Robert Wilson and His Collaborators*, New York: Theatre Communications Group, 1989.

3 Knowles published *Typing* (1974–7) in 1979 (New York: Vehicle Editions). In 1985 *The Knowles Drawings Book: Christopher Knowles, Drawings* was published as part of an exhibition organized by Wim Beeren and Elgrig de Groot (Rotterdam: Vitgeverij Bebert).

WORKS CITED

Deak, Frantisek (1974) 'Robert Wilson: *The Life and Times of Joseph Stalin'* (photo series). *TDR* 18, 2 (T62).

Trilling, Ossia (1973) 'Robert Wilson's *KA MOUNTAIN.'* *TDR* 17, 2 (T58).

18

VESSEL
The scenography of Meredith Monk

An interview by Brooks McNamara

T53, 1972

Meredith Monk's *Vessel* was performed in New York City several times during the month of October 1971. Each of the three sections of *Vessel* – Overture: Open House, Handmade Mountain, and Existent Lot – took place in a different environment in or near Greenwich Village. The performers included members of Monk's company, The House [founded in 1968], and about forty others, primarily student-participants. Music was composed by Monk for voice, electric organ, dulcimer, accordion, kazoo, Jew's harp, and mouth harp. The result was a piece that one critic termed 'a major work in an art form for which there is no proper name.'

Behind *Vessel*, which Monk labels an 'opera epic,' lies a very personal concept of performance. Since the 1966 production of *16 Millimeter Earrings*, all of Monk's pieces have been attempts to create what she calls 'composite theatre' or 'non-verbal opera,' a performance form in which voice, movement, costumes, lights, film, objects, and environments are blended together into an artistic whole, with all elements working together and none taking precedence over the others. [. . .] In *Vessel* as in *Needle-Brain Lloyd* [1970], Monk solves problems of time, space, and focus by developing techniques for live performance that are closer to the work of the filmmaker than to that of the theatre director.

Like most of Monk's pieces since 1967, *Vessel* was designed for what she calls 'specific sites' – existing architectural spaces or natural environments rather than conventional theatres and stages. The first of the 'specific sites' productions was *Blueprint*, presented in 1967, in which a moving frieze of human figures inside a building and on the roof was glimpsed through windows and a door by an audience seated outside. Later productions included *Tour: Dedicated to Dinosaurs*, which was performed in the halls and rotunda of the Natural History Museum of the Smithsonian Institution, and *Tour 2: Barbershop*, which used the three galleries of the Chicago Museum of Contemporary Art.

Sections of *Juice*, produced in 1969, took place on the ramps and in the galleries and stairwells of the Guggenheim Museum; at the Minor Lathom Playhouse; and at Monk's loft in the East Village. Like *Juice*, *Vessel* was spread over three separate architectural sites: Monk's own loft; the Performing Garage, a former truck garage in New York's SoHo section ordinarily used by Richard Schechner's Performance Group; and a vast parking lot surrounded by high brick walls a few doors down Wooster Street from the Garage.

At the end of the first section of *Vessel*, the audience boarded a bus for the Performing Garage where they saw Part Two. To see the final part of *Vessel*, which took place in the parking lot, spectators had to return to Wooster Street on another night. The idea of a mobile audience, first used in the two 'tour' pieces, and later in *Juice*, was explored again in *Vessel*; the trip from loft to Garage to parking lot paralleled in its literal movement through time and space the epic movement of Monk's opera. At each stop on the journey, the audience encountered the same or similar characters, objects, and events. But in each space they were reorganized and revealed in new ways. [. . .]

The interview that follows touches to some extent on all aspects of *Vessel*. But the concentration is on Monk as scenographer, dealing with problems of costume, properties, light, sound, and environment. Monk's scenography involves more than just radical use of theatre materials; it approaches theatre production without preconceptions about objects, or space, or light, and it suggests fundamental questions about the function of theatre architecture, design, and technology in contemporary performance.

McNamara: First let's talk about the loft on Great Jones Street, which you used for the first part of *Vessel*. Can you describe it for me?

Monk: It's about a hundred feet long and twenty-five feet wide. It has a very low ceiling, about nine feet high; it's a long narrow alley, with gray wood floors, white walls, white ceiling, two skylights, and windows at both ends. It suggests a tunnel, or a long narrow space in Renaissance perspective, with the floorboard going toward a vanishing point. One end, usually completely empty, is where I do movement; the other end has my living quarters – basically a living-room space.

McNamara: Why did you decide to use your own house for the first part of *Vessel*?

Monk: Since the nature of my work has a lot to do with unconscious imagery and fantasy, I'm very interested in grounding it in what I call 'reality space.' Constructing a realistic set doesn't interest me; what I'm interested in much more is using a reality situation and putting unusual images in that setting as counterpoint. The piece here in the loft is grounded in reality, but the images and the figures are strange. Because of that grounding in reality, the effect is surreal. When the performance moves later to the Performing Garage, it's almost totally in another world. Then when we move to the parking lot for the third section, the performance goes back to reality set against fantasy.

McNamara: What did you do to change this space from your house and workshop into a place to perform something?

Monk: Well, basically, I put the audience down in one end of the room, and I had them looking all the way down the loft into my living room.

McNamara: When I saw the first part of *Vessel*, people were concentrated at one end of the room and there was a space which, at least during the first part of the performance, wasn't used, a space maybe twenty feet deep that created a kind of gulf between the actors and the audience at the other end.

Monk: Yes. Like a moat. The irony of the situation is that this section of the performance, which could be the most personal since it's my own house, was actually the most remote. Instead of becoming the most intimate part of the piece, it was the least intimate because I'm putting a bracket around my living situation by making it so that you are actually looking into a real room, but from a great distance away. [. . .]

But what I was trying to do here, by lighting different areas at different times, was to see if I could continually transform the space and keep the audience from ever seeing what the whole space was like. When we got to the Garage, the attempt was just the opposite. There, the whole space was exposed, all at once. And all shifts of focus were done by the performers and their placement, but in the house, focus was shifted because we lit up a certain area of the room. That was a physiological shift of focus, whereas in the Garage the performers themselves shifted the focus of your eyes.

McNamara: To what extent did you change the living portion of your loft for the production?

Monk: I took one table out.

McNamara: What about lights?

Monk: The lights that I used in the performance were right there; they were the lights that I use in my living room. For example, in the living area there's a desk on one side with a 150-watt white bulb over it; there's a lamp on the other side of the room which has a 75-watt light bulb; and there's a 40-watt pink light bulb in a lamp on the shelf. We are dealing with this house, and there are no real stage effects or stage lights in it. It has a kind of primitive quality – people pulling light cords and turning on light switches. And in the Garage, even though we were using stage lights, I tried to keep that same kind of simplicity, because I can't stand tricks; I hate theatrical tricks. In a sense, there's no design, but only functions.

We also used a kerosene lantern which we moved around to light some scenes. The moving light idea is picked up later on, particularly in the third part. The structure of the third part is almost a combination of the two pieces that came before, because lights don't just light up and then go away as they do in the loft. In the loft one area will be lit, and the light is turned off; then another area will be lit, and the light is turned off. It's pointillistic, it's linear, in terms of time. In the parking lot, it's more an accumulation of light, and you actually do see the entire space more than you do in the house. But it's not like the Garage, where the space is lit overall. [. . .]

Each character – there are five of them sitting in the living room – is dressed in a very grotesque black costume. They're just sitting there; the image that we have, you know, is of people who have been in the loft for centuries, eons – as though they were in a castle waiting. And each person, one by one, leaves the room and goes into the kitchen and changes into a costume that has a much more specific character, a king, or a wizard – but they're very personal, very specific. And they come out and stand under a 200-watt bulb. They pull on the light cord, it's an overhead light, and they perform a scene. It's a small indication of what they're going to do in the Garage, a kind of introduction. Then they turn the light off and go back into the kitchen, change into their black clothes, and sit down again in the living room.

The house section was very much a black and white tapestry – not quite black and white because there was a bit of color, but it had a dull tone, almost the idea of black and white film. Then, when you get to the Garage, it's Technicolor. For example, the madwoman who comes out and starts laughing in the loft had a greenish-grayish wig on, but then when she's in the Garage, she's got a bright red wig. The same image, except that it's color. And that's the way all of the images are.

McNamara: A number of properties were handled or brought on in the loft – a rake, I remember, at one point. How did you choose the properties? Were they things you liked? Were they simply available things? Or was there an artistic reason for your choices?

Monk: Well, actually I used objects in this piece which interested me a lot, and I used them like notes in a musical score. There's a repetition of certain objects that later serve different functions in different parts of *Vessel*. There's a woman with a rake in the loft; then when you go into the Garage the king's scepter is a rake, and when you go into the parking lot, the soldiers' weapons are rakes. It's like using the rake almost as you would use a note in a piece of music. Or it's like using it as an overlay, a transparency that gradually discloses levels of the object itself.

McNamara: In a sense, then, you do the same thing with properties that you did with the space; you're using found objects in a found space.

Monk: In the first section of the loft, objects are not of primary importance because I'm simply using objects already in my house. But later in the Garage there are many more things, more objects because the space is more abstract. For example, in the Garage, the madwoman, Lanny Harrison, has a kettle she puts herbs into. There is the cutting up of the vegetables; Monica Mosley doing calligraphy on a board; Danny Sverdlik mixing the blue mixture; Mark Monstermaker reading a book. Those are objects and activities. And all of them are almost like everyday activities, but there is a twist to them, a kind of irony.

McNamara: Would you talk about the costumes?

Monk: I'm not really interested in made costumes, or in constructing cos-tumes. I'm really going against a kind of abstract tendency; I may come back to a certain kind of abstraction, but right now costumes to me always just look like costumes. When we were working on the Garage piece, for example, a costume designer made one of the costumes. She really put a lot of effort into it, but it absolutely did not work, because it looked like a costume. And what was nice about the other people's costumes was that they looked like clothing – even though you wouldn't see those people walking down the street. That's absolute fantasy.

McNamara: Once again, the fantasy seems to come through the strange juxta-position of real things.

Monk: I always want to have a grounding in reality; I always need to have something that grounds because some images I use are so far away from reality, and I am trying to deal with simultaneous realities. So I try to make as much contrast as possible.

McNamara: At the end of the first section, what happens?

Monk: The cast rented a bus and we get into the bus and go down to the

Performing Garage, and the audience stays and has wine. Instead of keeping their distance, the audience can enter my house. Then the bus comes back for them and they go down to the Performing Garage. The bus is painted blue and has red and yellow stripes. Inside it has rugs all the way through, seats along the side, a few seats in the back of the bus, and a lot of space to sit on the floor. It's very warm and cozy. I was happy about it.

McNamara: What were you trying to do with the bus in terms of the whole performance?

Monk: I called *Vessel* an epic because of the sense of journeying in the whole piece. Not only did I want the content of *Vessel* to be a journey, but the point of having the audience move from one place to another in one evening is that the audience is also on an epic, you know, they are literally going through the motions of traveling.

McNamara: So that each of the three spaces you use is a station on the journey, with its own specific character, and the bus is the connecting link.

Monk: Yes. We had actually thought of having performers on the streets along the way from one place to the next so that you would see them from the bus. But I realized that just looking at New York City out of the windows of a bus after having been through one theatrical experience and going to another is enough in a way. I was very determined to do this piece in New York City. That was very important to me, somehow. And I feel that the section in my house in some ways is the most like New York City. Because you're so aware of the traffic that's going by, and the sirens. It's like a little world filled with people in black sitting in a room; it's a little world absolutely closed off, but everything around it is just going on and on, and on. Every time a sound cuts into the silence, it cuts it like a knife.

McNamara: How do you use sound in the first part at the loft?

Monk: Well, I am dealing with silence as a base and then working mostly in terms of contrasts – sometimes silence and then cutting to a very sharp sound; sometimes silence and then gradations of sound like somebody lighting a cigarette. In other words, you become more and more aware, but sometimes you become more aware by gradations or increments of sound, and sometimes the sound is just cut into very sharply. *Vessel* is structured like a piece of music; you *hear* how the piece is structured as much as you see it. That's the way I'm working now; not only am I working with music in terms of my own music, but in terms of everything I do in performance. There's lots of repetition of sound motifs like the three knockings, and the bell ringing. And all of the singing that I do with the organ has the same kind of texture even though there are different emotions and very different kinds of sound in it. But it all has the same texture, so it's like a repetition. And because of the stillness in the house all the incidental sounds become magnified. [. . .] If I don't teach people to hear in this piece, then I feel that I've failed, because I believe that hearing – the absolute expansion of auditory perception – is what the piece is about.

McNamara: When you get to the Garage you discover that the environment left over from the Performance Group's *Commune* has been changed substantially. The old environment was basically a series of towers made out of wood which surrounded the room. What did you do with it and why?

Monk: We connected the scaffolding and made an overall Gestalt, a mountain of sorts, by hanging and draping white muslin. It's a mountain but it also looks like a clipper ship, a birthday cake. And it's very primitive. The second section of the piece is called Handmade Mountain, and we wanted very much that quality for the whole Garage, that's why we did it ourselves. I much prefer to show what I am doing. No one *designed* that mountain. We did it ourselves. In my group are weavers, and calligraphers, and people who dye fabrics – that is our group's sensibility.

McNamara: Could you go on a little bit more about the idea of showing what you do?

Monk: I really like a certain kind of theatricality; I don't want to have people in blue jeans. In some ways, we're not showing everything we do; we're not doing a thing where we're stripping down to our jeans and work shirts. That's a different way of stripping down. I think our costumes were the kind of theatricality that I'm talking about. There's a kind of wryness to them. There's a kind of wryness to the whole Garage piece. It's not childish, it's child-like, and I think that's what we're trying for, not to lose those things.

   [. . .] The reason I chose the Performing Garage in the first place was that I had had an idea for a long time of doing a living tapestry piece, related to a medieval two-dimensional kind of visual perception. Even though the section in the loft is a depth perception, incidentally, it also has a lot to do with two dimensions. It's not sculptured. [. . .] *Vessel* is dealing with a filmic kind of visual idea: in the house, the audience is looking down a long tunnel; in the Performing Garage it is all straight up and down, vertical; and the parking lot used in the third part is all flat. In the first section you're looking down a corridor at an event beyond a wall, beyond a moat; in the Performing Garage, things happen up and down; and in the third part, in the parking lot, you're looking from right to left. It's like a map, or like a Cinemascope screen, or a scene photographed with a wide-angle lens.

McNamara: What were you trying to do with light at the Garage?

Monk: Stage lights were available and it seemed that I should use them. But it is the most simple and direct use of them, and it is obvious that that's what it is. There's no attempt to create illusionistic lighting. Strangely, even though all the lights I used in the loft were ordinary household lamps, I would say the effect there was more illusionistic than at the Garage. In the loft, because of the darkness, the audience never sees the reality of the space, so it's as though I'm creating an illusion in a way.

McNamara: Why not just use work lights in the Garage?

Monk: I don't like that kind of 'scientific' look. I just wanted whiteness. The room is covered with white muslin so the whole sense of the space is white. Pieces of muslin are draped from tower to tower, and hang straight down like flaps to cover parts of it. Sometimes the scaffolding shows through – there are little rooms or cabinets between the pieces of muslin. The whole feeling is angular; it's as though the structure comes to a point on the top. [. . .]

   I think it has to be clear how the figures work against each other. Each of the people has a cubicle. There's one person, Ping Chong, who's the traveler, who takes a path from one side of the scaffolding all the way through the mountain, around to the other side of the scaffolding, and then around the back of the audience. You don't see him for a while, and then he starts coming around again. We call that 'rounds.' So you get the feeling in the Garage of a kind of cyclical time situation, whereas in the house you get the feeling of time stopping, being absolutely suspended. There are a number of people on the mountain, spread out all over it, and they do different activities at the same time. It's orchestrated in such a way that perhaps two people will be doing the same activity in unison, and the others will be doing other activities; then everybody will be doing the same activity. So that when you're in the audience, your eye keeps shifting.

During the first 'round,' for example, each character has five activities that he can choose from; and in the second 'round' three more are added. I don't set it; I don't tell a certain person to wave at a certain point, for instance. So what you get are combinations like a slot machine. You'll have three people doing the same thing at the same time, and all of a sudden your eye starts lining things up. At other times you shift your focus, depending on which person draws your attention. It is similar with sound. Each of the performer's activities involves some kind of sound and your attention is drawn by it. So the madwoman is throwing herbs into a bowl, but she really has marbles in her hand, and you hear them clink.

McNamara: Could you describe what happens when you go out of the Garage at the end of the second part?

Monk: You walk half a block away to a parking lot. The way we use the parking lot, it is a wide and not a deep space. It is probably a block wide and a third of a block deep. The audience sits on bleachers at one end. On one side, across the street, is the Canal Lumber Company and on the other side, across another street, is a church, St. Alphonsus, and you can see the tops of both buildings over the brick walls that enclose the parking lot. Straight ahead of the audience is a candy factory, an old building with a faded sign on it and a few straggly trees at its base. The ground is all asphalt, and there are eight trucks lined up facing the audience.

McNamara: Out of all the possibilities that existed for you, why did you choose the parking lot for the third part?

Monk: I was trying to find an outdoor space that had a specific New York ambience. We had done a pastoral piece, in Connecticut, involving some of the same material and large groups of people – a pastoral piece, on lawns, with trees and horses and a Victorian house and everything. But I didn't want to work with a park in New York. It didn't make any sense to me. I'm not dealing with politics except in a very subtle sense. But one level of *Vessel* has to do with people opening up their eyes to New York. The park just doesn't have anything to do with the New York ambience, at least on our level. Our economic level, our lifestyle, has most to do with complex interior spaces. This particular parking lot was the best of the large spaces I had seen. I knew I was going to be using many people and I wanted a pageant-like quality to the third part.

McNamara: Can you explain how you use light in the third part?

Monk: I was trying to use every kind of light source that I could think of that was portable. So, there are five camp-fires, there's a lamp, there are two sun guns, which are power packed – in other words, these are power belts to which lighting instruments are attached so that people can carry them and run around with them. They are usually used for filming movies at night. There is a welder, and a red traffic flare. There is a kerosene torch, and lights from across the street in the church. And there are the lights from the micro-bus and the motorcycles that are driven through the parking lot. [. . .]

McNamara: What about the lights from the church across the street? I became aware after a while that the porch of the church was lit up, and that there were characters doing things there. What was the function of this?

Monk: It's like expanding the environment until you're aware of more and more in that parking lot. When you think you've got to the limits of the parking lot, the two brick walls, your eye moves across the street, expanding even more.

I'm working like a filmmaker. I don't know why. That seems to be the way I think; the flash forward section of the first part is an example. I'm doing live movies. Or that's what I think they are. And there are many more ambiences I would like to explore this way – like a mountainscape, or a desertscape, or water, a lake. I'm really interested in dealing with those things as theatrical materials. I'm just not dealing with theatres anymore.

19

FOREMAN'S *PAIN(T)* AND *VERTICAL MOBILITY*

Kate Davy

T62, 1974

> All of my art is concerned with the problem of consciousness, the structure of
> consciousness, and specifically, with the problem of making art.
>
> Richard Foreman

In order to deal with an artist's rehearsal techniques, it is necessary to discuss a
particular system or process; in Richard Foreman's work process is important.
Foreman has been producing his plays for five years and, although there have been
changes, his aesthetic and style have remained distinctively constant; partially
because he is concerned with the problem and process of making art. He wants the
spectator to notice not only the 'art that is made' but also that 'art is being made.'
'The realm of art is trying to be clear about its materials which in turn, as you
watch it, helps you to be clear about your own watching.' Hence, Foreman's art is
basically self-referential in that it treats as subject the process of art. This involvement with process can be seen in the making of his two recent works *PAIN(T)* and
Vertical Mobility: Sophia = (Wisdom) Part 4. The plays were performed in repertory [after a three-month rehearsal period] during April and May 1974. Because
there is no collaboration in this work – every aspect of Foreman's art is done for
himself and by himself – his creative process includes writing the text, designing
and building the setting and props, recording the tape score, directing the
rehearsals, and conducting the performances. [. . .] Because Foreman is not concerned with a virtuosity of acting, he prefers to work with non-actors and uses
anyone who wants to participate in his productions.

At first there seemed to be nothing extraordinary about Foreman's rehearsal
procedures; he passed out scripts to the performers, assigned the speaking roles,
and began what appeared to be traditional 'blocking' rehearsals. The rehearsal
time for *PAIN(T)* and *Vertical Mobility* was entirely devoted to placing the performers on stage, because for Foreman 'placement is nine-tenths of the staging.'
However, his staging approach and the process involved in his 'placement' are quite
different than that of traditional theatre, as well as that of other experimental
theatre groups.

The approach is different partially because, in addition to staging the script,
Foreman stages the process of writing. 'I'm basically interested in staging what's
going on in my head while I'm writing the play.' Although he is most often
described as primarily a visual artist, he personally feels that his scripts are

complete and self-sufficient. The words of the text do not function as mere background for the visual placement of the performers but are an integral part of his staging of how the mind operates when writing a play.

When he writes, Foreman thinks about the 'kind of room' and the 'feel of the space' that the play exists in. He sees the props and other things in the room and the 'activities of the body.' He does not think of the characters' personalities or faces because 'I really think they are all me.' The characters are shades, 'like De-Chirico figures with the faces wiped out,' that come and go in his consciousness. In one line, a character may be a 'real flesh-and-blood Rhoda, who is someone I know, saying a real thing to me' and in the next line 'Rhoda may become an echo, sort of a melody in my mind, of a certain aspect of the woman.' Often, a line spoken by a character is actually Foreman's reaction to the line he has just written.

> *Voice:* Oh, it says what happened to Max's red feet.
> *Rhoda:* Why am I thinking about it now?

Foreman's texts are very personal and self-referential, because they are a documentary of his consciousness in the act of writing.

THE SPACE, SETTING, AND PROPS

> Theatre is about the text and the performer relating to the given architectural space. That's where the key to my performances is.
>
> *Richard Foreman*

Vertical Mobility and *PAIN(T)* were rehearsed and presented in the same large, rectangular loft. The space was divided across its width. An audience seating section (bleachers) was placed behind and between two poles at one end of the space, with the stage area directly in front of it. The spectators viewed the stage in a traditional picture-frame arrangement, with the two poles providing a proscenium. These two poles were architectural features of the actual place – the loft. When building the setting, Foreman takes the play's space and superimposes it on the architecture of the given, actual place. He builds the play's décor so that the actual places shows through. Hence, both places are evident simultaneously and overlap each other. His intention is to clarify the space so that when a performer is placed in a specific position, the spectator can see exactly where that body is in spatial relation to both the setting and the theatre/loft. 'Rehearsal is all a matter of placement in context. The crucial thing is making each moment completely clear.'

[. . .] When rehearsals began, the *Vertical Mobility* setting had already been designed and built, while the *PAIN(T)* setting, except for a few moveable set pieces, had not been designed. Foreman soon decided that *PAIN(T)* needed a setting of its own; it was based on the *Vertical Mobility* setting and took shape during the rehearsal period. [. . .]

During the rehearsal period many set pieces and props were invented and added to the basic design. Foreman is not a skilled carpenter, and yet he built most of the setting and props himself. 'I want everything to look as if I myself made it.' Whether or not an object appears slick and professionally built does not concern him, because he is involved with the process of building. When he makes a bed or a wall, he wants the spectator to notice how they were put together and just what decisions were made in the building process.

In all of his technical work, Foreman aims for *bricolage*. The term *bricoleur* is used by Lévi-Strauss to define a kind of handyman who invents in the face of specific circumstances, using whatever means and materials are available. Before and during the rehearsal period, Foreman devised several uses for a large quantity of white sheet material. It was used to make the curtains that comprised the basic setting, and it covered the long narrow table, pyramids, and other objects throughout both plays. Rhoda wore it as a headdress that trailed on the floor. It was used to make long, draping flags, and to cover performers lying on the floor. In *Vertical Mobility*, a ghost costume, a toga, a nightgown, and nightcap were made from it. A stage direction at the end of *PAIN(T)* read, 'Enter people under white sheets.' [. . .]

THE PLACEMENT PROCESS

> While the texts are carefully written, the rehearsal process is a trying of every conceivable alternative to make the text say what I think it secretly wants to say.
>
> *Richard Foreman*

Perhaps the most distinguishing feature of rehearsals was the meticulous attention to, and accumulation of, detail. Foreman controlled every aspect of the work. The performers neither improvised nor initiated activity. The director did not explain to them 'why' it was necessary to carry out an activity in one way rather than another – they seldom asked questions and rarely suggested solutions. He expected of the performers only that they write down all their actions, positions, and memorize them; and carry them out as precisely as possible. Often what seemed to be an instruction to a performer – 'Register how the word relates to the action (pause)' – was actually Foreman in the process of thinking out loud or talking to himself. His staging process is closer to that of an artist working in private – painting, writing, or sculpting – than that of a theatre director.

The rehearsals are rather austere and can be very tedious for the performer, because Foreman's placement process involves rigorous attention to the most minute details of staging. He works until every moment is completely clear in the course of the piece. Basically, placement involves the careful blending of three fundamental elements: (1) content – the implications of actions and positions in relation to dialog and the functioning of the consciousness in the process of making art; (2) space – the actual place the piece is performed in and the designed space of the play; (3) performers – the physical relation of the performers to all the visual elements combined. [. . .]

For the most part, Foreman's instructions to the performers were simple and direct. Often he would demonstrate how a certain position should look or how an action should be done. He instructed them to deliver the lines flatly and in a normal speaking voice. No attempt was made to project or interpret the lines. Occasionally, in order to inject a moment of color, he gave a performer a specific way to deliver a line, telling them to do it like 'a schoolteacher scolding a child' or 'in a sing-song manner.'

Foreman's placement procedure resembles that of a painter: 'I tend to think in a very frontal, picture-plane way.' Many of his visual arrangements are composed of pictures and tableaux that emphasize the two-dimensional picture plane. When he staged the first dance sequence in *Vertical Mobility*, he arranged four performers standing next to each other, a few feet apart, in the same plane across the stage facing the audience. A second row of four performers was positioned in the same manner a few feet behind the first row. Foreman paced out the dance for the performers and described it as 'a sort of Groucho Marx flapping of the arms, etc. . . .'

[. . .] The dance was accompanied by music. Before he staged the dance, Foreman recorded a banjo instrumental on one channel (track) of the tape. He distorted this sound by recording the music at a slower than normal speed and by adding a sound 'overlay'; he recorded an additional sound on a second channel of the tape. Foreman placed the microphone close to his mouth and repeated a brief whistle on the dominant beat of the banjo music. Thus, the four dominant beats that the performers danced to were accentuated by added sound. [. . .]

Foreman described the dancers as 'large hostile birds' and told them to 'glare at the audience in a hostile manner' throughout the dance, 'essentially asking the spectators what they are doing about this piece of art they are watching.' The performer forces the spectator to notice where he is by implying with his stare 'I am here, where are you?' 'Having to notice where one is is very exhilarating.' This technique is related to the Brechtian alienation effect and is employed to distance the viewer from the performance. Foreman wants the spectator to savor the work from afar rather than become involved with it as he is involved with events in life.

In addition to static pictures and movement across and through the space, placement may involve the slight, subtle movements of a performer. In another scene from *Vertical Mobility*, Kate Manheim (Rhoda) performed a sequence of words and positions sitting in a chair that directly faced the audience. Foreman worked with her for several hours so that her feet, legs, torso, arms, hands, and head were placed in the essential and most precise positions in relation to the words she delivered. Equally important was the direction in which her eyes were focused with each position. Each shift in position was slight but very exact. For example, Manheim said, 'Weight,' 'Ramp,' 'Airplane,' 'Caught,' 'Ice,' 'Tilt,' 'Cave,' 'Avenue,' with pause between each word. Foreman altered the position of her body in relation to each word – feet to one side, one foot on the chair, head tilted, eyes looking down, legs spread, one hand on opposite thigh, mouth open. At one point he told her to move her lips silently and then said to himself, 'This is much better, much more neurotic.' Foreman explained to her that the timing had to be exact and the positions precise because 'there is a big difference in the slightest shift in position.' [. . .]

Another distinctive feature of the rehearsal process was the continuous addition of 'framing devices.' A framing device is anything that punctuates, frames, emphasizes, or brings into the foreground a particular word, object, action, or position. For example, in *Vertical Mobility* a crew person attached a string to one wall, about three feet from the floor, drew it horizontally across the stage, parallel to the floor, and attached it to the opposite wall. Max, one of the principal characters, was lying on the floor, and he raised his leg so that his toe touched the string. At a rehearsal, Foreman added a 'frame' to the foot by instructing a crew person to attach a rectangular piece of white material to the string directly behind the foot – framing the foot.

Sometimes framing devices were added to [other] framing devices and used simultaneously. A picture and a frame were built into the rear wall of the *Vertical Mobility* setting. At one point in the play the picture popped out of the frame leaving the frame and a square-shaped opening. Later, Sophia stood behind the wall, looking through the opening so that her face was framed. During a rehearsal, Foreman added the beam of a flashlight so that her face was also framed by a small circle of light.

Two flashlights mounted on a board, controlled from above and behind the spectators, were used to spotlight individual faces and objects throughout both performances. In rehearsal, Foreman experimented with aiming the flashlight beams while deciding which elements he wanted to emphasize. For example, in *PAIN(T)*, a performer was lying on the floor in the rear of the space with a lighted chandelier on the floor next to him. The lights were dim; there was activity occurring downstage. After several rehearsals, Foreman added a small beam of light around the face of the performer lying in the rear. This device helped to emphasize the depth of the space and at the same time bring the face 'closer.'

A built-in framing device shared by both plays was a small mirror hanging close to the ceiling, facing the audience, and angled towards the floor. Spectators could watch the activity occurring on the floor in the reflection of the mirror. However, because of the size, the mirror reflected and framed only fragments of the total action.

Foreman experimented with many framing devices, but his primary vehicle for framing lines and activity was the tape-recorded words, music, and noises that accompanied every rehearsal and performance. Although a few noises were specified in the text, most were added during rehearsals; they included foghorns, thuds, pings, boings, glass shattering, drum rolls, bells, whistles, and screams. For example, Foreman added these sounds to the dialog in *Vertical Mobility*:

Rhoda: (Pause.) He cannot speak openly, huh. (Pause.) Oh, Max, I do not recognize –
Max: What?
Rhoda: the room. *A 'ping' added against the word 'room.'*
Max: Look. (Pause.) It became very beautiful. Oh, Rhoda. *A 'thud' added against the word 'beautiful.'*
All: Shhhhhh.
Max: (Pause.) We are now in Paradise. *A 'thud' added again to the word 'paradise.'*
Rhoda: I know it.
Max: (Pause.) Is it beautiful enough?
Rhoda: No. *A loud 'No!' added immediately after Rhoda's 'No.'*

Often noises were added to provide cues for the performers. At one rehearsal, Foreman told them 'For the change (in position) I'll put in a boing.' Until he got around to recording the sound, he shouted 'cue!' Eventually, his shouting became part of the piece, and the 'boing' was never added. Several times during the performance, Foreman shouted 'cue' from his booth behind the bleachers.

For the most part, the tape-recorded words and speeches in both plays were not written in the text but were improvised and added during the rehearsal period to clarify sections that Foreman felt needed explanation. Most of the voices were his. For example, after a few weeks of rehearsal, Foreman added a tape of his voice to the beginning of each play: 'This play is about making art (pause) from a certain energy (pause) which most people use (pause) most of the time' (*PAIN(T)*), and, 'The play focuses on Max who has given up writing . . .' (*Vertical Mobility*). At several points in *Vertical Mobility*, Foreman added, 'The important word is . . . showing.' The 'important word' would change with each repetition depending on which word Foreman wanted to bring to the foreground.

The tape allowed Foreman to interrupt the performance and address the spectator directly. 'It's like sitting there next to somebody and saying, "Look, don't you see this?" And "Are you overlooking that?" ' He continued to add to the tape recording throughout the rehearsal period, and, because he wanted the spectator to understand what the plays were about, many of the tapes took on an 'explaining' function. [. . .]

While *Vertical Mobility* evolved gradually and without major changes in the setting and text, *PAIN(T)* sustained radical changes during the rehearsal period. Foreman tried a different approach to staging each scene almost every night. By the end of the fourth week of rehearsals, he was at a peak of vacillation with the piece. When he came to rehearsal he told the performers that he was going to try some experiments with the fifth scene. The scene involved Rhoda and Eleanor positioned on the bed. The stage direction read: 'Now both on a high, rolling table, each head at a different side, legs together and overlapping.' The bed was placed center and parallel to the audience, a few feet from the front row, making the space very shallow and crowded. First, Rhoda and Eleanor were to say the lines through long, narrow, cardboard tubes. Foreman watched this for a few minutes, said, 'This is no good,' and eliminated the tubes. He added music and instructed the performers to look at each other when saying the lines. Next, he discarded the music and told them to look upstage and deliver the lines. Finally, when nothing appeared to be working out, he said, 'There is something about these positions that doesn't make sense with these lines.' He changed it all again, deleting many of the lines from the text. At the next rehearsal he said, 'I've been doing my homework and have finally figured out how to deal with the second part of this play.' He added the lines that were deleted at the previous rehearsal, changed the position of the bed, and worked on the scene again. It wasn't until the seventh week of rehearsals that *PAIN(T)* began to take shape and appear as it would in its final form.

Because the setting was not complete when rehearsals began, the placement process was affected by the adding and subtracting of both large set pieces and props. After a few rehearsals, Foreman added a tent structure, shaped like a tower and made from the same white material mentioned earlier. It was hung from the ceiling and extended to the floor with an opening so that a performer could stand inside of it. He tried different ways of using the tent, but eventually it was eliminated and did not appear in the final production. Since it was always true that performers were placed in strict relation to set pieces and props, the placement of performers was restaged if an object was added or discarded.

Individual performers also had an effect on the placement process. For example, the performer playing Ida in *PAIN(T)* was replaced by a different performer midway through the rehearsals. Positions were changed somewhat because of the visual difference between the two people. This was true partially because, with the exception of a few deliberately constructed costumes, the performers wore the same clothes in performance that they wore every night to rehearsals. Hence, the colors a performer usually wore affected the way Foreman placed him in the space.

In rehearsal, Foreman works solely to please himself rather than a prospective audience. 'Most theatre is built on people trying very consciously to manipulate the audience's response. I'm certainly not trying to do that. Really, I'm just trying to make an object that I'll end up loving.' Along with the work of many other artists, his pieces have been labeled 'experimental theatre.' An experiment is defined as a 'test, trial, or tentative procedure' carried out in order 'to discover or prove something.' The experimenting in Foreman's work occurs only in rehearsal. Consequently, when the rehearsal period is over, the testing is over, and his plays are exactly as he wants them to be.

20

PEARLS FOR PIGS
Program notes

Richard Foreman

T158, 1998

Editors' note: The following are the program notes for *Pearls for Pigs*, written, directed, and designed by Richard Foreman. It premiered at the Hartford Stage in Hartford, Connecticut, on 4 April 1997 and was presented at the Tribeca Performing Arts Center in New York City from 1 December 1997 to 4 January 1998.

OK, I could be wrong (just like everybody else), but it might be useful to let you know my current thoughts on what happens in my plays, and specifically, *Pearls for Pigs*. It's true, there is no 'story' in the normal sense. But there is definitely a SITUATION. The situation in *Pearls for Pigs* is that the leading character, the Maestro, after a long career, realizes he hates the theatre. And what he hates it for is the way in which it suppresses the possibility that impulse – human impulse – might be allowed to disrupt the performance. I realize this echoes established themes of Pirandello and/or Artaud – but I don't claim to be thematically unique – indeed my aesthetic is solidly in the mainstream of much twentieth-century poetry, painting, etc. There is no story in my plays, because IMPULSE is set free to deflect normal linear development. Linear, narrative development in the theatre always ends with a denouement, which delivers a 'meaning' – i.e., moral. Perform in such-and-such a way, and such-and-such are the results. This kind of narrative, this kind of logically arrived at 'moral' conclusion, is in fact a way of reinforcing the spectators' behavioral conditioning – conditioning provided by the world which exists 'as we have been conditioned to perceive it' by physical reality, society, inherited psychological patterns, etc. Such a world disciplines, orders, and imprisons a wide and potentially fruitful range of human impulses towards diversity and invention. My theatre is a theatre of SITUATION and IMPULSE. To the extent that impulse is policed and suppressed (by society or by the super-ego), we suffocate. Ah, do I propose that a good society (or a good way to live one's personal life) is to let impulse run free? No, I do not. But I do propose that the more desirable human condition is that where one is able to avoid stasis – spiritual and emotional stasis – by continually subjecting oneself to the nonstatic 'unbalanced' state where impulse is continually permitted to introduce a creative 'wobble' to the straight and narrow of 'well-disciplined' mental life. IMPULSE, of course, need not just mean hitting someone on the nose – it may also mean reaching for an unsettling idea, or letting words surface from the unconscious. The point is – ART IS THE PLACE TO ALLOW THIS, WHICH CANNOT REALLY HAPPEN IN LIFE, TO HAPPEN IN ITS FULL, RICH, RADIANT, ABUNDANT GLORY. In *Pearls for Pigs*, we can mentally dance with Maestro as he follows the impulse to turn his doctor into the underwater explorer that haunts his dreams. We can ride inside his emotional rollercoaster as impulse turns his nose into an object that shines in the spiritual dark even as it makes him feel ridiculous. But – HERE'S THE IMPORTANT PART – these manifestations of impulse are not just narrated – THE SAME IMPULSE THAT PUSHES THE CHARACTER INTO 'ACTING-OUT' ALSO TWISTS AND CONTROLS THE ARTISTIC STRUCTURE, so that the form and sequencing of the play itself reflects that impulsive, usually suppressed, energy of the human mental/emotional apparatus.

Fig. 20.1 Rehearsing *Pearls for Pigs*. (Photo by Paula Court.)

And it's that isomorphic relationship between form and content that often perplexes people about contemporary art. Why not – for easier comprehensibility – show characters acting impulsively with a normal narrative structure? But, of course, that happens all the time in drama and film and the novel. But there now exists a large group of so-called 'difficult' or transgressive artists who believe that such a strategy no longer suffices to introduce a powerful and effective 'impulse' therapy to audiences desperately trying to control their own impulsive tendencies – for fear they will interfere with their ability to lead efficient lives in the industrialized world's highly organized and demanding society. So art work that presents impulsive behavior within a normal narrative allows the spectator to 'maintain control' as it were – godlike in his/her ability to set the 'other' of disruptive impulse within the safe prison of 'moral-delivering "meaningful" narrative.' But narrative and meaning themselves churned up and fragmented by impulse – this hopefully provides the spectator with a 'disorientation massage' that perhaps brings him/her back into contact with a deep part of our mutual human self. One might object: But what you propose sounds like a recipe for 'anything goes,' so why are we to believe the results may as well be nonsense rather than the therapeutic aesthetic you describe? Ah, well, history I suppose will decide. (Does it always tell the truth?) It is as difficult, finally, to justify one's art to someone who has no taste for it, as it is to justify one's choice of a beloved to those who 'can't see what he sees in such an uninteresting person!' I can only assure you that 'anything goes' is as far from our procedures as one can imagine. Ten weeks of maddeningly slow and deliberate rehearsals changing and changing everything dozens of times until each 'irrational' cell seems to me to have a 'coherence' within the overall structure that is firmly in place as a successful string quartet. Believe it or not, lucidity is my overriding concern – lucidity in the framing and ordering of each 'impulsive' and disruptive moment of dialogue and action until – for me at least – this so-called 'impenetrable' piece of theatre sparkles like a diamond.

21

AIDS AND AVANT-GARDE CLASSICISM
Reza Abdoh's *Quotations from a Ruined City*

John Bell

T148, 1995

> I carry the ruined city under my skin.

Abdoh and Abdoh 1995: 1

> I admire your optimism. My pessimism is only a form of optimism. I would like things to happen differently from the way they do and I find myself weeping over ruins. Then I think that the ruins have great and surprising beauty and stimulate men in some unexpected direction within art. Cities in solid gold must sleep beneath the sands.

Cocteau 1972: 410

Reza Abdoh's work appears on the grid of late twentieth-century American theatre as both consummation and regeneration of the avant-garde tradition that has characterized innovative Western theatre since French symbolism's rejection of realism 100 years ago. Abdoh's work, and in particular his 1994 production *Quotations from a Ruined City*, fits into the continuum of American experimental theatre that, since the end of World War II, has led from the opening wedge of new theatre practices created by the Living Theatre, John Cage, and Merce Cunningham in the 1950s; through the Judson Church performances of Yvonne Rainer and others, 1960s happenings, and the politicized experimental theatre of the Vietnam era; to the high postmodernism of Robert Wilson, Richard Foreman, and the Wooster Group. Abdoh's productions, working in the same vein of image–text–sound performance that, since the days of Lugné-Pöe's Théâtre d'Art has stood as the constant antithesis to Western stage realism, have appeared in New York, Los Angeles, and in Europe as a culmination of modernist and postmodernist theatres' fragmented, multimedia collage technique, but also, in decided contrast to the content of postmodern performance, as a significant step outside (or beyond) the disconnected neutrality postmodernist theatre cultivated as its ideological means of survival.[1]

Abdoh approached his subject matter – the workings of American culture and American life in the post-cold war age of AIDS – as an outsider: a queer, HIV+, émigré artist of color, born in Iran and educated in London and Los Angeles, who was, as he described it, 'an addict for American culture':

> I'm obsessive about it, and it makes me angry. [. . .] I'm just amazed at the thickness of this culture. It's just so latent with thoughts and ideas that either are related or unrelated, but are nevertheless very rich. I find it very powerful culture, and I like to critique it and, in a sense, see where it's heading and where it can head.
>
> (Abdoh 1994a)

Abdoh's last works, including *Quotations from a Ruined City*, were not universally acclaimed, even by audiences predisposed to avant-garde performance's traditional tactics of abstraction and nonlinearity. Responses to his shows typically ranged from devoted adulation to almost complete rejection. In the latter category, one Los Angeles-area critic called Abdoh's AIDS-centered *Bogeyman* (1991) 'a tedious, repetitive series of noisy temper tantrums' in which 'few cliché turns of performance art are left unstoned'; while another termed the show 'as banal as anything produced by the commercial mainstream,' and called Abdoh 'the Andrew Lloyd Webber of the counterculture set.'[2] In New York, a critic reviewing *Quotations from a Ruined City* for the *New York Native* noted Abdoh's 'undeniable talent,' but termed it 'much too self-conscious of its avant-garde roots' (Cole 1994: 33). The *New York Times* reviewer said *Quotations* was 'a weary checklist of atrocities, couched in a fragmented treatise on enduring inhumanity,' a production that 'gives the impression of stoned channel-surfing through television on a particularly grisly news day' (Brantley 1994: C20). The opposite (and equally fervid) response was represented by the *Village Voice* critic James Leverett who, writing at the time of the *Voice*'s Obie awards, called Abdoh 'one of a scant handful of artists working in the theatre anywhere today who can create pieces big enough, passionate enough, complex, profound, and original enough to qualify as significant responses to what we feebly call contemporary reality' (1994: 100).[3] If Abdoh did not receive an Obie in 1994, Leverett added, it would prove how 'the sclerosis' of New York theatre 'has become total mummification' (*ibid.*). Abdoh did not receive the award.

Reza Abdoh's assaultive combination of nonstop live action, startlingly rich yet enigmatic text, very loud music, and surprising bursts of disconnected film and video images appeared to some audience members like the obscure rantings of an avant-garde muse gone over the edge into baroque indulgence. While Abdoh's penchant for 'great visual eloquence' was generally praised by admirers and detractors alike, critical opinion fell on either side of the question of what it all means: whether Abdoh was creating coherent theatre, or, as Ondrej Hrab, the director of Prague's Archa Theatre said to me upon seeing Abdoh's *Tight Right White* (1993), simply 'vomiting ideas.' Abdoh's presentation of image and sound certainly had the explosive, excretive quality of Hrab's metaphor. The question about whether Abdoh was a 'theatrical genius or just another crank peddling a vision' (Cole 1994) is answerable when one considers the meaning of the symbolic fragments forming what Robert Sember calls an 'unstoppable river of information,' Abdoh's 'catastrophe that takes an hour and a half' (Sember 1994). Experiencing *Quotations from a Ruined City*, as Sember sees it, is like being caught in a controlled explosion of information made that much more powerful by its tight compression of symbols and its ability to work on several different levels simultaneously. The images in Abdoh's theatricality register in the psyche on a subliminal level to connect with each other and with the bank of images anyone exposed to United States-based mass culture carries with them, willingly or unwillingly. [. . .]

QUOTATIONS FROM A RUINED CITY

Abdoh's *Quotations from a Ruined City* is a 90-minute multimedia spectacle performed by twelve members of his Dar A Luz ensemble. Centering action on a raised downstage platform bordered by a low, white picket fence and separated from the audience by eleven horizontal strands of barbed wire, *Quotations* is a 1994 state-of-the-world address, a *theatrum mundi* incessantly presenting Abdoh's paradoxical point of view: the perpetual outsider who happened to be, as Abdoh described himself, 'a TV junkie,' immersed in and fixated on the multiple levels of signification in which American culture does its work (Abdoh 1994b). Two male couples form the primary character focus of the show. Tom Fitzpatrick and Tony Torn, dressed first as Puritans and later as modern businessmen in corporate ties and blue blazers, are the capitalist would-be entrepreneurs of a postapocalyptic world. Tom Pearl and Peter Jacobs, initially dressed all in white and then in green shirtwaist dresses, are the queer lovers locked in a sometimes abusive relationship. These two couples are in transit through the ruined city.[4]

SENSORY OVERLOAD

Quotations is a construction of sequences alternating repetitive tableaux, group and solo scenes, and frenetic dance numbers choreographed in a frontal, MGM-movie musical style by Ken Roht. Abdoh skillfully designed stage images from his rich visual vocabulary, which combined costume, objects, gesture, and a raw, physical acting style in an incessantly compelling high theatricality. [. . .]

In addition to the downstage platform and a floor-level upstage playing area, Abdoh completed the performance space with two video monitors and two rear-projection film screens, both hung above the stage. These sporadically burst into a profusion of found images with startling intensity, an intensity matched (or bettered) by the similarly jarring montage of sounds that burst out aurally.[5]

Abdoh's basic technique here seems to be sensory overload – the controlled explosion of information coming at the audience on multiple levels. For example, near the end of the play the entire cast stands downstage left, dressed in Boy Scout uniforms (some with skirts instead of shorts), and sings a folk song, 'When I First Came to This Land,' with accompanying hand gestures. The video screens show a succession of farm animals (pig, goose, goat, etc.) sitting in a suburban living room. On the platform stage left, naked, the two lovers at the center of the show's focus (Tom Pearl and Peter Jacobs) 'simulate,' as a stage direction puts it, 'tender fucking,' quite realistically. The odd pastoral serenity of the uniformed Boy Scouts (men in skirts, women in shorts) singing an immigrants' song in the company of barnyard animals is in itself so striking that on several occasions during performances I witnessed, half the audience did not even notice the two lovers' graphic intercourse. The stage was so loaded with other images, and the audience so ener-vated by the experience of that preceding 80 minutes, that the startling scene of homosexual lovemaking simply existed on the periphery. This is probably how Abdoh wanted the image to work onstage: queer sexual congress presented not as a centered, solo action sensationally seizing our eyes, but as an everyday act of passion: decentered, simply occupying its own space, just part of the terrain.

TEXTS

Like the images, the texts of *Quotations from a Ruined City*, written by Abdoh and his brother Salar Abdoh,[6] are similarly disjointed, equally powerful. Coming in short torrents rather than in developed scenes, the shards of words, whether spoken in curious monolog, strained dialog, or in short, sharp repetitive shouts, are rich and poetically evocative. For example, in the opening dual monolog introducing Tony Torn and Tom Fitzpatrick as patriarchal white men in suits who wander the terrain of the play, each actor is contained in a metal booth upstage of the main performance platform, dressed in Puritan costume, a spotlight focused tightly on each face as it peers out the cubicle's small window. Torn and Fitzpatrick move their mouths; but their voices (like almost all the voices in *Quotations*) project from the speakers overhead, prerecorded and out of synch. The actors' heads also appear on the video screens, one to a monitor, prerecorded and also mouthing the words, out of synch:

> *Tony:* The ruin is infested nowadays.
> *Tom F:* My consistency lies in one thing and one thing only.
> *Tony:* I carry the mask of tired souls like an old pro.
> *Tom F:* I'm a goddamn partner! I'm a goddamn partner! Now let me in!
> (Abdoh and Abdoh 1995: 109)

Abdoh insisted he was 'not a playwright' but 'a dramatist in the form of [. . .] symbolist poetry, or symbolist writers' (1994a). [. . .] Founded on decidedly non-Western roots (fourteenth-century Islamic mystic poetry and the powerful ritual of Shi'i Muslim Ta'ziyeh plays), filtered through his queer/immigrant/dysfunctional-family perspective, combined with a sensible knowledge of European and modern-ist classicism (Aristotle, Wagner, Verdi, Poe, Duchamp), and, most importantly, completely immersed in heavy doses of American popular culture, Abdoh creates a symbolic theatre language intimately familiar with American culture but tempered with the skeptical gaze of the outside observer.

The Abdoh brothers' writing at the opening of *Quotations from a Ruined City* is cryptic and evocative, the initial brushstrokes of a vast surrealist landscape painted with words. But unlike texts of high postmodern playwrights, whose meaning is obscurely inner-directed or clearly nonrepresentational, the Abdohs' lines frankly attempt to communicate situation and feeling by means of the evocative poetic image. The men dressed as Puritans continue to whisper:

> *Tony:* You ask yourself, What is more likely to cause bits and pieces of American corporations to become available? Easy. Leverage. If a company can't meet its debt payments, it makes itself vulnerable. If the company cannot meet its debt payments, it will be forced to sell off assets to the highest bidder.

Tom F: I return to the ruin . . . because I am done romancing the gutter. That sort of horseshit is for yellow-bellied boys and girls who think dirt is appealing. Anyhow, it turns out I'm too damn clumsy for the fabled streets.

Tony: So you are back at the old ruin.

Tom F: But Floyd, the cat who used to run this place isn't here anymore. By the way, I want your picture.

Tony: Say I have a picture. You want that picture, but I don't want to sell my house. I love my picture. Then I take a large mortgage out on my house. I then lose my job and am desperate for cash to avoid defaulting on my mortgage. Now I am not just willing to sell my picture to you. I'm desperate to sell my picture to you. You may even get it at a knockdown price. This isn't just idle metaphor.

(1995: 109)

The Abdohs' disembodied voices here continue to paint in the terrain of the play – the ruined cities of the West after the 'triumph of capitalism,' the body facing ruin from disease – as well as the play's dominant emotions: sense of loss, anger, confusion, desire. [. . .] Reza Abdoh's passionate yearning to communicate is at odds with high postmodernism's mistrust of communication, a mistrust which most often appears as irony. Abdoh's work, ultimately un-ironic, has earnest ambitions similar to those of 1960s experimental theatre, but (as I shall examine below) actually more like the politically nuanced ambitions of avant-garde theatre before World War II.

HORRORS OF WAR

The fifty-two scenes constituting *Quotations from a Ruined City* are mostly centered on American themes and American places, specifically Los Angeles and New York (although it is not correct to say that the play 'takes place' in any specific locale), with periodic forays into Bosnia and Iraq. This geographic range is matched by the show's mythic chronological range, which begins with the patriarchal Tony and Tom F. in Puritan dress, and ends with them in modern blazers and ties. Civilization, or more accurately, civilizations, are not happy bearers of progress here. The scene titles of *Quotations* give an idea of the pain and meanness each different locale, each different milieu, is capable of doling out to its inhabitants or its enemies: 'Shackle Tableau,' 'Ear Pull Section,' 'Impalement,' 'Body Bag Sequence,' 'Dental Torture,' ' "I'm Dying. No You're Not" Sequence,' 'Electrocution Sequence,' and 'Eye Tube Text/Nose Measuring Sequence.'

One of the most uncomfortable sections of the production, and one which most specifically directs itself to contemporary political events, is the 'Impalement' scene, a narrative early in the show that describes (but does not depict) the torture of Mustafa, a Bosnian Muslim, by Serbians. A herd of life-size cutout sheep has been set up on the platform stage; overhead on the video monitors is a montage of amateur-looking video footage of Beirut and Sarajevo – the most extensive literal images of ruined cities in the show. Broken up into short lines, the gruesome description of Mustafa's torture is spoken in alternating phrases by Fitzpatrick, Torn, Pearl, Jacobs, and Sabrina Artel, as each actor in turn picks up one of the sheep to drop off the upstage side of the platform:

Tom P: On the ground was an oak pole, two and a half meters long, with a sharp iron point.

Tony: When they ordered Mustafa to lie down he lowered his head, then the Chetniks walked up to him and started stripping off his coat and shirt.

Sabrina: Then they tied each of his legs with a rope.

Tom P: Two Chetniks pulled his legs wide apart.

Peter: Another Chetnik rested the pole against two logs so the pole's top was between Mustafa's legs.

Tony: He pulled a short, wide dagger out of his belt, kneeled before the outstretched body of Mustafa and cut the cloth of his trousers between his legs to widen the opening where the pole would enter the body.

(1995: 114–15)

And so on. The first scene interruption is '12 seconds of sound': excruciatingly loud industrial shrieks. The projected images shift from video to black and white film, including footage of a cymbal player. The scene resumes, is interrupted for 16 more seconds of the same aural assault, and then concludes with a description of Mustafa, impaled on the pole six feet above the ground, growling, 'Chetniks I hope you die like dogs . . . die like dogs . . . die like dogs.'

The vivid description of torture causes the audience immediate discomfort. This is due to a number of factors, perhaps most importantly the fact that, despite his uninhibited capability of presenting such images, Abdoh shows nothing of what is being described. Instead, the audience is forced to imagine. The visual field balances the actors' aggressive competition for the cutout sheep with the video images of shelled-out modern buildings. These juxtaposed visual images of ordinary daily life (the pastoral sheep, the actors doing their work, the calm and distanced documentary effect of the home-video footage of blasted architecture) make the textual horror that much stronger.

Despite the constant presence of the Bosnian War in news media and hints of potentially increased U.S. and U.N. military involvement in it, the war hardly surfaced in New York avant-garde theatre during the winter of 1994.[7] So Abdoh's powerful focus on it was unusual, a reminder that disastrous international political situations could be legitimate subject matter for theatre. However, Abdoh, who might be expected to support the Muslim and multi-ethnic side of the conflict against the recrudescence of European racist ideology in the Serbian operations of 'ethnic cleansing,' did not approach the issue with the simplistic zeal (mistakenly) ascribed to agitprop theatre. Abdoh's response to the atrocities of the Bosnian War was distanced, nearly nonpartisan, almost elegiac. A few scenes before the 'Impalement' section, Artel, clad in a Puritan matron's costume, wields an axe while reciting a definition of 'Chetnik' (the Bosnian name for Serb militants, originally applied to fascist Serb paramilitary groups in the Second World War). Artel's definition is biting, but hyperbolically extreme:

Sabrina: (*enters with an axe*) 'Be civil, will you!' Chetnik: The word derives from the one used for troop. There are several features characteristic of Chetniks. They tell lies. They are Serbs. They massacre the Bosnians – Through slaughtering, killing, burning, raping, and robbing the Chetniks hope to conquer the country of Bosnia. The Chetniks are defenders of the Serbian cause. The Serbian cause is all things Serbian: men, women, birds, fish, plants, and the Serbian Crow. Serbian Crow. Serbian Crow.

(1995: 110)

Abdoh's political position here is complicated. While on the one hand he pushed his theatrical images into the controversial area of partisan politics (a move always suspect in American theatre, except when the politics express accepted ideologies), he simultaneously stepped back to critique all politics: the inhuman use of torture as well as the simplistic cant of the political ideologue seeking to define her/his opponent as evil. In this way, Abdoh retained some of high postmodernism's skepticism of politics in general, and yet dove into the messy area of post-cold war geopolitics without hesitation.[8]

SPIRITUAL REDEMPTION

However discomforting such scenes are, they are in fact complemented (opposed is too optimistic a word) by exuberant, if not joyous, dancing; by the occasional tenderness of the Pearl/Jacobs interchanges; and above all by the mystical spiritualism of two 'Arabic Prayer' scenes. (The first incorporates a text from the Koran in Arabic, the second a poem by Rumi, in Farsi.) The scenes do not offer an appealing Hollywood-style 'happy ending on earth,' but instead the possibility of some kind of spiritual redemption on a different plane, in a different world. This spiritual possibility is increasingly frequent in Abdoh's post-HIV+ work, especially when that work deals with the question of death. In an interview with Andrea Vaucher, Abdoh said:

> I think death exists in the fourth dimension. Not as a reality or a concept that exists or brings to an end, but as something that provides the opportunity for regeneration. That might sound inanely Christian or godly. I don't mean it to. But within the framework of destruction and construction – within the framework of that dialectic where things are destroyed, ideas are destroyed, lives are destroyed or self-destroyed – within that framework, ideas and people and thoughts and objects are reconstructed. Within that dialectic, even in the fourth dimension – beyond time, beyond space – there is the need for that kind of regeneration. Otherwise you are in a state of stasis. And that's not what the fourth dimension is about. It's totally the opposite.
>
> (in Vaucher 1993: 223)

Spiritual redemption is not impossible in Abdoh's world, but it is difficult to achieve, apparently as remote a concept as the mystic poem by Hafiz written out in gold Arabic calligraphy on black placards; or the recitations from the Koran and the poetry of Rumi: all messages of spiritual rebirth hinted at, yet left untranslated for uncomprehending American audiences. Redemption does seem possible, materializing in odd, reassuringly tender moments in Abdoh's production, often as 'traditional culture': Middle-Eastern dances (choreographed by Abdoh), an Anglo-American folk song ('When I First Came to This Land'), an African American spiritual ('Gonna Build a Mountain'), or even a Frank Sinatra classic ('All the Way') sung with only a hint of irony by Ken Roht.

PUNCTUATING THE SPECTACLE

Quotations from a Ruined City's longer imagistic texts, and its sometimes slow and even quiet scenes, are countered by sudden slogans shouted in the midst of short bursts of light, movement, and sound which Abdoh used to punctuate his fuguelike structures. Artel, in her Puritan-woman costume, lip-synchs 'Be civil, will you!' at three separate charged moments early in the play, her axe sometimes replaced by an upraised hammer. Later, Abdoh had Torn and Fitzpatrick interject an equally fervid 'No don't do that!' / 'Let them be!' eleven times into a Pearl/Jacobs dialog about Napoleon's demise and the advantages of learning a plumber's trade. (The scene reappears later in the play with only five such interjections.) Typical of Abdoh's indirect, layered theatremaking, the Torn/Fitzpatrick lines don't comment on the dialog they interrupt so much as on the accumulated horrors that have already occurred – and will occur again soon.

Sometimes, such repeated cadences dispense with words altogether, as when a recording of frogs and crickets interjects itself between two scenes: laying down an intense but brief aural recollection of 'nature.' At other times, Abdoh's incessant and purposefully repetitive theatrical punctuation is essentially visual. For example, an 'Opening Movement Sequence' (a breathtaking, choreographed group dance) appears at the top of the show, following the first Fitzpatrick/Torn dialog. Five scenes later, it appears again, performed double-time, immediately after a brief reprise of Fitzpatrick and Torn's opening cubicle scene. Similarly, an 'Electrocution Sequence' appears three different times during the play: Pearl and Jacobs, the two lovers, approach, and then touch the strands of barbed wire separating the audience from the stage. Their immediate electrocution is accompanied by a painfully harsh blast of light and sound, and then five tape-recorded peals of a large, sonorous bell, each bong sounding in a brief flash of intense green light overhead. The light illuminates Ken Roht in profile, clad in boots and his khaki Boy Scout skirt, silently flailing his hands and feet.

All the dances in *Quotations* (mainly choreographed by Roht) function similarly. Inspired by MGM movie musicals, they feature the whole company in frenetic, frontal chorus lines on the downstage platform. Attention tightly focused on the audience (as in Broadway production numbers), the group executes tight choreographies to the classic jazz music of either Charles Mingus ('Boogie Stomp Shuffle') or the Dirty Dozen Brass Band ('Jazz Juice'). Roht's dances combine unison footwork and daffy tap-influenced hand gestures, but whereas the gestures in 'legitimate' musicals illustrate the meaning of the dances, or simply signify the dancers' carefree abandon, in Abdoh's production the splayed-out hand gestures are disconnected from the traditional musical's strained presentation of bliss; defamiliarized, they appear to the audience as form. The dancers, uncompelled to smile at the audience, reinforce this, their faces free to strain with exertion. The seven MGM-style dances punctuate and counter the hardness and brutality of the other scenes, not with easy, effervescent joy – or even sensuality – but with sober buoyant energy that somehow preserves the promise of joy, even if at present it must be deferred.

REPETITION AND INTENT

Reza Abdoh turned away from linear plot development in 1986 with the *Medea* he directed in a Los Angeles recreation center; *Quotations from a Ruined City* was his most successful combination of nonlinearity and effective theatricality. Unlike minimalist theatre, which tends to shun content as well as linearity, Abdoh's work reveals his obsession with imparting relevant information; he admitted, 'I usually have something to say' (1994b). However, is it possible to say something, to impart information, without telling stories, without engaging in plot? Like 1970s minimalism, avant-garde movements of the early twentieth century often allowed the form of their work to stand as message, an effective strategy at a moment when abstraction and collage – simply by themselves – could produce splendid outrage in audiences unaccustomed to considering such forms as 'real' art. Abdoh's work, at the other end of the century, abides in a very different environment, addressing an audience almost exclusively immersed in montage, collage, and the intense symbolism of advertising, especially through television. Faced with a culture in which abstraction and collage are normative, Abdoh combined nonlinear structure with subversive subject matter in *Quotations* to address issues of patriarchy, religion, intolerance, will, and desire. In order to deliver various fragments of content through nonlinear structure, Abdoh used repetition and variation on many different levels.

Repeated dances, phrases, images, and sounds – especially when they call up unpleasant images of ugly, brutal humanity – are wearying. But they succeed in defining a landscape, in creating a theatrical world which, Abdoh has shown, mirrors the real world all too well. Abdoh's fugue structure balances repetition with variation skillfully enough to maintain audience interest. His sense of theatricality, cultivated since he was a teenager in London, enabled him to pull off the difficult feat of making nonlinearity theatrically compelling.

And despite Abdoh's embrace of disorienting, seemingly chaotic structure, there is in fact a little story, a little progression, a little character development, a little plot – as there must be when the same characters appear on stage for 90 minutes.

By the end of *Quotations*, Torn and Fitzpatrick have transformed from Puritan dress to modern suits, and then (worn down by the abuses of the play to weary, disheveled businessmen) to rumpled shirtsleeves, ties askew, both wearily leaning on long staffs. They slap each other – for Abdoh, a typical act of abusive intimacy – but then drop their staffs and kiss.

They and the rest of the cast, except Pearl and Jacobs, crank up their 'Final Dance,' a last frenetic clog and tap dance in which couples (one performer on each side of the stage) methodically remove the eleven strands of barbed wire separating them from the audience. This is a preparation for their last burst of activity, a leap offstage into the audience for a final exit through the house. Pearl and Jacobs slowly approach each other, fall to their knees, and embrace in a single spotlight, as their taped voices recite the last speech, a dream:

> *Tom P/Peter:* I am in a beautiful garden. As I reach out to touch the flowers they wither under my hands. A nightmare feeling of desolation comes over me as a great dragon-shaped cloud darkens the earth. A few may get through the gate in time. Remember. Remember. We are bound to the past as we cling to the memory of the ruined city.

> (1995: 135–6)

At the end, *Quotations from a Ruined City* turns, as it has intermittently throughout the performance, to a tender personal moment, probably important for Abdoh as it was for Abdoh's characters. The smallest modicum of 'story' here – the slight development of the Pearl/Jacobs relationship, the consistency of their love – is extremely romantic and peaceful, a bittersweet coming together. It is not a 'real' happy ending, but a passably happy one, not unlike what Hollywood might do if it made 1990s MGM-style musicals about queer young men finding strength and spiritual redemption. But Abdoh was not content to let romance reign alone. Following the men's embrace, the last illuminated image is four larger-than-life-size sides of beef hanging upstage: dead meat.

HAFIZ AND SYMBOLISM, TA'ZIYEH AND DEATH

[. . .] Abdoh's method of creating 'realities that [are] multilayered' (Abdoh 1994a) was not an extemporized gesture, but a considered strategy drawing not only from MGM movie musicals by means of Duchamp [see the author's interview with Abdoh, *TDR* 39, no. 4, 1995] but from the structures of Persian poetry and Islamic ritual theatre.

Hafiz is considered the premier lyric poet in the Persian language (Hillman 1976: 2). [. . .] Abdoh used one of Hafiz's mystic poems about eternity in *Quotations*, its Farsi characters calligraphed in gold letters on large, black, stick-mounted cards topped by a reclining crescent. But it is clear that Persian poetry was not only a textual and thematic touchstone for Abdoh, but a structural one as well. [. . .] Influenced by Sufi mysticism, Hafiz's pantheistic poetry employs an elaborate, conventionalized symbol system that in many ways conflicts with orthodox Islam because of the poems' hedonistic bent. All of Hafiz's couplet-based *ghazels* have at least three levels of signification, working simultaneously as celebrations of love and wine, as Sufi mystic theology, and as sexually symbolic odes to a divine male lover (Avery and Heath-Stubbs 1952: 8–9). [. . .]

The other major Iranian cultural influence on Abdoh's work was Ta'ziyeh, the Shi'i Muslim tradition of processions and martyr plays performed annually during the ten-day Muslim festival of Muharram (see Beeman 1982; Chelkowski 1979; and Riggio 1988). [. . .] Formally, Ta'ziyeh features a broad, stylized acting technique emphasizing histrionic gesture and declamatory speech. Each Ta'ziyeh play of the ten-day cycle is a mourning ritual centered on the liminal event of death – of Husayn (grandson of Muhammad and an Imam of Shi'i Islam), or of specific members of Husayn's family and entourage. [. . .] Ta'ziyeh, for Abdoh (1994a), was

a very powerful form of theatre. It's not even really theatre, it's a ritual. It's mystical and at the same time it's very theatrical. It's very simple but very theatrical and complex and it's as if it's in a hyperreality – you know it's all hyper. And I think that's probably the most important connection between it and my work.

As in Hafiz's poetry, part of Ta'ziyeh's 'hyperreality' consists of its ability to exist simultaneously in three different modes of time and space ('literal,' 'representational,' and 'non-time') which 'totally interpenetrate each other' (Beeman 1982: 121). Ta'ziyeh's depiction of 'real' events in heightened circumstances so fraught with emotion that they provoke a true Greek tragedy catharsis was emulated by Abdoh, who wished to bring the same kind of experience to his audiences, although they may not 'believe' in the ritual efficacy of theatre the way Shi'i audiences in Iran believe in Ta'ziyeh. This made Abdoh's search for a collective sensitive nerve in his audience that much more intense, and when he found the nerve, he produced shocks. [. . .]

Abdoh saw in Ta'ziyeh 'a certain kind of struggle to reach divinity,' to reach 'purification and redemption, through the act of sacrifice and through the act of performance' (1994a). The act of sacrifice Ta'ziyeh focuses on, of course, is death, and the way death is treated in Ta'ziyeh has important ramifications for the contemporary theatre of death which AIDS has engendered, and of which Abdoh's post-HIV+ plays are an important part. In Ta'ziyeh, death is an inevitable end and the details of its process are the center of dramatic focus. [. . .] Mass-media performances of death in the West tend to cheapen its effects, to sensationalize the passing and then quickly forget about it: to trivialize, in most cases, its metaphysical importance. But Ta'ziyeh [. . .] focuses on the act of death, pauses over its minutiae, ponders its meaning, and, as Abdoh has said, finds redemption and significance in it.

Quotations from a Ruined City, also focusing on the nature of decay and death, was an intensely personal response by Abdoh to his own approaching end. The deaths in Ta'ziyeh are martyrs' deaths; this is also an important link to Abdoh's theatre. Martyrdom raises the importance of death to a higher level; unjust, yet not unexpected, the martyr's death immediately assumes significance in a greater context, becomes meaningful on a different, higher plane. Abdoh transferred Ta'ziyeh's method of making great sense of death from an environment (Iran) and religion (Islam) no longer hospitable to him, to a new context in a society struggling over the meaning of AIDS.

AIDS AND POSTMODERNISM

Abdoh's theatre work, especially his post-HIV+ productions with Dar A Luz, marks a significant break with high-postmodernist theatre as represented by Wilson, Foreman, and the 1980s work of the Wooster Group. Postmodern cultural theory of the 1980s proposed or rationalized a retreat from point-of-view as a logical response to the collapse of aesthetics into politics. At that time, Hal Foster, for example, argued that engaged political art, 'locked in a rhetorical code,' was 'problematic' in late twentieth-century Western society, where 'there can be no simple representation of reality' (1985: 155). [. . .] In postmodernist theatre the refusal to fix meaning is concurrent with a steadfast attention to form over content, or, when the question of content becomes inevitable, with the embrace of irony as the only viable point of view.

[. . .] The AIDS epidemic changed the nature of avant-garde performance irrevocably, forcing artists to consider and analyze not only the horror of the killing disease, but the social and political implications of government and corporate responses to the epidemic, as well as the questions of homophobia and racism inevitably linked with the AIDS crisis. The unavoidable presence of death through AIDS engendered artistic response, just as the Vietnam War in the 1960s, the rise of fascism in the 1930s, and the horrors of World War I in the 1910s had engendered avant-garde political theatre throughout this century. Beginning with the brilliant political performance actions of ACT-UP, and the AIDS-conscious works of such gay men as Larry Kramer, Marlon Riggs, Robert Mapplethorpe, and David Wojnarowicz, a whole body of late twentieth-century avant-garde performance came into definition, a body of work which, once again, demanded that common individual concerns connect to larger social and political issues. This change of focus is probably the single most important factor in the development of what might inelegantly be termed post-postmodernist performance.

The signs of this change are evident in the work of Ron Vawter (d. 1993), one of the American avant-garde's most brilliant performers. One of Vawter's last works, his solo performance *Roy Cohn/Jack Smith*, differed greatly from such Wooster Group productions as *Route 1 & 9* and *North Atlantic*. *Roy Cohn/Jack Smith*'s depiction of two very different HIV+ gay men – one (Cohn) steadfastly denying his sexuality, the other (Smith) openly using it to help in the joyous creation of Queer Theatre – used the whole range of postmodern performance techniques refined by the Wooster Group, wedded them to a surprisingly realistic (almost naturalistic) aesthetic, and produced a theatre production brilliantly combining both personal interests and political concerns (see Bell 1992a). Reza Abdoh similarly established the presence of AIDS within a larger grid of social, cultural, and political power relations, but Abdoh had more time onstage than Vawter or Smith to focus and develop his analysis of the meaning of AIDS. [. . .]

'STRUCTURAL STABILITY' OF THE AVANT-GARDE

To the alarm of some of his critics, Abdoh's work actively and consciously recycled twentieth-century avant-garde performance techniques just as, in true postmodern fashion, it actively and consciously deconstructed and recycled images and sounds from the juggernaut of United States mass-media culture. In *Quotations from a Ruined City*, the barbed wire separating the audience from the stage echoes the Living Theatre's similar use of chain-link fence in its 1963 production *The Brig*.[9] Abdoh's use of strong, white, audience-focused stage lighting and obliquely signifi- cant scenic elements refers to the work of Richard Foreman. *Quotations*' sudden manic dance sequences and persistent video images follows Wooster Group tech- niques. There is something of both Robert Wilson and Peter Brook (two early influences) in the flow and scale of Abdoh's work, and his lugubrious, cryptic dialog scenes, in turn, suggest both Beckett and Genet. Abdoh himself acknowl- edged particular debts to Duchamp and Breton, as well as to symbolist poetry.

The problem with Abdoh's work, according to some critics, is that he recycled avant-garde techniques into pastiche constructions only capable of quoting the far greater works of recent postmodernist theatre. This point of view parallels the critique of avant-garde art as an attack on the institution of bourgeois art (Schulte- Sasse 1984: xxxvii), an attack that – despite all its intentions – inevitably reinforces that very institution. According to Peter Bürger, for example, avant-garde art never developed its own style precisely because the whole purpose of avant-garde was (and is) to negate style (1984: 18). Bürger sees avant-garde productions as one-time- only gestures, 'acts of provocation' which, once completed, defy repetition or variation (56). Once Duchamp has made a urinal a 'work of art,' there is no reason to repeat the gesture, nor, furthermore is the gesture even artistically pos- sible. From the viewpoint of this critical position, avant-garde production *by defin- ition* has no chance of developing continuity (i.e., a continuing theatrical language) and its successful works cannot or should not help engender others.

The 'one-time-gesture' theory of avant-garde art precludes an understanding of avant-garde technique as a repository of tradition and continuity. The approach does, in some ways, help clarify the historical avant-garde's sometimes oppositional relationship to normative culture and power, but only partially, since it fails to take into account the important ways avant-garde techniques have infused themselves into normative culture, for example into fascist and other forms of state-approved art; or into mass-media aesthetics, where a urinal (or at least a toilet) *will* appear again as a work of art, as the animated centerpiece of a bathroom disinfectant advertisement whose aesthetics are based on classic avant-garde techniques: collage, montage, and radical juxtaposition. Second, the one-time-gesture theory denies the possibility of a developing avant-garde aesthetic – the possibility of a developing avant-garde tradition – which is what Reza Abdoh's work represents.

Abdoh's construction out of fragments is not only typical of postmodernist structure and of the modernist avant-garde in general, but characteristic of even older (and similarly misunderstood) traditions of European art going back to the baroque, as Walter Benjamin pointed out in *The Origin of German Tragic Drama*:

> That which lies here in ruins, the highly significant fragment, the remnant, is, in fact, the finest material in baroque creation. For it is common practice in the literature of the baroque to pile up fragments ceaselessly, without any strict idea of a goal, and, in the unremitting expectation of a miracle, to take the repetition of stereotypes for a process of intensification. The baroque writers must have regarded the work of art as just such a miracle. And if, on the other hand, it seemed to be the calculable result of the process of accumulation, it is no more difficult to reconcile these two things than it was for the alchemist to reconcile the longed-for miraculous 'work' and the subtle theoretical recipes. The experimentation of the baroque writers resembles the practice of the adepts. The legacy of antiquity constitutes, item for item, the elements from which the new whole is mixed. Or rather: is constructed. For the perfect vision of this new phenomenon was the ruin.
>
> (1977: 178)

Abdoh's productions are similarly 'baroque' in the affirmative sense of the term Benjamin sought to establish in his recuperative study of seventeenth-century German drama, similarly concerned with contemplating the meaning of ruins and asserting that meaning through emblems and symbols rather than through realism. Different, perhaps, from the theatre Benjamin was analyzing, Abdoh's productions tethered their multileveled symbolism to their director's harsh intent to 'say something' through performance; this purpose puts his theatre in sync with the politicized avant-garde theatres of the twentieth century.

Avant-garde performance, beginning with symbolism in the late nineteenth century, placed itself outside the existing structures of modern theatre because of its desire to oppose rationalism and realism. Avant-garde theatre artists discovered existing traditions of nonrational, nonrealistic performance in 'low-culture' Western theatre and in Asian and African theatre, and stole or recycled elements of those performance traditions to create their own symbolist, futurist, dadaist, constructivist, Ballets Russes, Bauhaus, Ausdruckstanz, and modern dance productions. This technique allowed avant-garde artists the dangerous possibility of shopping in the supermarket of international culture, but denied them the privilege of working from a solid performance *langue* in order to create their individual *paroles* (a privilege which non-Western performance practices did share with normative Western performance traditions such as realistic drama). Frantisek Deak, writing about Prague School approaches to theatre, clarifies this problem of avant-garde performance practice:

> In avant-garde theatre, the breaking of particular conventions is often present, but the investigation of the avant-garde theatre's own assumptions, conventions or

'language' does not occur because the opposite of 'language,' the individual innovative act ('speech' in Saussurian terms), is of primary importance. Only in the strongly
codified theatre forms of the oriental and folk theatre is the distinction of language
and speech clearly visible.

(1976: 90)

At the close of the twentieth century, however, avant-garde performance
has indeed established a language, an aesthetic tradition built from a hundred
years of piecing together performance fragments and shards of performing techniques into what Abdoh called 'a kind of a vocabulary that everybody sort of
shares' (Abdoh 1994a). In 'Dynamics of the Sign in the Theater' Jindrich Honzl
refers to the 'structural stability' of 'theaters with a centuries-old tradition'; a
'constancy of structure' which 'causes theatrical signs to develop complex
meanings' (1986: 79). While a solidified structure might be thought to inhibit
innovation, in Honzl's opinion 'the immutability of the structure's key points
does not necessarily impoverish its expressivity because within this traditional
structure subtler and finer changes can take place' (80). What we ought to consider is the fact that 'avant-garde' theatre has now created its own century-old
tradition. [. . .]

Instead of seeing conventional cultural 'language' as a unitary monolith best
opposed by individual 'speeches' of deconstructed theatre productions, Abdoh's
work has opposed conventional culture and the power structures it represents by
posing avant-garde style as its own 'language,' a tradition of performance as
dependent upon its particular structure as Western opera, wayang kulit, or Yoruba
ritual are dependent on their structures. Working confidently within the established
theatre language of the twentieth-century avant-garde, Abdoh freed himself to
return to political, social, and spiritual content in a way normally unavailable to
high-postmodernist performance. In this sense, Abdoh's work has confounded the
view of avant-garde performance as gesture. Instead, like the productions of any
artist working within an established (but mutable) frame, Abdoh's theatre demands
to be considered as a particular combination of and variation on existing forms.
With Abdoh's Dar A Luz productions, avant-garde performance becomes 'classic,' and the creative possibilities of the avant-garde artist play in a very different
space than they did at the previous turn of the century.

QUOTATIONS AND 'THE SPECTACLE OF AIDS'

Timothy Wiles writes that in 340 BCE the Greek actor Polos 'made a great impact'
in the role of Sophocles' Electra 'when he carried the ashes of his own son into the
theatre in the urn supposed by Electra to carry the ashes of Orestes' (Wiles 1991:
13). Performance in our time makes a similar impact, as HIV+ artists who decide
to talk about AIDS put the questions of disease and death before their audiences.
The subject of AIDS has naturally found form in solo monolog, the signature
technique of performance art in the 1980s. Abdoh himself made brilliant use of the
form in 'a very personal monolog' (Abdoh 1994b) performed by Mario Gardner
in *Quotations from a Ruined City*:

> *Mario:*   [. . .] And when the graves start yielding up the dead, I'll rise like Christ in
> drag and you best not offend me with your innocence, sister, because I bet you could

tease a queen to death without half trying, so stop trying and let me tell you something. You reckon I ought to have a lot of regrets, my orgasm like being directly plugged in my hypothalamus socket and all, and my body in ruins after years of abuse but I have just one regret: I never made a drop of whiskey in all my life and if I last long enough I'll remedy that. And the preacher came in right after my old buddy left. Asked me if I was ready to go. Ready to go? I put my mascara on, my lipstick on and my yellow pumps and I snapped back. I'll go when I'm good and ready. There were so many things I wanted to say to my old buddy. But this haze I'm in bedimmed from the ailment and all. I just sort of wander in and out of things. I did tell him I love him though. I remember telling him that. I never could have told him years back. Even though I should have. Funny how men folk have trouble telling each other things like that. Until the pale horseman starts to gallop by the door. Gallop. Gallop. Gallop. Gallop. Gallop.

(Abdoh and Abdoh 1995: 127)

In Abdoh's work, the AIDS monolog does not stand alone, but is instead a theatrically effective moment in a multidimensional spectacle. *Quotations from a Ruined City*, a theatre production suffused at almost every instant with the sense of AIDS, is, surprisingly, not specifically about AIDS. Instead of following the performance artist's strategy of intense self-focus, Reza Abdoh decenters AIDS to focus instead on: the institutional abuses of patriarchy as familial and social authority; the nature of queer identity and its role in and against normative society; the conflicts of New World Order capitalism as they materialize in urban America; the dangers of combining religious fundamentalism with politics and economics (fundamentalist Christianity, fundamentalist Islam); the persistent presence and importance of folk culture, especially in contrast to mass-media performance; and how the deconstruction of mass-media culture can help create a radical critique of that culture.

AIDS is not the central focus of *Quotations from a Ruined City*, but it infuses the work, operating (unnamed) as a central metaphor of ruin, the ruin of the body encompassing and standing for the ruins of modern society. Gordy and Floyd, the lovers and central characters of *Quotations*, are never defined as HIV+, but they seem to be, could be, probably are, especially in the context of the horrid hospital scene where medical treatment slips over into torture. [. . .] Their bodies are signs of the HIV+ body, and not so much symbols (signs with an arbitrary relationship to an abstract signified) as they are indices (signs pointing to the physiological whole that is their referent). They represent Abdoh's HIV+ body; the bodies of other company members who may be HIV+; the bodies of gay men and all those at risk; the bodies of everyone who faces death.

Like a poem by Hafiz, or a surrealist collage, Abdoh's theatre not only works simultaneously on different levels of reality, but *believes* in those different levels. In this way, one of the most romantic scenes of *Quotations from a Ruined City* is the 'Medieval Hyperzone,' where Tom Pearl's character, apparently ill, and having removed a green dress he has been wearing, slowly and painfully stumbles naked from stage left to stage right, where Peter Jacobs stands, wearing only a medieval helmet and holding an upraised sword. An aria from Wagner's *Tannhäuser* plays, the two film screens above are filled with factory images, and Jacobs' sword implies some violent conclusion; but the scene completes itself with a dramatic release

189

when Jacobs drops the sword and Pearl falls into his arms. The abusive violence that seems always to characterize Abdoh's depiction of love dissolves in an embrace. In the Medieval Hyperzone love is possible, and this possibility on a distant level of existence implies hope for the same on our immediate level of existence. [. . .] *Quotations from a Ruined City*, according to Fitzpatrick, marked a change in Abdoh's HIV+ work:

> When we started to get the text, finally, after two and a half weeks of making the framework, he came back to rehearsal [after a bout of pneumonia] looking very spectral and ill indeed, and was so pleased at how the company had functioned creating the framework, and he could drop the stuff in. We got the text and we started to do it fast and loud, *à la* the old shows, *à la Bogeyman* and *Hip-Hop* and *Law of Remains*. And he said, 'No, no, not like that. I want this to be very slow, painfully slow.' 'But what about the old way, the fast and loud way?' – God, I can never remember quotes – [Abdoh said] something like 'I think I've gone beyond that now,' which was just like signaling the end of an era. And we all went 'Thank God, man!' 'Cause' it's hard to do it that fast and that loud.
>
> (Fitzpatrick 1994)

If *Quotations* subsumed the anger of earlier post-HIV+ productions under an encompassing late-century *theatrum mundi* seen from the decaying center of Western economic, political, and image-making power, this strategy in no way diminished the centrality of AIDS in the work. It did, on the other hand, create a brilliant theatrical response to what Simon Watney has called 'The Spectacle of AIDS': the 'carefully and elaborately stage-managed [. . .] sensational didactic pageant' performed ubiquitously through Western European and North American mass-media culture and through AIDS 'education,' in which the diseased bodies of gay men are ritually expunged from a dominant sociopolitical structure bent on reenshrining the patriarchal family as the 'national family unit,' a 'private' model for 'public' social organization (Watney 1993: 209). The ongoing spectacle of AIDS focuses on the homosexual body as the 'source' of disease, disease that specifically 'threatens' other physical bodies, but more importantly, metaphorically threatens State, Family, and Society. *Quotations from a Ruined City* is a different sort of spectacle, in which Reza Abdoh presented the same elements in reverse symbological order. In Abdoh's spectacle, State, Family, and Society are centers of critical attention, while the HIV+ body coexists on a more metaphoric level.

Quotations from a Ruined City marks two related shifts in late twentieth-century performance. Its first shift, from postmodernist political detachment to post-postmodernist political engagement, is made possible by its second shift: a recognition of the 'structural stability' of avant-garde theatre techniques since their inception in the 1890s. Working within the theatricality of those techniques, Abdoh also moved beyond postmodernist performance's reliance on irony as a dominating sensibility. *Quotations from a Ruined City* returns not only to an engagement with issues characteristic of other political theatres of this century, but to the ritual focus on death, birth, and renewal that characterizes Ta'ziyeh and other folk theatres. Finally, Abdoh even recovered romance, in *Quotations'* penultimate image of the two lovers embracing on the floor. The two lovers are most certainly doomed; the hanging sides of meat which are the production's ultimate image underline that fact. Nonetheless, in an artful quotation from Hollywood-style sensibilities, Abdoh here indulged in hope, not necessarily on the grand scale of political and social renewal, about which Abdoh was too realistically skeptical, but on the smaller, more important scale of personal relations, which hinge on the possibility of love.

NOTES

1   My use of the term 'postmodernist theatre' in this essay avoids dealing with the different strategies of feminist and queer performance, which, although often sharing performance techniques with high-postmodernist theatre, cannot as easily afford disconnected neutrality. For queer and feminist theatre, the mere existence of the performance takes on inevitable political overtones, whether or not those are taken up as thematic subjects.

2   Critics Tom O'Connor and Cliff Gallo, quoted in Stayton (1992: 28).

3   A similarly adulatory review was written for the *Voice* a couple of months earlier by Elinor Fuchs (1994).

4   Tom Fitzpatrick described his conception of the pairs: 'I haven't ever investigated any further than to think, well, we are apparently the capitalistic, Puritan, lard-ass, Wall Street mother-fuckers of America and the world, and Tommy and Peter are not. They, I assume, are the counter-revolutionaries, the suspectedly homosexual lovers; they're definitely our enemy, within the framework, I guess, of this postapocalyptic universe' (1994).

5   It is hard to overestimate the importance of sound for Abdoh's productions. Tom Fitzpatrick said that one of the practical reasons Abdoh used lip-synched voices throughout *Quotations* was to meet the demands of the existing aural element, the recorded music: 'Reza's experimenting with [lip-synching], but it's also, it's mainly, a budgetary concern. He couldn't afford Lavalier mikes for all of us, and therefore [the actors' voices] had to be recorded to get over the level of the music. Because the music is exactly the way he wants it. So it's the only way he could do it' (1994).

6   Salar Abdoh is a poet and novelist living in California whose works as of this writing are largely unpublished. *Quotations* was his first theatrical collaboration with his brother.

7   Exceptions were an exhibition by émigré Bosnian artists; a symposium on Bosnia by New York artists and activists; and the Bread and Puppet Theatre's *Fly or Die*, based on the testimonies of Bosnian rape victims.

8   A further example of this complexity is the 'impalement' text itself. Abdoh (1994b) insisted that he found the text in a French journal, and at first hearing it sounds like the first-person testimony of a contemporary refugee. (First-person testimonies by Bosnian women raped by Serbian men were highly publicized at this time.) But as [. . .] Lenio Myrivili has pointed out to me, the impalement story is in fact based on Ivo Andric's acclaimed 1945 novel of Yugoslavian history, *Na Drini Cuprija* (*The Bridge on the Drina*). [. . .]

9   This connection was uncannily underlined in the New York production of *Quotations* by the presence of longtime Living Theatre actor Tom Walker as the Arab Man.

WORKS CITED

Abdoh, Reza (1994a) Interview with author. New York City, 18 February.

—— (1994b) Interview with author. New York City, 4 April.

Abdoh, Reza, and Salar Abdoh (1995) '*Quotations from a Ruined City*.' TDR 39, 4 (T148): 108–36. Manuscript dated 16 June 1994.

Andric, Ivo (1959) *The Bridge on the River Drina*, trans. Lovett F. Edwards. New York: Macmillan.

Auslander, Philip (1987) 'Toward a concept of the political in postmodern theatre.' *Theatre Journal* 39, 1 (March): 20–34.

Avery, Peter, and John Heath-Stubbs (1952) *Hafiz of Shiraz*. London: John Murray.

Barthes, Roland (1977) 'Death of the author.' In *Image, Music, Text*, 142–8. New York: Hill and Wang.

Beeman, William O. (1982) *Cultural Performances of Cummunication in Iran*. Tokyo: Institute for the Study of Languages and Cultures of Asia and Africa.

Bell, John (1992a) '*Roy Cohn/Jack Smith*.' *Theater Week*, 9 March: 12–13.

—— (1992b) '*The Law of Remains*.' *Theater Week*, 23 March: 15–16.

—— (1993) '*Tight Right White*.' *Theater Week*, 16 April: 14–15.

Benjamin, Walter (1977) *The Origin of German Tragic Drama*, trans. John Osborne. London: Verso.

Brantley, Ben (1994) '*Quotations from a Ruined City*.' *New York Times*, 3 March: C20.

Bürger, Peter (1984) *Theory of the Avant-Garde*, trans. Michael Shaw. Minneapolis: University of Minnesota Press.

Chelkowski, Peter, ed. (1979) *Ta'ziyeh: Ritual and Drama in Iran*. New York: New York University Press.

Cocteau, Jean (1972) 'Letter to Americans.' In *Cocteau's World: An Anthology of Writings by Jean Cocteau*, trans. Margaret Cosland, 397–411. New York: Dodd, Mead & Company.

Cole, L.C. (1994) 'Angrier than thou.' *New York Native*, 14 March: 33.

Deak, Frantisek (1976) 'Structuralism in theatre: the Prague School contribution.' *TDR* 20, 4 (T72): 83–94.

Fitzpatrick, Tom (1994) Interview with author. New York City, 30 March.

Foster, Hal (1985) 'For a concept of the political in contemporary art.' In *Recodings: Art, Spectacle, Cultural Politics*, 139–55. Port Townsend, WA: Bay Press.

Fuchs, Elinor (1994) 'A vision of ruin.' *Village Voice*, 15 March: 91–2.

Hillman, Michael C. (1976) *Unity in the Ghazels of Hafiz*. Minneapolis: Bibliotheca Islamica.

Honzl, Jindrich (1986) 'Dynamics of the sign in the theater.' In *Semiotics of Art*, ed. Ladislav Matejka and Irwin R. Titunik, 74–93. Cambridge, MA: MIT Press.

Leverett, James (1994) 'Ghosts of Obies past.' *Village Voice*, 31 May: 100.

Riggio, Milla, ed. (1988) *Ta'ziyeh: Ritual and Popular Beliefs in Iran*. Hartford, CT: Trinity College.

Savran, David (1986) *The Wooster Group, 1975–1985: Breaking the Rules*. Ann Arbor: University of Michigan Research Press.

Sember, Robert (1994) Personal communication with author, 21 September.

Schulte-Sasse, Jochen (1984) 'theory of modernism versus theory.' Foreword to Peter Bürger, *Theory of the Avant-Garde*. Minneapolis: University of Minnesota Press.

Stayton, Richard (1992) 'Hellraiser: the shock tactics of Reza Abdoh push audiences to the edge.' *American Theatre* 8,11 (February): 26–33.

Vaucher, Andréa R. (1993) *Muses from Chaos and Ash: AIDS, Artists and Art*. New York: Grove Press.

Watney, Simon (1993) 'The Spectacle of AIDS.' In *The Lesbian and Gay Studies Reader*, ed. Henry Abelove, Michèle Aina Barale, and David M. Halperin, 202–11. New York: Routledge.

Wiles, Timothy (1991) *The Masks of Menander: Sign and Meaning in Greek and Roman Performance*. New York: Cambridge University Press.

22

WOMAN, MAN, DOG, TREE
Two decades of intimate and monumental bodies in Pina Bausch's Tanztheater[1]

Gabrielle Cody

T158, 1998

You're right in demanding that the artist have a conscious relation to his work, but you are confusing two ideas: solving a problem and posing a problem correctly.

Anton Chekhov, Letters to A.S. Suvorin

Choreography too will reassume tasks of a realistic nature. It is a mistake of recent time that it has nothing to do with the depiction of 'people as they really are.' [...] In any case a theater that bases everything on Gestus cannot do without choreography.

Bertolt Brecht, Little Organon

All life Murphy, is figure and ground.

Samuel Beckett, Murphy

There is an eerie and seductive moment, right at the beginning of Pina Bausch's 1994 revival of *Two Cigarettes in the Dark*, when Mechthild Grossmann enters the stage in an evening gown, crosses down to the audience, and with the masterful delivery and conspirational tone of a career hostess declares: 'Why don't you come in, my husband is at war.' It's difficult not to want to follow this urban Clytemnestra into the gruesome psychic antechambers of Bauschland, to eat her promise. And we do, perhaps because we know we are guests, hungry for the emotional carnage we are about to witness. Now another woman in an evening gown appears. But Helena Pikon does not fit into her dress like a hand in a kid glove. Pikon's anorexic body convulses, spasmodically exposing a boy's chest as she tries to expiate her unspeakable trauma and escape the large stage enclosure. She runs, she falls, she moans. When a man in a tuxedo enters, he tries to keep her down. He shouts at her in French to stop crying, and hits her. Shortly after, another woman in an evening gown enters and urinates in a corner of the stage. Then another man in a tuxedo screams at her and rubs her nose in the urine. Men are also subjected to greater and lesser public humiliations by the women, and by other men.

Bausch's Wuppertal Tanztheater, now in its second decade, is famous for its depictions of the violence in the relationship between the sexes, the plight of the individual subjected to annihilating institutional authority, and the anguish inherent in attempting to enter the physical memory of childhood. Her dancers' brutal encounters occur in vast, neohistorical compounds and are often underscored by popular music from the 1930s and 1940s, perhaps a mock-nostalgic reference to the deadly world of her parents' generation, the slick decadence of German fascism. These are some of the codas that critiques of Bausch's work tend to enshrine. But what are the vestiges of Bausch's tracks on the landscape of contemporary performance?

Like Tadeusz Kantor, Marguerite Duras, and Peter Handke, Bausch is interested in the drama *before* language intervenes and choreographs plays which, in many ways, dramatize the psychic scars Auschwitz and Hiroshima have engraved on the collective imagination. As she puts it, 'I try to find what I can't say in words, although I know it, I am looking to find what it is' (in Kisselgoff 1985: C4). Her productions are noted for their stunning, visceral, and apocalyptic environments: a stage surface covered with dead leaves (*Blue Beard*, 1977); a flooded stage (*Arien*, 1979); a grass floor (*1980*, 1980); a field of carnations bending in the wind (*Tanzabend Nelken*, 1982); a concrete wall that crumbles onstage (*Palermo, Palermo*, 1990). The setting of *Two Cigarettes in the Dark*, first produced in 1985, is composed of three gigantic glass cases inlayed into proscenium walls. One is filled with water and goldfish, the second with exotic fauna, and the third with desert sand and cacti. In a more recent piece, *Nur Du* (*Only You*, 1996), the stage is transformed into a transplanted forest of redwoods. The function of this bottled naturalism is hauntingly commemorative. Nature is artificially (and some might argue, morbidly) preserved in these lush wastelands. Animals also make their way into Bausch's surreal landscapes, but only to highlight the human body's mythic entrapment. Barking German shepherds reined-in by ominous guards patrol the false Eden of *Tanzabend Nelken*, recalling images of Nazi Germany. A life-size hippopotamus is desperately wooed by a woman whose love for him is not reciprocated in *Arien*. A black poodle appears and disappears in *Two Cigarettes*, padding gingerly on stage and off, as if to punctuate the world's flippant indifference to the humiliations taking place onstage.

Bausch is leery of sociopolitical explanations for her kinetic phantasms. Her responses to what have become well-known generalities about her work are always meticulously cautious: 'I can only make something very open, I'm not pointing out a view. There are conflicts between people, but they can be looked at from each side, from different angles' (in Hoffman 1994: 12), or, 'You can see it like this or like that. It just depends on the way you watch [. . .] You can always watch the other way' (in Hoghe 1980: 73). Ideological motives for her hypernaturalism are equally egregious in light of Bausch's ostensibly simple purpose: 'I think that this is beautiful: real things onstage – earth, leaves, water' (in *ibid.*: 68).

PATHWAYS TO A NEW THEATRE AESTHETIC

Bausch's footfalls are at once banal and philosophical, reverent and irreverent routines on the ground of Being. Her most quoted observations are 'I am not so much interested in how people move as in what moves them' (in Manning and Benson 1986: 43) and 'The work [. . .] is about relationships, childhood, fear of death, and how much we all want to be loved' (in Price 1990: 325). One might be tempted at first to assume that Bausch is praising pure feeling over the emotional detachment of formalism; certainly Bausch, among other Germans of her generation, has reexplored the subjectivist tradition of *Ausdruckstanz*, the dance of expression epitomized in the 1920s by the movement choirs of Expressionistic choreographers such as Rudolf Laban, Oskar Schlemmer, Mary Wigman, and Kurt Jooss – Bausch's mentor during the 1960s. As Raimund Hoghe puts it, 'In the theater of Pina Bausch one can experience many ways of looking, of becoming aware of one's subjective way of watching humans, relations, situations [. . .] there are many ways of seeing something within oneself as well as within others' (1980: 73). But I also suspect that Bausch wants to be taken quite literally when she speaks of a *mise-en-scène* based in what 'moves' people. She asks, that is: What emotions or psychic wounds physically shape the body's public and private trajectories? From what parts of the body is history recalled?

Bausch says only that the stories of her plays are about human relations: '[. . .] I have tried to see them and talk about them. [. . .] I don't know anything more important' (in Hoghe 1980: 65). Her subjects are people on the street, in everyday life: 'The way somebody walks or the way people carry their necks tells you something about the way they live or about the things that have happened to them' (*ibid.*). Similarly, idiosyncrasies are what she searches for in her actors: 'I pick my dancers as people. I don't pick them for nice bodies, for having the same height. [. . .] I look for the person [. . .] the personality' (in Loney 1985: 14). In brief, Bausch seems to be primarily interested in the choir of her dance company as an expression of the histories of individual bodies in relation to the larger cultural history of the body. [. . .] 'The history of what has been written in this form: as injuries, as hopes, as disappointments, as any experience at all' (Kirchman 1994: 42). Johannes Birringer suggests that Bausch's dialectical theatricality is rooted in social practice: 'The borderline in Bausch's tanztheater is the concrete human body, a body that has specific qualities and a personal history – but also a body that is written about, and written into social representations of gender, race, and class' (1986: 86).

In this sense, Bausch's aesthetic motive – often linked with Mary Wigman's[2] – might in fact be closer to Valeska Gert's.[3] As Susan Allene Manning and Melissa Benson suggest, Gert, like Wigman, 'confounded the conventional image of femininity projected by Isadora Duncan and other female soloists, but she did so in the spirit of satire and parody rather than as a means for transcending everyday reality' (1986: 38). [. . .]

Gert's dismissal of movement choirs as isolated communities of feeling in a compromised culture was politically astute and prophetic. Laban's choirs (sometimes as large as 1,200 participants), which originated after World War I, had been designed for communities to come together in the spirit of a festival. Later, they 'straddled social dance and theater dance' mainly through the efforts of Laban's students, who involved trade unions and church groups in their making (Manning and Benson 1986: 35). But under the Third Reich, when Goebbels's Ministry of Culture took over the arts and established new standards for dancers, such as proof of their Aryan origin and a return to German sources, *Ausdruckstanz*, or expression dance, was adopted as a prime propagandist aesthetic. And while Jean Weidt and Kurt Jooss, for instance, took positions against Hitler and went into exile when he came into power, a number of Laban's students – including Wigman – were coopted by the ministry (Manning and Benson 1986). Their works became exemplary vehicles for Nazi propaganda. Wigman was featured, along with Harold Kreutzberg and Gret Palucca, at the opening [of the] Olympic Games in Berlin in 1936. [. . .]

Like Gert, who during the late 1920s had asked Brecht to define epic theatre and received the pithy answer 'what you do' (Manning and Benson 1986: 38), Bausch dramatizes the *Gestus* of showing and the technique of *Verfremdung* through a 'specific application of the comic' (Servos 1981: 438). Bausch often breaks the monumental scale of her mythical environments and the emblematic gestures of her figures by interrupting her physical narratives and introducing the intimacy of cabaret talk, the tension of unmatrixed performance. Her actors periodically walk downstage and share personal stories or jokes with the audience. In *Arien* the same joke is told twice: 'A man came to the circus manager and asked him if he needed a bird imitator. "No" answered the circus manager. Then the man flew away through the window.' Bausch comments on a plethora of preexisting dance forms and, in so doing, deliberately undercuts the dancer's 'expressive self.' Her parody of the classical ballet repertoire is a case in point.

In *Two Cigarettes* a man holds a woman by her arms and legs and uses her posterior literally to crack the peanut he has placed on the stage floor. Through this kind of commentary, as Kay Kirchman argues, 'Pina Bausch is worlds away from the essentially romantic cosmology of expressive dance and the naive belief in building a counter world in the aesthetic of the dancing figure' (1994: 40). It is through the self-referential irony of postmodern pastiche that Bausch keeps her audience distanced and engaged. In the finale of *Two Cigarettes*, the entire company make their way, on their asses, to a door stage right, swaying in unison to Ravel's *La Valse*. But the last moments of this ten-minute exhilarating *lazzi* amount to nothing more than a massive pile-up at the door. Bausch's 'impossible' ending obstructs the possibility of complacency: the laugh is on us for craving the pleasure of aesthetic transcendence.

[. . . As] David Price notes, 'What distinguishes Bausch [. . .] is her development of an art form based upon a binary opposition that does not reproduce an either/or dichotomy; instead, Bausch's productions are both dance and theater' (1990: 322). Her tanztheater aesthetic can be defined only by what it is not. It is not dance in the conventional sense, since her dancers seldom dance. It isn't orthodox theatre in that dialogue does not sustain her drama. Instead, repeated gestures, sounds, smells, and random utterances do. As Bausch puts it, 'Our work is a mixture of elements [. . . : people] dance; people talk; others sing. We use actors [. . .] and we use musicians in the works, it's theater, really' (in Loney 1985: 19). Her tanztheater plays require a multilingual spectatorship, an alternate willingness to see and hear, which is why attempts to encompass her work are inevitably refracted through the graffiti of this century's most radical theories of performance: Artaud's cruelty, Brecht's alienation, Grotowski's confrontation, and Schechner's environmental theatre.

'SHE CAN MOVE LIKE SHE'S MADE OF RUBBER'

Bausch has been repeatedly chided for the gratuitous violence in her work, espe-cially as it pertains to female bodies. But Bausch is a pioneer in a dance aesthetic that confronts the cultural and historical significance of bodies by pushing her dancers to their physical limits and stretching *Gestus* to the breaking point of meaning. The body is Bausch's stage, yet, unlike the redemptive promise of ordeal art,[4] Bausch never falls prey to the notion of *returning* to an essential Real. Bodies, for her, seem to be enclosures with no issue.

'She can move like she's made of rubber,' recalls an old conservatory professor about her former pupil (in Langer 1994: 46). Bausch was born in 1940 in Solingen, a small town near Wuppertal, where her parents owned a tavern. She began her dance studies when she was 15, at the Folkwangschule. She was taught by Kurt Jooss, a former student of Mary Wigman's. [. . .] Jooss asked Bausch to be a soloist in his new Folkwang Ballet in Essen. There, Bausch choreographed pieces for Bar-tók's *Fragments* and Dorner's *In the Wind of Time*. Jooss asked her to take over the Folkwang Studios in 1969. [. . .]

A major turning point came in 1975, when Bausch staged Brecht and Weill's *The Seven Deadly Sins* and *Don't Be Afraid*, a compendium of songs from *The Three-penny Opera, Happy End*, and *The Rise and Fall of the City of Mahagonny*. These works – which required actors and singers as well as dancers – placed Bausch firmly at the intersection of expressive ballet and cabaret theatre. They also deepened Bausch's exploration of the sadomasochistic terms of heterosexual power relations. [. . .] Three of Bausch's most celebrated works followed in the late 1970s. *Café Müller* (1978) is a recollection of childhood, the memory of a daughter whose parents ran a bar. Bausch usually dances the main role. She remains on one side of the stage, recalling events that took place at the café, while on the other side her dancers act out the dream's content (Sullivan 1998: 45). *Kontakthof (Difficult Place)*, created the same year, is a searing indictment of the effects of the specta-tor's gaze on a self-conscious postmodern body trained for media acts (see fig. 22.1). *Arien* (1979), takes place on a flooded stage and dramatizes the fantasmatic space of memory (see fig. 22.2). As in most of her mature works, Bausch uses the musical principle of repetition as her primary structuring device, simultaneity as her main compositional tool. A mournful saxophone plays 'Stormy Weather' as men and women in bathing suits and beach robes dance, take pictures of each other, and literally immerse themselves in the atmosphere of a group on holiday. But Bausch's haunting themes soon make their way into this ostensibly benign seascape. A woman courts an indifferent hippopotamus, a man dances with a dead woman, a group of men turn a row of inert women into grotesque window man-nequins by dressing and coifing them while a sadistic master of ceremony forces them each to say 'ha.' The women all finally lose themselves in a disturbing cacophony of brutally commissioned utterances.

From early in her career, Bausch has exposed the power relations inherent in erotic negotiations, classical dance training, and theatrical representation. By the mid-1970s, she specifically inscribes the conflict between the sexes (Manning 1986), and by the 1980s her work examines gender as a compulsory performance. Bausch's distancing techniques are used in large part to explore the power relations of gendered bodies in representation. Price argues that '[h]er repeated movements

Fig. 22.1 Dance 'Cattle call' in Bausch's *Kontakthof*. (Photo by Gert Weigelt, courtesy of Princeton University Library.)

Fig. 22.2 The Brooklyn Academy of Music Opera House stage is transformed into a pool of ankle-deep water for *Arien* by Pina Bausch. (Photo by Ulli Weiss, courtesy of Princeton University Library.)

signify that behavior between men and women is reamed, culturally coded and determined, and just as inadequate as it is inept' (1990: 329). Bausch self-consciously uses mimesis as a grotesque form of mimicry and 'undermines the referent's authority' (Diamond 1989: 62). In *Kontakthof*, the 'signs' of gender are estranged through countermimicry, [. . .] but she also recognizes, as Judith Butler does, that those who fail to 'do' the signs of gender right are punished (Butler 1990). Bausch's pieces invariably dramatize the notion that:

> Gender is not a fact, the various acts of gender create the idea of gender, and without those acts, there would be no gender at all. [. . .] This repetition is at once a reenact-ment and reexperiencing of a set of meanings already socially established; it is the mundane and ritualized form of their legitimization.
>
> (Butler 1990: 277)

Bausch's plays are fraught with figures whose site of struggle is the relationship between their body and culturally sanctioned cloaks of legitimization. Women often tug at girdles and suffer high heels; men are shown to be restless, uncomfort-able in the deadly uniformity of suits and ties. And when men cross-dress, they appear equally endangered. In *Two Cigarettes*, a man enters in an evening gown but almost immediately takes it off. He stands in the middle of the stage in his under-wear and high heels unable to move. He finally removes the women's shoes, dons flippers, and enters the aquarium, where he immerses himself in water. Repeatedly, Bausch entrusts her dancers with what would appear to be the ludicrous and annihilating exercise of performing gender 'well,' that is, of expressing gender as a correlate of biological sex. In *Kontakthof* Bausch mercilessly spoofs this 'corporeal project' by requiring her company to face a movie screen on the back wall and view a documentary film on the mating rituals of ducks.

Bausch also calls conventional proxemics into question. Marianne Goldberg (1989: 111) describes a moment in Bausch's 1984 piece *Auf dem Gebirge hat man ein Geschrei gehört* (*On the Mountain a Cry Is Heard*) this way:

> In a prelude, the performers run as if terrorized through the area behind the audience [. . .] including us in the frame of their action. [. . .] Suddenly, a gang of men in white shirts and black trousers brutally force a resisting man and woman together into a kiss. This scene of enforced sexuality is repeated over and over to a fanfare of strident, heroic classical music. The grotesque portrayal of phallic/patriarchal sexuality develops into sadism that permeates the piece. Billie Holiday sings about a pastoral scene in the American South that is disrupted by the 'sudden smell of burning flesh.' The burning flesh serves as a metaphor for the performers' display of violence and pleasure in a theatrical marketplace. Sometimes vulnerability is tinged with black humor. Two women in flouncy green dresses perform 'innocent' cartwheels that reveal their underwear and sexy little dance phrases that make them available commodities.

In moments such as these Bausch openly confronts the complicated motivations of our desire and explores the genesis of performative acts by examining the power relations underlying representation. A woman in *Kontakthof* asks a male member of the audience for a quarter in order to ride the electric hobby horse on the side of the stage; this brief negotiation and her subsequent performance of sexualized passivity – in which she blankly gazes at the audience as she rocks to the horse's artificial cadence – expose the tacit rules of a representational economy which regards femininity as a compulsory public service. Right before the intermission of *Two Cigarettes* Mechthild Grossmann comes down to the audience and repeats in a monotone 'fifty cents, cinquente centimes, fifty cents, cinquente centimes.' We are once again publicly implicated as 'members of the economy of onlookers,' and, as Bausch puts it, 'we must look again and again' (in Birringer 1986: 87, 91). Her theatre is difficult and funny precisely because it lays bare the messy, inherently unequal, and costly business of representation, which, as Peggy Phelan reminds us, 'is almost always on the side of the one who looks, and almost never on the side of the one who is seen' (1993: 25). If art is made at a cost, then our complicity in its making is what Bausch, in part, would like us to experience.

As Heiner Müller noted, in Bausch's theatre, 'the image is a thorn in the eye and bodies write a text that defies publication, the prison of meaning' (in Daly 1986: 56). Bausch's dancers acknowledge and often literally confront the audience with physical and psychic scars, rendering the viewing body culpable for its presence, accountable for what it sees, painfully aware of its own dissecting eye/I. Bausch asks her performers to play themselves in scenes based on exercises and improvisations, located around a specific emotion. Their work takes place in real time, and through painful exertion. In *1980*, a woman skips around the stage fifty times, repeating the phrase 'I am tired' until her body is overcome with exhaustion. In *Palermo, Palermo*, Francis Viet plays 'Stormy Weather' on a sax as votive candles drip wax onto his flesh. In *Bandoneon* (1980), a dancer puts veal steaks in her shoes and dances *en pointe* as blood oozes out of them. In *Gebirge*, a man in a leotard and tiara suddenly whips across the stage stopping only to ask the audience, 'Why are you looking at me?' The performance in *Kontakthof* consists of a repeated audition; as in a dream, Bausch's automated dancers form single-sex 'cattle call' lines and auction their bodies off to us exposing teeth, profiles, arms, and legs. As Manning suggests, these are 'images of narcissism and self-display' (1986: 68). But the repeated gestures also refer to the malignant pageant our gaze helps to produce. [. . .] In moments such as these, Bausch seems to be simultaneously drawing on Artaudian notions of the divided body of Western history – a primal cry for lost unity – and eliciting Brecht's much hoped-for 'tears from the brain.'

Bausch's 'theatre of experience' to a great extent precludes a hermeneutic scheme in that 'change is brought about through experienced necessity instead of intellectual insight' (Servos 1981: 440). Yet her work 'refer[s] the spectator directly to reality' (437) because it 'aims for an emotional involvement in the formation of problems, not in the characters' (439). It offers itself to the 'comprehension of the seekers, the archeologists and the physionomists' through *all* the houses of the body (Kirchman 1994: 42, 40). Bausch's performance texts are often punctuated by verbal lacerations, avowals, confessions, or testimonials. But speech is never at the service of exposition or communication. Rather, words act as spontaneous emissions, states of mind and being, utterances that simply make audible the traces of a moment. The brilliance of Bausch's plays – and their potential as radical practice – is that they dramatize bodies which at once signify and escape signification (Diamond 1989) and whose embodied 'stories' take us outside of discourse, into the visceral and chaotic Impossible-Real of love, art, history. Because mimesis is regarded by Bausch as the malignant reproduction of self-alienating acts, the drama of her performers' bodies is shown to exceed a representational system that no longer contains them.

Yet, while Bausch in a general sense borrows from modernism's arsenal of confrontational devices, she is decidedly postmodern in that she does not depict the possibility of altering the social world she so boldly dramatizes. Her resistance to declaring her position, or providing a moral compass in her work, has led to serious indictments.[5] [. . .]

Bausch's plays are about loss on a primordial level. Her works take place in the aftermath of the certainties connected to love, belonging. They are about self-division and, therefore, 'reconciliation [. . .] can only be dealt with in her pieces as a (mainly unattainable) quest,' as Kay Kirchman writes. This concept of physicality manifests itself as a collective body, as the release and tracing back of the divided self to the aesthetic figure of an original unity' (Kirchman 1994: 40). Bausch's mediating ideology is precisely that there is no mediating ideology. For her to provide one would be to succumb to the very myths of transcendence she is deconstructing.

THE FISH OUT OF WATER STORIES, OR A THEATRE OF THE HISTORY OF THE TOTALITY OF THE BODY?

Bausch's tanztheater, in many regards, bypasses programmatic motives. Her work, for one, is profoundly metatheatrical and dramatizes the ontology of performance. In this sense, Bausch's plays can be linked to Beckett's drama of the collective unitary self in the wake of Cartesianism. Beckett's fiction and theatre dramatize the bankruptcy of positivism, the need for alternate paths to the knowable. As Beckett put it, speaking of *Endgame*:

> The crisis started with the end of the seventeenth century, after Galileo. The eighteenth century has been called the century of reason . . . they give reason a responsibility which it simply can't bear, it's too weak. [. . .] Now it is no longer possible to know everything, the tie between the self and things no longer exists. [. . .] *One must make a world of one's own in order to satisfy one's need to know, to understand, one's need for order.*
>
> (in McMullen 1994: 200; emphasis added)

[. . .] Like Beckett's protagonists, split off from their environment and enacting the homeless condition of their division through the impossibility of being there, where the being is (can such a place exist?), Bausch's use of her stage (the house of the body) exposes her dancers/our consciousness (the house of the mind), and repeatedly dislodges ontological certainty. She/they/we ask 'Who am I?' but the answer remains issueless.

Bausch's texts are demanding and compelling for the same reasons Beckett's are. She has found her own provisional order to satisfy temporarily our desire to know, and she offers her kinetic theatre of primordial sounds and gestures as a means to master the failure of knowable answers.

Bausch dramatizes the credo of Beckett's *The Unnamable* – 'I'm locked up, I'm in something, it's not I' – in part, through the repeated failures of her dancers to embrace binary logic and perform gender 'successfully.' But her work also draws on the recurring use of animals, and her fish-out-of-water stories are comical expressions of the cogito's deadly work, the hell of split ontology. A man tells a shaggy-dog story about training his pet fish to live on land. His goldfish dies when he returns it to water. As Goldberg notes about Bausch's 1984 *Gebirge*:

> [I]f the stage is covered with the dirt of a mountainside, many of the gestures are derived from swimming, rowing, or canoeing. Forming a line seated on the ground, groups of men or women mime a crew boat skimming across water. A woman flaps her whole body like a fish out of water; [. . .] This incongruity creates a friction between stage action and scenography that indicates fantasy [. . .]. [But] the displacement of this amphibian society onto dry land continually estranges even the most mundane action.
>
> (1989: 110)

[. . .] But if the place of the body is elusive, so too is the body of place. What is the ontology of place, and how can it be represented in any truthful sense? Bausch's *Only You* is intentional mimicry, rooted – as the title suggests – in 1950s Americana and based on temporary and arbitrary observations: mimicry. One senses that Bausch fears, as Phelan puts it, that '"the thing itself," (you, me, love, art), will disappear before [she] can reproduce it' (Phelan 1997: 12). As Rolf Hemke (1997: 37) noted when seeing the production in Germany:

> Here, love means kissing at school, between ice creams and cheerleaders. Scarcely developed images fly past. [. . .] But there is something rotten in these United States. Someone tries to climb the walls of the theatre, another piles up as many chairs as possible on a woman. A black streetsweeper wants to paint a white woman. [. . .] In the score, we first hear today's hits, then boogies from the fifties and sixties, and Latin American rhythms. Relationships between the sexes remain at the dance school level. When couples come on, they look like dummies in the windows of department stores. Either that or they let themselves go in terrible bursts of anger: 'Are you bored?' she asks, cutting the straps of a sleeveless top. Perhaps the shock of the impossibility of meeting is what gives us the impression that this is Pina Bausch's coldest work.

But how could Bausch really ever meet the subcutaneous, and catastrophic, racial history of the West other than through recycled cultural clichés? Even her evocation of nature references a kind of cowboy nostalgia for a time when nature was vast, full of the romantic promise of its own expendability:

> For the set, Peter Papst planted giant trees from the California forests. When during the solos of the second part, six monumental trunks stand on the stage, they make the dancers look like miniature people or models symbolizing the essence of solitude. [. . .] Autumn leaves rain down.
>
> (Hemke 1997: 37)

Bausch's necessary cruelty extends to her use of 'real' nature, torn from its organic root and bluntly placed in the artificial enclosure of a theatre. This gesture – the mythical rendering of a catastrophic, global displacement – is in and of itself her most powerful metaphor for the fragmentation of our condition through the cultural repression of organic bodies. Such violence can seem tasteless to some. Gitta Honegger (1990: 57), for instance, eloquently recalls her interior monologue while viewing *Gebirge*:

> The most shocking moment [. . .] happens [. . .] when the company members drag out about 40 huge pine trees and dump them all over the stage. They use them for a few

minutes to play little games of childlike seductions and hide-and-seek, and then they pull the trees off the stage again. [. . .] The scene is fraught with irresponsible cruelty. The felled trees, their needles still lusciously green, look like fresh corpses, beautiful and pathetically tragic – abused. I feel sorry for them. A cathartic effect in the end? No, I am angry. Angry at Bausch. I can't accept the fact that in order to show us what we are, the artist must resort to the same deadly ruthlessness.

These gestures are irresponsible, but not gratuitously so. Like the damaged bodies of her dancers, and the damaged body of history, Bausch never forgets that the body of nature 'bares the livid scars of dislocation, dissection and injury' (Kirchman 1994: 40). It is not that her repossessed animals, earth, trees, water, and leaves are merely out of place, inappropriately colonized, but rather that we no longer have a knowable, organic connection to them: we have forgotten ourselves in relation to them. Bausch demonstrates that nature is an abandoned 'object of hopeless yearning,' nothing more at present than an aestheticized luxury (Kirchman 1994: 40). The cost, to Bausch, of this repeated showing, is that her audience may tire of her ruthless and extravagant spectacle. This danger is exemplified by Jacques Roue's brief article on Bausch's 1995 Paris tour entitled, 'To Go See, or Not To Go See Pina,' in which he wonders if her redundant work is still worth viewing. Bausch's 1997 piece *The Window Washer*, which premiered at the Brooklyn Academy of Music, was inspired by a stay in Hong Kong. Commissioned and predominantly financed by the Hong Kong Arts Festival Society and the Goethe Institute in Hong Kong, this new work, in which 'confessional monologues have been largely replaced with pure dance solos' (Kisselgoff 1997: BI), has also drawn ambivalent responses. Anna Kisselgoff remarks, 'for the first time, the underlying effort is beginning to show. [. . .] There could have been a better way to edit the piece, which is not as much long as it is padded' (*ibid.*).

But padding, whether aesthetic or prosthetic, is a defense against the Real. Bausch, clearly, has little interest in the belief that bodies can be authentically located or truthfully reproduced. Whatever the merit of *The Window Washer*, it is self-consciously packaged to reflect the packaging of bodies, the packaging of desire. Papst's backdrop this time is of billboards and neon signs. Bausch contrasts the frenzied rush of her dancers' bodies – as if projected toward the nearest shopping mall super sale – with the repeated and seemingly futile gestures of a lone window washer. As Kisselgoff (1997: B5) concludes, this work is once again about the cost of representational economies:

> If Ms. Bausch is concerned with the futility and hope of human existence, then she has not done badly with her metaphor of a window washer faced with miles of glass skyscrapers in Hong Kong. [. . . But] when the characters rush around offering drinks and fruit to the audience, they do so because they come from one huge duty-free shop of a city where the seller aims to please.

Bausch's is a theatre of traces, culminating out of and into aftermaths. The embodiment of her substance is that she does not have a 'system' of notation *or mise-en-scène*. Her repertory will most likely die with her (Sullivan 1994: 47). In this sense, Pina Bausch – a quintessential witness of the postmodern condition, whose pieces are fraught with images of consumerism and waste – may be writing the truest, most credible naturalism of our time, a painful shorthand for the ecological drama Chekhov inaugurated over a century ago. The ending of *Two Cigarettes in the Dark* provides a mock answer to the felled trees of history's cherry orchards, as Grossmann, wearing an evening gown and opera gloves, a cigarette hanging from her mouth, splits wooden coat hangers with an ax and later pitches hay, while the company applauds her efforts.

NOTES

1 My title partially borrows from Susan Allene Manning's essay in *TDR* 30, no. 2 (T110): 'Interestingly, this mode juxtaposes two extremes of scale, the monumental and the intimate' (66).

2 This connection is made because Kurt Jooss, Bausch's mentor during the 1960s, had studied with Wigman before the war.

3 Bausch has on numerous occasions become impatient with imposed links between her work and that of Wigman and Jooss. In 1985, for instance, she told Glenn Loney: 'I never saw Mary Wigman or Harold Kreutzberg. Never. Not even in films; pictures only. But I certainly saw Martha Graham, and I studied the Graham technique. Of course because of the school where I studied and worked in Essen, the Folkwang, I had a long experience with Kurt Jooss, and he was wonderful as a teacher. [. . .] I studied with Jooss, yes, but I had many teachers. You can say I'm eclectic, but what is eclectic? [. . .] I don't like to call what I do a "system". [. . .] Whatever I saw, whatever I learned, I have *digested* it all. Oh, I could have a system if I wanted to make one up. But I don't want to do that; every time, I want to try new things. For every production I want to try something different' (1985: 17, 19).

4 As Peggy Phelan notes in *Unmarked: The Politics of Performance*, ordeal or 'hardship' art offers the promise of redemptive meaning in that it 'shares a fundamental bond with ritual' because it 'invoke[s] a distinction between presence and representation by using the singular body as a metonymy for the apparently nonreciprocal experience of pain. This performance calls witnesses to the singularity of the individual's death and asks the spectator to [. . .] share that death by rehearsing for it. ([. . .] The Catholic Mass, for example is the ritualized performative promise to remember and to rehearse for the Other's death)' (Phelan 1993: 152). Bausch, on the other hand, like Beckett, seems to suggest that the joke is on us for seeking ourselves through the Other. For them absence is absence; theirs is a theology of the absent.

5 For an interesting discussion of critical responses to Bausch during the 1980s, see 'What the critics say about tanztheater' in *TDR* (*TDR* 1986: 80–4).

WORKS CITED

Anderson, Jack (1996) 'Pina Bausch? Funny? Yes. And sad.' *New York Times*, 5 October: 13, 18.

Birringer, Johannes (1986) 'Dancing across borders.' *TDR* 30, 2 (T110): 85–97.

Butler Judith (1990) 'Performative acts and gender constitution: an essay in phenomenology and feminist theory.' In *Performing Feminism: Feminist Critical Theory and Theatre*, ed. Sue-Ellen Case, 270–82. Baltimore: The Johns Hopkins University Press.

Daly, Ann (1986) 'Tanztheater: the thrill of the lynch mob or the rage of a woman?' *TDR* 30, 2 (T110): 46–56.

Davies, Paul (1994) 'Three novels and four nouvelles: giving up the ghost be born at last.' In *The Cambridge Companion to Beckett*, ed. John Pilling, 43–66. Cambridge: Cambridge University Press.

Diamond, Elin (1989) 'Mimesis, mimicry, and the the the True-Real.' *Modern Drama* 32, 1: 59–72.

Goldberg, Marianne (1989) 'Artifice and authenticity.' *Women and Performance* 4, 2: 104–17

Hemke, Rolf C. (1997) 'Pina Bausch: where does the dance begin?' *UBU Scènes d'Europe, Revue Théâtrale Européenne* 7 (July): 36–7.

Hoffman, Eva (1994) 'Pina Bausch: catching intuitions on the wing.' *New York Times*, 11 September.

Hoghe, Raimund (1980) 'The theatre of Pina Bausch.' *TDR* 24, 1 (T85): 63–74.

Holden, Stephen (1985) 'When avant-garde meets mainstream.' *New York Times*, 29 September.

Honegger, Gitta (1990) 'Form as torture: found meanings between Bausch's and Kantor.' *Theater* 17, 12: 56–60.

Kirchman, Kay (1994) 'The totality of the body: an essay on Pina Bausch's aesthetic.' *Ballet International/Tanz aktuell Heft* 5: 37–43.

Kisselgoff, Anna (1985) 'Pina Bausch dance: key is emotion.' *New York Times*, 4 October: C1, C4.

—— (1997) 'Man as a window washer and a metaphor for futility.' *New York Times*, 6 October: B1, B5.

Langer, Roland (1994) 'Compulsion and restraint, love and angst: the post-war German Expressionism of Pina Bausch,' trans. Richard Sikes. *Dance Magazine* June: 46–8.

Loney, Glenn Meredith (1985) 'I pick my dancers as people.' *On the Next Wave, Brooklyn Academy of Music* 3, 1–2: 14–19.

McMullen, Anna (1994) 'Samuel Beckett as director: the art of mastering failure.' In the *Cambridge Companion to Beckett*, ed. John Pilling, 196–208. Cambridge: Cambridge University Press.

Manning, Susan Allene (1986) 'An American perspective on Tanztheater.' *TDR* 30, 2 (T110): 57–79.

Manning, Susan Allene, and Melissa Benson (1987) 'Interrupted continuities: modern dance in Germany.' *TDR* 30, 2 (T110): 30–45.

New York Times (1936) '100,000 roar frantic greeting to Hitler at opening Olympic Games.' 2 August.

Phelan, Peggy (1993) *Unmarked: The Politics of Performance*. London: Routledge.

—— *(1997) Mourning Sex: Performing Public Memories*. London: Routledge.

Price, David W. (1990) 'The politics of the body: Pina Bausch's Tanztheater.' *Theatre Journal* 42, 3: 322–31.

Roue, Jacques (1997) 'Pina à voir ou ne pas voir.' *Saisons de la Danse* 265: 6.

Servos, Norbert (1981) 'The emancipation of dance: Pina Bausch and the Wuppertal Dance Theater,' trans. Peter Harris and Pia Kleber. *Modern Drama* 231, 4: 435–47.

Sullivan, Scott (1998) 'The laugh is on us.' *Newsweek*, 13 June: 45–7.

TDR (1986) 'What the critics say about Tanztheater.' *TDR* 30, 2 (T110): 80–4.

23

HAIKU IN THE FLESH
Oguri's theatre of transmutation

Meiling Cheng

2000

BWL in L.A.

Naoyuki Oguri's career as a Los Angeles-based, live art practitioner is fascinating in its seemingly inconsonant components.[1] A Japanese national, Oguri has settled in L.A. because this happens to be the cultural site that could support his work as a full-time artist. Having established himself in the United States, he still clings to Japan, which has now become a regular stop in the itinerary of his international performance tours. Although Oguri regards himself as a dancer/choreographer, he functions more closely as a performance director, a maker of *mise-en-scène* that demands a comprehensive control of the theatrical matrix (that is, the time–space–action–performer–audience circuit of theatricality). His performance art excels as dance, but it exceeds the normative range of dance to encompass theatre: a choreographer as a director. The press often identifies Oguri and his company Renzoku's performance works as 'butoh,' which is perhaps the most popular Japanese post-war live art form known to the West (see Klein 1988). Oguri himself, nevertheless, acknowledges only a brief encounter with the charismatic butoh founder Tasumi Hijikata. He prefers to trace his artistic lineage, instead, to Body Weather Laboratory (BWL), a school of kinetic training methods founded by Hijikata's younger contemporary Min Tanaka.

The sense of incongruity characteristic of Oguri's artistic biography also extends to his aesthetic. As his kinetic methodology dictates, Oguri's dance/theatre pieces actively engage the performing bodies in eccentric and strenuous motion. I find his artistic direction most distinctive, however, in its treatment of non-motion and in its non-interventionist tendency. The former displays protracted moments of still-ness where even a 'regular' breath feels like an abrupt happening; the latter allows the performers to inhabit the theatrical present as if their human bodies were no different from the external environment.

These 'inconsonant components' in Oguri's art practice result largely from his particular cultural location. In a city where immigration and diasporic trans-plantation constitute a major cultural ethos, Oguri's career path, exceptional as it is, points to the paradigmatic existence of an international artist working in the field of performance. His task here lies in negotiating his native cultural heritage with the onset of foreign stimuli in the new host environment while exploiting the multimedia potentials of his art practice. A successful solution he has applied so far pivots on the non-verbal basis of his chosen performance mode. He was able to cultivate a corporeal vocabulary that eludes the language barriers of different nations and draws inspirations from multiple cultural sources. The art medium's transcultural condition frees the artist from having to confront an either/or scenario: he does not have to forfeit his Japanese legacy for his residency in the contemporary American art world. Thus, Oguri transcends his own cultural limits not through an act of substitution but through one of aggregation, adding his South Central trenchcoat to his Tokyo fundoshi and mixing Beatles pop lyricism with Kaoru Abe's esoteric effulgence.[2]

It is important to recognize that the process of 'transculturation' affects, if to varying degrees, both the migrating subject and the host environment. Whereas Oguri's cultural location has resituated his *body weather* performance in a North American, multiethnic, and post-industrial urban *laboratory*, his contribution as a performance maker – who routinely choreographs, designs, directs, and performs self-authored dance theatre pieces – also stands to disrupt the pedigree of Western auteur-directors in twentieth-century theatre. What was once other has become part of the same; what is deemed 'the same,' then, may have always already muffled or concealed the inflected otherness within. How many Oguris were/are there already in the bloodline nominally termed 'Euro-American directing'? Perhaps the

Fig. 23.1 The 1998 premiere of Oguri's *thestreamofconsciousness*. (Photo by Roger Burks, courtesy of Meiling Cheng.)

Fig. 23.2 The 1998 premiere of Oguri's *thestreamofconsciousness*.
(Photo by George Sandoval, courtesy of Meiling Cheng.)

label 'Euro-American' could only designate a geographic location, the 'where' rather than the 'how' of an artist's work. On this note, the following essay assesses Oguri's intrusion into the cumulative façade of 'sameness' identified as 'Euro-American directing,' probing a subtle disruption instigated more by the artist's lived circumstances than by his will.

OGURI AND RENZOKU

Oguri began performing as a solo artist in 1984 by enacting concept-based happenings on the streets of Tokyo. He was intrigued by the famed Anti-Art (*Han-geijutsu*) performances of Hi Red Center and its cofounder Genpei Akasegawa's highly publicized trial in 1964. Akasegawa was convicted of forging counterfeit 1,000-yen notes, even though those notes were only printed on one side. During the trial, the suspect identified himself as 'a Happening artist'; he further turned the judiciary procedure into a quasi-art exhibition by demonstrating sample performances and inviting many artists and critics to appeal on his behalf (see Paik 1994: 77–81). Akasegawa's renegade spirit was shared by another iconic personality in Japan's postwar era: Tatsumi Hijikata, the secretive artist/dandy who, together with another master dancer/choreographer, Kazuo Ohno, founded *Ankoku Butoh* (the stamping dance of utter darkness).[3] Unaware of Ohno's practice until much later, Oguri decided to take a few dance workshops with Hijikata, who was, by then, in semi-retirement from the stage.

If Oguri's exposure to the legend of Akasegawa affirmed his affinity with an idea of art, then his experience with Hijikata lent him a form of artistic expression that would become his aesthetic discipline. As Oguri remembers, his initiation into dance came from watching his father's sweaty back at work. This unspeakable nostalgia revisited him while he observed Hijikata, who offered a name to his hitherto unidentified obsession: 'It is Dance' (Oguri 1998). Through Hijikata's recommendation, Oguri began formal training with Min Tanaka, who was the principal dancer in *Ren-ai Butoh-ha Teiso: Foundation of the Dance of Love* (1984), a piece choreographed by Hijikata and presented in Tokyo. Tanaka had been conducting Body Weather Laboratory workshops since 1978 and in 1981 he founded the company Mai-juku, in which Oguri participated between 1985 and 1990. Thus, Oguri owes his artistic debt more to Tanaka's BWL than to Hijikata's Ankoku Butoh. Tanaka, however, prefers to identify himself as 'the legitimate son of Tatsumi Hijikata.'[4] There is then a certain connection – aesthetic or otherwise – between BWL and Ankoku Butoh.

Similar to other butoh masters, Tanaka urges his disciples to branch out and found their own schools and performance troupes elsewhere. Oguri followed this tradition and in the early 1990s, with his life and career partner Roxanne Steinberg (an L.A. native), brought the BWL work to L.A. Out of their first BWL participants, they formed a company called Renzoku (a Japanese word meaning 'continuum') in 1993, while taking up artistic residency in La Boca, a chapel-turned-warehouse performance space located inside Sunshine Mission/Casa De Rosas in South Central L.A.

BEFORE OR AFTER THE ATOMIC FLASH?

Body Weather Laboratory consists of a three-part training program that starts with 'rigorous mind/body, muscle/bone training,' to 'specific stretching and relaxing exercises concerned with breathing and alignment,' to 'explorations designed to sharpen focus and develop the scope of expression through the body' (Oguri 1998). In its commitment to discovering and cultivating the maximum potentials of the human body in stillness and movement, BWL upholds butoh's affirmation of 'the dance which lies *within* the body' (Klein 1988: 27). BWL further highlights the body's interactions with the external surroundings. The latter emphasis is specified in Oguri and Steinberg's statement that their BWL research investigates 'expression through the body within different environments'(1998).

Coincidentally, BWL's focus on the circumstantial juxtaposition between the 'soft' body and the 'hard' environment recalls a terrifying image memorialized in Fumio Kamei's film *Ikite-iteyokata* (*The Shadow on the Stone*): 'the preserved silhouette of a man burned into a rock by the atomic flash' in Hiroshima.[5] Before pursuing the connection further, I must confess that neither Tanaka nor Oguri has mentioned the influence of this image on BWL. While BWL, similar to butoh, grew out of Japan's postwar experimental art scenes, it is impossible to isolate a single image as the catalyst for all the post-Hiroshima art forms transmitted from Japan to the world. I nevertheless find this image of a human imprint on a rock surface an unexpectedly telling metaphor for Oguri's approach to BWL, reinterpreted through the theatre directed by him.

Abstracting from its catastrophic history, a human imprint on a rock provides a singular image for Tanaka's elusive coinage 'body weather.' Tanaka has never fully articulated the conceptual foundation for Body Weather Laboratory. Perhaps following Hijikata's resistance to theory, Tanaka merely offered the evocative term itself, along with some specific training methods. Based on my own conception, then, BWL involves at least three thematic propositions: (1) The *body* is troped as a microcosm with its different climate zones (*weather*) – the body as a thermokinetic landscape that generates both heat (thermo-) and motions (kinetics). (2) The *body* (as a microcosm) is placed within the *weather* (as the macrocosm), which is in turn a metaphor for the uncontrollable environment. (3) The *body* is merged with and becomes (part of) the *weather*; the *body* (perceived as a mere object with temperature) is assimilated into the *weather* dynamics. This last proposition stands in closest proximity to the post-Hiroshima image of the human profile on the rock, which demonstrates the power of an immeasurable (nuclear) force that managed to *mineralize* a human body at a split second, the second that equalized all weather zones.

Combining the first two propositions brings us to a common theatrical situation where a performer – as a microcosmic body weather – enacts a work at an open rather than an enclosed site. The *weather* at this open site is the performative condition confronting the performing *body*; the performance is literally an experiment in the *body weather laboratory*. This scenario offers us an angle to read Oguri and Renzoku's pieces, for the company often performs outdoors, raising the stake of their BWL work. The choice for an open performance site subjects the dancing bodies to the contingencies of an uncertain environment/weather, while it simultaneously renders that open environment a live set for their performance. The performing bodies are read as specific thermokinetic landscapes juxtaposed with a larger landscape; there is a free circulation of multifarious weather zones in between these bodies and amid the weathered environment that sustains and frames them.

The montage of moving flesh with an extensive, unframed site addresses the investigation of BWL; it also contributes to an innovative use of space in the theatrical matrix. Take, for example, *A Flame in the Distance* (1997), a collaborative piece between Renzoku and the Illustrious Theatre Orchestra, directed by Shane Cadman. The piece was performed in the California Plaza, the outdoor common in a shopping mall built on the Bunker Hill area in downtown L.A. Like a basin carved into mountains of architecture or a large clearing in an urban jungle, California Plaza is surrounded by sleek skyscrapers, commercial and institutional high-rise buildings, and adjacent to the Museum of Contemporary Art (designed by the Japanese architect Arata Isozaki). The two collaborating directors in this piece, Oguri and Cadman, fully utilize the site by composing a performance trajectory that, through action rather than spoken instruction, leads the audience from one section to another. The performers – in this case including both Renzoku and the Illustrious Theatre Orchestra – become the moving 'body weather' that animates the apparently inert built environment. Since the performance starts at dusk (8 p.m. in September when the last daylight still lingers in L.A.), a most dramatic body weather experiment consists of the change from the gradually fading natural light to the even brilliance of electric lights, together with the actual drop in the surrounding temperature.

The body being absorbed into the weather – as per my third thesis regarding BWL above – appears as a preternatural performative trait in Oguri's theatre. Through what I might call an aesthetics of *animistic transmutation*, Oguri and the performers directed by him often identify with the creatures they embody, the props they use, the themes they represent, and the environment they inhabit to such an extent that they become perceptually fused with these others.

Such an aesthetic process of animistic transmutation is of course not a new invention by BWL. It echoes an ancient Japanese theatre technique practiced for centuries by Noh actors who purport to be possessed by the spirit of the masks that barely cover their whole faces (see Keene 1966; Maruoka and Yoshikoshi 1975; Komparu 1983). The practice reflects the Shintoistic belief in animism, which envisions a cosmos of natural objects and landscapes teeming with the spirits that endow them with gradations of divinity. The actors in Noh are therefore able to cohabit the stage with their masks, costumes, and symbolic props (such as the fan) as equals. Further, they are ready to be *animated*, hence transmuted, by these nonhuman others. The premodern and indigenous belief in animism has retained its hold on Ankoku Butoh, even though the dramaturgical symbolism of Noh was rejected by Hijikata and Ohno (Klein 1988: 5–23). It was a tragic irony that, before Ankoku Butoh or BWL, such a spiritual belief had already suffered a strange imitation, like a horrific or mocking quotation, in the violent spectacle of Hiroshima. The human subject who had suffered the fate of becoming a profile on a rock in Hiroshima had also undergone a process of transmutation, one that occasioned a qualitative change in his body by melding it with the rock's calcareous substance: the man and the rock have become equals in that fusion.

ANIMISTIC TRANSMUTATION: LIQUID FLAMES

Whether Oguri was inspired by the premodern Japanese heritage of animism or by the post-Hiroshima shadow on the stone or by something else entirely, I have witnessed this process of animistic transmutation performatively achieved by Oguri and Renzoku. In performance, Oguri and his dancers seem to be able to surrender their humanities to the impetus of the moment, which leads them to become a tree, a pair of high heels, a fixture on the wall, the wind, or a monkey/duck in the mud. To me, such a fusion between mutually alien others is a core experience in *A Flame in the Distance.*

The piece happened in the fall, a time-frame that inspired Oguri to link it broadly with the *Obon* holidays in Japan. *Obon* is a week-long celebration in August in commemoration of the ancestral dead. People would carve potatoes into different animal shapes, with tooth-picks serving as the legs. At the end of the week, they put the sculpted potatoes in the water so that the dead ancestors could ride on the animals to the ocean. Legends have it that exactly after *Obon*, the fireflies suddenly all disappear. Indeed, images of fireflies, flightiness of being, and quickened ghosts enliven the body weather of *A Flame in the Distance.*

The action begins in a side pocket of the California Plaza, centering on a small, flat, and low fountain base built with a couple of concrete-paved concentric circles on the ground. Numerous water holes, now dry, appear as metal rings on the concentric circles. As the audience sits on concrete steps opposite the fountain, four dancers from Renzoku (Lakshimi Aysola, Boaz Barkan, Jamie Burris, and Dona Leonard), dressed in white and each holding in their mouths a string attached to a white balloon, move slowly from different corners in low squatting positions. Accompanied by a solo clarinet, the dancers survey their joint geography in their halting routes and eventually join Oguri, who has been dancing a gyrating solo on the fountain base. The white balloons, promptly released, disperse into the graying sky; in a distance, they look like fireflies carrying their contained flames in an autumn journey. A sound of explosion suddenly occurs, then another, and another, building a rhythmic chant. They are the sounds of motors pumping out water from the metal rings. The streams rush out in such a velocity and diffusion that they look like splendid fireworks, with the dancers at times cowering under and at times exulting over these liquid flames. A transposition of two opposing elements (water and fire = water as fire) is perceptually realized in a sonic, visual, and haptic drama of fluctuating motions and temperatures.

Whereas the performative transposition of natural elements provides a highlight for the opening sequence of *A Flame in the Distance*, an emotional admixture of contrary moods – such as melancholy and jubilation, solitude and plenitude – demonstrates a different kind of animistic transmutation in this BWL performance. Prompted by the nomadic dancers, the audience moves to California Plaza's central courtyard, which revolves around a huge square pond connected with a dam. Renzoku dancers, now changed to black, pick up canvas water buckets with their mouths and promenade around the waterfront. They move like grazing cows or donkeys on the bank, while Oguri walks across the pond, disappearing into the darkness. In a pavilion next to the pond, the six musicians with the Illustrious Theatre Orchestra (including Scott McIntosh's clarinet, Greg Adamson's cello, Arthur Bowansky's violin, Cadman's and Ron Shelton's keyboards, and John P. Hoover's bass clarinet) present a minimalist melody evoking Catholic mass motifs. The dancers with buckets cruise into the pond, gradually lowering their bodies until only their heads and buckets are floating above the water. Like a random assembly of spectres, their apparitions emerge in encrypted contrast with the steel-and-glass urban environment that encases their kinetic rituals.

The particular visual geography of the performance site comes into vivid play at this juncture in *A Flame in a Distance*. Similar to other spectators who scatter around the stairs and the upper level of the shopping mall, I watch the action from a *distance*, for we are all blocked by the boundary of the pond. Such a physical distance heightens the equivocality of our perceptual dramas. Against the grandiose urban landscape and the illuminated pond, the floating objects in the water look lonesome, like hapless birds caught in the waves. Viewed from a different mindset, however, they also look like full-blown lilies, at home in their elements. Now, Oguri's solitary figure, as if out of thin air, appears on the upper-middle level of the dam, dancing his way down while other dancers are veering upwards. The moment they join cues the dam to come alive: a magnificent waterfall cascades from the top of the aquatic plateau to immerse the dancers in its grandeur.

TO SEEM OR NOT TO SEEM

The three conceptual propositions for BWL with which I coordinate my readings of Oguri and Renzoku's performances merely sketch out some points of departure for meditation – Zen-like or not. To me, a most extraordinary dimension in Oguri's directing is the philosophical space it affords to my thought even as I chart the 'body weather' of my perceptions. The process of animistic transmutation noted above could have happened only in the realm of perceptions, for the dancers remain intact after their performance ends, unlike the post-Hiroshima profile on the rock. The climate of my perceptions is manipulated by the ability of these performers to empty out their human wills and to become continuous with their surroundings, existing as unintrusively as a blade of grass in a meadow or a sand painting in a desert. Without the benefit of an external force like the atomic flash, these dancers seem to be able to turn that violence inward, letting it implode like a breath-holding tranquility: they endure their own progressive fossilization with patience and intensity. I am induced into a state of reverie not by their appeal to my attention but by the absence of that appeal, which encourages my perceptions to *lapse* sporadic-ally only to be shocked by the minutest mutation in the unfolding spectacle – 'ah, he has moved from squatting to an asymmetrical crouch but when did it happen?'

The question of *when* looms large in my perceptual lapses, which are enabled by the prolonged sense of time on which Oguri's choreography operates. He allows non-motion to thrive without fearing the audience's distraction. A predominant effect of such temporal prolongation is *syncopation*: the players and viewers seem never fully harmonized in their speeds/beats of perceptions.[6] There is then a dis-placement of narrative certainty in Oguri's thermokinetic theatre. He uses a body language eluding semantics. That language, rid of its desire for a seamless communication, further abets the eccentricity of those syncopated (mis-stressed) perceptual beats.

On the whole, Oguri's non-interventionist aesthetics reinforce what I can best describe paradoxically as an *active stance of passivity*, which permits multivalent actions to unfold without the imperious control of an authorial commentary. 'Let-ting be be the finale of seem,' the suggestive verse from William Carlos Williams, applies aptly to Oguri's artistic direction, which consciously indulges the theatrical realm of metaphors (seem) to be inhabited by the often unmarked, ephemeral, and inexplicable flow of embodied behaviors (be). Herbert Blau has taken this famous verse from Williams in a different direction in his brilliant essay 'Letting be be finale of seem,' arguing on the behalf of 'seem' that 'Letting be was never the finale of seem, only a nuance, the readiness which may not be all but as much as we've got if we're lucky to have that' (1977:72). My take on 'be' and 'seem' here places stress on their varying degrees of ostentatious display; the former emphasizes the exhibited state of non-contested existence; the latter accentuates the intentionality of authorial intervention. The paradox of Oguri's directing lies in his construction of a negative presence in performance, yielding much freedom to my contemplation precisely by declining to insist on my hermeneutic engagement. His non-*seem* animates my being *be*.

NOTES

1 Portions of this essay are taken from chapter 7 of my forthcoming book *In Other Los Angeleses: Multicentric Performance Art* (University of California Press, 2001). All biographical and historical information concerning Oguri and Renzoku is based on my interviews with Oguri and Roxanne Steinberg on 10 November 1998 and 23 September 1999. I also interviewed Sherwood Chen, a dancer who sometimes collaborates with Renzoku, on 11 December 1997. Naoyuki Oguri goes by his family name alone in his performance works.

2 Trenchcoats and fundoshi (a kind of loincloth worn by Japanese wrestlers) are frequently featured costume pieces in Oguri and Renzoku's performances. The Beatles song 'Abbey Road' (1969) and Kaoru Abe's 'Partitas' (1973) were included in Oguri and Renzoku's *'behind eyeball' Fu-Ru-I (sift) # 2* (1995).

3 See Klein 1988; Goodman 1971; *TDR* 1986; Nanako and Martin 2000.

4 Cited in http://www.radio.cz/archa/tanbio.html. This website also contains a brief biography of Tanaka. See also the interview with Tanaka by Bonnie Sue Stein (1986).

5 Paul Schimmel makes the transcultural influences of the avant-garde apparent. For example, he cites the fact that the French action artist Yves Klein attributes the source of his 'anthropométries' (body paintings) to this body/rock image that he witnessed during a 1953 visit to Hiroshima (Schimmel 1998: 31).

6 I pay homage to Gertrude Stein here for the concept of syncopation. In her essay 'Plays,' Stein writes, 'The thing that is fundamental about plays is that the scene as depicted on the stage is more often than not one might say it is almost always in syncopated time in relation to the emotion of anybody in the audience' (1998: 3).

WORKS CITED

Blau, Herbert (1977) 'Letting be be finale of seem: the future of an illusion.' In *Performance in Postmodern Culture*, ed. Michel Benamou and Charles Caramello. Madison, WI: Coda Press.

Goodman, David (1971) 'New Japanese Theater.' *TDR* 15, 3: 154–68.

Keene, Donald (1966) *No: The Classical Theatre of Japan*. Tokyo and Palo Alto: Kodansha International.

Klein, Susan Blakeley (1988) *Ankoku Buto*: *The Premodern and Postmodern Influences on the Dance of Utter Darkness*. Ithaca, NY: East Asia Program, Cornell University.

Komparu, Kunio (1983) *The Noh Theater: Principles and Perspectives*. New York: Weatherhill.

Maruoka, Daiji, and Tatsuo Yoshikoshi (1975) *Noh*, trans. Don Kenny. Osaka: Hoikusha.

Nanako, Kurihara, and Carol Martin, eds. (2000) Special issue featuring Hijikata and postwar Japanese theatre. *TDR* 44, 1 (T165).

Oguri, Naoyuki (1998) Press packet.

Paik, Nam June (1994) 'To catch up or not to catch up with the West: Hijikata and Hi Red Center.' In *Japanese Art after 1945*: *Scream against the Sky*. New York: Harry N. Abrams, in association with the Yokohama Museum of Art, The Japan Foundation, The Guggenheim Museum, and San Francisco Museum of Modern Art.

Schimmel, Paul (1998) 'Introduction.' In *Out of Actions*: *Between Performance and the Objects 1949–1979*, ed. Paul Schimmel. Los Angeles: The Museum of Contemporary Art.

Stein, Bonnie Sue (1986) 'Min: Tanaka: farmer/dancer or dancer/farmer: an interview.' *TDR* 30, 2 (T110): 142–51.

Stein, Gertrude (1935) 'Plays.' In *Lectures in America*. New York: Random House.

TDR (1986) Special issue on butoh. *TDR* 30, 2 (T110).

Part III

THEATRES OF COMMUNITY AND TRANSCULTURATION

24

INTRODUCTION TO PART III

Gabrielle Cody

As discussed in the General Introduction to this volume, the genesis of directing is attributed to nineteenth-century efforts to produce a unified vision on stage. Technologies of vision together with general alienation in industrialized urban society generated an increasing polarization between viewer and viewed, which in turn contributed to a drive toward a director who could find 'a collective focus for theater in an atomized society' (Cole and Chinoy 1976: 14) – primarily through visual unity. The twentieth century, however, would witness a profound split in attitudes toward unity as well as toward vision. While realistic directors like Lee Strasberg would still privilege an 'angle of viewing,' directors such as Artaud would strive for a profoundly communal experience expressed through an exploration of primal gestures and ritual effects. Indeed, in Artaud's theater, sound is significantly more important than vision (see the Artaud letters in Chapter 15). The so-called unity of an image on stage, which tends to exacerbate the separation between viewer and viewed, began to face profound criticism. How can the 'stamp of individuality' Cole and Chinoy cite as marking early directing practice foster true collectivity – a collectivity perhaps understood as collaboration or exchange? Eventually, the irony that the generation of 'collective' harmony should be sought through an individual director and his imposed singular point of view led some twentieth-century directors to see their role not as individual artists but as spokespersons for a mutually generative ensemble (see Shank, Chapter 25 below).

Part III is devoted to expanding the exploration begun in Parts I and II, by looking at directors (or ensembles) whose work is involved in articulating (or critiquing) twentieth-century notions of unity, community, or collectivity. Directors here foster counter-cultural collectivity, attempt to express global community, and/or, conversely, critique the notion of 'global community' as inherently riddled with the historical traumas of colonialism or the nomadic power of contemporary global capitalism. Critical Art Ensemble, for instance, jettisons the role of individual director entirely, seeing the thrall to the individual artist as complexly expressive of the concerns of capital, of which they are profoundly critical. Grotowski's work in intensive actor training ultimately led him to abandon 'theatre' altogether and explore a communal experience much closer to ritual.[1] Thus the essays offered here examine works which build or critique community by: (1) generating new community *within* an ensemble through 'collective creation' (Shank) or through intense actor training (Grotowski); (2) seeking community or universality by breaking the boundaries between seemingly disparate cultural practices (Brook, Mnouchkine); or (3) inviting a critical analysis of the 'community' in which art display happens (Fusco and Gómez-Peña, Critical Art Ensemble).

Part III features essays on practitioners whose work formally or thematically addresses the politics of place and global culture. Grotowski, Brook, Mnouchkine, Fusco/Gómez-Peña, and Critical Art Ensemble have all, in quite different ways, radically challenged the conventions of Western literary theatre – in some cases by adopting Asian metaphysics and modes of performance, in others by working with Brechtian techniques of estrangement, and in still others by plumbing the emotional 'magic' of heightened theatricality or, in Grotowski's terms, actor 'sacrifice.' We are interested in how we enter this new millennium with renewed interest in testimony, chorus, and ensemble, as well as reinvigorated connections between theatricality, collectivity, and activism. If, as Cheng suggests in relation to Oguri in Part II, '[t]he human subject who had suffered the fate of becoming a profile on a rock in Hiroshima had also undergone a process of transmutation, one that occasioned a qualitative change in his body by melding it with the rock's calcareous substance,' we might wonder at the afterlife of such a melding. What kind of fusion or transmutation takes place when Oguri makes butoh-identified theatre in California? Is it American butoh-theater in L.A.? Or Japanese butoh-dance in America? Or some other transmutation animating our 'Euro-American' practices?

Western directors have long romanced Eastern forms to generate the very genre we call Euro-American directing – Lugné-Pöe, Meyerhold, Brecht, Brook, Mnouchkine, Bausch, LeCompte, and others. (See Mnouchkine, Chapter 28 below, on how 'theatre *is* Eastern.') Given the co-determinacy of this genre as well as the contemporary transnationality of the art world (among worlds), the borders determining national categories are as riddled with quotation and overlap as are the borders distinguishing 'directing' from 'choreography.' Or rock from flesh. We could, of course, just as easily have included Oguri in *this* section, for these very reasons. As Richard Schechner reminds us, culture is never 'pure,' indeed, it is never 'itself' (1989: 151). However, as Bonnie Marranca suggests, it is crucial to push beyond the East/West binary and also examine intercultural spaces *within* Europe and North America (1988: 6). The fraught transculturation Sharon Marie Carnicke describes in her essay 'Stanislavsky Uncensored and Unabridged' (Chapter 3 above) is a forceful reminder that twentieth-century theatre in North America – indeed, entire schools of acting and directing in the 1930s, 1940s, and 1950s, such as those put forth by Strasberg and Meisner – were largely the product of an interested Anglo-centered *translation* industry: monetarily motivated reinterpretations of Stanislavsky, Boleslavski, Soloviova, and Michael Chekhov.

But the problematics of Euro-American practice, its historical dependence on the East to retheatricalize the Western stage from early modernism on, seemed to us one of the defining, if controversial gestures of this century. To be sure, the work of several of the artists included in this section has inspired passionate debate around the distinction Carl Weber draws between 'acculturation' and 'transculturation.'

As Weber puts it, 'transculturation could indeed be defined as the deconstruction of a text/code and its wrenching displacement to a historically and socially different situation' (1989: 19). Not a Kabuki *Lear*, but rather a bolder displacement of the *Lear* fable into a completely new environment; for Jan Kott, the difference between Mnouchkine's 'Kabuki-derived performance style' in presenting Shakespeare plays to French audiences and Kurosawa's *Ran* (Weber 1989: 18). Brook's work has yielded similar reproaches. In an issue of *Yale Theater* in 1988 almost entirely devoted to Brook's production of the *Mahabharata*, Rustom Bharucha 'talks back' to Brook's so-called 'exchange among people of different cultures' (see Schechner's interview with Brook, Chapter 27 below). From the position of 'native' he assails the sinister market economy of cultural importation:

> Peter Brook's *Mahabharata* exemplifies one of the most blatant (and accomplished) appropriations of Indian culture in recent years. [. . .] [The] reordering of non-western material within an orientalist framework of thought and action, which has been specifically designed for the international market. [. . .] What disturbs me most is that it exemplifies a particular *kind* of western representation that negates the non-western context of its borrowing.
>
> (1988: 7–8)

Brook's somewhat self-indicting notion that 'Geography is bunk' or that geography and history can cease to exist in rehearsal (see Chapter 27) may strike some as what Coco Fusco calls here 'happy multi-culturalism.' Fusco's 'The Other history of intercultural performance' (Chapter 29 below) poignantly underlines Bharucha's critique of Brook *within* North American culture. While the performance art piece Fusco and Guillermo Gómez-Peña created was initially intended as a satirical commentary on Western concepts of the 'exotic, primitive other,' the artists quickly realized that their mock ethnographic, site-specific exhibition of two *undiscovered* Amerindians in a cage was not only taken seriously by most audiences – internationally – but the two artists were also angrily critiqued by spectators and museum administrators alike for the 'moral implications' of their performative deception.

Fusco's account of her own and Gomez-Peña's experiences as fake exhibitors brings to the surface not only the productive dangers of interactive performance, but the massive ideological implications of the avant-garde's fascination with new and 'undiscovered' territories. Fusco's point is stunningly blunt: the origins of intercultural performance in the West are rooted in ethnographic exhibition. Similarly, Fusco calls on us to remember that the break with realism which the avant-garde made possible in radical ways originated as an imitation of the 'primitive.' Once again, by including directors as diverse as Grotowski, Brook, Mnouchkine, and Gómez-Peña/Fusco it is our intention to invite debate about culture, place, voice and the colonial unconscious in theatrical works exploring community, communities, and spaces in between.

NOTE

1 The essay in this section (Chapter 26) concerns Grotowski's early work with actors. The link to communal experience may not be immediately apparent. On the lifetime work of Grotowski and his later Theater of Sources and Objective Drama periods, see Wolford and Schechner (2000).

WORKS CITED

Bharucha, Rustom (1989) 'Peter Brook's *Mahabharata*: a view from India.' *Yale Theater* 19, 2: 6–20.

Cole, Toby, and Helen Krich Chinoy, eds. (1976) *Directors on Directing*, rev. edn. Indianapolis: Bobbs Merrill.

Marranca Bonnie (1989) 'Introduction.' *Performing Arts Journal* 33–4: 5–8.

Schechner, Richard (1989) 'Intercultural themes.' *Performing Arts Journal* 33–4: 151–62.

Weber, Carl (1989) 'AC/TC currents of theatrical exchange.' *Performing Arts Journal* 33–4: 11–21.

Wolford, Lisa, and Richard Schechner (2000) *The Grotowski Sourcebook*. London: Routledge.

25

COLLECTIVE CREATION

Theodore Shank

T54, 1972

The group, rather than the individual, is the typical focus of the alternative society, and this is reflected in the structure of the new theatre organizations, their manner of working, and their theatre pieces. The collective creation of theatre pieces has become the method of conceiving and developing works in the alternative theatre. Society has become increasingly specialized and competitive. This is reflected in an established theatre based on competition and a theatrical method that focuses on individual specialists, such as playwright, director, and star actor. In reaction to the fragmentation of the established society, which for many has become disorienting, the alternative society has sought wholeness. This is evident in many ways, including its focus on group living and group activities, and in its theatre, which is based on the cooperation of a creative collective.[1]

Instead of the two-process method of the traditional theatre – a playwright writing a script in isolation and other artists staging it – the new theatre practices a one-process method, wherein the group itself develops the piece from initial conception to finished performance. The typical member of a new theatre group is not merely a performer, but a person with broader creative response abilities, who may not distinguish between the work of performer, director, designer, and playwright, but who applies his creative energies to the making of a theatre piece, whatever that might involve. While some in the group will provide more leadership than others, the works that result are truly the expression of the group, not simply of a playwright or director.

Improvisation is the principal technique. It is used to train members of the group to work creatively and collectively, and to suggest initial conceptions for new pieces. It is the means by which embryonic conceptions are developed into finished productions. Sometimes, the improvisational exercises themselves become the performance. Despite the use of improvisation by nearly every group, each develops its own unique method that may change somewhat from work to work as they experiment with new conceptions and new means of expressing them. One of the chief ways their methods differ is from the source of or the means of discovering an inceptive idea for a piece: (1) from exercises; (2) from a social, political, or aesthetic problem; (3) from a text or painting; (4) from working with an object or materials; or (5) from a script by someone within the group. The groups may also vary in their means of developing the piece – through discussion, research, improvisation. And they are also distinguished by the circumstances of performance, which may be completely determined in rehearsal and set before performance, may be improvised within a scenario, and may involve spectators.

Some groups work with sensitivity exercises and theatre games until something that interests them begins to emerge. That idea may be developed further through improvisation and sometimes a scenario or a script is written down as they work. A group which has created several pieces in this way is **T.O.C. (The Other Company** [founded in l968]) in London which is part of an organization called Inter-Action established 'to make the arts more relevant to local community life.' The director of T.O.C., Naftali Yavin, described the development of *The Pit* [l968], which was their first piece:

> We worked for about six months with the people I had chosen after looking for them for a year. Just work-shopping on ways and methods (most of them improvised) of approaching and opening up people and getting from them more and more as performers, breaking down barriers. So we were working on a technique and at the same time just working on the human being as a creative individual. Then what we discovered was that the process which we had gone through in those six months can be interesting to other people because it is a very human process. So we started to recall our sessions, and we designed the special exercises and rituals along those lines. The process we had been through became the three stages of *The Pit* – meeting, master–slave relationship, and the possibility of love.

The structure in which the performance takes place resembles a large box without a lid constructed of flats with windows on all four sides through which the audience of thirty-four can view the action. The performers improvise within a scenario which involves them in personal confrontations with each other, including insults, slaps, and spitting. When these frictions are resolved, the barriers between the performers and the spectators are removed and interaction between these two groups takes place. The same rituals and exercises are done at each performance, but they are not predetermined in detail and of course the interaction with the audience varies considerably. [. . .]

Christianshavnsgruppen in Copenhagen has theatrical and social goals very much like those of T.O.C. The group has conducted workshops in prisons, hospitals, and schools and has gained insights into ways of involving audiences in their productions. At the beginning of *Muddermanden* (*The Mud Man*) [produced in l970], the audience is admitted to a room where there are many objects with which they can entertain themselves – finger paints, costumes to put on, food and wine. Only after the spectators have begun to use these objects do the performers enter the room and, using only nonsense sounds, engage the spectators in a series of games, including blind-man's buff, a group dance, and trust exercises. The performers are alien creatures who must gain the confidence and friendship of the audience.

[. . .] In *Muddermanden*, there was no director. Bent Hagested, one of the leaders of the group, explained the relationship of their objectives to their methods:

We try to make moving politics, to show how people can be together with each other, a new way of being in contact with other people . . . We no longer have a director, we simply have ideas, the five of us, and we work them through and try them on the public . . . We try to make theatre and to change society, and of course, we must start with ourselves. Trying not to have a director is part of that, but it's damn difficult.

The **Dancers' Workshop of San Francisco** has worked in a variety of ways as its director, Ann Halprin, continues to challenge herself and the group to fulfill more effectively her idea of the artist as 'a guide who works to evoke the art within us all' (*TDR* T41). She attempts to find ways of involving Workshop members and the audience in the creative process (see fig. 25.1). Sometimes the audience has been involved on an equal basis with the performers in sensitivity exercises. In 1971, she told me the group was trying to develop a work '*with* the audience rather than *for* the audience so that it would be an expression of the community.' The announcement for a series of preview performances at the studio stated that their purpose was to offer people an opportunity to respond to the new piece and 'feedback that response into the ongoing development of the work.' She had devised a means by which the audience could participate in the usual function of director. During some of the preview performances, a microphone was passed among the spectators for their comments, enabling the performers to hear several opinions as they worked. Most often, however, the ideas of the audience were expressed only in the discussion of the performance which the group calls 'valuaction.' [. . .]

More and more Ann Halprin has come to think that 'each community is its own art' and therefore it is essential that if the spectator is a part of the community he must participate in creation of the work.

Fig. 25.1 Ann Halprin explaining the score for one of her pieces at the Dancers' Workshop of San Francisco. (Photo by Theodore Shank, courtesy of Theodore Shank.)

*

Some groups begin work on a piece with a specific idea or a problem in mind. The idea becomes the focus for their discussions and improvisations, which attempt to find the most effective means of developing and expressing the idea. One group that works in this way is **Orbe-Recherche Théâtrale** in Paris directed by Irene Lambelet and Jean-Philippe Guerlais. In creating *Oratorio Concentrationnaire*, their first group-developed piece, they attempted to find expression for what they felt about 'violence, the inevitable violence from biblical times to our own.' Numa Sadoul, a young poet who was a performing member of the group, described their way of working:

> We have an idea and we search for a corporal expression. It is not yet developed in our minds, it is very vague, and with our bodies we improvise or search for the real direction of our idea. We have confidence when we are working together, even when what we do is ridiculous, and we often search not knowing where it will lead.

In developing this piece, Orbe worked five to seven hours a day, seven days a week. Each day began with an hour of exercises, which focused on voice, body, respiration, and concentration. These exercises also helped to develop what the group calls 'the intelligence of the body,' instinctive physical responses that can keep them from being hurt when performing the extremely vigorous physical feats they demand of themselves. [. . .] Sometimes, after the general exercises, the group worked together on special exercises for certain parts of the body. The remainder of the rehearsal was spent in 'research for the piece.' The movement was developed through improvisation – Nazi concentration camps serving as the strongest image. The text was then written to go with the movement. Except for the music, all creative work was done by the performers.

In attempting to express their horror at certain atrocities past and present, the group avoided the usual theatrical artifices. Instead of stage make-up they used walnut stain, which takes several days to wear off, and the pain their faces expressed was actual. The physical stress on the performers 'is like running 10,000 meters as if it were a hundred.' Such torture was their way of making *Oratorio Concentrationnaire* a real experience, not only a theatrical one. [. . .]

Mabou Mines, a New York-based group [established in 1970], worked for twelve months in developing *The Red Horse Animation* [produced in 1970] (see fig. 25.2). Lee Breuer, the director of the group, described the process:

> We started with a couple of basic ideas that interested all of us. First, the idea of working horizontally on the floor so that the audience would look down on the image allowed us to work in two planes 90 degrees apart. This permitted a kind of cinematic structure, because when you are standing up and then lying down it is the equivalent of a camera angle being changed. The other idea that we started with was that we wanted to deal with the image of the horse.

The group's name is also the name of the Canadian mining town where they train and rehearse, and it was there that the actual work on *The Red Horse Animation* began. Phil Glass, who composed and directed the music, worked with Lee Breuer and the three actors during the entire twelve months of rehearsal. They began with photographs of horses:

> We worked on the Muybridge book on the movement of the horse.[2] We worked with that book for three months . . . The piece is actually a lot about the way we rehearsed

Fig. 25.2 Mabou Mines' *Red Horse Animation.* **(Photo by Theodore Shank, courtesy of Theodore Shank.)**

it. There are many things in the performance that are analogous to the performers building the horse itself. As rehearsals went on, the piece became more and more abstract; as various tensions come in, the idea tends to get lost . . . The script was written along with the rehearsals over the entire period. We would work on dialogue that I had written the night before . . . Another thing that we were experimenting with was taking a narrative, like the story of building a horse, and changing the medium – it would be verbal, then it would be simply movement, then it would be four minutes of music, then it would be back to text and movement, then it would be wholly text. We wanted to see if we could get this very very tricky association process where a person could follow the story in music, then follow it in movement, then in narrative, and still have a through-line continuity. It's not so hard just to put one form against another, but to tell a story through changing media, not combining them but going from one to another is what we wanted. We specifically did not want the mixed-media bag, we wanted something cleaner and harder.

[. . .]

The Dutch group **Bewegingstheater** (Moving Theatre) [founded 1965], better known by the abbreviation Bewth, developed a piece on the idea of death.[3] For several years the group, led by Frits Vogel and Luc Boyer, had been performing their collectively created pieces which explored new concepts of movement to express abstract fantasies from the subconscious. In the fall of 1969, they decided to suspend performances in order to devote more time to research. The following summer I talked to Luc Boyer about *Strong and Pliable* [1970], the piece that resulted from this research:

For a long time Frits had the idea of doing something around the idea of death – dead bodies and funerals, losing limbs or parts of your bodies. At the first rehearsal we tried to think about embalming. How would it be to have an embalmed body? How would it be to move around as a dead body? How would it feel to touch dead skin? It sounds very morbid but, well, it was very morbid. These exercises were sort of a source of inspiration . . . But more and more we got away from the idea of death because, even in Bewth itself, there was a feeling that it was too dangerous. We felt there were a lot of taboos still, and we were not ready for it. So we tried to find other things, very small facets of maybe death, maybe life itself. [. . .] At first we rehearsed only for ourselves, then we had some real performances. Then we dropped the performances and only held open rehearsals because there was a kind of dualism within us – when working only with the group, we were very sincere, it was very personal and we were very close to each other; but as soon as there was an audience we became exhibitionists, and that was the wrong way of working, especially in *Strong and Pliable*. Our other plays were quite structured, although there was room to improvise; but in *Strong and Pliable* everything was unknown because the audience was to be involved with us in the trance. That was why we limited the audience to sixty people . . .

We tried to get into the most real trance possible just by repeating one very simple movement, by trying to hold one rhythm. We took as an example the African dances. They go so far and they get so close to what they are doing that they lose their intellectualism. . . . We felt that when somebody is in a trance he can do more things than in a normal state. So we repeated over and over the same movement until we could do something else and still be in the trance. We had to try not to be disturbed by the audience, and that's why we wanted to make the audience feel and react with us. We also wanted them to join in so as to get new impulses. Since there was no structure and no plan, the circumstances and the atmosphere were important. If the audience was a good one, it would have great influence on the whole direction of the performance. At the same time we had to be alert to what the audience would do and to other members of the group as the play developed. So every rehearsal was research. It was never the same on another night.

There are a number of politically motivated theatre groups, of course, that begin with a political problem or situation.

The **AgitProp Theatre**, for example, has been working in London since the fall of 1968 (see fig. 25.3).[4] Chris Rawlence, the unofficial leader of the group, explained that they 'aim to be an instrument in the collective realization of the socialist revolution.' They arrange performances through tenant associations, labor unions, and other community organizations, and perform on such occasions as rallies, meetings, and strikes. They refuse to participate in theatre festivals or other theatrically focused occasions. They present their works at 'scenes of actual or potential action.' [. . .]

We start off by taking an issue that we want to deal with or that an organization has asked us to deal with, and we talk it round. Depending on the length of the play, whether it's going to be done indoors or outdoors, the amount of time, and our political knowledge on this subject, we try to read a lot of books so we can make the thing flawless. We take perhaps a week, two weeks, three days. [. . .] It's been our experience so far . . . that you can't improvise without a structure . . . When you really know the framework of what you're dealing with, then you can start improvising and possibly change a lot that you had previously thought out; but to improvise from scratch on something like collective bargaining is impossible. So we talk, and from group discussion will emerge the line or ideas that we will try out.

[. . .] Chris Rawlence comes very close to serving [the function of a director], and he usually is the discussion leader. The pieces are developed through discussion and improvisation. Long enthusiastic discussions on political theory take place at the

Fig. 25.3 The AgitProp group performing outdoors in London. (Photo by Theodore Shank, courtesy of Theodore Shank.)

beginning of most rehearsals. These discussions attempt to find an image or a speech that accurately and vividly expresses a particular political concept. Similar discussions also may occur in the midst of a rehearsal in reference to a particular action or line. Sometimes the speeches are written down as they work. Everyone, including Chris, performs.

Like a good political cartoon, the pieces made by AgitProp are incisive political analyses with a viewpoint, and they are funny. Most are about fifteen minutes long and are completely set in rehearsal. Often they provide the impetus for action by their audiences. For example, one day when I talked with them they had just performed their *Housing Play* at a neighborhood meeting in an attempt to raise the awareness of the spectators regarding their capitalistic landlords. The discussion following their performance led to the organization of a tenants' association and a rent strike.

[. . .]

Sweden, the Western country that has perhaps come closest to achieving the socialist ideal, has some of the most active political theatre groups. Bibi Nordin, one of the original founders in 1965 of the **Narren Theatre** in Stockholm, explained that 'this socialized democracy is a bluff. The government has been in power thirty-six years, and all the important things that they said they wanted to do either have not been done or they were done and are now being taken away.' The Narren Theatre has been trying not only to create pieces that present information and raise political consciousness but to make the ideals of socialism work practically within the group.

In 1969, the group decided that they wanted to make a play about Cuba and the revolution, so Hans Hellberg and Bibi Nordin went to Cuba to do research. The following winter the entire group spent three weeks together in a house in the country and developed *The Girl from Havana*. Bibi described their difficulties:

> There was so much material. We began to read the Cuban history, and that was so exciting that we began working through the centuries toward the revolution. We came to the revolution, but we didn't get through it. We built it up like a circus with such characters as Uncle Sam and Dona Espana. El Dictatore and Rebello were like clowns. . . . It was the most important piece we had done, but it was not very good. It was important because it was the beginning of something.

The following winter the group toured throughout Sweden and ended by performing in northern Sweden for striking miners. The situation, the problems of solidarity and making the strike work, intrigued the group.

> Some of us stayed there and lived with a miner's family for six or seven weeks. We weren't performing then, we were just studying to make a play about the strike. But we have put it aside to work on a play about solidarity – it's part of the strike situation, really, but it's our situation too.

The work started with the group using a script by one of the members, but this was quickly shelved. They began to work improvisationally.

> We take a person and put him in different situations and see how he reacts. The framework is to see how these people (a shop girl, a miner, for example) are changed during the course of the strike.

The workers of northern Sweden were also the subject of a piece that was developed by some of the younger members of the company of the **Royal Dramatic Theatre**, the theatre in Stockholm associated with Ingmar Bergman. The rebel group began their 'extra-curricular' work in 1968 with *Gypsy*, a group-developed piece based on material about the position of gypsies in Swedish society. The following year, the group became interested in factory workers because of a sociologist's report which showed that virtually no workers attend performances at the established theatres. The group wanted to do a piece that would genuinely be for the workers, and they decided that research would be necessary. [. . .]

The group made interviews in the morning and rehearsed in the afternoon and evening. They talked about what they had learned from the interviews and other sources and discussed the possibilities of using the material in scenes and songs, and someone would then volunteer to write the song or scene. This would then be presented to the group for discussion again.

The workers were involved in the rehearsal process as well. At least once a week, the group had an open rehearsal for the workers, who came and told them what was right and wrong with their work. When the play was about two-thirds finished, the group rented a school in the workers' district and presented what they had done for the workers' comments. [. . .]

The inceptive ideas for the theatre pieces of some groups come from various sources outside the group. Jerzy Grotowski's Theatre Laboratory in Poland [1959–76] and Eugenio Barba's Odin Theatret in Denmark [1964–present] have used classical plays, the San Francisco Mime Troupe [1959–present] has made a piece based on Bobby Seale's book *Seize the Time* [1970], works of fiction such as Lewis Carroll's Alice stories have been used by the Manhattan Project [founded 1968] and others, a painting by Hieronymus Bosch served as a starting point for *Bosch's Balls* by Bewth, and trial transcripts have provided the bases for other group-created productions. Regardless of the initial inspiration, if the culminating theatre piece is successful it is uniquely that of the group, and the original will have been completely assimilated into the new work or it will have served only as a creative stimulus.

The **Freehold Theatre Company** in London [1969–73], like Grotowski [see Chapter 26 below], focuses on the actor, and its workshops emphasize psychophysical exercises designed to free the actor for expression. Also like the Polish group, most of its productions were developed using classical plays as starting points. In the very beginning, the group attempted to work without a director. Nancy Meckler, who subsequently became the director, explained what happened:

> We rehearsed a play, and there was to be no director, but what it really amounted to was that one person had an idea and was able to impose it. You couldn't say in the end that it hadn't been directed.

A workshop–rehearsal, which I attended, lasted from 11:00 a.m. until 5:30 p.m. with one break of less than an hour. The morning session involved calisthenics, gymnastics, acrobatics, and psychophysical exercises. [. . .] An exercise that is done by everyone in the group is 'The Cat,' which probably comes from Grotowski's exercise of that name. It is a sequence based on the movements of a cat waking up and stretching, but it becomes more strenuous, involving headstands and somersaults. It can be done many ways, and by concentrating on different words while doing it – for example 'sun' or 'water-lily' – it may express different feelings. [. . .]

Following a short break for lunch, the group reassembled to work on their next production. [N]on-verbal sounds and abstract movement were [. . .] used to express images, feelings, and an environment for the new piece. This is the method used by the group even when the starting point is an established play such as *Antigone* [staged in 1970 at the Royal Court]. Nancy described the process:

> Say two people are going to do a scene that they haven't done before . . . Somebody throws the lines out to them one at a time; when they hear the line they take it and do whatever they like with it, often using a kind of extended speech. They experiment between themselves as the lines come to them. . . . They end up doing things to each other, saying things in certain ways that they never would have thought of doing; but they do it at the moment because they are just trying to cope with the situation as the mind comes to it.

The objective is somewhat like that of Grotowski: an attempt to eliminate the conscious mind between the stimulus and the impulse so as to avoid the mask of clichés that the conscious mind tends to rely upon.

During these improvisations, Nancy makes notes on those things that might be used in the production or which seem to have a potential for further development. After twenty minutes or so of improvisation around maybe five lines, she stops it, and there is a general discussion about what has just been done. Then the same actors, or perhaps different ones, repeat the process with the same lines but concentrating on those directions or images which in the first attempt, or through discussion, seemed to have the most interesting possibilities. While it is Nancy who guides the actors and selects elements for the production, thereby developing the conception, all the other members of the group contribute in a significantly creative way by their improvisational work.

Approximately four months of rehearsals such as this, five days a week, went into the preparation of *Antigone*. The piece is a collage of Sophocles, added speeches written specifically for the production, and sections developed entirely through improvisation. Scenes were deleted, added, and rearranged to suit the intent of the group. An indication of the extent to which the completed work was their own is the fact that the Freehold, because of *Antigone*, was the first group instead of a playwright to receive the John Whiting Award for 'new and distinctive development in dramatic writing.'

Emilio Galli, the Peruvian director of **Group N3** in Paris, believes it is essential 'to put aside all plastic elements' and focus on the actor. 'Man is enough to make the creation, nothing else is needed.' However, he considers it important to eliminate the 'mystique of the actor' and to find a kind of movement that can express something beyond the psychological reality of the characters. One means he has used to accomplish these goals is multiplication of characters. In *Hamlet, Structure 1*, eight actors, including some women, played the title role.

> One actor gives only one perspective. Multiplication of the roles, as in Cubist painting, is richer and shows much better the different perspectives.

A manifesto by Emilio included in the program for this production explains further his deviation from the traditional theatre:

> The creative energy of the participant will no longer be employed for the illustration of a text so as to identify with the characters of the psychological theatre.

This psychological detachment of the spectator is intended to allow him to 'reflect upon the problems' of society presented in the work so that 'he takes a position and adjusts his behavior, his attitude, and frees himself from himself.' The techniques used in rehearsal and in performance are intended to achieve this detachment and to eliminate the mystique of the actor. He does not believe the actor 'can mix his personal problems with the character's problems.' To avoid this psychological approach he focuses on the respiration column, using the body 'as a musical instrument' as well as a 'scenic element in motion.' White mask-like makeup, phonetic distortion, and body percussion also deter the actor and spectator from psychological involvement and serve as important means of expression. He believes that 'the distortion of speech and gesture provides a new language of signs, of graphics, and of music, which is much richer than traditional theatre language.' [. . .]

Several times during the last few years I have directed **group-developed productions** at the Davis Campus of the University of California. One of these, *The Crimes and Trials of the Chicago 8 – 1 + 2*, had as a starting point the Chicago events of August 1968, at the time of the U.S. Democratic Convention and the subsequent trial. I announced that anyone could participate who was willing to commit himself to the project for approximately nine months. At the beginning, there were forty-five; of the twenty-three who stayed to the end, a quarter were black.

At every rehearsal two or three participants would each present an image from the trial or Convention events that he had developed into a structure providing a focus for improvisation by the entire group. The person responsible for each structure directed the improvisation. When the results seemed promising, we spent more time on them in another session. Sometimes these improvisations were silent pantomimes, sometimes non-verbal sounds were used, sometimes the performers ad libbed, sometimes sections of dialogue from the trial transcript were added.

Often the structure presented by a member of the group was related not only to the trial but to his own experience. One that developed into the opening section of the production was the entrance of the judge and other trial participants, which was like a parade for a returning military hero with heckling by the defendants in the crowd. Another was by a student who felt the authoritarian and condescending attitude of the judge toward the defendants paralleled that of some teachers to their students. Eventually, this improvisation developed into one of the sections of the piece in which the courtroom is also a classroom, the judge a teacher, the defendants students rebelling against the judge–teacher, and the members of the prosecution teacher's pets, who accept the control of the judge–teacher. Dialogue was selected from the trial transcript – intimidating speeches for the judge–teacher and revolutionary speeches for the defendants–students. [. . .]

After ten weeks of work we had notes on approximately fifty improvisations. From these, eighteen were selected and put in an order. Two were divided into several parts to be used at different places in the piece, and some of those chosen were actually combinations of several improvisations that seemed to work together. For the first time we had an overall structure.

At this time two decisions were made in an attempt to give the work a greater sense of honesty. First, it was decided that everything spoken during the perform-ance would be from the trial transcript and that the audience would be informed of this. They would also be told that what was said had been edited, rearranged, and reassembled. Second, there would be no attempt to hide the identity of the per-formers. The audience would see them before the performance as the students they were, and during the performance these students would be illustrating their felt version of what went on in the Chicago streets and courtroom. Since they would demonstrate this like someone telling a story (as opposed to being the characters in the story), an actor would not be associated with one character throughout the performance but would suggest a number of different characters. [. . .]

At the beginning of the final ten-week period attention was given for the first time to who would play what role in what section. This was determined without regard to sex or race but considering the unique qualities of each performer. In the final form of the piece, Judge Hoffman was played in more sections by women, both black and white, than by men. Abbie Hoffman at different times in the pro-duction was played by blacks and whites of both sexes. [. . .] Rehearsals then focused on further polishing, detailing, pacing, and clarifying the tone of each section. The resulting production was not a linear, story-focused piece, but more an accumulation of bizarre, kaleidoscopic images dramatically structured to express our reaction to those emotive events in Chicago.

Ever since the Happenings of the late 1950s, visual artists have had a significant impact on the works produced by the alternative theatre and on the methods used by some of the groups. While these groups may begin with ideas from outside, their work with visual materials serves an important function in developing their productions.

Half of the eight performing members of **G.S.T. (Gruppo Sperimentazione Teatrale)** in Rome are painters, who during the day make various scenic objects that are to be used in the group's productions. When the group begins to make a new piece by reading and discussing a well-known work of fiction, this work serves only to provide a focus for early discussions, and the resulting piece bears little resemblance to it. Work on the G.S.T. production *Baron Munchausen* began when the group read the book, which ostensibly relates the fantastic Gulliver-like adventures of the eighteenth-century soldier and traveler. The group then met to discuss their impressions and attempt to find an acceptable approach. How the piece developed from that point was discussed in an interview with the director, Mario Ricci, and Deborah Hayes, a member of the group who is from the United States.

> *Deborah:* Someone has an idea for a starting point, usually Mario, and we begin to work simultaneously on the scenic objects and the action. While we work on the action, the objects are thought about even if they aren't actually built.
>
> *Mario:* We often start off thinking about how an object will work, and then, as the object gets built, there are economical or practical reasons why it is changed. It is almost always different from what we initially thought it would be. So the object imposes on us as director and actors, and we must comply with its demands. The objects have as much or more personality than the actors.

In one part of this production, a large Chinese dragon swallows a performer, sounds recorded in a Chinese restaurant are heard, the dragon is lighted up inside to disclose six performers eating Chinese food with chop sticks, the lights inside go out and the dragon regurgitates the performers one by one. As with some other objects, the dragon had been built before the group knew how they were going to use it. [. . .]

Another group in Rome, **Space Re(v)action**, directed by former painter Giancarlo Nanni, sometimes uses Dada scripts for their inceptive ideas, sometimes works of fiction, and sometimes images that come out of improvisations with objects such as ropes or a large rock. Very early in the process of developing a piece, sometimes before other members of the group are working, the director begins making a series of drawings. These are colorfully painted rather subconscious eclectic impressions of the images that come to mind as he begins to develop his conception for a production. [. . .] The drawings are not shown to the actors until their work is well along because Giancarlo thinks the drawings might 'limit their own inventions and fantasy.' His objective in rehearsals is to free the actor so that he can be inventive rather than relying on techniques. 'I don't tell the actors what they have to do. I just try to make them able to do what they want.' [. . .]

Giancarlo says that he never plans a scene before going to the theatre for rehearsal. They simply start working, and he organizes what happens. There is no separation between acting and the scenic aspects of a production. Rehearsals are concerned with everything that will go into a production. Their approach 'is always through the materials.' All aspects of the work are developed simultaneously almost as if the group were making a collective sculpture from found materials.

> When we start to do a play we are eight people going around in the town thinking about the play. So when we come to the theatre, almost everyday somebody brings something he found in the street or at home that he thinks is useful for the play. And then we rehearse, but we don't separate the making of costumes and the rehearsal. Making the costumes is rehearsal. For example, someone is trying movements in a costume he has already made. His movements give to someone else an idea which relates to another part of the play.

The production may continue to develop even after performances begin – new costumes or makeup, different movements, changed words. However, this is not thought of as performance improvisation. The performances, in general, are set, but the performers are free to improve upon the work.

When Giancarlo began working with the actors on *A come Alice* (*A is for Alice*) [1970] he had made some drawings, but there was no script.

> We could have gone on working without a script, but the actors said, 'We don't have a script.' So at night I went home and started writing down the lines. But I took only the dialogue, not the narration. From *Alice's Adventures in Wonderland* I took nine adventures, and from *Through the Looking Glass* I took five. I also used another book by Carroll, *The Game of Logic*. And then I took a speech from Rabelais, where Pantagruel says he would like to play at this and this – a very long speech with many sexual references. This was said by Alice. One thing I did was redistribute some speeches. For example, I took from Humpty Dumpty his speech about the power of words and gave it to Alice. So it was not a new script in the sense of using different words; I used the same words to make a new play. [. . .]

In the fall of 1971, Giancarlo was invited to spend two months developing a production with students at the Davis Campus of the University of California. In keeping with his belief that everyone has potential creative ability, he accepted all who wanted to work. At the first session, Giancarlo told them to do whatever they wanted to do. He was disappointed when many of them went on stage and began doing pantomimes they had done or seen before, miniature performances that came from a kind of surface exhibitionism usual in auditions. He wanted to get to know the performers so as to make use of their own unique qualities; but they consciously interposed something else, a trick, rather than reveal themselves by letting what they did come up from their subconscious. It is the same problem that has concerned Grotowski, Ann Halprin, and others. In subsequent rehearsals, Giancarlo provided one or two props – a network of ropes, long sticks, a large rock or a plastic drop with holes – that helped to transfer the performer's focus from himself to an object and resulted in improvisations that were more honest expressions of themselves. [. . .]

Some groups begin work on a piece with an idea about a character or characters which they wish to explore and develop. The **People Show** in London sometimes works this way.[5]

The People Show, a group of four and sometimes five performers, denies being a group because they rehearse together as little as possible. They are interested in retaining their identity as individuals because they feel that a group stifles individual creativity and soon everyone is doing the same thing. They have no director or leader.

Work on a piece begins, whenever possible, with a visit to the place where they will perform in order to discover all the possibilities the space might offer both inside and out. Then, working separately, they develop their own images, often beginning with a character. They come together a few days before the first performance to find points where their individual work might intersect, to discuss possibilities, to determine a framework which is an order of events, and to build a set. Each of them works on that part of the set which is determined by the images he has developed. This is very important because they can build it in such a way as to include the means of performing their own work. In the process of building the set, they discover new possibilities and come to understand what the others are doing. The performances are improvised within the framework that has been determined, but the framework is not very strict, and can be changed in the course of a performance. According to Jose Nava, a painter from Mexico who began performing with the group in 1970, 'the idea is to develop the frame so that it can be changed, otherwise you limit yourself.' Productions are never set, they are dropped before this happens. [. . .]

In West Berlin, the **Hoffmann's Comic Theatre** [founded 1967] also begins work on many of its pieces by determining the characters to be used in the piece. This political group worked for several years to develop contemporary stereotype characters that can serve the same function for them that Il Dottore, Pantalone, Il Capitano, and others served for the *commedia dell'arte*. Their contemporary stereotypes include a capitalist-boss figure, a young male worker, an older male worker, etc. There is a mask for each of the characters. Each actor in the group has one or two specialties: for example, one might play sons and young workers, another can do fathers and older workers. Pieces are created by taking these stereotypes, talking out a brief scenario involving them in a situation, and improvising the performance. *Rita and Paul* is the story of a young factory worker who is in love with the owner's daughter. Both fathers disapprove and try to separate them. Rita runs away and comes to Paul, who tells her she can't stay because her father will fire him and keep him from getting another job. Rita's father finds her at Paul's house and fires both Paul and Paul's father. Rita tells Paul she doesn't love him anymore and goes home with her father. Paul and his father forget their differences and try to figure out together what can be done about such a rotten system. This piece is performed for young factory workers approximately 16 to 19 years old. The performance ends when the actors take off their masks and ask the workers what the solution is. The audience is encouraged to use the masks and act out the way they would behave or the way they think things should be. The obviousness of the scenario makes it easier for the workers to participate – they know the situation very well. Peter Mobius, one of the members of the group, feels that the masks enable the workers to say things about their problems that they would otherwise not be able to say. [. . .]

The most significant difference between the working methods of the new theatre and traditional methods is that the pieces are created through a single process from inception to completion somewhat as in the visual arts. This change demands broader creative responsibility than is required of those in the established theatre, who are narrowly specialized. Each participant contributes to the development of the conception for a piece and takes part in the search for materials and techniques to express the conception. Often each member of a group combines the specialized traditional functions of playwright, director, designer, etc. The leader of such a group, rather than possessing the specialized abilities of a director in the established theatre, must possess the same creative skills as the other members and in addition be able to stimulate and focus their creative energy. This might be accomplished by providing structures within which the group can improvise, by leading and directing discussion, or by providing objects and environments with which the group can work. Nearly always the leader selects from what the group has created and helps to organize it. Sometimes the leader has no official recognition; sometimes the leadership rotates from one member to another; often the leader is also a performer. Moreover, it is frequently necessary for the leader to become a kind of teacher because the members of the group usually come from schools and universities, where they have been trained in the methods of the traditional theatre, or from established theatre companies, and they have had little opportunity to develop the broad skills necessary in a creative collective. They may be skillful performers or technicians, but they often lack the conceptual ability that is requisite to their participation in the making of a work without the aid of a script.

NOTES [ADDED BY EDITORS]

1 This essay as published in 1972 did not provide a lot of information on dates and places. We tried to discover what became of specific theatre groups post-1972. This effort was interesting, but in some cases quite frustrating. Some groups left little trace while others, such as Mabou Mines, went on to become extremely prolific and influential theatres and are still in operation today. In our opinion, this essay stands as a kind of letter from 1972, making apparent the degree to which 'collective creations' were widespread and influential – often, and somewhat ironically, an effort of 'directors' (and interestingly, such theatres did have directors) to collaborate completely.

2 Eadweard Muybridge, *Animal Locomotion*. 1887.

3 Bewth, was founded in 1965 and created work at least through 1991.

4 AgitProp Theatre, founded in October 1968, has survived the turn of the century. However, they changed their name to Red Ladder Company shortly after being founded.

5 Founded in 1965, the People Show is still active today.

26

AN INTERVIEW WITH GROTOWSKI

Richard Schechner, Theodore Hoffman, Jacques Chwat, Mary Tierney

T41, 1968

Editors' note: This interview was conducted on 1 December 1967 in New York. Polish director Jerzy Grotowski had just completed a four-week course (four days a week, five hours a day) at New York University. Present at the interview were Theodore Hoffman, Richard Schechner, Jacques Chwat, and Mary Tierney. Chwat served as Grotowski's interpreter during both the course and the interview. Both Hoffman and Schechner observed and – to the degree that it was possible – participated in the NYU course.

Schechner: You often talk about the 'artistic ethic,' what it means to live the artistic life –

Grotowski: During the course I did not use the word 'ethic,' but nevertheless at the heart of what I said there was an ethical attitude. Why didn't I use the word 'ethic'? People who talk about ethics usually want to impose a certain kind of hypocrisy on others, a system of gestures and behavior that serves as an ethic. Jesus Christ suggested ethical duties, but despite the fact that he had miracles at his disposal, he did not succeed in improving mankind. Then why renew this effort?

Perhaps we should ask ourselves only: which actions get in the way of artistic creativity? For example, if during creation we hide the things that function in our personal lives, you may be sure that our creativity will fail. We present an unreal image of ourselves; we do not express ourselves and we begin a kind of intellectual or philosophical flirtation – use tricks and creativity is impossible. [. . .]

The creative process consists, however, in not only revealing ourselves, but in structuring what is revealed. If we reveal ourselves with all these temptations, we transcend them, we master them through our consciousness. That is really the kernel of the ethical problem: do not hide that which is basic, it makes no difference whether the material is moral or immoral; our first obligation in art is to express ourselves through our own most personal motives.

Another thing which is part of the creative ethic is taking risks. [. . .] That means we cannot repeat an old or familiar route. The first time we take a route there is a penetration into the unknown, a solemn process of searching, studying, and confronting which evokes a special 'radiation' resulting from contradiction. This contradiction consists of mastering the unknown – which is nothing other than a lack of self-knowledge – and finding the techniques for forming, structuring, and recognizing it. The process of getting self-knowledge gives strength to one's work.

The second time we come to the same material, if we take the old route we no longer have this unknown within us to refer to; only tricks are left – stereotypes that may be philosophical, moral, or technical. [. . .]

The third thing one could consider 'ethical' is the problem of process and result. When I work – either during a course or while directing – what I say is never an objective truth. Whatever I say is a stimulus which gives the actor a chance to be creative. I say, 'Fix your attention on this,' search for this solemn and recognizable process. You must not think of the result. But, at the same time, you can't ignore the result because from the objective point of view the deciding factor in art is the result. In that way, art is immoral. He is right who has the result. That's the way it is.

But in order to get the result – and this is the paradox – you must not look for it. If you look for it you will block the natural creative process. In looking only the brain works; the mind imposes solutions it already knows and you begin juggling known things. That is why we must look without fixing our attention on the result. What do we look for? What, for example, are my associations, my key memories – recognizing these not in thought but through my body's impulses, becoming conscious of them, mastering and organizing them, and finding out whether they are stronger now than when they were unformed. Do they reveal more to us or less? If less, then we have not structured them well. One must not think of the result and the result will come; there will be a moment when the fight for the result will be fully conscious and inevitable, engaging our entire mental machinery. The only problem is when. It is the moment when our living creative material is concretely present. [. . .] The principle is that the actor, in order to fulfill himself, must not work for himself. Through penetrating his relationship with others – studying the elements of contact – the actor will discover what is in him. He must give himself totally.

But there is a problem. The actor has two possibilities. Either (1) he plays for the audience – which is completely natural if we think of the theatre's function – which leads him to a kind of flirtation that means that he is playing for himself, for the satisfaction of being accepted, loved, affirmed – and the result is narcissism; or (2) he works directly for himself. That means he observes his emotions, looks for the richness of his psychic states – and this is the shortest way to hypocrisy and hysteria. Why hypocrisy? Because all psychic states observed are no longer lived because emotion observed is no longer emotion. [. . .] Then the actor looks for something concrete in himself and the easiest thing is hysteria. He hides within hysterical reactions: formless improvisations with wild gestures and screams. This, too, is narcissism. But if acting is not for the audience and not for oneself, what is left?

The answer is a difficult one. One begins by finding those scenes that give the actor a chance to research his relationship with others. He penetrates the elements of contact in the body. He concretely searches for those memories and associations that have decisively conditioned the form of contact. He must give himself totally to this research. In that sense it is like authentic love, deep love. But there is no answer to the question, 'love for whom?' Not for God who no longer functions for our generation. And not for nature or pantheism. These are smoky mysteries. Man always needs another human being who can absolutely fulfill and understand him. But that is like loving the Absolute or the Ideal, loving someone who understands you but whom you've never met.

Someone you are searching for. There is no single, simple answer. One thing is clear: the actor must give himself and not play for himself or for the spectator. His search must be directed from within himself to the outside, but not for the outside.

When the actor begins to work through contact, when he begins to live in relation to someone – not his stage partner – but the partner of his own biography, when he begins to penetrate, through a study of his body's impulses, the relationship of this contact, this process of exchange, there is always a rebirth in the actor. Afterwards he begins to use the other actors as screens for his life's partner, he begins to project things onto the characters in the play. And this is his second rebirth.

Finally the actor discovers what I call the 'secure partner,' this special being in front of whom he does everything, in front of whom he plays with the other characters and to whom he reveals his most personal problems and experiences. This human being – this 'secure partner' – cannot be defined. But at the moment when the actor discovers his 'secure partner' the third and strongest rebirth occurs, a visible change in the actor's behavior.

It is during this third rebirth that the actor finds solutions to the most difficult problems: how to create while one is controlled by others, how to create without the security of creation, how to find a security which is inevitable if we want to express ourselves despite the fact that theatre is a collective creation in which we are controlled by many people and working during hours that are imposed on us.

One need not define this 'secure partner' to the actor, one need only say, 'You must give yourself absolutely,' and many actors understand. Each actor has his own chance of making this discovery, and it's a completely different chance for each. This third rebirth is neither for oneself nor for the spectator. It is most paradoxical. It gives the actor his greatest range of possibilities. One can think of it as ethical, but truly it is technical – despite the fact that it is also mysterious.

Schechner: Two related questions. Several times you told students – particularly during the *exercises plastiques* (which I will describe later) – to 'surpass yourselves,' 'have courage,' 'go beyond.' And you also said that one must resign oneself 'not to do, not to do.' First question: what is the relationship between surpassing oneself and resigning oneself? Second question – and I ask them together because I feel they are related, though I don't know why – several times when we were working with scenes from Shakespeare you said, 'Don't play the text, you are not Juliet, you didn't write the text.' What did you mean?

Grotowski: [. . .] When I say 'go beyond yourself' I am asking for an insupportable effort. One is obliged not to stop despite fatigue and to do things that
we know well we cannot do. That means one is also obliged to be courageous.
What does this lead to? There are certain points of fatigue which break the
control of the mind, a control that blocks us. When we find the courage to do
things that are impossible, we make the discovery that our body does not
block us. We do the impossible and the division within us between conception
and the body's ability disappears. This attitude, this determination, is a training for how to go beyond our limits. These are not the limits of our nature, but
those of our discomfort. These are the limits we impose upon ourselves that
block the creative process, because creativity is never comfortable. If we begin
really to work with associations during the *exercises plastiques'* transforming
the body movements into a cycle of personal impulses – at that moment we
must prolong our determination and not look for the easy. We can 'act it' in
the bad sense, calculating a move, a look, and thoughts. This is simply
pumping.

What will unblock the natural and integral possibilities? To act – that is, to
react – not to conduct the process but to refer it to personal experiences and to
be conducted. The process must take us. At these moments one must be
internally passive but externally active. The formula of resigning oneself 'not
to do' is a stimulus. But if the actor says, 'Now I must decide to find my
experiences and my intimate associations, I must find my "secure partner,"'
and so on, he will be very active, but he will be like somebody confessing who
has already written everything out in pretty sentences. He confesses, but it's
nothing. But if he resigns himself 'not to do, not to do' this difficult thing
and refers himself to things that are truly personal and externalizes these, he
would find a very difficult truth. This internal passivity gives the actor the
chance to be taken. If one begins too early to conduct the work, then the
process is blocked. [. . .]

If the actor wants to play the text, he is doing what's easiest. The text has
been written, he says it with feeling and he frees himself from the obligation
of doing anything himself. But if, as we did during the last days of the course,
he works with a silent score – saying the text only in his thoughts – he unmasks
this lack of personal action and reaction. Then the actor is obliged to refer to
himself within his own context and to find his own line of impulses. One can
either not say the text at all or one can 'recite' it as a quotation. The actor
thinks he is quoting, but he finds the cycle of thought which is revealed in the
words. There are many possibilities. In the Desdemona murder scene we
worked on in the course her text functioned as erotic love-play. Those words
became the actress's – it didn't matter that she didn't write them. The problem
is always the same: stop the cheating, find the authentic impulses. The goal is
to find a meeting between the text and the actor.

[. . .]

Schechner: A lot of work in the course and, as I understand it, in your troupe is
concerned with the *exercises plastiques.* I don't want to translate this term
because the work is not exactly what we understand in English as 'body
movement.' Your exercises are psycho-physical; there is an absolute unity
between the psychical and the physical, the associations of the body are also

the associations of the feelings. How did you develop these exercises and how do they function in the training and in the *mise-en-scène?*

Grotowski: All the movement exercises had, at first, a completely different function. Their development is the result of a great deal of experimentation. For example, we began by doing Yoga directed toward absolute concentration. Is it true, we asked, that Yoga can give actors the power of concentration? We observed that despite all our hopes the opposite happened. There was a certain concentration, but it was introverted. This concentration destroys all expression; it's an internal sleep, an inexpressive equilibrium: a great rest which ends all actions. This should have been obvious because the goal of Yoga is to stop three processes: thoughts, breathing, and ejaculation. That means all life processes are stopped and one finds fullness and fulfillment in conscious death, autonomy enclosed within our own kernel. I don't attack it, but it's not for actors.

But we also observed that certain Yoga positions help very much the natural reactions of the spinal column; they lead to a sureness of one's body, a natural adaptation to space. So why get rid of them? Just change all their currents. We began to search, to look for different types of contact in these exercises. How could we transform the physical elements into elements of human contact? A great play with one's partner, a living dialogue with the body, with the partner we have evoked in our imagination, or perhaps between the parts of the body where the hand speaks to the leg without putting this dialogue into words or thought. These almost paradoxical positions go beyond the limits of naturalism.

We also began to work with the Delsarte system. I was very interested in Delsarte's thesis that there are introverted and extroverted reactions in human contact. At the same time I found his thesis very stereotyped; it was really very funny as actor training, but there was something to it so I studied it. We began searching through Delsarte's program for those elements which are not stereotyped. Afterwards we had to find new elements of our own in order to realize the goal of our program. Then the personality of the actor working as instructor became instrumental. The physical exercises were largely developed by the actors. I only asked the questions, the actors searched. One question was followed by another. Some of the exercises were conditioned by an actress who had great difficulty with them. For that reason I made her an instructor. She was ambitious and now she is a great master of these exercises – but we searched together.

Later we found that if one treats the exercises as purely physical, an emotive hypocrisy, beautiful gestures with the emotions of a fairy-dance develop. So we gave that up and began to look for personal justification in small details, by playing with colleagues, using a sense of surprise, of the unexpected – real justifications which are unexpected – how to fight, how to make unkind gestures, how to parody oneself, and so on. At that moment, the exercises took life.

With these exercises we looked for a conjunction between the structure of an element and the associations which transform it into the mode of each particular actor. How can one conserve the objective elements and still go beyond them toward a purely subjective work? This is the contradiction of acting. It's the kernel of the training.

There are different kinds of exercises. The program is always open. When we are working on a production we do not use the exercises in a play. If we did, it would be stereotyped. But for certain plays, certain scenes, we may have to do special exercises. Sometimes something is left from these for the basic program.

There have been periods – up to eight months – when we have done no exercises at all. We found that we were doing the exercises for their own sake and we gave them up. [. . .]

At this point in the interview Mr. Grotowski agreed that descriptions of a few exercises might be included. A description is dangerous because imitations based on a written record can lead to severe distortions. Once, during a discussion in the course, a student asked Mr. Grotowski how his work could be continued after he was gone. He replied that the class could continue the exercises but that if he returned after five years and found them doing the same work it would mean they had proceeded incorrectly. The exercises are personal; they develop around certain principles but their exact physical shape depends upon the individual performer. The basic principles are: (1) to relate the physical to the psychic; (2) to surpass fatigue; (3) to follow one's innermost associations; (4) to avoid 'beauty' and 'gymnastics.'

One relates one exercise to the next. In this sense there is only one exercise – a continuing, incomplete, related research into the relationship between the physical and the psychical.

The head roll   The head is pivoted on the neck and rolled around in both clockwise and counter-clockwise motion. This can cause some pain at first, as all the exercises can.

The body roll   The torso is pivoted from the base of the spine and rolled around in both clockwise amd counter-clockwise motion. At the most extreme backward position, the back is arched and fluid.

The pelvic roll   Much like the stripper's 'bump and grind.' The pelvis is rolled both in clockwise and counter-clockwise motion.

The shoulder flex   Each shoulder individually is raised and then dropped in three distinct steps. One seeks the balance of the skeletal frame and muscles.

The shoulder-stand   This is somewhat like a head-stand. The face is laid against the floor with one arm and hand under the upper torso, palm up. One rotates the body so that the knees approach the hand, which is held as in a normal head-stand. One proceeds to lift the body as in a normal head-stand, balancing on the cheek, shoulder, and flexed hand and arm. One seeks the balance in a variety of positions, rotating the pelvis, stretching the legs upward, and so on. The 'result' is not important: one must seek, during each step, the body's balance.

The cat One begins by lying flat on one's stomach. Not asleep, but ready for activity. First one opens the eyes, looks to each side, up and down. Then one flexes a shoulder, then the next. Then one raises the shoulders so that the back forms an arch from the top of the spine to the heels. In one motion one lifts up into the reverse arch, as a cat stretches upon awakening. One tests and flexes the entire body. Then one rotates the pelvis in a full circle, maintaining floor contact only with the feet and the hands. Then one brings a leg up against the side of the body, pulling it toward the torso with all one's strength. While maintaining the power, bringing the upper leg and thigh toward the body, one begins a counter-force pushing the lower leg and foot away from the body. As the lower force increases the leg kicks away from the body. Repeat with the other leg. Stretch upwards once more, resume the pelvic rotation, and then make contact with the floor again, first with the lower leg and then progressively with the rest of the body, keeping the back arched and fluid. Lower each shoulder and then the head.

There are other exercises. Somersaults and rolls, head-stands, back-bends. An important – perhaps the most important – exercise cannot be described, since each actor will adapt it personally. One takes the elements of the exercises and, forming movements with the hands, begins to relate these to one's most personal associations. [. . .]

In watching Mr. Grotowski work with the students one was struck most by his intense personal concentration on each, his avoidance of formulas and generalized solutions. He spoke, laid hands on people, followed them around, and watched with deep intensity. [. . .]

Grotowski: [These exercises] do function as tests. If an actor has blocks, the underdeveloped parts of his body are very visible. One can also observe the blocks in the association work. For example, in a physical exercise it is necessary to evoke a partner, to live for him, take the stimulus from him – all the functions of dialogue. Blocks in this process are clearly visible during the exercises. In the somersaults, the actor who hesitates, who will not take risks, will also hesitate at the culminating moment of his role. [. . .]

Schechner: I want to move now into another area, *mise-en-scène*. [. . .]

Grotowski: At the beginning, when I worked in the conventional theatre, I thought that the most important thing was to avoid the rivalry between theatre and film. So I asked myself: how can we have a meeting between actors and audience which is a real one, an exchange, something that cannot be done in film or on TV?

That was not concrete enough, so I began with completely naive things.

Actors spoke directly to spectators, or actors played in the entire hall including where the audience was supposed to be. Then it became necessary to change everything. I found a young theatre architect, Gurawski, who was also possessed by this idea of transformation. We collaborated, agreeing always that if one has a problem one seeks an associate, the theatre is always a troupe. I can't do everything in this troupe, but I can stimulate each member of it and be stimulated in return. [. . .]

[W]hen we did Marlowe's *Dr. Faustus*, we found a direct word-for-word situation. The dramatic function of the spectators and the function of spectator as spectator were the same. For the first time we saw authentic spontaneity. The audience was treated as Faustus' invited guests, people whom Faustus seeks so that he can make an analysis of his own life. The spectators sat around a long table and Faustus, with the other people from his life, arranged for them a flashback production. It was absolutely concrete. For example, he said, 'Now you will see the scene of when I first met the devil. I was sitting in a chair like this, and I was listening to a song.' Then there is the song and in front of the spectators a woman comes in. The confession was authentic because the actor really mobilized the associations of his life. At the same time he made Faustus' confession with the text, he accomplished his own very drastic but disciplined confession.

There were waves of movement in the room. Faustus never waited for answers from the spectators, but he observed their eyes and we saw them turn red or pale, one could hear their breathing; something real was happening.

Before *Faustus* we staged Wyspianski's *Akropolis*, where we got the same thing but weren't conscient. *Akropolis* is a classical play organized around a Polish sanctuary, the Royal Palace of Krakow. During the night of the Resurrection, the figures on the royal tapestries come to life and play out episodes from the history of Europe and Poland. At the end there is Christ's Resurrection (he is Apollo at the same time) and a triumphant procession forms to liberate Europe.

All very good, we said. But the Royal Palace is not a sanctuary anymore; it is not what it was in the nineteenth century: the cemetery of our civilization. That's why Wyspianski called the Royal Palace the Akropolis: it was Poland's ruined past. We asked ourselves painful and paradoxical questions. What is the cemetery of our own civilization? Perhaps a battleground from the war. One day I knew that without a doubt it was Auschwitz. At Auschwitz all nations encountered each other: Greeks, Poles, Jews, French – all the tribes were there waiting for something, but the Messiah never came for those who were killed.

We organized it all into the rhythm of work in the extermination camp, with certain breaks in the rhythm where the characters refer themselves to the traditions of their youth, the dreams of their nations – the dream of freedom, of normal life which for them was impossible. Each dream was broken, each act was a paradox. For example, the love between Helen and Paris. They were homosexuals (a common occurrence in prisons) and their love scene was watched by all the prisoners who laughed. The final procession was the march to the crematorium. The prisoners took a corpse and they began to cry, 'Here is our Savior.' A procession with organized hysteria. They all fell to the ground in exhaustion during this song of triumph.

We did not wish to have a stereotyped production with evil SS men and noble prisoners. We cannot play prisoners, we cannot create such images in the theatre. Any documentary film is stronger. We looked for something else. What is Auschwitz? Is it something we could organize today? A world which functions inside us. Thus there were no SS men, only prisoners who so organized the space that they must oppress each other to survive. [. . .]

No realistic illusions, no prisoners' costumes. We used plain costumes made from potato sacks and wooden shoes. These were close to reality, a reality that is too strong to be expressed theatrically. How did we cope with this danger? The rhythm of the actors' steps functioned as music, every moment was organized in tempo and volume so that the shoes became a paradoxical musical instrument which, in that situation, was much more terrible than a direct image.

The prisoners worked all the time. They took metal pipes that were piled in the center of the room and built something. At the start, the room was empty (except for the pile of pipes) and there was a seating arrangement for the audience. By the end of the production the entire room was filled, oppressed, by the metal. The construction was made of heating pipes. We didn't build a crematorium but we gave the spectators the association of fire. It was indirect, nevertheless afterwards the spectators said that we had built a crematorium.

Certain scenes typified the kind of unity I am talking about. The marriage of Jacob and Rachel, for example. A prisoner takes a piece of pipe, there is nothing else, and he begins to look for a woman. He touches the pipe as if it were a woman. It's funny to the other prisoners and another prisoner answers as if he were a woman. For the first prisoner it is the pipe that has answered. The marriage procession is that of tragic farce. A man and a woman – a man and a pipe – and they begin to sing songs of marriage that are very well known in Poland. At that moment a very authentic process begins in the actor, a return to life – no more buffoonery. Then the marriage procession, laughter and songs, and the rhythm of the wooden shoes.

These scenic elements – pipes, shoes, wheelbarrows, costumes – were very intentionally found. It is no accident that the famous Polish designer, Szasna, who spent 1940 to 1945 at Auschwitz, picked these elements. He has always been called abstract. The scenic elements of *Akropolis* were not abstract, but neither were they realistic. These elements were concrete objects, things from bad dreams, but all completely 'untheatrical.' Szasna found these objects in flea markets and junk shops.

The actors did not play prisoners, they played what they were doing – people plunged into absurd work, oppressed by a detailed routine that was insupportable. They referred back to their memories and their personal contacts with happier days and, at the culminating moments, these associations were stopped by this absurd work which was not even the real work of the exterminating camp.

Each actor kept a particular facial expression, a defensive tick which was elaborated with facial muscles without makeup. It was personal for each, but as a group it was agonizing – the image of humanity destroyed.

The spectators sat throughout the room. They were treated as people of another world, either as ghosts which only got in the way or as air. The actors spoke through them. The personal situation of the spectators was totally different from that of the characters. The spectators functioned both as spectators and within the context of the play. They are in the middle and at the same time they are totally irrelevant, incomprehensible to the actors – as the living cannot understand the dead.

Finally, [in] *The Constant Prince*, [. . .] we put the spectators in a voyeuristic relationship to the production. They were watching something prohibited. The room was constructed so that the audience was almost hidden behind a wall. They watched something much lower down – as medical students observe an operation, a psychic surgery – and there was no relation whatsoever between actors and spectators. None.

One could see over the wall the heads of the audience, and one could observe the rhythm of these heads and, at certain points, the rhythm of breathing. Some of my foreign disciples were deceived. They said, 'You are a traitor to the idea of osmosis between the spectator and the actor.' I am always ready to be a traitor to an absolute rule. It is not essential that actors and spectators be mixed. The important thing is that the relation between the actors and the spectators in space be a significant one.

If the contact between the spectator and the actor is very close and direct, a strong psychic curtain falls between them. It's the opposite of what one might expect. But if the spectators play the role of spectators and that role has a function within the production, the psychic curtain vanishes. [. . .]

Schechner: My question about textual montage is really one about your attitude toward the text. I think you know the question I want to ask.

Grotowski: The initial montage is done before rehearsals begin. But during rehearsals we do additional montage all the time. The principle is the following – it is very clear if you understand the creative situation of the actor – one asks the actors who play Hamlet to recreate their own Hamlet. That is, do the same thing that Shakespeare did with the traditional Hamlet. [. . .]

Every great creator builds bridges between the past and himself, between his roots and his being. That is the only sense in which the artist is a priest: *pontifex* in Latin, he who builds bridges [. . .]. It's the same with the creativity of the actor. He must not illustrate Hamlet, he must meet Hamlet. The actor must give his cue within the context of his own experience. And the same for the director. I didn't do Wyspianski's *Akropolis*, I met it. I didn't think or analyze Auschwitz from the outside; it's this thing in me which is something I didn't know directly, but indirectly I knew very well.

One structures the montage so that this confrontation can take place. We eliminate those parts of the text which have no importance for us, those parts with which we can neither agree nor disagree. Within the montage one finds certain words that function vis-à-vis our own experiences. The result is that we cannot say whether it is Wyspianski's *Akropolis*. Yes, it is. But at the same time it is our *Akropolis*. One cannot say that this is Marlowe's *Faustus* or Calderon's *Constant Prince*. It is our *Faustus*, our *Constant Prince*. All the fragments of the text which were unnecessary were eliminated, but we interpolated little. We did not want to write a new play, we wished to confront ourselves.

It's a meeting, a confrontation. That's why there must be little inter-
polation. But there is rearrangement of words, scenes. We organize the event
according to the logic of our cues. But the essential parts of the text – those
which carry the sense of the literary work – remain intact and are treated with
great respect. Otherwise there could be no meeting.

[. . .]

27

TALKING WITH PETER BROOK

Richard Schechner, Jean-Claude Carrière, Joel Jouanneau, Georges Banu[1]

Translated by Anna Husemoller

T109, 1986

THE REALITY OF ZERO

Richard Schechner: When in 1970 you began the International Centre for Theatre Research in Paris you started working with non-English-speaking actors from several cultures – African, Asian, American, European. Why did you form this kind of company?

Peter Brook: The big step came in 1965 when within the Royal Shakespeare Company a group emerged exploring the 'other languages' of theatre. Within a theatre dominated by the obsession with spoken language, my so-called 'Theatre of Cruelty Group' explored communicating with sounds and syllables. I began exploring also the possibility – and techniques – of exchange among people of different cultures. Then in 1968, at the invitation of Jean-Louis Barrault, head of the Théâtre de Nations, I went to Paris to direct a workshop with people from different cultures with very different backgrounds.

In that workshop I saw some very special possibilities. Yoshi Oida and Barry Stanton worked on *The Tempest*, one playing Ferdinand and the other Miranda, so there was a change of sex, of size, of language. I saw – as Henry Ford might have said – that geography is bunk.

Each human being carries with him/her all the continents, but each only knows one of them. So when a person with one known continent and a mass of dark continents meets someone else whose condition is the same, and they communicate, there is an illumination for each.

Schechner: This need to communicate interculturally connects your work with Eugenio Barba's, Jerzy Grotowski's, Tadashi Suzuki's, Wole Soyinka's: a search for cultural synthesis.

Brook: In every travel, in every meeting, I find the same dichotomy in every Third World country: do we allow ourselves to be influenced by outside models or do we return to our own sources? Obviously to be invaded by outside models – whether these are the old models of colonial theatre or the new ones of experimental theatre – doesn't solve anyone's problems. Nor does returning to folklore. Every Third World country passionately lives this difficulty.

But it seems to me that people ignore another possibility: the reality of zero, the moment when any group anywhere in the world comes together – at the first rehearsal, at the fifteenth rehearsal, at the first meeting with an audience. At that absolute and pregnant moment, geography and history cease to exist. From this zero can come an infinity of forms, provided one is aware of the qualities each person carries. Within zero nobody is a blank sheet, everybody carries her/his own baggage. If, when those baggages are projected into this living, pregnant void, instead of a cultural preoccupation there is a dharmic preoccupation, then different, individual strands of expression can find their way into this zero moment.

Schechner: Let's go back to 1968. Yoshi is working with you. What other members of the *Mahabharata* company have been with you for a long time?

Brook: Bruce Myers and Andreas Katsulas since '70, Mireille Maalouf since '73, Toshi Tsuchitori since '73, Alain Maratrat since '74.

Schechner: Obviously you've built a company with a core.

Brook: Since '74.

Schechner: And then there is the archeology of your performances, the conscious layering of several cultures. Your shows recapitulate your travels and research. The acting styles, scenographic effects, narrative themes. And the way the *Mahabharata* rearticulates elements from earlier works. Take fire, which is so spectacular in *Mahabharata*, so delicate in *The Ik*. Or the carpet on which the musicians sit – didn't that come first from Iran? The *Mahabharata*'s French dialogs are spoken by performers of many different cultures who retain distinct regional acting styles while collectively playing out a Sanskrit epic. In one scene Australian Aborigine *didgeridoos* are played. For me, at that moment, the performance actualized the cultural layerings of India herself: Melanesian, Harappan, Vedic, Sanskritic, Hindu, Muslim, English, Contemporary.

Brook: You're making me think about things which I don't think about analytically but only intuitively.

I've the greatest suspicion of mixing cultures. There's nothing I condemn more than a cultural salad. That is not what we do at the Centre. There's a misunderstanding that suddenly in 1970 I broke with a whole life and, like Gauguin, went off somewhere. Looking back at my life I see my precise steps.

In 1969 I was doing *Midsummer Night's Dream*. Although for ten years I had been doing experimental work, with the *Dream*, for the very first time, I played something out of the theatre. It was also the first time I had the idea of saying during rehearsals, 'Now let's go and play this for an audience.' So we took *Dream* into a community center near Stratford. I decided not to take any of the props or elements we had been rehearsing with, which in *Dream* were vital. We went into a hall with no focus, no shape, no artificial light, and for everyone it was a revelation, this different flow of energy coming directly from the audience.

Then came the work in the Roundhouse where we re-improvised shows in a completely new way. And at the Centre where we were working under conditions that we did not know in advance. This brought us to the start of a long series of events in Persia, Africa, France, Australia, and California, playing in daylight. I remember Bruce Myers in Africa being very moved by the fact that after ten years as a professional actor he was for the first time actually seeing the faces of the audience.

You understand, maybe more than anyone, how radical a change the playing in daylight was. The quarry in Avignon where we do *Mahabharata*, the daylight, the all-night performance – all stem from that first day when for the first time we shared not only space but light with the audience.

In Persepolis we related to the sun going down; we started the second part of *Orghast* at four in the morning. We had to build great bonfires because there was no other light. *Orghast* ended with Claude Confortes coming over a hill leading a cow with its bells tinkling as dawn broke. In the same way I remember standing near a duck pond in Iran – and now I see the link between that and the water in *Mahabharata* fifteen years later. There was the pond, and goats, and a little teahouse. At the back of that teahouse there was a garden, and I thought, 'This is where I would like to play *Midsummer Night's Dream*.' And although the logistics of taking the Royal Shakespeare Company into a small teahouse near Shiraz were obviously ridiculous, the idea was there. But even if we did *Dream* there the audience of villagers could not come to grips with Shakespeare's play because of the language barrier. This barrier is only relative when you do the sort of prestige tours to festivals and cities. Out of this realization came *Orghast*, which was an experiment with the vibratory power of ancient languages. Directly after doing *Orghast* in Persepolis we went into two villages. In one we did a pure improvisation in the ru-hozi style. Ted Hughes suggested a theme of the bride and bridegroom. This worked very well with the local people because everyone could understand the basic images – boy, girl, parents. We used a made-up language. We then wanted to try the same experiment with *Orghast*. We re-adapted a folk version of *Orghast*. It was very exciting for us to put it into a ruined building on the outskirts of a village. But the communication was nil, because the premises of *Orghast* were far too abstract and intellectual to reach the villagers.

So there was the contradiction we had to resolve. Why was the first carpet show so totally successful while *Orghast*, which came from a much deeper search, was so hermetic that not even a change of style could open it up?

Then in 1973 I and eleven actors went to Africa where we learned to de-intellectualize our work. We learned to play outside theatre conditions without formulated concepts. What you open yourself to is the grabbing by everything that God gives at that moment. Whether it's the fall of a sparrow, which literally happened when we were with the Teatro Campesino, or any other 'accident': what the light is giving you, what the elements are giving you, what the presence of the audience does or what you can get from another actor who is less than a foot away. All these only flow if you are in the state of improvisation, having no concept whatsoever to start with, but letting concepts develop out of the work.

Schechner: No concepts?

Brook: And knowing that nothing happens at all if there isn't a technique, but the technique is not a know-how, it's a practice. So we start by learning how to sustain an improvisation decently for about two minutes. Four years later our best improvisation was about two hours. What this meant was that bit by bit we were in the absolute opposite of the best interior theatre conditions where everything is based on preparing known means to attain known goals. We were working in a variety of conditions in a variety of cultures. What was most important for an acting group was to receive from life within very different cultures. We went to Africa not because the Africans were far away and different from us, but because they carried within them a very high culture. We could have gone into any number of villages in France and found people very different from ourselves, but we would not have found people whose culture was so rich.

My basic method in traveling is never to take any notes. After a certain time everything drains through a filter of memory until in the end – let's say for instance, out of the million extraordinary impressions I've had of India – time goes by and I find while working on the *Mahabharata* that water and fire and earth remain, not having been flooded out by too many details. The same with the didgeridoos – out of Australia remains the sound of the didgeridoo which finds its place naturally in the Indian world.

[. . .]

Schechner: Of all the intentionally intercultural productions I've seen, your *Mahabharata* is the finest example of something genuinely syncretic. I think your success is due to two things. First, your long experience of moving from culture to culture so that your home base is now relational rather than cultural. Peter Brook's 'home' is at the intersection of cultural energies rather than in Paris.

Brook: Exactly. That's what I mean by the 'reference zero.' The life within zero is relational.

Schechner: Second, the *Mahabharata* tells such a powerful story, is so full of dramaturgical needs, that each action is called forth concretely by a particular need.

Brook: In 1966, just after *Marat/Sade*, I did *US*, a play about Vietnam. In the middle of our work a young Indian, Asif Currimbhoy, came by with a short, six-page play on the *Bhagavad Gita*. At that time I had never read the *Gita*. [. . .] Years later, about '73, when I started working with Jean-Claude Carrière on *Timon of Athens*, which he adapted, we started talking about future projects. And I said, 'There is something that can make a play of our times. All I know is this central image. Let's consult a great friend who's a Sanskrit scholar.'

So I asked this scholar to come over. I said to him, 'Tell me more about the Indian work where a warrior says, "I am not going to fight."' To tell us who that warrior was, who he was fighting, and why he couldn't fight took my scholar friend three months. And so we received the *Mahabharata* in the traditional way, orally. My friend didn't tell us the epic in a linear way. He would say, 'We must meet again tomorrow, because this warrior's chariot driver is Krishna and I must tell you the scene where Krishna is lying asleep and the two opposing leaders – Arjuna and Duryodhana – come to him . . .' 'Yes but,' I said, 'why are Arjuna and Duryodhana at war with each other?' And he'd have to tell me – and so bit by bit unfolded the entire Vyasa *Mahabharata*.

Schechner: How did you prepare the particular theatrical event I saw in the quarry near Avignon?

Brook: This is where the ten years of preparation comes in. After our encounter with the *Mahabharata* orally, Jean-Claude wrote a first version – simple play length, two hours. He wrote without reference to anything except his own memory. We looked at this and said, 'This is an exercise between us. Now we really start work.' Then began a process parallel with all the other work we were doing – reflecting lots of the work we'd done over the ten years. The Kerala Kalamandalam troupe gave us Kathakali workshops without costumes or makeup. We played *Ubu* to them and they played *Mahabharata* to us.

Then we went to Costa Rica, where on a Saturday morning as a children's play we did our first public improvisation of 'The Game of Dice' from the *Mahabharata*. There are five people in the company who remain from that. During that time Jean-Claude and I decided our basic through-line was to tell the Pandava–Kaurava story. In India they don't need this – everyone knows the basic story. They can perform variations and fragments. The second condition we gave ourselves was not to talk at all about length or a date for the premiere.

Then we ran an international workshop mainly on the relation between certain kinds of music and the French text. For this Jean-Claude wrote his first fragments, two or three pages, a speech, some dialog that we sang to, danced to, and dramatized with or without music. After that began a series of journeys to India.

Schechner: Where did you go?

Brook: We went to Udipi – straight to Yakshagatla at a Krishna temple. Then down to Cananore for Teyyam, then to the Kalamandalam for Kithakali – a long night of only *Mahabharata*. From there across to Madurai just to hit a big festival. In Madurai we went into the forest to rehearse the scene with Shiva in the forest. From Madurai to Madras, from Madras to Kanchipuram for a meeting with a Shankara. Then on to Calcutta for a whole day with Habib Tanvir, his actors, and his storyteller. Magnificent. He told story after story, which was thrilling for the actors. Being so close to the material, they could follow his every inflection. From Calcutta to Benares. Then we returned to Paris.

For *Mahabharata* we did an enormous number of auditions. This was good for Jean-Claude because these auditions were working sessions. Every time he wrote a scene we could try it out, take it back, reject it, rewrite. He was rewriting through the whole rehearsal period. Which of course is terrifying for actors dealing with such an enormous package of material. They would master a scene, but Jean-Claude and I would arrive the next morning and say, 'Well, that scene's out.'

Through to today that's how we've been working.

Schechner: How did you decide to do the play in three parts?

Brook: Gradually, through a process of evolution, the essential takes over and the unimportant falls away. So gradually it grew to nine hours, and from nine hours came a decision to divide it in two. Then we thought to break it into three parts. Then we felt we'd present it both ways – in three parts and as a single all-night performance. [. . .]

MANY PERSPECTIVES, MANY POINTS OF VIEW

Brook: In the heart of the *Mahabharata* is destruction. When it starts, the *Mahabharata* is apparently only about the gods, giving us the impression of an imaginary enchanted tale which really doesn't concern us. But little by little the mythical characters 'descend,' they get involved with conflicts of ambition, love, jealousy, pride. The myth becomes theatre – theatre of war. We are faced with the truth of violence and suffering, the same war as always. The *Mahabharata* is of our time.

There is war, this inexplicable impulse to massacre – but also one always hears a profound interior voice speaking of self-understanding. The *Mahabharata* heroes are forced to confront both the impulse to kill and inner voice. They must understand more than just the shock of events, they must strip away illusion even as they are taught everything is illusion.

Jean-Claude Carrière: Everything is illusion except thought. Even the gods are destructible. There's no utopia, no ideal.

Brook: Unlike optimistic or pessimistic or analytic works, the *Mahabharata* doesn't propose any solution. The collective and the individual destiny is announced all the time by Krishna, who tries to prevent while declaring that it will – it must – happen. Krishna is a challenge to our moral senses, but he is not negative. He is not a fatalist. Christianity resolved these contradictions with the doctrine of Grace. Indians tell me I was born in the Kali Yuga, the era of destruction. How did I wind up here and now – I would prefer to have been born earlier. They tell me the only short-cut is to go to the end of yourself. And they show me how Pandavas, at the end of their exile in the forest, disguised their most secret thoughts and how Arjuna the warrior becomes a transvestite to escape a curse.

Carrière: The work on *Mahabharata* was empirical, not analytical. Some scenes took months or years to find, and we're not finished yet. Others came together in less than a week's rehearsal.

Brook: We extracted sixteen main characters from the poem, and put a lot of importance on Vyasa, the storyteller who tells the tale to a young boy while a scribe writes it all down. From the start we used these Brechtian techniques, offering many perspectives, many points of view.

Carrière: In the troupe there are sixteen different nationalities. This allows us to show themes freed from any particular culture. There is only one Indian, the actress Mallika Sarabhai. If we had tried to make a wholly Indian production the barrier would have remained, or if we had taken only Africans the universal aspects would have not been so strongly felt. We avoided realism – for in that tradition how could a white actor have a black daughter or a 75-year-old Japanese man father a European baby? Bengali filmmaker Satyajit Ray once thought of making a *Mahabharata*, but he gave it up because he could not assemble a coherent troupe. In the movies, if you need elephants, you need elephants. But in theatre the elephants can all be in a valley, out of view: you don't need even a single elephant.

Joel Jouanneau: After the *Iks* and the *Conference of the Birds* comes the *Mahabharata*. Back to India. Does this mean back to the source? Is India esthetically important for your work?

Brook: Esthetically important, certainly not. I've always tried to get closer to the roots. The source is always the same. The branches of a tree extend out in different directions, but they all come out of the same trunk. This was how I was led to the Persian source in the *Conference*, then to Shakespeare, and now to the *Mahabharata*. There is a very strong bond between what is covered up, or hidden, and the surface, even if the surfaces or appearances are very different. Fortunately this is true, because nothing is more boring in life – even more so in theatre – than to keep seeing the same shapes and forms over and over again. Of course with the *Mahabharata* we were affected by Indian culture, its shapes and forms, but as far as only taking into account its esthetic, or worse, exotic interest, I would have to say an outright no.

Jouanneau: And what about the trips back and forth to explore the culture, like those you took to Africa?

Brook: It's all very simple. Every one of us tries more or less to be a complete being. This, however, is impossible. We are only fragments of that being. But in order to grasp what we could be, we need a model, image, and if we were to look at the whole world, we would say that the myriad cultures and races compose a puzzle. The African, the Japanese, the Indian, the French are some of the pieces of this puzzle. If we had to determine which puzzle pieces were inferior or superior to others we would arrive at an impasse. This we know very well, but if all differences and specificities were to be considered, we would look for what is most beneficial to all in each one. We could then attempt to reconstruct the puzzle. This is what I try to do in my work . . .

Jouanneau: But the relationship between the West and India also has a history. The colonial era is with us in our memory, also the myth of Gandhi, Kathmandu in the '60s, and the music of Shankar digested by George Harrison: our fascination for the Orient, and most particularly India, is continuous. Where is the *Mahabharata* in this context?

Brook: Let's take a concrete example. In India, there are two very important epics. The *Ramayana* is performed all over India, but the story of Rama is so specific that to represent it in the West would not make sense. Most audiences would not have the frame of reference to understand the characters. With the *Mahabharata* it is different. The work is Shakespearean in the true sense of the word. Its form is essentially Indian but based on universal conflicts and ideals.

Jouanneau: But dealing with such a huge work, you had to make many choices. What criteria did you use?

Brook: The play represents many years of work with Jean-Claude Carrière. In truth, ten years. We finished the first version seven years ago, and we've been working every day for the past three. With this text, there's no other possible method. If we had been sloppy or clumsy, the result would have been sloppy as well. The selection we made was intellectual or theoretical. The only basic method we used was what I call 'sifting.' At the beginning, we were blinded by this epic – its hundred characters, its twelve volumes. So we had to distill it until we could see clearly. It is like an opera chorus that appears to be an anonymous mass the first day you work with it but then two days later the confusion lessens, and finally after two weeks you know everyone's individual capacities. With the *Mahabharata* the first choice we made was simple: that is, the central story – the fratricidal war within a family (which leads to hundreds of digressions) was the main thread. Then we sifted. For example, two out of the twelve volumes in the *Mahabharata* consist wholly of Bhishma's death-bed speech, a purely theoretical discourse on the essence of life. You need five or six days to read just this text. We kept this character in, but in our play he tells a very simple story within a two-minute span.

Jouanneau: Your production takes nine hours. [. . .] The *Mahabharata* took ten years of work. How did you work on the actual production when your actors for the most part did not know the book? How were you able to reduce the gap – which must have been large – between what you learned in your preparatory work, and the actors' lack of knowledge?

Brook: The audience has the same problem. The audience is not prepared either. People sign a tacit contract with us, saying, 'I'm at your disposition for two, three, or nine hours.' In that time we have to transmit what took the actors months of work to do. It's the same process for the director in relation to the actors. The first thing I had to do was spark an interest for the subject in the actors. An actor is not necessarily in harmony with a work. Sometimes he is with his role, but if he were to focus his work only on the passage that he interprets, this could throw the production off-balance.

Therefore we worked as a group for a long time to create a well-known team. At the first meeting I made clear I would do a lot of the talking first because the *Mahabharata* was so unfamiliar but that later it was necessary for the relationship between director and actors to be reversed, that everyone would retrieve their independence. If we had kept up the relationship we had at the beginning, it would have led to what I detest: a totalitarian attitude over a group. But with the *Mahabharata*, it was possible to begin with a senti-mental democracy within the working team, because spontaneity in such conditions could not have produced a thing. I should add that I did the staging as late as I could, because I wanted to explore possibilities with the actors and do more sifting. In this production, I didn't make definitive choices in the staging of certain scenes until the last day.

Jouanneau: Was this the reason you rejected scenery in the conventional sense of the word, whether at the Bouffes du Nord or the quarry near Avignon?

Brook: I've worked extensively in the past with complex scenery which at times I designed myself. Then I came to a very simple conclusion: it is wrong to conceive of scenery as fundamental to staging. Scenery is not now a part of my conception of a play, whereas at one time scenery was a determining factor of the production. Today I believe directing is above all the living relationship that should be established between the text, the actors, and the audience. But when I asked myself if I should abolish scenery I said no, it should be the bridge between staging and the space.

According to the great tradition in theatre, that is, theatre from the past two or three thousand years in the diversity of its forms all around the world, scenery is an extremely minor element. It only exists in theatres which must be sheltered from the wind and rain, which takes place inside a building. There scenery plays the role of stimulant. But I don't use expressionist scenery that takes on a narrative role as important as actors' eyes or gestures. Making scenery more important than the actors is an outmoded idea, good maybe for cinema but not for theatre.

[. . .]

Georges Banu: How did you put together your company for the *Mahabharata*? For example, for the five Pandavas, it looks as if you cast the actors so that each would incarnate a certain aspect of humanity.

Brook: I never start off with schematic ideas. I did not do casting *à la* UNESCO. I worked by searching and sifting. Marie-Hélène Estienne looked for actors everywhere. We set up multiple auditions; we saw hundreds of people; we traveled a lot; we went to Dakar to meet Senegalese actors. We attended certain performances in Paris to see African actors from other countries. The need to have actors who spoke French imposed practical limits. Beyond that, I kept my usual criteria: that an actor be interiorly open to the subject, exteriorly open to collective work. [. . .]

Banu: For the *Mahabharata*, you concentrated the space more than you usually do. There is less action in the audience's space. You presented the Kurukshatra war as if the spectators had to see it while remaining detached, not directly involved.

Brook: That's right. First, there was the extensive collaboration with Chloe Obolensky. For months, we worked on the basic elements of the staging. Like always, something that appears simple is, in fact, a result of all kinds of abandoned ideas, because simple solutions do not present themselves right away. We thought we would need platforms to indicate different areas; we thought about surrounding the stage with water, etc. By a process of elimination, little by little, we kept the idea of the arena, but only after getting rid of things like doors and windows which we originally used.

When I work, I always have two things in mind: to do what is right for the work and to do what is fresh. For example, we exhausted certain possibilities of the Bouffes du Nord. We waited to let the ruin-like beauty of the Bouffes, which is the true beauty of the theatre, stand out. However, the Bouffes was becoming sordid, dirty and needed a new, luminous touch. The walls were repainted to remove the somber, tragic dimension so needed in *Carmen*. For *Mahabharata*, the walls are luminous – this meant months of work for a team of painters. In the environment there are two axes: a pond and a little river. Sometimes the whole arena – covered with earth – is bordered by fire. The result is a scenography that expresses itself through the natural elements of earth, air, water, and fire, but its apparent simplicity results from a long maturation.

Acting in the house is an effect, and, like everything else, it exhausts itself. Beyond the need for freshness is another thing. In plays like *The Cherry Orchard* or *Carmen* the images are close enough to us now so that the audience can really believe it belongs to either of these worlds. A small provocation of the imagination and we believe that we're in the same house as Ranevskaya. But in the *Mahabharata*, the war has to be treated on two different levels. We show battle scenes close up. But while we wanted to say that this war is in our world, it is not there all the time. To show the war of the *Mahabharata* is not to show a nineteenth- or twentieth-century war.

Banu: The music is very active. It plays its role like music in Oriental productions: it participates fully and develops a dialog with the action. The
musicians are present, visible, and incorporated into the production.

Brook: I experimented a lot at the beginning, because I felt that for the nine
hours of performance we would need considerably varied music. I even
wondered whether I would need a composer this time. I looked around, but
besides Richard Peaslee, I never found a musician who was like writer Jean-
Claude Carrière, that is, someone who is both a super-specialist in his domain
and totally involved with what we are doing. (I had this relationship with
Marius Constant, it is true, but Oriental music is not at all his specialty.) I saw
composers from the Mid-East and India, but either the composer was completely in the Western tradition or had nothing to propose beyond what came
naturally from improvised music.

   The music's richness and participation comes from Toshi Tsuchitori. He
lived two years in India, walking from one place to another, listening to all
sorts of music. We ended up with music that wasn't quite Indian, or non-
Indian, a kind of music that has the 'taste' of India. The team had to arrive
at a certain tonal color. This color was the product of the musicians' avid
research. For example, Kim Menzer went to India for three months to learn
how to play the nagaswaram. He is the only European capable of reproducing
this sound. Kim is an excellent woodwind player, but it took him three months
to get a sound out of the nagaswaram. [. . .]

Banu: You make the poet Vyasa the one who guides us through the story. But
Alain Maratrat portrays Vyasa as a troubadour, a wandering artist, and not at
all like a great artist who knows the secrets of the world. Was it your aim to
contrast Vyasa's situation and his image?

Brook: This was our goal. We observed Indian theatre extensively. We had to
be open to the Indian way of storytelling. It was obvious from the start that
we had to eliminate classical Indian art at all levels: in acting, in dance, in
song, in music. For this art was only accessible to certain Indians who have
been devoted to it for many generations. On the other hand, we saw that in
India there was another style of theatre, another way, Indian as well, to tell the
Mahabharata, which exists everywhere: popular form. This popular style is
exactly our own, and we call it in our terminology a 'carpet show.' It's *Ubu* – –
the same acting, the same climate. And we wanted the *Mahabharata* to be
both very close to our audience and at a certain distance. We mustn't speak
from above but from below. That means we had to begin at a level of very
natural contact.

   As for Vyasa, we could have presented him as an old impressive guru, a 70-
year-old yogi who tells the story. But I don't know any actor capable of that.
And we would have to place ourselves permanently at this level. The other
possibility was to do something that would come out of our own work, that
is, by introducing a storyteller who would be from the other side, a French-
man. Right from the start of the play, Maurice Benichou, who is also
French, as Ganesha establishes a direct contact with the audience. During
the first rehearsals, we started the play with those two not as characters but
as people who speak with the audience. We changed it, but the first idea was
to speak directly to the audience. Then we felt that it was more touching to

see Vyasa answering the questions of a child, addressing himself to the audience. [. . .]

Banu: The role of the child is very important, but at the same time, what struck me was that you do not give him very much liberty. In John Heilpern's book on your journey to Africa, *Conference of the Birds*, you said: 'the presence of the child immediately brings with it a sense of liberty.' But here I thought more of those pictures of children I have observed in Oriental scenes. I had the impression of a great contrast between the fragility of the child and the extraordinary mission it was charged with.

Brook: That's correct. The child is there to receive and to give us that which is in the *Mahabharata*. It is a story told to 'someone.' In the Sanskrit *Mahabharata*, the story is told to a young king who is about to make 'sacrifice.' He is about to massacre all the serpents in the world. He is interrupted during this sacrifice and told the story of his ancestors, so that he will understand what awaits him in the future. The whole *Mahabharata* is told for the sake of a young man who prepares himself for life. In a certain kind of theatre you would have a young king. But if you begin with a young king, everything is at such a distance that you neither identify with him nor are moved by the story. But a child touches us directly. And it is clear that the role of this child is to listen to the story. You feel that he is listening, that he asks questions. You feel that for the child in all of us there's a lesson to be learned from these fabulous adventures from another era.

In the *Mahabharata* there is an appeal to a positive attitude. The *Mahabharata* tells a history that is as somber, tragic, and terrible as our contemporary situation. But thanks to the tradition, the attitude people have faced with this situation is not negative, not Spenglerian. It is not pessimistic negativity, despair, or protest. It is something else. It is a way of life in a world in a catastrophic condition without losing contact with that which allows man to live and fight in a positive way. What does 'positive' mean? It is a word that takes us back to our starting point. And very concretely, that brings us to the heart of the *Bhagavad Gita*: do you stand back, do you act, or what? The question, 'or what?' is everyone's question today, and to it the *Mahabharata* gives no answer. It simply gives immense nourishment.

NOTES [ADDED BY EDITORS]

1   Part of this interview was first published in *Le Monde*, Special issue, Avignon, July 1985, in an article by Mathilde La Bardonnie.

28

BUILDING UP THE MUSCLE
An interview with Ariane Mnouchkine

Josette Féral

Translated by Anna Husemoller

T124, 1989

Ariane Mnouchkine is one of the best-known directors in France. She founded Théâtre du Soleil in 1964 and has been its director for twenty-five years, becoming a leading figure in today's theatre. The following interview took place in March 1988 at the Cartoucherie, home to Théâtre du Soleil, during a performance of Mnouchkine's production of *Indiade* by Hélène Cixous. As we talked, we could hear drums, gongs . . . the whole music of the *Indiade* emanating from the background.

ARE THERE THEORIES ABOUT ACTING?

Féral: Ariane Mnouchkine, I know right away that you are going to answer my first question by saying that there are no theories about acting.

Mnouchkine: I do not know if I would say that. I know that I myself do not have any, maybe because I am not in the position to develop a theory on acting. I may not ever be capable of developing a theory about acting. Because in fact the idea of a theory of acting involves a written development of the theory of acting and a practice of acting. That is to say that we, directors and actors, put into practice the practice – we don't practice the theory. I think that if there is no theory of acting, at least there are theoretical laws that we may find, curiously enough, in all traditions of acting. It is true that the term 'theory of acting' does not seem fundamentally wrong, but it seems always somewhat imperialistic and pretentious. I prefer to use fundamental laws which we sometimes know but then sometimes lose and forget. It is only practice that all of a sudden can make law or tradition rise to the surface. I will not say then that there is no theory of acting; on the contrary, there have been many of them. Of course, what interests me in these multiple theories are the essential laws that are common to all of them.

Féral: In the 1960s there were several theories of acting that everyone referred

to: Bertolt Brecht, Antonin Artaud, Jerzy Grotowski, for example, represented a very important historical moment together in the evolution of
theatre. They were theoreticians, some of them being practitioners, and others
not. Artaud, for example, was not a practitioner in the same sense as Brecht.
On the other hand, what he said about theatre had enough weight to influence
a whole epoch. Actors today, beginning actors in their formative stages, are
quite unequipped because these masters are not masters for us today.

Mnouchkine: They were not the only ones. There were people like Stanislavski
of course, and Meyerhold. But there were also people in France who wrote
absolutely essential things: Jacques Copeau, Charles Dullin, Louis Jouvet. If
you were to read them again, you would notice that there are things in Copeau
that you find in Zeami, and that is what is interesting, moving, not so much
reassuring but comforting. You can then see that Zeami wrote in fifteenth-
century Japan what Copeau wrote in twentieth-century Europe. And Brecht,
as original and ideological as he may be, fully rediscovers in his least logical
moments traditional elements of Oriental theatre. You are right, I will not
differentiate between master-of-thought practitioner and master-of-thought-
nonpractitioner because from what we know even Artaud, for example, failed
in practice. He failed probably because he did not have the physical or the
mental strength to produce what he wanted. But what he wrote was so close to
practice, so lucid on the practice he discovered – on the practice of Balinese
theatre – and makes such a strong translation into theory that his work ends up
being quasi-practice.

Féral: Would you say that Stanislavski, Brecht, and Artaud have one thing in
common, and that is that the laws they attempt to uncover rest upon a vision
of a theatrical act in its essence?

Mnouchkine: I would not put Artaud and Brecht on the same scale. Artaud is
closer to the foundations than Brecht. Brecht gave laws of a certain type of
theatre, sometimes of course with fundamental laws that can be found in all
types of theatre. I believe that Artaud had a much deeper conception of the
function and mission of the actor, less political and more metaphysical.

Féral: Nowadays, we seldom refer to Artaud, just as we seldom refer to Brecht.
Is it because we have surpassed them or is it because we have assimilated
them?

Mnouchkine: Neither! No! I think it is because they are for now – [the phone
rings and we break off].

SUCH MYSTERIOUS FUNDAMENTAL LAWS!

Féral: Can we turn back to these fundamental laws which govern theatre
throughout the world? It seems that theatre practices, in the East and West,
are universal. Even if techniques vary from one place to another, they are
governed by fundamental laws. What are these laws?

Mnouchkine: Do you want me to make an inventory of them? [We laugh] How
shall I tell you? They are so mysterious and so volatile. Sometimes we have the
impression that a rehearsal goes by and we've forgotten laws we thought we
knew perfectly the day before. All of a sudden during a rehearsal there is no
more theatre. An actor cannot act, a director cannot help an actor anymore.

We ask ourselves why and we cannot understand. We have the impression we are respecting the laws and actually all of a sudden we realize that we have lost the essentials, for example, being in the present. I believe that theatre is the art of the present for the actor. There is no past, no future. There is the present, the present act. When I see young students work on what they call the 'Stanislavski method,' I am surprised to find how much they go back to the past all the time. Of course Stanislavski talks about the character's past: where does he come from, what is he doing? But the students are not able simply to find the present action. So they go back and I always tell them, 'You enter leaning backwards, weighted by all this past, while in the theatre only the moment exists.'

I think that the greatest law is probably the one that governs the mystery between inside and outside, between the state of being (or the feeling as Jouvet would say) and the form. How do you give a form to a passion? How do you exteriorize without falling into exteriority?

How can the autopsy of the body – I mean the heart – be performed by the body? My slip of the tongue is revealing because the autopsy of the heart must be performed by the body. An actor or actress worthy of the name is a kind of autopsy-er. His or her role is to show the inside.

Yesterday was beautiful. There was a short debate with high schoolers who were theatre majors and all very young. They did not stop asking me the same question, 'Why is there so much emotion?' They were talking about the moment in *Indiade* when Nehru says, 'I am afraid.' A small young woman hardly 15 years old asked me this question, then a boy did the same. So we asked ourselves the question together. Why? How could a young Frenchwoman of 15 be moved all of a sudden by a particular scene of Nehru's? And we said that this was something specific to theatre: the memory of the unlived. That is, a young Frenchwoman who has not lived is capable, by the grace of the theatre and the actor, to understand and recognize what she has in common with a 60-year-old man who is from a country that has 400 million inhabitants and to understand his fear. We were happy about this discovery. And we said this is what theatre is all about. That is: when an actor succeeds in making the unknown familiar and making the familiar enchanting and moving. [. . .] You ask me, 'What are the laws?' If I knew them all the time, I would not have to ask myself what I say everyday in rehearsal, 'Okay, now, what is theatre? Are we going to succeed in producing a moment of theatre today?'

EMOTION COMES FROM RECOGNITION

Féral: You talk about emotion from the actor's point of view, but doesn't emotion exist for the spectator as well?

Mnouchkine: The emotion is different in the two cases. For example, Indian theatre offers something very beautiful from this point of view. There are big theoretical books on the subject. There is Zeami, of course, but there is also an Indian book [the *Natyasastra*], an enormous work that gives the theory of the whole Indian theatre. There we can find some laws that I find extraordinary. For example, there are different words to define the emotion of the actor and the character [*bhava*] and the emotion of the spectator looking at the actor [*rasa*]. I find in Western theatre, in the acting style of certain actors, an ability to bring together what should be their emotion, which should be a part of the action, and what the emotion of the spectator should be. These are the good moments. The good moments are when all of a sudden a spectator has tears in his eyes while what the actor acts out is a moment of enthusiasm, happiness, and laughter. Why do you all of a sudden start crying with joy or recognition?

Féral: Because you perceive at this very moment the exactitude of what is happening. It is the truth of the moment we experience, independently from what is expressed.

Mnouchkine: Exactly, the emotion comes from recognition. From the fact that it is true.

Féral: This recognition is not solely that of the subject matter, of that which is said, or the life that is acted out, but it is recognizing the exactitude of what goes on on stage, grasped in the actor's performance. What is astonishing about the Théâtre du Soleil is that so often the actors hit it right. There is something in their gestures that recalls the necessity or urgency of the moment. They are so efficient, we recognize theirs as the only gesture that could have been performed at that very moment with that much precision. This brings us back to one of the laws that you talked about earlier. You said that the actor must be present.

Mnouchkine: Wait, I did not say 'be present' but be in the present. The theatrical act occurs in the moment and once this happens, something else happens.

Féral: We talk a lot about a concept we borrowed from the East which people like Eugenio Barba use in their work with the actor: the actor's presence. It is a very difficult notion to grasp but as a spectator I can identify an actor who has presence and one who hasn't.

Mnouchkine: Presence is something you state, but I myself have never worked with this idea. I would not be able to tell an actor to 'be present.' On the other hand, what I do know, what I try to tell the actor, is that he should be in his present, in his action, in his emotion, in his state of being, and in the versatility of life as well. These are the lessons Shakespeare gives. With him we can begin a verse in a murderous rage, have a moment of forgetfulness of this rage simply to be happy about something in the text, then fall back into a strong desire for vengeance, and all of this in two verses – in a few seconds, therefore in the present. The actor truly playing such a verse is 'hyper-present.' Present to the second.

As for the actual concept of the actor's presence . . . There are actors who are present, and others less. It comes with talent. There are no bad actors who have presence, unless it's bad presence, and presence increases with the capacity of the actor to be naked.

Féral: How do you help an actor to be in the present? Do you use a technique? Do you have a method? Is your method a form of listening?

Mnouchkine: I believe that there are no techniques. There are methods and I believe every director has one, maybe an unconscious one. I believe I have one, but I do not know it. The last word you said is very important: 'listening.' I believe that I know how to do that well. There, that is the only thing that I can say. I think I know – no – I would not even say that I know, but I love, I love to listen, and I love to look at the actors. That I love with a passion. I think that is already a way to assist them. They know that I never tire of listening to them, of watching them, but how do I help them? I do not know.

Féral: In one of your texts you wrote, 'You must build up the muscle of the actor's imagination.' This nourishment you feed the imagination is a form of assistance.

Mnouchkine: I encourage the expression 'building up the muscle.' When I work with very young actors one of the first questions I ask is, 'What do you think is the actor's most important muscle?' Of course no one thinks of it, and so I tell them it is the imagination. And it can be conditioned, worked on.

Féral: How do you proceed?

Mnouchkine: With sincerity, with emotion. By acting, really by acting, not by the memory, I don't believe in that. You have to be able to have visions little by little, to be a visionary, to see what they talk about, to see where they are going, where they are, to see the sky above them, the rain, to take in the emotion of another and to believe in it.

We are trying to talk very seriously and very severely about theories of theatre, but really the essential theory is that you have to believe in it: believe in what we act, what we are, what we incarnate; and believe in the emotional

Fig. 28.1 Nirupama Nityanaudau and Simon Abkarian
as Iphigenia and Agamemnon in the 1992 production of
Les Atrides. (Photo by Martine Franck/Magnum,
courtesy of The Brooklyn Academy of Music.)

trouble, in one's strength, one's anger, one's joy, one's sensuality, one's love, one's hatred, whatever you want . . . but you have to believe in it.

The common misinterpretation of Brecht is that we thought he said you shouldn't believe in it. Brecht never said that. He said you should not deceive.

I think there is something in the actor's work that obliges him or her not to fall back into childhood but out of childhood. He must divest himself of all made-up images which go against the work of the imagination. These made-up images are clichés or crutches where there is no emotion.

Féral: But this imagination must nourish itself somewhere. It is not enough for the actor to say to himself, 'I will believe in it' to believe in it.

Mnouchkine: There has to be a true situation to start from. I will not say a pretext because we know that it is possible to improvise from this. But there has to be a theatrical situation and a desire to create a character. There has to be invention, discovery.

WE MUST HAVE THEATRE THE FIRST DAY

Féral: Does work on character happen alone? In a group? In discussions?

Mnouchkine: Nothing ever happens alone. The work happens from the beginning by acting. For us, there is never, never any work at a desk.

We read the play once and the next day we are already on the stage. The actors can decide to try all the characters they want for several weeks, even several months. They have old bits of costume at their disposal to disguise themselves and they begin. And we act right away. We must have theatre the first day.

Féral: Are there any points of reference that can be used to start off with? Do actors keep the memory of what they have done on stage so that the good things they have found during improvisation are retained? Or is it simply a period of exploration?

Mnouchkine: There is a period of exploration but the good things remain when they are really good. This is what you were saying about the precision of gesture, the evidence of gesture. The gesture is not what remains because things are fixed much later. But we will know that such and such a character has this type of gesture, that he is a little like this. Then we will discover something else. Because one of our most important laws is to keep it firmly in our mind that all the characters, all of them, have a complete soul. We realize it is a little dogmatic to say that each character in a play contains all the others. There is a little of Prince Hal in Falstaff, a little of the father in the son, a little of the fiancée in the fiancé, a little of Juliet in the nurse, a little of the nurse in Juliet . . . Everyone is complete. Because otherwise we do not progress. [. . .]

Féral: Do you make a psychological study of the characters? I am asking you this because in the *Indiade* we don't have the impression that the characters have a psychology. We have the impression instead that the characters are from the theatre, presented as theatrical constructions, with a complexity, but without day-to-day psychology. They are emblems. They are motivated by signs rather than by psychology.

Mnouchkine: We flee daily life. We do not talk of psychology but rather of the characters' souls. Not of their psychology. But they have emotions, sensations. They are cold, they are hungry, they are proud, they want power, they don't want it, they are stubborn. Each one of them has their way of being, their own world. Nicolas Boileau said, 'the truth is not always verisimilitude' and verisimilitude is not necessarily true. This can be precisely understood in a historical play. That is, what happens happens. These characters experienced it, oriented it, or made it happen. It was with their psychology, as you say, that the events took place. But there is no question about it, the theatre is not supposed to represent psychology but passions, which is totally different. Its role is to represent the soul's different emotional states, and those of the mind, the world history. In the Théâtre du Soleil, psychology has negative meaning. When I say to the actors, 'Watch out, that is psychological,' it's a criticism. They know very well what I am saying – I mean their performance does not reach truth, it is slow, complicated, and narcissistic. Contrary to what we believe, psychology does not pull toward the interior, but toward the interior mask.

THEATRE IS EASTERN

Féral: There is no tradition of gesture in the West. Many directors must look for this tradition in the East. You yourself in the Théâtre du Soleil have to find inspiration from Asian theatres. What are you looking for?

Mnouchkine: Theories that have marked all people of theatre. They have marked Artaud, Brecht, and all people of theatre because it is the source of theatre. I think that we go East to look for theatre. Artaud said: 'Theatre is Eastern.' This thought goes very far. He does not say, 'There are Eastern theories that are interesting for theatre.' He says, 'Theatre is Eastern.' I believe Artaud is right. So I tell the actor to go look for everything in the East. Both myth and reality, interiority and the exteriorization, and the famous autopsy of the heart by the body we talked about. We also go to look for the nonrealism or theatricality. The West has only given birth to the *commedia dell'arte* – and even this comes from Asia – and to a certain type of realism which great actors escape from. It is true that a great actor, even when he is in a realistic theatre, succeeds, I do not quite know how, in not being realistic himself. But it is difficult.

Féral: Theatre is in need of traditions?

Mnouchkine: It needs sources and memory. It needs to be worked on in order to allow the depths and origins to come to the surface. You can't easily say that we need traditions. We have them. Lineages exist and they belong to us completely, even beyond national borders.

Féral: How do you choose your actors?

Mnouchkine: I meet with a lot of young actors in person. There is a lot of opportunity to select. The workshop is one of the times when selection takes place, although not the only one, because I do not do it from that perspective. I do not know how I choose the actors. First, I choose people that make an impression on me. People who make an impression on me in a human way before an artistic way. I choose people who move me, like ones where I sense a strength, innocence, fantasy, gaiety, and also rigor from the beginning.

Féral: Do you sometimes make a mistake?

Mnouchkine: Yes! But not very often. My mistakes are bad ones because it is very bad to make a mistake in a group. When I notice it in time, it's easy to patch up. But sometimes this provokes moments of crisis. Still, I would say that in twenty-four years, my major errors have not been more than the fingers of one hand. There were plenty of little mistakes, but minor ones. There were people whose place turned out not to be at the Soleil, but that was harmless. People who attempted to upset the group, and thereby did upset the group, were very rare.

Féral: You have said that the duty of every director is to make workshops for actors. Is this because actor training in school is not sufficient?

Mnouchkine: Yes, there is schooling but it is insufficient when you consider the demand. There are one or two good schools in France which take thirty to forty students each year. And then even the students who have gone through the schooling need to continue to work. When they do not act, they lose their adaptability.

WE DO NOT INVENT THEORIES OF ACTING ANYMORE

Féral: Why don't you put your theories about acting in writing?

Mnouchkine: First of all, my area is not writing. Also I sincerely think that everything has been said already and in an extraordinary fashion. A little like Jean-Jacques Lemetre, our musician at the Théâtre du Soleil, who replied when someone asked him if he invented instruments: 'You do not invent instruments anymore, you transform them, you rediscover more, but you do not invent them anymore. They have all been invented.' I, too, reply that you do not invent theories of acting anymore. The problem is that theories exist but they have been buried at the same rate as they have been pronounced. Let the young students read Zeami, Artaud, Copeau, Dullin, Jouvet, also Brecht . . . Everything is there. And let them do theatre. We do not need to say more.

29

THE OTHER HISTORY OF INTERCULTURAL PERFORMANCE

Coco Fusco

T141, 1993

In the early 1900s, Franz Kafka wrote a story that began, 'Honored members of the Academy! You have done me the honor of inviting me to give your Academy an account of the life I formerly led as an ape' (1979: 245). Entitled 'A Report to an Academy,' it was presented as the testimony of a man from the Gold Coast of Africa who had lived for several years on display in Germany as a primate. That account was fictitious and created by a European writer who stressed the irony of having to demonstrate one's humanity; yet it is one of many literary allusions to the real history of ethnographic exhibition of human beings that has taken place in the West over the past five centuries. While the experiences of many of those who were exhibited is the stuff of legend, it is the accounts by observers and impresarios that comprise the historical and literary record of this practice in the West. My collaborator Guillermo Gómez-Peña and I were intrigued by this legacy of performing the identity of an Other for a white audience, sensing its implications for us as performance artists dealing with cultural identity in the present. Had things changed, we wondered? How would we know, if not by unleashing those ghosts from a history that could be said to be ours? Imagine that I stand before you then, as did Kafka's character, to speak about an experience that falls somewhere between truth and fiction. What follows are my reflections on performing the role of a noble savage behind the bars of a golden cage.

Our original intent was to create a satirical commentary on Western concepts of the exotic, primitive Other; yet, we have had to confront two unexpected realities in the course of developing this piece: (1) a substantial portion of the public believed that our fictional identities are real ones; and (2) a substantial number of intellectuals, artists, and cultural bureaucrats have sought to deflect attention from the substance of our experiment to the 'moral implications' of our dissimulation, or in their words, our 'misinforming the public' about who we are. The literalism implicit in the interpretation of our work by individuals representing the 'public interest' bespeaks their investment in positivist notions of 'truth' and depoliticized, ahistorical notions of 'civilization.' This 'reverse ethnography' of our interactions with the public will, I hope, suggest the culturally specific nature of their tendency toward the literal and moral interpretation.

When we began to work on this performance as part of a counter-quincentenary project, the Bush administration had drawn clear parallels between the 'discovery' of the New World and his New World Order. We noted the resemblance between official quincentenary celebrations in 1992 and the ways that the 1892 Columbian commemorations had served as a justification for the U.S.'s then new status as an imperial power. [. . .]

Out of this context arose our decision to take a symbolic vow of silence with the cage performance, a radical departure from Guillermo's previous monolog work and my activities as a writer and public speaker. We sought a strategically effective way to examine the limits of the 'happy multiculturalism' that currently reigns in cultural institutions, as well as to respond to the formalists and cultural relativists who reject the proposition that racial difference is absolutely fundamental to aesthetic interpretation. We looked to Latin America, where consciousness of the repressive limits on public expression is far more acute than here, and found many examples of how popular opposition has for centuries been expressed through the use of satiric spectacle. Our cage became the metaphor for our condition, linking the racism implicit in ethnographic paradigms of discovery with the exoticizing rhetoric of 'world beat' multiculturalism. Then came a perfect opportunity: in 1991, Guillermo and I were invited to perform as part of the Edge '92 Biennial, which was to take place in London and also in Madrid as part of the quincentennial celebration of Madrid as the capital of European culture. We took advantage of Edge's interest in locating art in public spaces to create a site-specific performance for Columbus Plaza in Madrid, in commemoration of the so-called Discovery.

Our plan was to live in a golden cage for three days, presenting ourselves as undiscovered Amerindians from an island in the Gulf of Mexico that had somehow been overlooked by Europeans for five centuries (see figs. 29.1 and 29.2). We called our homeland Guatinau, and ourselves Guatinauis. We performed our 'traditional

Fig. 29.1 Fusco and Gómez-Peña, *Two Undiscovered Amerindians Visit . . .*, 1992 – 4. (Courtesy of Coco Fusco.)

Fig. 29.2 Fusco and Gómez-Peña, *Two Undiscovered Amerindians Visit . . .*, 1992 – 4. (Courtesy of Coco Fusco.)

tasks,' which ranged from sewing voodoo dolls and lifting weights to watching television and working on a laptop computer. A donation box in front of the cage indicated that for a small fee, I would dance (to rap music), Guillermo would tell authentic Amerindian stories (in a nonsensical language), and we would pose for Polaroids with visitors. Two 'zoo guards' would be on hand to speak to visitors (since we could not understand them), take us to the bathroom on leashes, and feed us sandwiches and fruit. At the Whitney Museum in New York, we added sex to our spectacle, offering a peek at authentic Guatinaui male genitals for $5. A chronology with highlights from the history of exhibiting non-Western peoples was on one didactic panel, and a simulated *Encyclopaedia Britannica* entry with a fake map of the Gulf of Mexico showing our island was on another. After our three days in May 1992, we took our performance to Covent Garden in London. In September, we presented it in Minneapolis, and in October, at the Smithsonian's National Museum of Natural History. In December, we were on display in the Australian Museum of Natural History in Sydney and in January 1993, at the Field Museum of Chicago. In early March, we were at the Whitney for the opening of Biennial, the only site where we were recognizably contextualized as an artwork. Prior to our trip to Madrid, we did one test run under relatively controlled conditions in the Art Gallery of U.C.-Irvine.

Our project concentrated on the 'zero degree' of intercultural relations in an attempt to define a point of origin for the debates that link 'discovery' and 'Otherness.' We worked within disciplines that blur distinctions between the art object and the body (performance), between fantasy and reality (live spectacle), and between history and dramatic reenactment (the diorama). The performance was interactive, focusing less on what we did than on how people interacted with us and interpreted our actions. Entitled *Two Undiscovered Amerindians Visit . . .*, we chose not to announce the event through prior publicity or any other means, when it was possible to exert such control; we intended to create a surprise or 'uncanny' encounter, one in which audiences had to undergo their own process of reflection as to what they were seeing, aided only by written information and parodically didactic zoo guards. In such encounters with the unexpected, people's defense mechanisms are less likely to operate with their normal efficiency; caught off guard, their beliefs are more likely to rise to the surface.

Our performance was based on the once popular European and North American practice of exhibiting indigenous people from Africa, Asia, and the Americas in zoos, parks, taverns, museums, freak shows, and circuses. While this tradition reached the height of its popularity in the nineteenth century, it was actually begun by Christopher Columbus, who returned from his first voyage in 1493 with several Arawaks, one of whom was left on display at the Spanish Court for two years. Designed to provide opportunities for esthetic contemplation, scientific analysis, and entertainment for Europeans and North Americans, these exhibits were a critical component of a burgeoning mass culture whose development coincided with the growth of urban centers and populations, European colonialism, and American expansionism.

In writing about these human exhibitions in America's international fairs from the late nineteenth and early twentieth centuries, Robert W. Rydell (author of *All the World's a Fair: Visions of Empire at American International Exhibitions, 1876–1916*, 1984) explains how the 'ethnological' displays of nonwhites – which were orchestrated by impresarios but endorsed by anthropologists – confirmed popular racial stereotypes and built support for domestic and foreign policies. In some cases, they literally connected museum practices with affairs of state. Many of the people exhibited during the nineteenth century were presented as the chiefs of conquered tribes and/or the last survivors of 'vanishing' races. Ishi, the Yahi Indian who spent five years living in the Museum of the University of California at the turn of the century, is a well-known example. Another lesser-known example comes from the U.S. – Mexico War of 1836, when Anglo-Texan secessionists used to exhibit their Mexican prisoners in public plazas in cages, leaving them there to starve to death. The exhibits also gave credence to white supremacist worldviews by representing nonwhite peoples and cultures as being in need of discipline, civilization, and industry. Not only did these exhibits reinforce stereotypes of 'the primitive' but they served to enforce a sense of racial unity as whites among Europeans and North Americans, who were divided strictly by class and religion until this century. Hence, for example, at the Columbian Exhibition of 1893 in Chicago, ethnographic displays of peoples from Africa and Asia were set up outside 'The White City,' an enclosed area celebrating science and industry.

Emerging at a time when mass audiences in Europe and America were literate and hardly cognizant of the rest of the world, the displays were an important form of public 'education.' These shows were where most whites 'discovered' the non-Western sector of humanity. I like to call them the origins of intercultural performance in the West. The displays were living expressions of colonial fantasies and helped to forge a special place in the European and Euro-American imagination for nonwhite peoples and their cultures. Their function, however, went beyond war trophies, beyond providing entertainment for the masses and pseudo-scientific data for early anthropologists. The ethnographic exhibitions of people of color were among the many sources drawn on by European and American modernists seeking to break with realism by imitating the 'primitive.' The connection between West African sculpture and Cubism has been discussed widely by scholars, but it is the construction of ethnic Otherness as essentially performative and located in the body that I here seek to stress.

The interest that modernists and postmodernists have had in non-Western cultures was preceded by a host of references to 'exotics' made by European writers and philosophers over the past five centuries. The ethnographic shows and the people brought to Europe to be part of them have been alluded to by such writers as William Shakespeare, Michel Montaigne, and William Wordsworth. In the eighteenth century, these shows, together with theatre and popular ballads, served as popular illustrations of the concept of the noble savage so central to Enlightenment philosophy. Not all the references were positive; in fact, the nineteenth-century humanist Charles Dickens found that the noble savage as an idea hardly sufficed to make an encounter with Bushmen in the Egyptian Hall in 1847 a pleasurable or worthwhile experience:

> Think of the Bushmen. Think of the two men and the two women who have been exhibited about England for some years. Are the majority of persons – who remember the horrid little leader of that party in his festering bundle of hides, with his filth and his antipathy to water, and his straddled legs, and his odious eyes shaded by his brutal hand, and his cry of 'Qu-u-u-u-aaa' (Bushman for something desperately insulting I have no doubt) – conscious of an affectionate yearning towards the noble savage, or is it idiosyncratic in me to abhor, detest, abominate, and abjure him? [. . .] I have never seen that group sleeping, smoking, and expectorating round their brazier, but I have sincerely desired that something might happen to the charcoal smoldering therein, which would cause the immediate suffocation of the whole of noble strangers.
>
> (in Altwick 1978: 281)

Dickens' aversion does not prevent him from noting, however, that the Bushmen possess one redeeming quality: their ability to break spontaneously into dramatic reenactments of their 'wild' habits. By the early twentieth century, the flipside of such revulsion – in the form of fetishistic fascination with exotic artifacts and the 'primitive' creativity that generated them – had become common among the members of the European avant-garde. The Dadaists, often thought of as the originators of performance art, included several imitative gestures in their events, ranging from dressing up and dancing as 'Africans,' to making 'primitive-looking' masks and sketches. Tristan Tzara's dictum that 'Thought is made in the mouth,' a performative analog to Cubism, refers directly to the Dadaist belief that Western art tradition could be subverted through the appropriation of the perceived performative nature of the 'non-Western.' In a grand gesture of appropriation, Tzara anthologized African and Southern Pacific poetry culled from ethnographies into his book, *Poèmes Nègres*, and chanted them at the infamous Cabaret Voltaire in Zurich in 1917. Shortly afterward, Tzara (1992: 57–8) wrote a hypothetical description of the 'primitive' artist at work in *Note on Negro Art*, imputing near shamanistic powers on the Other's creative process:

> My other brother is naive and good, and laughs. He eats in Africa or along the South Sea Islands. He concentrates his vision on the head, carves it out of wood that is hard as iron, patiently, without bothering about the conventional relationship between the head and the rest of the body. What he thinks is: man walks vertically, everything in nature is symmetrical. While working, new relationships organize themselves according to degree of necessity; this is how the expression of purity came into being. From blackness, let us extract light . . . Transform my country into a prayer of joy or

anguish. Cotton wool eye, flow into my blood. Art in the infancy of time, was prayer. Wood and stone were truth ... Mouths contain the power of darkness, invisible substance, goodness, fear, wisdom, creation, fire. No one has seen so clearly as I this dark grinding whiteness.

Tzara is quick to point out here that only he, as a Dadaist, can comprehend the significance of the 'innocent' gesture of his 'naive and good' brother. In the *Predicament of Culture* (1988), James Clifford explains how modernists and ethnographers of the early twentieth century projected coded perceptions of the black body – as imbued with vitalism, rhythm, magic, and erotic power, another formation of the 'good' versus the irrational or bad savage. Clifford questions the conventional mode of comparison in terms of affinity, noting that this term suggests a 'natural' rather than political or ideological relationship. In the case of Tzara, his perception of the 'primitive' artist as part of his metaphorical family conveniently recasts his own colonial relation to his imaginary 'primitive' as one of kinship. In this context, the threatening reminder of difference is that the original body, or the physical and visual presence of the cultural Other, must therefore be fetishized, silenced, subjugated, or otherwise controlled to be 'appreciated.' The significance of that violent erasure is diminished – it is the 'true' avant-garde artist who becomes a better version of the 'primitive,' a hybrid or a cultural transvestite. Mass culture caged it, so to speak – while artists swallowed it.

This practice of appropriating and fetishizing the primitive and simultaneously erasing the original source continues into contemporary 'avant-garde' performance art. In his 1977 essay 'New models, new visions: some notes toward a poetics of performance,' Jerome Rothenberg envisioned this phenomenon in an entirely celebratory manner, noting correlations between Happenings and rituals, meditative works and tantric models, Earthworks and Native American sculptures, dreamworks and notions of trance and ecstasy, bodyworks and self-mutilation, and performance based on several other variations of the shamanistic premise attributed to non-Western cultures. Rothenberg claims that unlike imperialism's models of domination and subordination, avant-garde performance succeeded in shifting relations to a 'symposium of the whole,' an image strikingly similar to that of world-beat multiculturalism of the 1980s. [. . .]

Redefining these 'affinities' with the primitive, the traditional, and the exotic has become an increasingly delicate issue as more artists of color enter the sphere of the 'avant-garde.' What may be 'liberating' and 'transgressive' identification for Europeans and Euro-Americans is already a symbol of entrapment within an imposed stereotype for Others. The 'affinity' championed by the early moderns and postmodern cultural transvestites alike is mediated by an imagined stereotype, along the lines of Tzara's 'brother.' Actual encounters could threaten the position and supremacy of the appropriator unless boundaries and concomitant power relations remain in place. As a result, the same intellectual milieus that now boast Neoprimitive body piercers, 'nomad' thinkers, Anglo compadres, and New Age earth worshippers continue to evince a literal-minded attitude toward artists of color, demonstrating how racial difference is a determinant in one's relation to notions of the 'primitive.' In the 1987 trial of minimalist sculptor Carl Andre – accused of murdering his wife, the Cuban artist Ana Mendieta – the defense continuously suggested that her Earthworks were indicative of suicidal impulses prompted by her 'satanical' beliefs; the references to Santeria in her work could not be interpreted as self-conscious. When Cuban artist Jose Bedia was visited by the French curators of the Les Magiciens de la Terre exhibition in the late 1980s, he was asked to show his private altar to 'prove' that he was a true Santeria believer. A critically acclaimed young African-American poet was surprised to learn last year that he had been promoted by a Nuyorican Poet's Café impresario as a former L.A. gang member, which he never was. And while performing *Border Brujo* in the late 1980s, Gómez-Peña encountered numerous presenters and audience members who were disappointed that he was not a 'real shaman' and that his 'tongues' were not Nahuatl but a fictitious language.

Our cage performances forced these contradictions out into the open. The cage became a blank screen onto which audiences projected their fantasies of who and what we are. As we assumed the stereotypical role of the domesticated savage, many audience members felt entitled to assume the role of the colonizer, only then to find themselves uncomfortable with the implications of the game. Unpleasant but important associations have emerged between the displays of old and the multi-cultural festivals and ethnographic dioramas of the present. The central position of the white spectator, the objective of these events as a confirmation of their position as global consumers of exotic cultures, and the stress on authenticity as an esthetic value, all remain fundamental to the spectacle of Otherness many continue to enjoy.

The original ethnographic exhibitions often presented people in a simulation of their 'natural' habitat, rendered either as an indoor diorama, or as an outdoor re-creation. Eyewitness accounts frequently note that the human beings on display were forced to dress in the European notion of their traditional 'primitive' garb, and to perform repetitive, seemingly ritual tasks. At times, nonwhites were displayed together with flora and fauna from their regions, and artifacts, which were often fakes. They were also displayed as part of a continuum of 'outsiders' that included 'freaks,' or people exhibiting physical deformities. In the nineteenth and early twentieth centuries, many of them were presented so as to confirm Social Darwinist ideas of the existence of a racial hierarchy. Some of the more infamous cases involved individuals whose physical traits were singled out as evidence of the bestiality of nonwhite people. For example, shortly after the annexation of Mexico and the publication of John Stephens' account of travel in the Yucatan, which generated popular interest in pre-Columbian cultures, two microcephalics (or pinheads) from Central America, Maximo and Bartola, toured the U.S. in P. T. Barnum's circus; they were presented as Aztecs. This set off a trend that would be followed by many other cases into the twentieth century. From 1810 to 1815, Euro-pean audiences crowded to see the Hottentot Venus, a South African woman whose large buttocks were deemed evidence of her excessive sexuality. In the United States, several of the 'Africans' exhibited were actually black Americans who made a living in the nineteenth century by dressing up as their ancestors, just as many Native Americans did dressing up as Sioux, whose likenesses, thanks to the long and bloody Plains Wars of the late nineteenth century, dominated the American popular imagination.

For Gómez-Peña and myself the human exhibitions dramatize the colonial unconscious of American society. In order to justify genocide, enslavement, and the seizure of lands, a 'naturalized' splitting of humanity along racial lines had to be established. When rampant miscegenation proved that those differences were not biologically based, social and legal systems were set up to enforce those hierarchies. Meanwhile, ethnographic spectacles circulated and reinforced stereotypes, stressing that 'difference' was apparent in the bodies on display. They thus naturalized fetishized representations of Otherness, mitigating anxieties generated by the encounter with difference.

[. . .] Our experiences in the cage have suggested that even though the idea that America is a colonial system is met with resistance – since it contradicts the dominant ideology's presentation of our system as a democracy – the audience reactions indicate that colonialist roles have been internalized quite effectively.

The stereotypes about nonwhite people that were continuously reinforced by the ethnographic displays are still alive in high culture and the mass media. Imbedded in the unconscious, these images form the basis of the fears, desires, and fantasies about the cultural Other. In 'The Negro and psychopathology' (1967), Frantz Fanon discusses a critical stage in the development of children socialized in Western culture, regardless of their race, in which racist stereotypes of the savage and the primitive are assimilated through the consumption of popular culture: comics, movies, cartoons, etc. These stereotypical images are often part of myths of colonial dominion (for example, cowboy defeats Indian, conquistador triumphs over Aztec Empire, colonial soldier conquers African chief, and so on). This dynamic also contains a sexual dimension, usually expressed as anxiety about white male (omni)potence. In *Prospero and Caliban: The Psychology of Colonization* (1990), Octave Mannoni coined the term the 'Prospero complex,' described as the white colonial patriarch's continuous fear that his daughter might be raped by a nonwhite male. Several colonial stereotypes also nurture these anxieties, usually representing a white woman whose 'purity' is endangered by black men with oversized genitals, or suave Latin lovers, or wild-eyed Indian warriors; and the common practice of publicly lynching black men in the American South is an example of a ritualized white male response to such fears. Accompanying these stereotypes are counterparts that humiliate and debase women of color, mitigating anxieties about sexual rivalry among women. In the past, there was the subservient maid and the overweight and sexless Mammy; nowadays, the hapless victim of a brutish or irrational dark male whose tradition is devoid of 'feminist freedoms' is more common.

[. . .] Not unsurprisingly, the popularity of these human exhibitions began to decline with the emergence of another commercialized form of voyeurism, the cinema, and their didactic role was assumed by ethnographic film. Founding fathers of the ethnographic filmmaking practice, such as Robert Flaherty and John Emerson, continued to compel people to stage their supposedly 'traditional' rituals, but the tasks were now to be performed for the camera. One of the most famous of the white impresarios of the human exhibits in the United States, William F. 'Buffalo Bill' Cody, actually starred in an early film depicting his Wild West show of Native American horsemen and warriors, and in doing so gave birth to the cowboy and Indian movie genre, this country's most popular rendition of its own colonial fantasy. The representation of the 'reality' of the Other's life, on which ethnographic documentary was based and still is grounded, is this fictional narrative of Western culture 'discovering' the negation of itself in something authentically and radically distinct. Carried over from documentary, these paradigms also became the basis of Hollywood filmmaking in the 1950s and 1960s that dealt with other parts of the world in which the U.S. had strategic military and economic interests, especially Latin America and the South Pacific.

The practice of exhibiting humans may have waned in the twentieth century, but it has not entirely disappeared. The dissected genitals of the Hottentot Venus are still preserved at the Museum of Man in Paris. Thousands of Native American remains, including decapitated heads, scalps, and other body parts taken as war booty or bounties, remain in storage at the Smithsonian. Shortly before arriving in Spain, we learned of a current scandal in a small village outside Barcelona, where a visiting delegation had registered a formal complaint about a desiccated, stuffed Pygmy man that was on display in a local museum. The African gentleman in the delegation who had initiated the complaint was threatening to organize an African boycott of the 1992 Olympics, but the Catalonian townspeople defended what they saw as the right to keep 'their own black man.' We also learned that Julia Pastrana, a bearded Mexican woman who was exhibited throughout Europe until her death in 1862, is still available in embalmed form for scientific research and loans to interested museums. This past summer, the case of Ota Benga, a Pygmy who was exhibited in the primate cage of the Bronx Zoo in 1906, gained high visibility as plans for a Hollywood movie based on a recently released book were made public. And at the Minnesota State Fair last summer, we saw 'Tiny Teesha, the Island Princess,' who was in actuality a black woman midget from Haiti making her living going from one state fair to another.

While the human exhibition exists in more benign forms today   that is, the people in them are not displayed against their will – the desire to look upon predictable forms of Otherness from a safe distance persists. I suspect after my experience in the cage that this desire is powerful enough to allow audiences to dismiss the possibility of self-conscious irony in the Other's self-presentation; and even those who saw our performance as art rather than artifact appeared to take great pleasure in engaging in the fiction, by paying money to see us enact completely nonsensical or humiliating tasks. A middle-aged man who attended the Whitney Biennial opening with his elegantly dressed wife insisted on feeding me a banana. The zoo guard told him he would have to pay $10 to do so, which he quickly paid, insisting that he be photographed in the act. After the initial surprise of encountering caged beings, audiences invariably revealed their familiarity with the scenario to which we alluded.

We did not anticipate that our self-conscious commentary on this practice could be believable. We underestimated public faith in museums as bastions of truth and institutional investment in that role. Furthermore, we did not anticipate that literalism would dominate the interpretation of our work. Consistently from city to city, more than half of our visitors believed our fiction and thought we were 'real,' with the exception of the Whitney, where we experienced the art world equivalent of such misperceptions: some assumed that we were not the artists, but rather actors who had been hired by another artist. As we moved our performance from public site to natural history museum, pressure mounted from institutional representatives obliging us to didactically correct audience misinterpretation. We found this particularly ironic, since museum staffs are perhaps the most aware of the rampant distortion of reality that can occur in the labeling of artifacts from other cultures. In other words, we are not the only ones who are lying; our lies simply tell a different story. For making this manifest, we are perceived as either noble savages or evil tricksters, dissimulators who discredit museums and betray public trust. When a few uneasy staff members in Australia and Chicago realized that large groups of Japanese tourists appeared to believe the fiction, they became deeply disturbed, fearing that the tourists would go home with a negative impression of the museum. In Chicago, just next to a review of the cage performance, the daily *Sun-Times* ran a phone-in questionnaire asking readers if they thought the Field Museum should have exhibited us, to which 47 percent answered no, and 53 percent yes (1993). We seriously wonder if such weighty moral responsibilities are leveled against white artists who present fictions in nonart contexts.

Lest we attribute the now infamous confusion we have generated among the general public to some defect of class or education, let it also be known that misinterpretation has filtered into the echelons of the cultural elite. [. . .] The trustees of the Whitney Museum questioned curators at a meeting prior to the Biennial asking for confirmation of rumors that there would be 'naked people screaming obscenities in a cage' at the opening. When we arrived at UC-Irvine last year, we learned that the Environmental Health and Safety Office had understood that Gómez-Peña and I were anthropologists bringing 'real aborigines' whose excrement – if deposited inside the gallery – would be hazardous to the university. This is particularly significant in light of the school's location in Orange County, where Mexican immigrants are often characterized by right-wing 'nativists' as environmental hazards. [. . .]

I should perhaps note here the number of people who have encountered this performance. We do not have exact figures for Columbus Plaza and Covent Garden, which are both heavily trafficked public areas; however, we do know that 1,000 saw us in Irvine; 15,000 in Minneapolis; approximately 5,000 in both Sydney and Chicago; and 120,000 in Washington, D.C. Audience reactions of those who believe the fiction occasionally include moral outrage that is often expressed paternalistically (i.e., 'Don't you realize,' said one English gentleman to the zoo guards in Covent Garden, 'that these poor people have no idea what is happening to them?'). The Field Museum in Chicago received forty-eight phone calls, most of which were from people who faulted the museum for having printed misinformation about us in their information sheet. In Washington, D.C., an angry visitor phoned the Humane Society to complain and was told that human beings were out of their jurisdiction. However, the majority of those who were upset only remained so for about five minutes. Others have said they felt that our being caged was justified because we were, after all, different. A group of sailors who were interviewed by a Field Museum staff member said that our being in a cage was a good idea since we might otherwise become frightened and attack. One older African-American man in Washington asserted quite angrily that it would only have been alright to put us in a cage if we had some physical defect that classified us as freaks.

For all the concern expressed about shocking children, we found that their reactions have been the most humane. Young children invariably have gotten the closest to the cage; they would seek direct contact, offer to shake our hands, and try to catch our eyes and smile. Little girls gave me barrettes for my hair and offered me their own food. Boys and girls often asked their parents excellent questions about us, prompting ethical discussions about racism and treatment of indigenous peoples. Not all parents were prepared to provide answers, and some looked very nervous. A woman in London sat her child down and explained how we were just like the people in the displays at the Commonwealth Institute. A school group visiting Madrid told the teacher that we were just like the Arawak Indian figures in the wax museum across the street. And then there have been those children who are simply fascinated by the spectacle; we heard many a child in Sydney, where our cage sat in front of an exhibit featuring giant mechanized insects, yelling, 'Mommy, Mommy, I don't want to see the bugs. I want to stay with the Mexicans!'

The tenor of reactions to seeing 'undiscovered Amerindians' in a cage changes from locale to locale; we have noted, for example, that in Spain, a country with no strong tradition of Protestant morality or empirical philosophy, opposition to our work came from conservatives who were concerned with its political implications, and not with the ethics of dissimulation. Some patterns, nonetheless, have repeated themselves. Audience reactions have been largely divided along the lines of race, class, and nationality. Artists and cultural bureaucrats, the self-proclaimed elite, exhibited skeptical reactions that were often the most anxiety-ridden. They sometimes have expressed a desire to rupture the fiction publicly by naming us, or they arrive armed with skepticism as they search for the 'believers,' or parody believers in order to join the performance. At the Whitney Biennial the performers of Dance-Noise and Charles Atlas, among others, screamed loudly at Gómez-Peña to 'free his genitalia' when he unveiled a crotch with his penis hidden between his legs instead of hanging. Several young artists also complained to our sponsors that we were not experimental enough to be considered good performance art. Others at the Whitney and in Australia, where many knew that we were part of the Sydney Biennale, dismissed our piece as 'not critical.' One woman in Australia sat down with her young daughter in front of the cage and began to apologize very loudly for 'having taken our land away.' Trying to determine who really believes the fiction and who doesn't became less significant for us in the course of this performance than figuring out what the audience's sense of the rules of the game and their role in it were.

People of color who believe, at least initially, that the performance is real have at times expressed discomfort because of their identification with our situation. In Washington and London, they have made frequent references to slavery, and to the mistreatment of Native peoples and blacks as part of their history. Cross-racial identification with us among whites was very common, but in London, a recently released ex-convict who appeared to be very drunk grabbed the bars and proclaimed to us with tears in his eyes that he understood our plight because he was a 'British Indian.' He then took off his sweater and insisted that Gómez-Peña put it on, which he did. In general, white spectators tended to express their chagrin to our zoo guards, usually operating under the assumption that we, the Amerindians, were being used. They often asked the zoo guards if we had consented to being confined, and then continued with a politely delivered stream of questions about our eating, work, and sexual habits.

Listening to these reactions was often difficult for the zoo guards and museum staff people who assisted us. One of our zoo guards in Spain actually broke down and cried at the end of our performance, after receiving a letter from a young man condemning Spain for having colonized indigenous Americans. One guard in Washington and another in Chicago became so troubled by their own cognitive dissonance that they left the performance early. The director of Native American programs for the Smithsonian told us she was forced to reflect on the rather disturbing revelation that while she made efforts to provide the most accurate representation of Native cultures she could, our 'fake' sparked exactly the same reaction from audiences. Staff meetings to discuss audience reactions have been held at the Smithsonian, the Australian Museum, and the Field Museum. In all the natural history museum sites, our project became a pretext for internal discussions about the extent of self-criticism those museums could openly be engaged in. In Australia, our project was submitted to an Aboriginal curatorial committee for approval. They accepted, with the stipulation that there be nothing Aboriginal in the cage, and that exhibition cases of Aborigines be added to our chronology.

Other audience members who realize that we are artists have chastised us for the 'immoral' act of duping our audiences. This reaction was rather popular among the British, and has also emerged among intellectuals and cultural bureaucrats in the U.S. I should here note that there are historical precedents for the moralistic responses to the ethnographic display in Britain and the U.S., but in those cases, the appeal was to the inhumanity of the practice, not to the ethics of fooling audiences, which the phony anthropologists who acted as docents in American Dime Museums often did. A famous court case took place in the early nineteenth century to determine whether it was right to exhibit the Hottentot Venus, and black ministers in the U.S. in the early twentieth century protested Ota Benga's being exhibited in the Bronx Zoo. Neither protest triumphed over the mass appeal of the spectacle to whites.

The literalism governing American thought complements the liberal belief that we can eliminate racism through didactic correctives; it also encourages resistance to the idea that conscious methods may not necessarily transform unconscious structures of belief. I believe that this situation explains why moralizing interpreters shift the focus of our work from audience reactions to our ethics. The reviewer sent by the *Washington Post*, for example, was so furious about our 'dishonesty' that she could barely contain her anger and had to be taken away by attendants. A MacArthur Foundation representative came to the performance with his wife and they took it upon themselves to 'correct' interpretations in front of the cage. In a meeting after the performance, the Foundation representative referred to a 'poor Mexican family' who was deeply grateful to his wife for explaining the performance to them. After receiving two written complaints and the *Washington Post* review, the director of public programs for the Smithsonian Natural History Museum gave a talk in Australia severely criticizing us for misleading the public. We have heard that he has since changed his position. What we have not yet fully understood is why so many of these people failed to see our performance as interactive, and why they seem to have forgotten the tradition of site-specific performance with which our work dovetails, an historical development that preceded performance art's theatricalization in the 1980s.

On the whole, audience responses have tended to be less pedantic and more outwardly emotional. Some people who were disturbed by the image of the cage feared getting too close, preferring instead to stay at the periphery of the audience. Barbara Kruger came to see us at U.C.-Irvine and went charging out of the gallery as soon as she read the chronology of the human display. Claus Oldenberg, on the other hand, sat at a distance in Minneapolis, watching our audiences with a wry smile on his face. The curator of the Amerindian collection at the British Museum came to look at us. As she posed for a photo, she conceded to one of our Edge

Biennial representatives that she felt very guilty. Her museum had already declined to give us permission to be displayed. Others found less direct ways of expressing such anxiety. A feminist artist from New York questioned us after a public lecture we gave on the performance in Los Angeles last year, suggesting that our piece had 'failed' if the public misread it. One young white woman filmmaker in Chicago who attended the performances showed up afterward at a class at the University of Illinois and yelled at Gómez-Peña for being 'ungrateful' for all the benefits he had received thanks to multiculturalism. She claimed to have gone to the performance with an African-American man who was 'equally disturbed' by it as she was. Gómez-Peña responded that multiculturalism was not a 'gift' from whites, but the result of decades of struggle by people of color. Several feminist artists and intellectuals at performances in the U.S. have approached me in the cage to complain that my role is 'too passive,' to berate me for not speaking and only dancing as if my activities should support their political agenda.

Whites outside the U.S. have been more ludic in their reactions than Americans, and they have appeared to be less self-conscious about expressing their enjoyment of our spectacle. For example, businessmen in London and Madrid had approached the cage to make stereotypical jungle animal sounds. However, not all the reactions have been lighthearted. A group of skinheads attacked Gómez-Peña in London and were pulled away by audience members. And scores of adolescents in Madrid stayed at the cage for hours each day, taunting us by offering beer cans filled with urine and other such delicacies. Some of those who understood that the cage piece was performance art have made a point of expressing their horror at others' reactions to us in private, perhaps as a way of disassociating themselves from their racial group. One Spanish businessman waited for me after the performance was over to congratulate me on the performance, introduced me to his son, and then insisted that I had to agree that the Spaniards had been less brutal with the Indians than the English. The overwhelming majority of whites who believed the piece, however, have not complained or expressed surprise at our condition in a manner that is apparent to us or the zoo guards. No American ever asked about the legitimacy of the map (though two Mexicans have to date), or the taxonomic information on the signs, or Gómez-Peña's made-up language. An older man at the Whitney told a zoo guard that he remembered our island from *National Geographic*. My dance, however, has been severely criticized for its inauthenticity. In fact, during the press review at the Whitney, several writers simply walked away just as I began.

The reactions among Latin Americans have differed in relation to class. Many upper-class Latin American tourists in Spain and Washington, D.C., voiced disgust that their part of the world should be represented in such a debased manner. Many other Latin Americans and Native Americans immediately recognized the symbolic significance of the piece, expressing solidarity with us, analyzing articles in the cage for other audience members, and showing their approval to us by holding our hands as they posed for photographs. Regardless of whether they have believed or not, Latinos and Native Americans have not criticized the hybridity of the cage environment and our costumes for being 'inauthentic.' One Pueblo elder from Arizona who saw us in the Smithsonian went so far as to say that our display was more 'real' than any other statement about the condition of Native peoples in the museum. 'I see the faces of my grandchildren in that cage,' he told a museum representative. Two Mexicans who came to see us in England left a letter saying that they felt that they were living in a cage every day they spent in Europe. A Salvadorean man in Washington stayed with us for an extended period, pointing to the rubber heart suspended from the top of the cage, saying, 'That heart is my heart.' On the other hand, white Americans and Europeans have spent hours speculating in front of us about how we could possibly run a computer, own sunglasses and sneakers, and smoke cigarettes.

In Spain there were many complaints that our skin was not dark enough for us to be 'real' primitives. The zoo guards responded by explaining that we live in a rain forest without much exposure to the sun. At the Whitney, a handful of older women also complained that we were too light-skinned, one saying that the piece would only be effective if we were 'really dark.' These doubts, however, did not stop many from taking advantage of our apparent inability to understand European languages; many men in Spain made highly charged sexual comments about my body, coaxing others to add more money to the donation box to see my breasts move as I danced. I was also asked out on dates a few times in London. Many other people chose a more discreet way of expressing their sexual curiosity, by asking the zoo guards if we mate in public in the cage. Gómez-Peña found the experience of being objectified continuously more difficult to tolerate than I did. By the end of our first three days in Madrid, we began to realize that not only were people's assumptions about us based upon gender stereotypes, but that my experiences as a woman had prepared me to shield myself psychologically from the violence of public objectification.

I may have been more prepared, but we were both faced with sexual challenges that transgress our physical and emotional boundaries during the performances. In the cage we are both objectified, or in a sense, feminized, inviting both male and female spectators to take on a voyeuristic relationship to us. [. . .] Interestingly, women have been consistently more physical in their reactions, while men have been more verbally abusive. In Irvine, a white woman asked for plastic gloves to be able to touch the male specimen, began to stroke his legs, and soon moved toward his crotch. He stepped back, and the woman stopped – but she returned that evening eager to discuss our feelings about her gesture. In Chicago, another woman came up to our cage, grabbed his head and kissed him. Gómez-Peña's ex-wife had lawsuit papers delivered to him while we were in the cage at Irvine, and subsequently appeared in costume with a video camera and proceeded to tape us for over an hour. While men taunted me, talked dirty, asked me out, and even blew kisses, not one attempted physical contact in all our performances.

As I presented this 'reverse ethnography' around the country, people invariably asked me how I felt inside the cage. I experienced a range of feelings from panic to boredom. I felt exhilarated, and even playful at times. I've also fallen asleep from the hot sun, and been irritable because of hunger or cold. I've been ill, and once had to be removed from the cage to avoid vomiting in front of the crowd. The presence of supportive friends was reassuring, but the more aggressive reactions became less and less surprising. The night before we began in Madrid, I lay awake in bed, overcome with fear that some demented Phalangist might pull a gun on us and shoot before we could escape. When nothing of that sort happened, I calmed down and never worried about our safety again. I have to admit I like watching people on the other side of the bars. The more we have performed, the more I have concentrated on the audience, while trying to feign the complete bewilderment of an outsider. Although I love the intentional nontheatricality of this work, I have become increasingly aware of how engaging in certain activities can trigger audience reactions, and acted on that realization to test our spectators. Over the course of the year, I grew fond of the extremists who verbalized their feelings and interacted with us physically, regardless of whether they were hostile or friendly. It seems to me that they have a certain braveness, even courage, that I don't even know I would have in their place. When we came upon Tiny Teesha in Minnesota, I was dumbstruck at first – not even my own performance had prepared me for the sadness I saw in her eyes, or my own ensuing sense of shame. [. . .]

WORKS CITED

Altwick, Richard D. (1978) *The Shows of London*. Cambridge, MA: Belknap Press.

Chicago Sun Times (1993), 19 January: 2.

Clifford, James (1988) *The Predicament of Culture*. Cambridge, MA: Harvard University Press.

Fanon, Frantz (1967) 'The Negro and psychopathology.' In *Black Skin, White Masks*. trans. Charles Lam Markmann. New York: Grove Press: 141–209.

Kafka, Franz (1979) *The Basic Kafka*. New York: Washington Square Press.

Mannoni, Octave (1990) *Prospero and Caliban: The Psychology of Colonialism*, trans. Pamela Powesland. Ann Arbor: University of Michigan Press.

Rothenberg, Jerome (1977) 'New models, new visions: some notes towards a poetics of performance.' In *Performance In Postmodern Culture*, ed. Michel Benamou and Charles Caramello, 11–18. Madison, WI: Coda Press.

Rydell, Robert (1984) *All the World's a Fair: Visions of Empire at American International Exhibitions, 1876–1916*. Chicago: University of Chicago Press.

Tzara, Tristan (1992) *Seven Dada Manifestos and Lampisteries*, trans. Barbara Wright. London: J. Calder.

30

NOMADMEDIA
On Critical Art Ensemble

Rebecca Schneider

T168, 2000

When an audience member enters the performance space for Critical Art Ensemble's *Flesh Machine* she might think she's stumbled upon a lecture in some biology hall of her past, except for the fact that the information is extremely up-to-date and ... delivered by artists. Dressed in lab coats, CAE presents information on medical and scientific practices in the field of eugenics, peppered by short performance sketches so that the 'class' will stay attentive. Unlike a parodic or distantiated performance of a lecture (recall Ron Vawter performing Clifton Fadiman in the Wooster Group's *Route 1 & 9*), CAE's opening is a lecture without overt irony. They *are* lecturing (which is not to say they are not performing).[1] Wanting their audiences to know some facts about contemporary eugenics practices, CAE has simply found the lecture to be both the gentlest and most reliable entry into what quickly becomes a more challenging event.

Opening with a lecture, emphasis is placed on the particular situation that many women face in regard to the political, social, and economic pressures to reproduce and raise children. In fact, for CAE biological reproduction is primarily an Ideological State Apparatus (Althusser 1979). From the start, the ensemble explain their own political position regarding issues of reproductive technology – as one member put it, they don't want to 'trick anyone.' Frontally and predictably staged, with all the trappings of traditional presentation, not only is this format a functional means of getting across a body of information, but the traditional theatre/lecture presentation panders to habit, providing, in CAE's words, a 'cushion for the impact of process theatre' which follows.

In the second part of the event spectators become far more involved – this is the 'lab' portion of biology class. Audience members participate in actual lab processes and encounter various models of artificial reproduction. This is CAE's attempt to include a tactile relationship to the material that goes beyond presentational language – what my junior high teachers called 'hands on.' But this is no pasting and labeling of leaves onto paper (my own memory of teenage bio). For this section, CAE built its own cryolab to house living human tissue for potential cloning so that audience members can become hands-on genetic engineers. But is this a theme park of cryopreservation, or the hard science itself?

In preparation for *Flesh Machine* CAE studied in biology labs to learn cryo-preservation and biopsy techniques. They lived with and documented a couple going through IVF treatment. They studied material science to learn how to build a cryo-lab. In the fall of 1997 they mounted their performance in Vienna at Public Netbase,[2] touring participants through the 'signage' of reproductive process (from theory to testing to representations of the process). Their aim was to reveal what they considered hidden eugenic agendas, agendas that become most apparent on the intimate level of the literal procedure. [3] To do this, they stumbled across that sacred line between hard science and soft art. When asked about the specifics of their study process, CAE gave me the following response:

> We didn't study 'seriously.' We are amateurs. However, to get to the political economy of this situation, and the sociological impact of these goings-on, you don't have to get a degree. We simply read lots of books and journals; spent a semester in cell biology lab (more like a participatory researcher in anthropology); spent two weeks living with a couple going through IVF; did numerous interviews with molecular biologists; had biologists (experts) check our work, and generally act as consultants. When we did *Flesh Machine* in Vienna, a team of biologists from the local university came to the event to check our work and show we were a fraud. They did not find one thing they could dispute, and were quite congratulatory about it too – although they were never too keen on our politics.

When I asked specifically which labs participated with them in their training, CAE provided the names of four U.S. labs, but asked that I not make them public as 'it could lead to problems for people who have been kind enough help us under the table.' I asked CAE these questions when *TDR* editor Richard Schechner was critical of the appellation 'study' to describe CAE's forays into hard science. Schechner was 'fearful of amateur dabbling being labeled "study."' He reminded me that 'Study comes hard, is not cheap, and doesn't yield to "I told you I did it."' Did CAE learn biopsy, or watch it and then mimic? I shared this concern with CAE, and was given the following response – a response that in many ways presents CAE's general principles in this and other projects succinctly:

> This is the very attitude we are struggling against – the crotchety academic defending his territory. Until myths such as 'we must suffer long and hard to learn about a model' are done away with (which is not to say that specialization should be done away with) there will never be interdisciplinarity, nor productive public dialogues on various knowledge bases. We are amateurs, and say so very proudly. Amateurism is a fundamental principle of tactical media work and nomadology in general. Amateurs move mountains – think of ACTUP for example – total amateurs, yet had an impact on AIDS policy (and I might say, for the most part, for the better). One of the functions of 'you must be an expert' discourse is to keep such movements from happening – listen to Big Brother – he knows best. Not all science is brain surgery (although they are the exalted scientists who are so much smarter than everyone else, so it must be). Most lab techniques, particularly the ones we learned, are monotonous and simple, and any idiot can do them. Contrary to expectation, the Human Genome Center is not a scientific think-tank with brilliant biologists scurrying about in *X-File*

surroundings; rather it is just a bunch of students from the general work study pool following Betty Crocker cake recipes. In *Flesh Machine* particularly, this was a myth that we were trying to break down. It's one reason why we had on-site labs, so the audience could see that science isn't magic, and that they the audience are easily smart enough to participate in this discussion if they so desire (and without suffering).

The second section of *Flesh Machine*, then, begins when the lectures end and the audience begins to mill about and attend to computers that stand about the space, available for audience members to check out a CAE CD-ROM. The CD contains a donor-screening test (abducted by CAE from an 'actual clinic'). Audience members sit at monitors and take the lengthy test to access their individual suitability to be further reproduced through donor DNA, cytoplasm, and/or surrogacy. If they 'pass' the test, they receive a certificate of genetic merit. Those who pass can be further examined through an interview with CAE followed by an actual taking of a cell sample by lab technicians at the site. These samples are then stored, if the audience member is willing, in CAE's cryotanks. The artists have been collecting photographs of audience members who 'pass' this standardized test and they claim that the similarities of those who are determined fit for reproduction is astounding. By now they can predict 'passes' just by looking at them: straight-looking whites, usually male.

After this hands-on, indeed cell-sharing, experience, the audience gathers for the close of the performance. This final section of *Flesh Machine* is intended to underscore the class politics, the economics, and the logic of human commodification involved in eugenics.

At this point, CAE presents a frozen embryo to their audience – an embryo that CAE adopted from a couple who no longer needed it. An image of the embryo is projected through a video beam onto a screen. The image has a clock marking the time the embryo has until it is evicted from its clinical cryotank. If enough money is raised to pay the rent on the cryotank through the performance, the embryo will live. If not, it will be 'terminated.'

Put another way, if no one buys the embryo, it dies.

CAE then takes donations from the audience. Needless to say, to date every performance has ended with the death-by-melting of the embryo. CAE claims that this part of the performance speaks for itself – though on more than one occasion the group has had to speak in the wake of their actions. In Vienna, for instance, they found themselves on national TV debating the ethical implications of embryo murder with an Archbishop live from Salzburg via satellite.

The group of artists who call themselves Critical Art Ensemble is concerned with 'tacticality' in an information age when power is radically dislocated from geography by the instant-time synapses of cyberspace and when colonizing 'penetration' seeks out new frontiers at the level of DNA. Their most recent concerns have pivoted on what they label the 'New Eugenic Consciousness,' but this interest in biotechnology grows out of their longer-standing agendas regarding post-national capitalism. CAE has repeatedly asserted that digital technology has enabled capital power to 'retreat' into cyberspace 'where it can nomadically wander the globe, always absent to counterforces, always present whenever and wherever opportunity knocks' (www.critical-art.net/ECD/Ch_1.html). How to fight nomadic power CAE-style? Fight it with dislocation and intermediality – perhaps nomad-mediality – an ever shifting, no longer simply hybridized, media tacticality.[4] If nomadic capital is absent to counterforce, the question becomes how to counter this absence-to-counter? By becoming nomadic. By appearing disappeared. Nameless, interfacing without facing, CAE set up a false corporation called BioCom and cast it onto the Web.[5] Art? Or capital?

CAE is a mixed-gender collective of five white 'new media' artists trained in various skills from book and performance to computer, film, video, photography, and critical theory. CAE's work has consistently been committed to the 'continuation of resistant cultural models.' While exploring and critiquing models of representation used in capitalist political economy to sustain what they call 'authoritarian policies' they have experimented with various organizational (versus primarily representational) strategies toward making art that intersects with activist practices. Because they resist precise location relative to genre and venue and artist identity their work questions the politics of location, specifically the politics which have historically located art via authorship, site, public/private space, media, price, frame.

Publishing and performing collectively and anonymously, CAE disseminate their works as broadly as possible (their books, if not their names, have circulated freely on the web). Their anonymity serves as a mark of their resistance to privatization – their collectivity does as well (see CAE 1998b). They are not secretive about their names. They simply do not use their names as signatures relative to their work. Similarly, they do not respect the signatures of other artists as 'Keep Out' markers of private property. Between 1988 and 1994, CAE began releasing object-oriented artists' books of plagiarist text poetry. The books, five in all, rapidly sold out – purchased by many library, university, and museum collections around the U.S.

While plagiarism draws lines of indebtedness to the historical avant-garde (one thinks of Brecht immediately), in other ways CAE is reminiscent of feminist collectives in the 1970s who refused to put forward a director or an author because of the critique of authority at the base of their efforts think and create differently. And like such collectives, CAE has firsthand experience that collective activity is against the grain of artworld production. Financial support favors individuals, as do art institutions. Several years ago they gave up grant writing as a waste of time. As they wrote in 1998, 'In spite of all the critical fulminations about death of originality, the artists, and the rest of the entities named on the tombstones in the modernist cemetery, these notions persist, protected by an entrenched cultural bureaucracy geared to resist rapid change' (1998a: 73). In art schools across the country, students are taught to accept the ideological imperative that artistic practice is an individual practice – there is 'no place where one can prepare for a collective practice' (74). Even in theatre schools the emphasis is rarely on ensemble. Though theatre is a model that carries within it a deeper imperative for ensemble work, more often than not that work is subsumed under the name of a director, an auteur, or a specific site. A roving band of anonymous actors without a playwright or director or stage is hardly the kind of collective one finds promoted in academies and so students, entering the profession with training, have most often already been trained against the grain of collectivity. [6]

CAE began in 1986, two years after the Guerrilla Girls formed their anonymous activist collective of 'artists and professionals.' Comparing the two groups can help to situate CAE's anonymity as similarly activist, but differently focused. The Guerrilla Girl mission is to expose racism, sexism, and homophobia in the art (and now theatre) worlds and they have done this through posters, statistical fact sheets, masked actions, and various publications. While the Guerrilla Girls were initially anonymous to protect their names, the necessity of their anonymity itself made a loud statement about the general blindspotting of artists of color, female artists, and queer artists precisely where art meets capital – the 'art scene' of galleries, funding, museums, reviews, shows, sales, and placement in history. Historically, women and people of color have not been *named* 'artists' and for such artists, then, to be rendered anonymous signals a troubled and suspect position. The broader sexed, raced, and gendered context that haunts names and continues to influence capital in the art establishment is what the Guerrilla Girl collective wants to *name* and *locate* (see Guerrilla Girls 1998).

From a similar perspective it would be possible to argue that for a collective of white people (such as CAE) to claim anonymity and emulate the fluid dislocation of capital while appropriating the work of others is nothing remarkably out of the ordinary historically, but rather a longstanding privilege of the larger propertied white collective. Most likely, however, CAE would agree and argue that they deploy such emulation in an attempt to make those operations explicit. Rather than struggle to name the unnamed, CAE names the operation of naming, struggling to expose the fact that the named artist (the 'star' individual) has long been circulated *as a name* to support a broader anonymous (unmarked) collective of (white patriarchal) privilege which reproduces its foundations by structurally facilitating institutional support for the cult of the individual artist.

Critical Art Ensemble began when two grad students at Florida State University collaborated on low-tech videos. In 1987, picking up new members, the group transformed into an artist and activist collective. Some of CAE's early projects between 1987 and 1993 include *Fiesta Critica* – a project launched in Indiantown, Florida. CAE interacted with Mayan migrant workers in the town and developed a set of pieces presented at an Easter fiesta, using their grant money to support the fiesta which otherwise would have been beyond the means of the workers. In *Cultural Vaccines*, CAE collaborated with Gran Fury on a multimedia event that critiqued U.S. policy regarding the HIV crisis.[7] Out of this exhibition the first chapter of ACTUP in Florida was created with CAE members as founding members. *Exit Culture* was a series of works developed for highway culture in Florida. The piece incorporated trucker poetry for CB, postcards for tourists, invisible performance, and bus-stop video. CAE traveled around Florida in a Winnebago for three days stopping only to perform at tourist sites, rest stops, and malls.

In 1994 CAE published *The Electronic Disturbance* with the Autonomedia Collective of Semiotext(e). The book was a broad-based critique of technology within pancapitalism and it immediately found a very wide audience. Hakim Bey called the book a 'manifesto for a new generation of artists' and Tim Druckerey heralded it 'required reading.' The book jumped to the no. 1 bestseller slot in nonfiction on the *Village Voice* alternative bestseller list. And indeed, it was available to download free off the Web. Suddenly CAE was deluged with offers to speak, perform, publish. *The Electronic Disturbance* was translated into German within a month of its appearance in English (works by CAE now appear in eight languages). *Electronic*

Civil Disobedience and Other Unpopular Ideas soon followed and CAE was on the road all over Europe and the U.S. and Canada.

In 1995 at a festival in Winnipeg, a woman showed a CAE member a photo of her child. While this quotidian exchange might not have been remarkable, this particular photo showed the child at the four-cell stage. The woman was a single parent who had conceived through invitro fertilizaion. The sighting provoked a turn in CAE's work from critiquing information and communications technology, with an emphasis on the Net, to addressing ideological problems associated with biotechnology.

This turn, which resulted in *Flesh Machine*, is interesting in part because CAE's critique of electronic technology had always included a critique of the blindspotting of the material and bodily effects of Net culture. One of the most riveting suggestions in *Electronic Civil Disobedience* (1996) concerns the futility of contemporary political activism based solely on present-body embodied actions. CAE believes, quite adamantly, that resistance at the level of bodies in the street is defunct. Such activism of the present protesting body (from sit-ins to marches to million-body appearances) is dependent, CAE argues, on an image of sedentary power: that is, power as centered in bunker-institutions, locatable and inhabitable, available for physical take-over. But power in pancapitalism has become nomadic, decentered (or at least multi-centered) and global, dislocated into the synapses of digitalia. In fact, CAE argues that the state has *given people the streets* (as a kind of 'false public' space) because power has itself gone nomadic through electronic networks. To take to the streets, today, they argue, is civil obedience – anticipated, sanctioned spectacle – prolonging the illusion that presence can have effect.[8]

CAE makes its primary concern one of tacticality regarding digital interruptions into pancapitalism's digital fluidity. Literalizing a certain poststructural insight, CAE maintains that direct political action in the form of civil disobedience cannot be effected through affects of *presence* in representational regimes. The days are over, they remind us, when 'castle, palaces, government bureaucracies, corporate home offices, and other architectural structures stood looming in city centres, daring malcontents and underground forces to challenge their fortifications' (in Dery 1998). As Mark Dery explicates CAE's position, these edifices that once housed power are now 'monuments to its absence.' Power is neither visible nor stable – thus effective resistance must make use of the invisible and unstable. CAE makes it clear that working in representational regimes is key to pedagogical resistance – and such resistance is important. But CAE makes a distinction between pedagogy and direct political action. For them, direct political action necessitates, today, invisibility and non-locatability, but pedagogical actions can slide into the space between location and dislocation, visibility and invisibility. *Flesh Machine* is largely a work falling into the category of pedagogy and thus should not be mistaken for direct political action, or for civil disobedience.

If power is neither visible nor stable, and if effective resistance must make use of the invisible and unstable, what kinds of instability does CAE deploy? For CAE, a longstanding device of instability is recombinance. In an essay in *TDR*, CAE cites the 'tradition of digital cultural resistance' as one indebted to a wide-ranging heritage of recombinance, some specifically digital, some generally 'avant-garde': 'combines, sampling, pangender performance, bricolage, detournment, readymades, appropriation, plagiarism, theatre of everyday life, and so on' (CAE 2000).

The disobedience that the digital offers is precisely a renewed deployment of the age-old disobedience of the thieving copy, a plagiaristic unsettling of the prerogatives of the ruse of locatable origin.

The benefits some theorists of the virtual see in the 'new' body – the degendered body, for example – is, according to CAE, shortsighted. To them, the promise that cyberspace might become a truly multi-sensual apparatus, unleashing myriad bodily pleasures released from policings of desire, ignores the fact that the technology is developed and released only under the auspices of intensive capital. 'Why would capital want to deliver what would essentially be a wish machine to its population?' asks CAE. 'Capital depends upon a consistent state of what the Situationists called "enriched privation." If satisfaction were ever offered to the public, the economy of desire would collapse overnight. A virtual wish machine is about as likely as capital legitimizing and insisting upon the use of heroin among its [working- and middle-class] population' (in Dee 1998).

CAE's invocation of Debord and the Situationists is a huge clue to CAE's indebtedness to 1960s radical performance politics – and an indication that it does not agree with the postmodern claim that the avant-garde is dead. *The Electronic Disturbance* relentlessly critiques traditional theatre and performance art – seeing much of it invested in a naval-gazing celebration of the 'solipsistic self' and citing the proscenium arch as the primary apparatus of that solipsism in a machinery of presence. But certain avant-garde art tactics they consider resistant – and useful for *pedagogical* actions. The Living Theatre and Happenings and general 1960s attempts to collapse the distinction between art and life are cited as offering 'tremendous help' by 'establishing the first recombinant stages.' CAE also cites Berlin Dada, Boal's Theatre of the Oppressed, feminist performance of the 1970s, and Guerrilla Art Action Group as inspirational. Though, as they claim in *TDR*, the art world regularly 'defanged' these movements, the lesson CAE takes from various radical theatres is the impact of the 'experiential,' of something called 'real life' (CAE 2000). They maintain the importance of an art that is 'looped back' into the immediacy of everyday life. Into and out of. The loop is important as they feel equally strongly that 'everyday life' cannot be art's exclusive terrain.

> CAE's interest in the Living Theatre stems from our belief that it offered a proto-postmodern model of cultural production. The group quite consciously located itself in the liminal position between the real and the simulated. Various behaviors were appropriated and redeployed so perfectly that, regardless of their ontological status, they had the material impact of the real. The Living Theatre performed the crisis of the real before it had been adequately theorised, and contributed to the conceptual foundation now used to understand and create virtual theatre. It helped make it clear that for virtual theatre to have any contestational value, *it must loop back to the materiality of everyday life*.
>
> (quoted in Dery 1998)

The turn to biotechnology from their earlier artwork on communications technology offered a site for a direct interrogation of the relations between digital capital culture and the 'loop' to material everyday life. CAE wanted their work on biotechnology to challenge the distinction between the simulated and the real – something that biotechnology itself challenges (think simply of Dolly the clone[9]).

In the tradition of the Living Theatre, they wanted to tap the contestational value in enunciating 'the loop.'

Intent on the real/virtual/real loop, then, CAE's deployment of digital models of recombinance is not a move to bankrupt the material body as site of political action, despite the fact that the 'street' has moved to the nonmateriality of the information highway. Rather recombinant resistance needs to be attentive, they argue, to the *body politics* of nomadic authoritarian power and its multiple deployments of the digital toward increased privatization – including the production of 'false public space' and the parallel production of privation for 'undesirable' or deviant bodies. Despite its nomadism and dislocation in terms of the national or geographic, capital still operates through the metaphorics of the frontier, which are, more precisely, metaphorics of penetration (the name of a new consortium of scientists and companies investing in cloning is 'Probio America'). For CAE the biological body – or the privatization, manipulation, and commodification of the *organic* – is the 'new frontier' for capital.

While theorists on the left and right have long been hip to the regulation of bodies under capital and the politics of the body as capital vis-à-vis production and reproduction, the 'new eugenic consciousness' makes the laboring body *seem* like an antiquated machine. CAE suggests that we distrust this equation. New Eugenics is a body radically disembodied – a body contained in a single sample, the body as digitized code – but still, perhaps, a future body designed relative to economics, regulating and managing a *white-collar* workforce. I asked one CAE member to make this point clearer to me – being a bit skeptical of the conspiracy theory that seemed to undergird the argument. The artist pointed to a large glass office building opposite my seventh-floor window in the financial district in Manhattan. We sat silently for a few moments and watched the workers inside. Floor upon floor upon floor of management – the ones with windows, the ones we could see, were middle-level executives – many of whom might be the clients of a corporation like BioCom, many of whom might 'pass' for appropriate genetic duplication, and many of whom might be able to afford the cost. It was hard for me to see exactly how *this* was a frontier – body upon body upon body, floor upon floor upon floor, the last thing from 'wild' let alone 'where no man has gone before.' But maybe it only takes a little thought. If this frontier is more cellular than it is geographic, still it nevertheless may be as far-reaching as other 'penetrations' have been in the history of capitalist expansion. Here, biotechnology, like some railroad to the interior, opens access like never before – making 'the body' available, differently, for theatres of empire.

CAE's point in *Flesh Machine* is direct: the new commodity market open for colonial expansion of property politics is taking place intra-bodily via reproductive biotechnologies. They advocate, through their nomadmedial highway dodgings between art, critical theory, digital production, performance, and the literal life/death auction of an embryo, a close analysis of linked apparati of reproduction (esthetic, digital, and biotechnical). They are not neo-luddites. They are very much manifesto-style avant-garde artists *of* technology. Their profound effort is pitched toward the faith that technological development can be shaped, designed, and deployed alternatively. They aim to provoke critical response.

Even, it seems, if some have to die in the process.

NOTES

1 See Jon McKenzie (2001) on the 'lecture machine.'
2 Subsequent performances took place at the Kappelica Gallery, Ljubljana; the Labor Gallery, Graz; Beursschouwburg, Brussels (at the Art and Science Collision); and at the Kiasma Museum of Contemporary Art, Helsinki.
3 CAE's notion of hidden agendas has a resolutely Marxist ring, though their angle on late capital's liquid structure – its nomadism – lands them more precisely in league with the anti-rationalist schizoanalysis of Deleuze and Guattari.
4 The word 'intermedia' was introduced into the arts lexicon by Dick Higgins in 1965 (see Higgins 1969, the essay dates from 1965). In describing artworks at the interfaces of established media and in the interstices between art and life, Higgins anticipated the postmodern preference for hybridity over formal unity and the challenge to 'art' as an ontologically pure and privileged category. Deploying intermedia, CAE's nomadmediality dislocates as well as interfaces.
5 BioCom is now a page on CAE's website at critical-art.net/biocom.
6 Of course there are ensembles of performers today who are very active: The Wooster Group, Split Britches, Brith Gof, East Coast Artists, Double Edge Theatre, SF Mime Troupe, Spiderwoman, Mabou Mines, Nature Girls, Goat Island, the Living Theatre, Great Small Works, and more. In the visual art world, collectives are much more foreign, for obvious reasons. In the theatre, groups are not dominant, but neither are they nonexistent. In fact, one of the tendencies the theatre inherited from the interaction with art that produced 'performance art' was the tendency toward solo creation.
7 Gran Fury is an artists' collective that emerged simultaneously with CAE and the Guerrilla Girls. Ironically named after the popular brand of car used by police, Gran Fury was closely tied to the ranks of New York AIDS activists. The mission was to use the medium of advertising to strike back against homo- and AIDS-phobia. Refusing to identify its members, Gran Fury wheat-pasted posters all over New York City. Perhaps most famous is the upturned pink triangle and 'Silence = Death' logo. *Kissing Doesn't Kill*, a video by the collective, aired on cable and MTV. A bus poster of the same title was banned in several cities because it featured multicultural imagery of gays and lesbians kissing.
8 That embodied protest as effectual might be a ruse of post-national power is reminiscent of Baudrillard's argument that the manufacture and media deployment of scandal is an empty ritual of authority engineered to maintain the ruse that capital and its governing body has conscience (1994).
9 See Schneider (2001).

WORKS CITED

Althusser, Louis (1997) 'Ideology and ideological state apparatuses.' In *Lenin and Philosophy and Other Essays*. London: New Left Books.
Baudrillard, Jean (1994) *Simulacra and Simulations*, trans. Shiela Faria Glaser. Ann Arbor: University of Michigan Press.
Critical Art Ensemble (1994) *The Electronic Disturbance*. New York: Autonomedia/Semiotext(e).
—— (1996) *Electronic Civil Disobedience and Other Unpopular Ideas*. New York: Autonomedia/Semiotext(e). http://www.critical-art.net
—— (1998a) *Flesh Machine: Cyborgs, Designer Babies and New Eugenics Consciousness*. New York: Autonomedia/Semiotext(e).

Critical Art Ensemble (1998b) 'Observations on collective cultural action.' *Artjournal* 57, 2: 72–85.

Dee (1998) 'Critical Art Ensemble. An interview.' *Fringecore* 4: 7–9.

Dery, Mark (1998) 'Vector block on Telecoms Avenue: Critical Art Ensemble interviewed.' *Mute* 10: http://www.metamute.com/issue10/dery.htm.

Guerrilla Girls (1998) *The Guerrilla Girls' Bedside Companion to the History of Western Art*. New York: Penguin.

Higgins, Dick (1969) 'Intermedia.' In *foew & ombwhew*. Barton, BT: Something Else Press.

McKenzie, Jon (2001) *Performing or Else*. New York: Routledge.

Schneider, Rebecca (2001) 'Hello Dolly Well Hello Dolly: The double and its theatre.' In *Psychoanalysis and Performance*, ed. by Patrick Campbell and Adrian Kear. New York: Routledge.

Part IV

MONTAGE, REITERATION, REVISION

31

INTRODUCTION TO PART IV

Rebecca Schneider

Anne Ubersfeld (1982) has suggested that directing is a semiotic writing over writing. On the stage, textual writing meets bodies texted in space, the texture of gesture and object, light and sound. Even where there is no playscript, faculties of *interpretation* come into play on the parts of directors, designers, actors, and the audiences they engage. To the degree that the theatre makes meaning, then, it is involved in quotation or reiteration. But what are the politics of quotation? Is quotation (as in saying a line or striking a pose) *always* angled toward interpretation or reinterpretation? Or re-reinterpretation? What happens when quotation is not 'faithful' to its supposed origin? Where, as Gerald Rabkin asked in 1985, is text located? And how many texts can dance on one stage? What happens when texts collide? When a playscript, for instance, meets a director's interpretation as one of open challenge rather than unquestioned reproduction?

One of the signatures of postmodern art practice has been the return to, or appropriation of, 'classic' texts or formal practices in the service of explicit reiteration and revision. If modernist practices, such as naturalism, sought to expose some truth or 'reality' underlying representation, postmodern practices often make representation *about* representation, in a sometimes dizzying concatenation of quotation as montage – where the relationship between the quoter and that which is quoted is highlighted, destabilized, and put into question by being *played*. Here, if 'reality' is explored it is often the reality of representation itself – or, in politicized postmodern theatre, the 'reality effects' of representational practices which ghost our habits of meaning-making (see Schneider 1997: 21–8). Emphasis shifts from the object or narrative as primary focus of attention and onto the dynamics of exchange between spectator, artist, and object – the *acts* of interpretation.

Of course, this type of theatre has roots that reach deep into modernism. While a precise parsing of modernism from postmodernism is sadly beyond the scope of this introduction (and a famously fractured and contestatory project), we are including here examples of directing strategies that have foregrounded fragmentation, citation, and polyvocal reassembly – what Suzan-Lori Parks and Liz

Diamond, drawing on jazz, here cite as 'rep and rev' – repetition and revision. These strategies would become quasi-signatures of postmodern theatre, in some tension with the 'revolutionary' aims of the modernist signatures they retrace. But, of course, as postmodernism is unimaginable without the modernism it posts . . . this posting is part and parcel (pardon the pun) of play put into play. The tangle of citation, the repetition and revision, is often hard to map, as in many ways the politics of mapping itself – of meaning making and history marking – are precisely opened for reevaluation.

We begin this section with Daniel Gerould's 1974 essay on Sergei Eisenstein's 1923 production of Ostrovky's 1868 comedy *Enough Stupidity in Every Wiseman* and with Eisenstein's own manifesto, 'Montage of attractions.' Like many revolutionary directors, Eisenstein was drawn to the circus as site of inspiration. As a form of 'popular carnival' circus contained a ready-made critique of bourgeois hierarchies. Also, as a montage form of disparate attractions it engaged in 'shock elements' that might wake a sleepy spectator out of his habitual repose. The emphasis for Eisenstein, even more than for his teacher Meyerhold, was on the possibility of 'radical new interpretation' (Gerould). That interpretation of a text might be made anew shifted the locus of effort away from faithful rendition and onto a directing practice *aimed at being precisely other than faithful*. This is what Eisenstein called a 'revolutionary modernization,' a revolution he articulated as a 'social reevaluation' (cited in Gerould below).

Investment in 'revolution' changed drastically across the twentieth century. World War II contributed profoundly to the 'incredulity' toward master narratives – utopian or otherwise – that Jean-François Lyotard cites as a defining stance of postmodernism (1984). Identity politics post-1968 increasingly challenged the terms of any unified voice for 'the people.' And the dismantling of the symbolic Berlin Wall symbolized a post-mortem for the 'project of modernity' that had generated a globe mapped according to boundaries between revolutionary agendas: East and West, North and South, Left and Right, Capitalist and Other.

Perhaps a result of any post-mortem is a preoccupation with ghosts. The replaying of classics as well as the replaying of the 'folk art of vulgar commercial entertainment' (Ludlam below) evident in this section are arguably preoccupied with the status of history as it returns in play. This is history not understood as a seamless master narrative, but as a fractured re-entry of remainders. This is a history sometimes understood, as in Charles Ludlam's queer Theatre of the Ridiculous, as a history of identifications, of role-playing and its discontents (see Stefan Brecht below; see also Diamond 1997). In Ludlam's theatre, as Brecht describes it, 'Removal of cadavers, necessitated by the high onstage death-rate, is done with exaggerated clumsiness; the corpse does not cooperate – but mostly the dead just sit up after a while, walk off, reparticipate in the action.'

The final essay of this section explores a piece of self-referential directing – that is, directing reflexively 'replaying' the history of directing – in a brief analysis of Schechner's 1997 production of Chekhov's *Three Sisters*. This final essay is the third to explore one of the ur-texts of naturalism as directed by different artists – Stanislavsky, Elizabeth LeCompte, and Richard Schechner. Thus, we have provided a kind of 'return' at the end of the book to its own beginning. Or, perhaps better said, a ghosting that is less a return to a beginning than a revolution: a troubling of the 'ends' of our endeavors.

WORKS CITED

Diamond, Elin (1997) *Unmaking Mimesis*. New York: Routledge.

Lyotard, Jean François (1984) *The Postmodern Condition*. Minneapolis: University of Minnesota Press.

Schneider, Rebecca (1997) *The Explicit Body in Performance*. New York: Routledge.

Ubersfeld, Anne (1982) *Lire le Théâtre*. Paris: Editions Sociales.

32

EISENSTEIN'S *WISEMAN*

Daniel Gerould

T61, 1974

Throughout the first decade of its existence, Soviet theatre sought inspiration and new directions in the popular arts. In the period after the Revolution, the most innovative Russian directors and writers turned to the clowning and novelty acts of circus and music hall, in an attempt to break with the traditions of bourgeois drama – its plotting, psychology, and domestic themes and in order to create a vital new political and propagandistic theatre with, they hoped, broad appeal to the masses.

The painter Yuri Annenkov, in his version of Tolstoy's *The First Distiller* at the Hermitage Theatre, Petrograd, in 1919, added clowns and variety acts, made hell into a circus, and turned the devils into acrobats. Vladimir Mayakovsky collaborated with the professional clown Vitaly Lazarenko in staging his circus scenario *The Championship of the Universal Class Struggle* (see T57) at the Second State Circus in Moscow. At the Folk Comedy Theatre in Petrograd from 1920 to 1922, Sergei Radlov wrote and staged a series of circus comedies and melodramas, hiring circus performers as actors, and using trapeze acts and flights over the audience on a tightrope in his search for a synthesis between the arts of theatre and circus. At the Factory of the Eccentric Actor, all productions were inspired by the popular arts; with the aid of a professional clown and cabaret artists, Grigori Kozintsev and Sergei Yutkevitch in 1922 presented an adaptation of Gogol's *Marriage*, which, in Kozintsev's words, was 'an amalgam of circus, cabaret, and cinema.'

Also in 1922, the year in which the Soviet avant-garde's circus tendencies reached a high point (and the year in which Eisenstein prepared *The Wiseman*), Vsevolod Meyerhold, the master of all the young directors, presented first *The Magnificent Cuckold* with its acrobatics and physical exercises and then *Tarelkin's Death*, composed of clown acts, gymnastics, and a denouement in which the hero made his escape by swinging across the stage on a trapeze. At just about the same time, even Alexander Tairov, in his production of Charles Lecocq's operetta *Girofle-Girofla*, utilized a wide range of circus and music-hall tricks.

According to Sergei Yutkevitch, 'The whole young generation of Soviet artists had turned toward minor genres, the kind of popular art which the aristocracy and bourgeoisie had scorned . . . the music hall, the circus, and the cinema.' For Kozintsev, the revolutionary excitement of the times explains why it was that the dominant theatrical modes took on 'the artistic forms of a great popular carnival,' since 'in the middle of every kind of privation a sort of fair was going on.' Above all, these young artists were in love with the circus, which they considered the highest and most difficult of all the arts because of its precision, discipline, and daring. The eccentric and eccentrism (circus terminology for novelty numbers exploiting the ludicrous, illogical, and surprising) flourished on stage in the early years of the Soviet theatre and served as a basis for a new system of acting. The *Soviet Small Encyclopedia of Circus* (Moscow, 1973) defines the eccentric as:

> An artistic device for pointedly comic portrayal of reality, consisting of intentional violation of logic, sequentiality, and interdependence among the events portrayed and of the alogical (from the point of view of generally accepted norms) behavior of the characters, with the result that the occurrences appear as though displaced from their usual positions and receive unexpected shifted meanings . . . The eccentric performer by the seeming illogicality and absurdity of his actions, presents happenings in an unexpected light, exposing their hidden truth (for example, the comic portrays a man who publicly repents the mistakes that he has made and beats himself on the breast; then leaving the platform, the 'orator' pulls out from his chest a metal tray with a pillow attached to it, which has protected his breast from the blows). After a series of logical actions, there can follow a displacement, which shows the senselessness of all that has gone before (for example, the performer carefully cleans his jacket, blows the dust off it, and then suddenly spreading it out on the ground, wipes his feet on it).

By the mid-1930s, from the dogmatic viewpoint of the new esthetic of Socialist Realism, the youthful Soviet experiments with the eccentric were repudiated or at least apologized for, even by those who had helped to create the movement. Clowning as the foundation for a style of theatre was now seen as a Bohemian Western import, negative and anarchistic in its rejection of the past traditions of realistic drama that had triumphed in Soviet artistic ideology. [. . .]

Eisenstein's period of work in the theatre corresponds exactly with the heyday of the eccentric actor. Arriving in Moscow in 1920, with a passionate interest in circus going back to childhood and a strong personal identification with clowns, Eisenstein began his association with the Moscow Proletkult, where he became one of the chief proponents of eccentrism in the theatre and, with *The Wiseman*, its most brilliant and radical practitioner.

The Proletkult – abbreviation for 'Proletarian Cultural and Educational Organizations,' which were established after the Revolution to foster art among the workers as the basis for the new socialist society – sought to promote a totally new kind of theatre, revolutionary in content and popular in form, whose aim was to be agitation and propaganda. It readily adopted and promoted the acrobatic acting style then in vogue. For his first production with the Proletkult, *The Mexican* (adapted from Jack London), Eisenstein worked officially only as a designer of costume and scenery; in fact, he not only created the circus clothes and formalized movements for the characters, but also staged the concluding boxing match as a genuine sports event in a boxing ring directly before the audience.

Subsequently for Foregger, with whom he next worked, Eisenstein continued his experiments with circus and music hall in the parodies of *Be Kind to Horses* and

The Scarf of Columbine, in which he projected (although never realized) an appearance by Harlequin from the auditorium on a tightrope. After a year's work with Meyerhold, Eisenstein returned to the Proletkult in 1922 to fulfill his ambition of creating an acrobatic theatre with his production of *The Wiseman*, which was given its premiere in Moscow on 16 April 1923. Based on Alexander Ostrovsky's nineteenth-century classic comedy *Enough Stupidity in Every Wiseman* (written and first produced in 1868 and variously translated into English as *The Diary of a Scoundrel* and *The Scoundrel*), Eisenstein's *Wiseman* used the original play simply as a starting point for topical political and social satire in the style of circus, music hall, and variety show.

Because of its irreverent treatment of a literary masterpiece and its flouting of theatrical tradition, *The Wiseman* touched off a controversy and polemic that was to last many years. In the essay 'Montage of attractions,' published in May 1923 in *Lef*, a left-wing experimental magazine under Mayakovsky's direction, Eisenstein, using the dense jargon characteristic of the movement, gives in condensed form the esthetic theory underlying the production and the whole eccentric school. Yevgeny Gabrilovitch recounts how, in a meeting at the House of the Press, Eisenstein justified such performances as the only course for the theatre in the new era:

> What do the masses and the Revolution want from the theatre? Only (answered Eisenstein) what goes back to the sources of traditional forms of popular spectacle: circus, fairground attractions. The new theatre must be a sort of 'montage of attractions,' that is to say of shock elements that strike and dazzle.

The year 1923 was the hundredth anniversary of Ostrovsky's birth, and at the celebration at the Maly Theatre, Anatoly Lunacharsky, the Commissioner of Education responsible for the direction of Soviet theatre, repeated his new slogan: 'Back to Ostrovsky' – a clear call for theatre workers to revise their negative attitudes toward the classic repertory. Eisenstein's response, in the form of *The Wiseman*, in which even the title of Ostrovsky's play was ironically shortened, seemed more in the spirit of Meyerhold's plea, 'No More Anniversaries!' than a genuine commemoration. In any case, *Enough Stupidity in Every Wiseman*, one of Ostrovsky's most sharply satirical plays with an ingenious plot full of surprises, lent itself well to the eccentric treatment, and, although some saw the production as an irresponsible sabotaging of artistic sanctity, Eisenstein was less concerned with undercutting Ostrovsky than with creating a new kind of theatre. Properly understood, according to Eisenstein's theory, all the stunts and tricks were designed to express the play's themes and ideas – in a radical new interpretation.

In 1928 Eisenstein wrote: 'My aim was to achieve a revolutionary modernization of Ostrovsky, i.e., a social reevaluation of his characters, seeing them as they might appear today.' Sergei Tretyakov – author of *Gas Masks* and *Listen, Moscow*, the next two plays to be directed by Eisenstein, and of *Roar, China*, produced by Meyerhold in 1926 – made the adaptation of Ostrovsky's play, while Eisenstein prepared the scenario. The text was entirely rewritten, expanded, and drastically revised; the characters were totally reconceived. Jokes, puns, and buffoonery were added; popular songs of the time interpolated; acrobatics, novelty acts, and clown shows inserted, as well as topical political allusions and references to local issues. At the Twelfth Party Congress in 1923, it had been declared: 'The theatre must also be utilized as a means for anti-religious propaganda.' Accordingly, Ostrovsky's satire on bigotry was developed into an anti-religious theme typical of agitational work at that time, making use of a comic priest, rabbi, and mullah. At the same time, bourgeois morality and ideas on art, the White emigration, and imperialistic spying and secret agents were mocked.

Besides the abbreviated title and central satirical theme, the general line of action (except for the finale or epilogue) also remained the same as in Ostrovsky, but the plot was transferred to the contemporary political world and took place in Paris among the circle of White Russian émigrés. The characters from the original play underwent the following changes: Mamaev became Pavel Mamilyukov-Prolivny (satirizing Pavel Milyukov, Foreign Minister in the Provisional Government, who emigrated at the time of the Revolution); Krutitsky was transformed into General Joffre, Marshal of France and Commander in Chief of French forces until 1916; Mashenka turned into a woman stockbroker, Mary Mac-Lac; Gorodulin became Goredulin, a Fascist; Kurcahev expanded into three hussars; Glumov was George the clown at one and the same time; and the clown in the red wig, who first appeared in the prologue (specially composed for the production) subsequently turned into Glumov's mother. Two other women's parts – Manyefa and Turusina – were played by men, and all the servants were played by one actor. Strictly circus characters were also added, such as the uniformed attendants and 'the act in the ring.'

Moreover, all the characters were assigned functions as clowns and acrobats at various points in the play. The actor–acrobats did triple somersaults on an imaginary horse, walked over the auditorium on high wires, jumped down in parachutes, and climbed up the ceiling on poles. For example, Yanukova (Mamaeva) did stunts at the top of a pole held by Antonov (Joffre–Krutitsky). These numbers required rigorous circus training, and considering that Eisenstein was using actors, not professional acrobats, the results obtained with less than half a year for training were spectacular.

Viktor Shklovsky, the Soviet critic, records that the acrobatics were absolutely genuine, holding great danger since neither nets nor safety wires were used. Grigori Alexandrov 'walked over the heads of the spectators on an inclined wire from the balcony to the lower stage. He almost fell once and was saved only by a member of the audience who raised his cane and thereby helped Alexandrov regain his balance and take the next step.' Shklovsky maintains that Eisenstein was so conscious of the tremendous risks that he occasionally ran out of the auditorium and hid in the basement during parts of the performance.

The playing area was especially designed for the performance so that everything resembling a conventional theatre was excluded. The Proletkult theatre was located in the former mansion of a millionaire businessman, which was built in pseudo-Moorish style on Kalinin Prospect (formerly Vozdvizhenka Street), and which, at the present time, is 'The House of Friendship with Foreign Countries.' The great hall used for the theatre was relatively small, but had a very high ceiling. The audience was placed on two sides in steep, semi-circular amphitheatres in front of which was the arena or ring, which was covered with a soft round mat-like rug where the action unfolded. The walls were hung with canvas, and there was a raised platform stage with curtain and ramps from which the characters appeared.

[. . .]

The eccentrism of the acting consisted of generalized metaphorical expression of emotions through physical action, combining techniques from *commedia dell'arte* and ancient farce. Portraying astonishment, the actor did not simply give a start – he did a double somersault. All metaphor became literal and physical. Eisenstein later amplified how this fundamental device operated:

> A gesture turns into gymnastics, rage is expressed through a somersault, exaltation through a salto-mortale, lyricism by a run along a tightrope. The grotesque of this style permitted leaps from one type of expression to another, as well as unexpected intertwinings of the two expressions.

Apparently such surprising stunts and unexpected twists made it difficult for the audience to follow the development of the action. Shklovsky complains that meaning and motivation disappeared and continuity was constantly broken, although the resultant theatricalism was greater than Meyerhold or Yevgeny Vakhtangov ever produced. When the circus artist Yevgeny Kumeiko reviewed the play, he reported that Tretyakov 'came on stage before the audience and narrated the content of the play and the meaning of its respective situation.' Also, the libretto, printed on the back of the program, gave a summary of the action.

Eisenstein's inventiveness was inexhaustible, and there was an endless flow of circus tricks that left the audience gasping and worn out from laughing. When Mamilyukov first appeared, he was followed by an automobile tire from which air was escaping. When Joffre–Krutitsky called on Turusina and tea was served, the servant carried a tray laden with various canned goods, and as he passed close to the spectators, his legs flew out from under him. The audience in the first rows let out cries of fear that soon changed to laughter and applause when they saw that the cans hung in midair, suspended on strings.

The Masked Man, Golutvin (as played by Alexandrov) – with green electric eyes, top hat, and floor-length detective's coat, like Harry Piel, popular sleuth of the time – made his famous descent from the balcony down to the stage at this point, holding an umbrella to balance himself on the tightrope attached to the sculptured cornice of the hall. The three question marks in the program point to the revelation that beneath the mysterious black mask Golutvin is actually a NEPman – a pejorative term for those who took advantage of the opportunities for private enterprise afforded by the New Economic Policy instituted in 1921 to restore the economy. Again Eisenstein used stunts as expressive visual metaphors. At that time, NEPmen were usually portrayed as pot-bellied, and thus it was a surprise to see a handsome, agile actor doing difficult acrobatic feats; thematically, these eccentric traits showed the adroitness, shrewdness, and ability to mimic the new bourgeoisie.

Film was used for the first time by Eisenstein in the production of *The Wiseman*, not only in the epilogue to show the theft of Glumov's diary, but also in the course of the play as trains and automobiles bearing the characters off to new horizons were flashed on a screen. The film epilogue was a parody of both newsreels, then in vogue, and American adventure films with their motorized chases. Glumov escapes in the film by climbing out a window. Pursued, he dashes off in a car, while Golutvin, in silk hat and evening dress, leaps from a moving plane into the car and eventually reaches the Proletkult theatre – at which point the live actor

Alexandrov breathlessly bursts into the auditorium holding the film. The film montage had previously transformed the chameleon-like Glumov into whatever his companion of the moment most wanted him to be: a dutiful donkey with his uncle Mamaev, a military cannon with General Joffre–Krutitsky, and an infant with his doting aunt Mamaeva. The film itself is another attraction, an eccentric number translated into a different artistic sphere, technique, and dimension. As if to mark this fact, at the end of the production, instead of appearing on stage for a bow to the applause of the audience, Eisenstein was shown on the screen smiling and turning from side to side, like the trademark Pathé rooster at the end of a feature film.

Furthermore, the montage principle was used not only for the film, but also in the construction of the play itself, in the very way that the scenes were put together. The juxtaposition of Scenes 8 and 9 of Act II illustrates how this scenic montage effect was produced. In the first, his uncle gives Glumov instructions as to how to woo his aunt; in the second, Glumov puts these instructions into operation. Instead of being played separately and consecutively, the two scenes were intersected and given simultaneously so as to sharpen contrasts of character, quicken tempo, and multiply comic possibilities. Years later, Eisenstein described how this montage had been worked out and what its purposes were:

> The scene with Mamaev takes place below, in the 'ring' as we called it then. The scene with Mrs. Mamaev takes place on the platform stage. And instead of a smooth change of scene, Glumov races from one to the other and then back again. He carries on a segment of dialogue with one in such a way as, having broken off, to continue the segment already started with the other. The final remarks of one series of segments, colliding with the beginning of the second, acquire new meaning, sometimes a punning play on words. The jumps themselves create something like caesuras between the ensemble play of separate moments. The presence of a third person, not taking part in the conversation and as if absent, gives additional effect of illustrative cutting to this or that remark in the dialogue of the two others.

As an example of this technique, Eisenstein cites the following use of cutting in *The Wiseman*. Speaking of his own wife, Mamaev told Glumov, 'She's a woman of passion.' At this point the actress playing Mrs. Mamaev made appropriate gestures and expressions, thus cutting into the conversation about her and transforming the scene into something new.

The Wiseman was undoubtedly influenced by Meyerhold, particularly by his production of *Tarelkin's Death*, which made extensive use of traditional fair and circus tricks and for which Eisenstein was an assistant director. However, in his own treatment of classic works, Meyerhold did not depart from the author's text no matter how original the interpretation. Comparing his own famous production of Ostrovsky's *Forest* in 1924 with Eisenstein's *Wiseman*, Meyerhold declared in 1939: 'My *Forest* turned out to be an absolutely naïve work in comparison with what he did.' The master recognized the importance of his pupil Eisenstein's experiment, which he characterized in these terms: 'The subject of the investigation was movement in its maximal expressiveness.'

Looking back at the production of *The Wiseman* from the perspective of many years, Eisenstein concluded:

First and foremost we must give credit to the basic principles of the circus and the music hall – for which I had had a passionate love since childhood. Under the influence of the French comedians, and of Chaplin (of whom we had only heard), and the first news of the foxtrot and jazz, this early love thrived. The music-hall element was obviously needed at the time for the emergence of a 'montage' form of thought.

33

MONTAGE OF ATTRACTIONS

Sergei Eisenstein

Translated by Daniel Gerould

T61, 1974; first published in *Lef,* 1923

1. THE THEATRICAL DIRECTION OF THE PROLETKULT

Just a few words. The theatrical program of the Proletkult does not involve the 'utilization of the values of the past' or the 'invention of new forms of theatre' but the abolition of the very institution of the theatre as such, replacing it with a showplace for achievements in the theatre or with an instrument for raising **the standard of training of the masses in their day to day life**. The real task of the scientific section of the Proletkult in the field of theatre is to organize theatre studios and to work out a scientific system for raising the standard.

All the rest that is being done is 'provisional'; to fulfill secondary, not basic, aims of the Proletkult. The 'provisional' runs along two lines under the general heading of revolutionary content.

1. **Representational-narrative theatre** (static, real-life – the right wing): the Proletkult's *Zori,*[1] *Lena,*[2] and a series of not fully realized productions of the same type – this being the direction of the former Workers Theatre with the Central Committee of Proletkult.
2. **Agit-attraction theatre** (dynamic and eccentric – the left wing): the direction promoted by me in collaboration with B. Arvatov, chiefly for the work of the touring company of the Moscow Proletkult. In its embryonic form, but with sufficient clarity, this direction has already been pointed out in *The Mexican*[3] – a production by the author of the present essay in collaboration with V. C. Smyshlyaev[4] (the First Studio of the Moscow Art Theatre). [. . .]
3. **The Wiseman**, begun by the Peretru[5] (and completed as a joint enterprise of the two companies), was the first work, in terms of *agit*, based on the new method of constructing a performance.

2. MONTAGE OF ATTRACTIONS

Since this concept is being used for the first time, it requires some explanation. The spectator himself constitutes the basic material of the theatre; the objective of every utilitarian theatre (agit, poster, health education, etc.) is to guide the specta-tor in the desired direction (frame of mind). The means of achieving this are all the component parts of the theatrical apparatus (Ostyzhev's[6] 'chatter' no more than the color of the prima donna's tights, a stroke on the kettledrum as much as a soliloquy of Romeo, the cricket on the hearth[7] no less than a salvo under the seats of the spectators). In all their heterogeneity, all the component parts of the theatri-cal apparatus are reduced to a single unit – thereby justifying their presence – by being attractions.

An attraction (in relation to the theatre) **is any aggressive aspect of the theatre**; that is, any element of the theatre that subjects the spectator to a sensual or psycho-logical impact, experimentally regulated and mathematically calculated to produce in him certain **emotional shocks** which, when placed in their proper sequence within the totality of the production, become the only means that **enable the spectator to perceive the ideological side of what is being demonstrated – the ultimate ideological conclusion.** (The means of cognition – 'through the living play of passions' – apply specifically to the theatre.)

Sensual and psychological, of course, are to be understood in the sense of immediate reality, in the way that these are handled, for example, by the Grand Guignol theatre: gouging out eyes or cutting off arms and legs on the stage – or a character on stage participating by telephone in a ghastly event ten miles away; or the plight of a drunkard who senses his approaching death, and whose cries for help are taken as delirium tremens – not in terms of the development of psycho-logical problems where the attraction is already the theme of the play itself – a theme that exists and functions even outside of the play's action provided that it is suf-ficiently topical. (This is an error into which agit-theatres fall, satisfied with only this kind of attraction in their productions.)

On the formal level, by an attraction I mean an independent and primary elem-ent in the construction of a performance – a molecular (that is component) unit of effectiveness in theatre and of theatre in general. It is fully analogous to Grosz's 'storehouse of images' or Rodchenko's 'elements of photo-illustrations.'

'Component': just as it is difficult to determine where the fascination for the hero's nobility (the psychological aspect) ends and the aspect of his personal charm (that is, his sensual magnetism) begins, the lyric effect of a series of scenes by Chaplin is inseparable from the attraction of the specific mechanics of his move-ments – so it is difficult to determine where religious pathos gives way to sadistic satisfaction in the scenes of martyrdom in the Mystery Play, etc.

An attraction has nothing in common with a trick. A trick, or rather, a stunt (it is time to put this term, which has been excessively abused, back in its proper place) is an accomplishment complete in itself in terms of a certain kind of craftsmanship (chiefly acrobatics). A stunt is only one of the kinds of attractions with its own appropriate method of presentation (or as they say in the circus – its 'sale'); since it signifies something absolute and complete in itself, it is the direct opposite of an attraction, which is based exclusively on an interrelation – on the reaction of the audience.

[. . .] A new method emerges – free montage of arbitrarily selected independent (also outside of the given composition and the plot links of the characters) effects (attractions) but with a view to establishing a certain final thematic effect – montage of attractions.

The way of completely freeing the theatre from the weight of the 'illusory imita-tiveness' and 'representationality,' which up until now has been definitive, inevit-able, and solely possible, is through a transition to montage of 'workable artifices.' At the same time this allows interweaving into the montage whole 'represen-tational segments' and connected plot lines of action, no longer as something self-contained and all determining, but as an immediately effective attraction consciously selected for a given purpose. The sole basis of such a performance does not lie in 'the discovery of the playwright's intention,' 'the correct interpretation of the author,' 'the true reflection of the period,' etc., but only in attractions and a system of attractions. Any director who has become a skilled hand due to a natural flair has intuitively used an attraction in some way or other, but, of course, not in terms of a montage or construction but 'in a harmonious composition' at any rate (hence even the jargon – 'effective curtain,' 'rich exit,' 'good stunt,' etc.). But what is significant is that what was done was only in the framework of logical plot probability ('warranted' by the play) and chiefly unconsciously. [. . .]

The film and above all the music hall and the circus constitute the school for the montage-maker, since, properly speaking, putting on a good show (from the formal point of view) means building a strong music hall-circus program, starting from the basic situation of the play. As an example, here is an enumeration of a portion of the numbers in the epilogue to *The Wiseman*:

> *Editors' note*: At this point in the essay Eisenstein includes a breakdown of twenty-five scenes in the epilogue. This list is published in its entirety in *TDR*. We have included the first ten scenes as well as the final two in order to give a sense of Eisenstein's 'montage of attractions' in production. The material in italics represents a supplement to Eisenstein's list. The supplemental information, which is also published in *TDR*, was reconstructed by the surviving participants of the performance: M. S. Gomorov, A. P. Kurbatov, A. I. Levshin, V. P. Shareuv, I. F. Yasykanov, under the general direction of M. M. Shtraukh.

1. Expository soliloquy by the hero. [*On stage (in the ring), Glumov, in a ('exposi-tory') soliloquy, tells how his diary was stolen from him and how this threatens him with exposure. Glumov decides to marry Mashenka quickly; he calls Mayefa (a clown) on stage and proposes that he appear as a priest.*]
2. Part of a detective film: (explanation of point 1 – the theft of the diary). [*The lights go out, on the screen is seen the theft of Glumov's diary by a man in a black mask – Golutvin. This is a parody of an American detective film.*]
3. Musical-eccentric act: the bride and three rejected suitors (according to the play, only one character) in the role of ushers: a scene of sorrow in the style of the song, 'Your Fingers Smell of Incense.' [*Light in the auditorium. Mashenka appears in a motoring outfit with a bridal veil in a crown, followed by her three rejected suitor officers. [. . .] In Eisenstein's original plan, this scene was sketched out as an eccentric xylophone number, with Mashenka playing on bells sewn like buttons on the officers' uniforms.*]
4., 5., 6. Three parallel clown acts, two sentences each (motif of payment for organizing the wedding). [*After the exit of Mashenka and the three officers, Glumov is on stage again. Three clowns – Gorodulin, Joffre, Mamilyukov – come running up to him one after another out of the auditorium, and each performs his*

circus number *(juggling with small balls, acrobatic leaps, etc.)* and demands payment for it. Glumov refuses and goes out. *('A clown act with paired sentences' – for each exit, there are two sentences of text: the comments of the clown and of Glumov.)*]

7. Feature act of the *étoile* (the aunt) and of the three officers (motif of the rejected suitors). Punning with a transition through the mention of an unsaddled horse (because of the impossibility of leading it into the auditorium – traditionally 'three as a horse.') [*Mamaeva appears, dressed in provocative splendor ('an* étoile*') with a circus whip in her hand and officers following her. Mamaeva wants to break Glumov's engagement and consoles the rejected suitors. After their remarks about a horse ('My friend the mare neighs'), she cracks her whip and the officers scamper about the ring. Two represent the horse, the third the rider.*]

8. Choral-agit song: 'The Priest Had a Dog,' to the accompaniment of the priest's 'bouncing ball' in the form of a dog (motif of the beginning of the wedding). [*The priest Manyefa is on stage; the wedding ceremony begins. All those present for the wedding sing: 'The Priest Had a Dog.' Manyefa performs a circus number ('the bouncing ball') portraying a dog.*]

9. An interruption of the action (voice of a newsboy for the exit of the hero). [*A newsboy yells through a megaphone. Glumov, leaving the wedding ceremony, runs off to find out whether his diary has appeared in print.*]

10. The appearance of the villain in a mask. A segment of comic film (a summary of the five acts of the play in the transformation of Glumov; the motif of the publication of the diary). [*The thief who stole the diary appears – a man in a black mask (Golutvin). The lights go out. On the screen, Glumov's diary is seen in the film. It tells about his behavior toward the mighty patrons and about his transformations into various temporary shapes (like into an ass with Mamaeva, into a tanker with Joffre, etc.).*]

[. . .]

24. The final feature act of the two clowns, who douse each other with water (traditionally) ending with the announcement 'the end.' [*A squabble arises between the two 'red noses'; one of them splashes the other with water, and he falls down with surprise. One of them announces 'the end' and bows to the audience.*]

25. A salvo under the spectators' seats as the final chord. [*At the moment the clown bows to the audience, there is a burst of fireworks under the seats in the auditorium.*]

NOTES [ADDED BY TRANSLATOR]

1 *Zori Proletkulti* was a performance by the Proletkult, in which the poetry of proletarian poets was dramatized. It was intended as an answer to Meyerhold's production in 1920 of Emile Verhaeren's *Les Aubes* (*Zori*).

2 *Lena* is a play by Velerian Pletnyov about events on the Lena River in Siberia in 1912. It was presented for the opening of the Moscow Proletkult Theatre in 1921. Eisenstein was one of the artists who worked on the staging.

3 *The Mexican* was a dramatization of a Jack London story. It was Eisenstein's first production

(with Smyshlyaev) at the Proletkult Theatre in 1921. Eisenstein also did the costumes and scenery.

4 Valentin Smyshlyaev was an actor and director from the First Studio of the Moscow Art Theatre. He worked with the Proletkult and wrote a book, *The Technique of Constructing a Stage Production*, published by the Proletkult. In 1923, he directed Shakespeare's *The Taming of the Shrew* at the MAT.

5 Abbreviation for the mobile troupe of the Moscow Proletkult Theatre.

6 Alexander Ostyzhev was a well-known actor of the period who appeared as Romeo, Othello, and in many other classic roles.

7 A reference to the dramatization of Dickens's *The Cricket on the Hearth* presented by the First Studio of the MAT in 1915.

34

CHARLES LUDLAM'S RIDICULOUS THEATRICAL COMPANY

Ron Argelander

T62, 1974

> When I was in conventional theatre, even when I was going to school, people thought my acting was too broad, too pasty. So I had to create a theatre where I could exist. I had to create, for my own survival, a world where I could take advantage of my talents.
>
> *Charles Ludlam*

In 1967, Charles Ludlam organized the Ridiculous Theatrical Company, patterning it after modern dance companies where composer and choreographer perform with the group. It was an actors' company, primarily composed of untrained actors, nonactors, and filmmakers. Most had experience working in 'underground' films, but few had any professional training. Ludlam was the only one of the group with extensive schooling and experience in acting, directing, and playwriting. [From 1967 to 1974] he has been responsible for writing, directing, and acting the lead roles in the company's plays: *Big Hotel* (1967), *Conquest of the Universe/When Queens Collide* (1968), *Whores of Babylon* (by Bill Vehr, 1968), *Turds in Hell* (by Ludlam and Vehr), *The Grand Tarot* (first version, 1969), *Bluebeard* (1970), *The Grand Tarot* (second version, 1971), *Eunuchs of the Forbidden City* (1971), *Corn* (1972), *Camille* (1973), and *Hot Ice* (1974). Today [1974], in addition to Ludlam, the Ridiculous Theatrical Company consists of John Brockmeyer, Jack Mallory, Lola Pashalinski, Black-Eyed Susan, Bill Vehr, Richard Currie, Robert Beers, Georg Osterman, and Stephen Sterne.

As head of the company, Ludlam has worked with the raw material of his fellow members – seeing what they did best or what was unique about them – and crafted plays around their talents. An intimate way of working has emerged based on a shared creative sensibility most like the activity of play – the kind of play children share in creating backyard fantasy drama. It is a sensibility that takes plots, dialog, and characters from movies, comics, and other familiar or personal sources. Role creation is everything except 'playing oneself' – it is disguise, sexual role switching, artifice, caricature, stereotype. And acting is broad and expressive but not 'good' or 'bad.'

Although Ludlam is credited with writing the company's plays, it is because of the way the company works that the plays are written. Members of the company are constantly exchanging ideas for plays, sharing desires for roles, inventing visual gags, and bits of business, watching each other in performances and making suggestions, and contributing lines of dialog and plot maneuvers that are added to the play. There are usually many ideas for plays being discussed among the members of the group simultaneously. Each idea is at a different level of development. Some, like the proposed *Jack and the Beanstalk* and *Fashion Bound*, are now awaiting the right time for production; others are still in the early stage of planning. 'For months and months before we even start rehearsing a play,' explains Jack Mallory, 'Charles will be talking about the next play and the play after that. The company discussed doing *Camille* for five years before getting around to doing it. We've been talking about *Hot Ice* for nearly two years.'

Usually the plot comes from a movie. 'None of us saw that much theatre,' says Ludlam. 'Most of our "theatrical" experiences were in the cinema; that's where we saw plot and began to develop our ideas about it.' Characters may also come from the film, but there is usually no attempt at imitation. Often, Ludlam's plots blend characters from several sources, and in piecing them [in montage] he designs a play to fit the members of the company.

Hot Ice, the company's most recent play, began with an idea that developed when Ludlam was living with a macrobiotic couple who believed in euthanasia – mercy killing. 'I never felt really comfortable with the idea,' says Ludlam. 'Some other friends of mine were involved with cryonics – low temperature biology; freezing people after death until a cure is found for their disease. These people I was living with thought cryonics was a big joke. We talked about it, and I sent away for some material. The whole idea of cryonics versus euthanasia began to evolve in my mind.'

The idea was discussed among members of the group, but it was not until Ludlam saw James Cagney's film *White Heat* that he found the cops-versus-gangsters form for the play, the main characters, and the basic relationship between them. 'The next day after I saw the movie, I drafted the plot outline,' says Ludlam. The outline was discussed by members of the group whenever they got together.

The characters and relationships between the members of the cryonics gang were in the film: the mother-and-son team, the epileptic seizures, the son's glamorous girlfriend, and the animosity between the mother and the girlfriend. John Brockmeyer could not play Max Mortimer as a 'Cagney' because of the great dissimilarity between them physically. Brockmeyer is tall and lanky. But imitation is not the way he (or the rest of the company) works in creating a role.

Redheaded Georg Osterman, the company's specialist in female impersonation, was the obvious choice for the 'Jewish princess' girlfriend. She became a gum-chewing slut in green silk hot pants and fox-fur jacket.

A second plot, involving Ramona Malone (Black-Eyed Susan) and an attempt to recover her forfeited heirloom diamonds, was interwoven through the cops-and-robbers story. Susan decided that her character should be 'wacky,' so she began to watch Burns and Allen reruns of television, developing lines, speech mannerisms, and an incongruity of thought like Gracie Allen. Lola Pashalinski wanted to do a bit she had seen in the movie *The House on 92nd Street* in which the mysterious Mr. Christopher was a woman in man's clothes. Her dark suit, tie, and hat disguise evolved from this.

Bill Vehr said that he would like to play a narrator and that a crime play would be a good opportunity for it, but he had no idea what the role would entail until Ludlam began to write it. 'I had never used a narrator before,' explains Ludlam, 'but I liked radio serials. I thought I'd use the narrator that way – the convention of the narrator would move it along. I wanted the quality of an action story in *Hot Ice*.'

There was only a scenario containing the names of the characters and a few pages of dialog when rehearsals began on *Hot Ice*. Most of the dialog was written by Ludlam, but it came gradually during rehearsal. The play got bigger night by night as he produced a few pages of dialog at a time. The company improvised dialog, plot maneuvers, and scenes in rehearsal; often, a scripted scene would burst into improvisation. 'A lot of times,' says Ludlam, 'an actor will improvise a whole thing, and he could never repeat it again. But I have total recall when it comes to dialog. So I go home and write it down word-for-word as he said it and hand it back to him the next night. It's a very intimate way of working. It involves many trips back to the typewriter, dragging the script that was written that morning into rehearsal and hammering it out on stage that evening. It makes the plays very organic and personal to us.' 'Some of the last part of this play was dictated right on stage at rehearsal,' Mallory explains. 'Charles said lines, and people memorized the lines in front of him.' It was not until the second month of rehearsals that there was a complete second act and run-throughs of *Hot Ice* could take place.

The ending of *Hot Ice* presented Ludlam with a major problem. All of the company's plays before *Corn* had ended tragically or with the characters suffering degradation or humiliation. '*Corn* was the turning point,' explains Ludlam, 'when I realized that the synthesis of opposites is the basic magic act. It's at the basis of all metaphysics. And I realized that this was what comedy had that tragedy didn't have. For me now, that is a major esthetic problem: how to have a happy ending. The Cagney film doesn't. The criminal undergoes a total transference when the agent relieves him of his seizure and actually loves him, but the agent remains the predator to the end and kills him. I found that extremely disturbing. To me the betrayal of love was so horrible that I couldn't get over it; I couldn't deal with it. The disturbing thing to me was that the cop betrayed the trust, and I couldn't play that, because I'm playing opposite John Brockmeyer, whom I love.' It also bothered Ludlam that, by the end of the film, the 'good guys' kill all of the 'bad guys.' This is one reason why two endings were developed and performed in *Hot Ice*.

'A lot of directors block before they go to the rehearsal, then they come in and dictate the movements as they visualize them. A lot of them work with models, miniatures, etc. I don't find that interesting,' states Ludlam. 'Being an actor myself, I can't see that it's any use in creating an exciting event.' As a director, Ludlam has tried to work with what is already there rather than from a preconception of what 'ought' to be there. 'Trying to realize a conception is just frustration,' he says.

Ludlam: [. . .] One little trick I do know about staging something is to interrupt the scene and start a discussion. Suddenly all the physical relationships change; people start leaning, talking, moving in a different way that is totally real to the way they are to each other, and then you see how the scene would be in real life.

Susan: Our rehearsals are comfortable because we take a playful approach. We enjoy ourselves. In creating a character, all of a sudden we'll do something outrageous – go out on a limb – and the people you're with begin to laugh, and that's an encouraging sign.

Ludlam: We try to break each other up a lot. [. . .] Breaking-up is an indication that the thing is working. That it's funny. It's part of the atmosphere of rehearsal – enjoyment.

But one of the most difficult things in rehearsing comedy, Ludlam points out, is that 'something that gets a laugh once, and you know it's good, may never get a laugh again during rehearsal, because the surprise is gone, or people have seen you do it so many times. There's a tendency to drop it before opening night, forgetting how funny it was the first time. That's a problem – keeping things in; instinct reminding the actors that something was good, that it worked; and to trust that it will be funny again for people who haven't seen it yet.'

Play is very much a part of Ridiculous rehearsals. Implicit in the idea of play is the ability to engage in and disengage from the activity at will. A certain intellectual detachment is maintained. [. . .] The gangster character, Max Mortimer, in *Hot Ice* has seizures that only his mother can eliminate with a massage. For John Brock-meyer, who played this role, the seizures became a problem. They were not funny but pathetic and weak. The character had to have them, however, because his disguised opponent, Buck Armstrong, would relieve him of them and gain his confidence. In rehearsals, Lola Pashalinski, as his mother, massaged the back of his neck to relieve the seizures. 'Then on night it came to me,' explains Brockmeyer, 'that she should be doing this [strokes his throat] because we used to do this in grade school [strokes his neck and spits].' From this [. . .] developed the bit in which Moms masturbated Max's neck during a seizure, and Max had an orgasm with saliva.

Ludlam's job as director/writer/actor is to encourage play, then fit the results into a script. Thus, the performances have a spontaneous playfulness about them even though they are set. [. . .] The most profound theme of his theatre is the business of role play – that roles are interchangeable, that personality is artifice in life, and that it can be changed or interchanged. [. . .] Ludlam recalls reading a book in college that left a strong impression on his approach to the craft of role creation. The author stated that before he learned one line he went to the costume room, stood in front of the mirror, found the costume, did the makeup, and, when the character was staring back at him out of the mirror, then he could begin to work on the role. 'I think it's that way for us,' Ludlam says.

This freedom allowed the actor in creating a role is, in Ludlam's words, 'terrify-ing to most actors. It's like having nothing to go on but yourself, an immediate situation, and your co-workers. The actor creates the role in a primary way – from his own imagination, wish-fulfillment, and fantasy life. It's your creation; it's more daring. This way there's a lot invested in our roles, and the risks are great working this way. In our company, there is virtually no risk, though, because we all work that way. Since we share this way of working, there's something going on that makes it possible to be that free. It is this relationship that we have, which is a very delicate one, and a unique one. I don't think it's something anyone could just set out to have. We didn't set out to have this kind of relationship. It grew out of many years of work, and it requires a special atmosphere. One has to create an environment where this can go on. It's really not something an actor can do completely on his own, without sympathetic co-workers who feel that way about it as well.'

One of the most striking characteristics of role-playing in the Ridiculous Theatrical Company is the fact that every member except Black-Eyed Susan (who, however, will have young-boy roles in the forthcoming *Fashion Bound* and *Jack and the Beanstalk*) has, at one time, played transvestite roles. The androgynous sexual sensibility that the members of the group cultivate frees them from any limitations on acting out any part of their fantasy life. Everyone in the company wants to play a character of the opposite sex – each for different reasons. Some because it is an extension of the way they themselves are in real life; others because it provides a contrast to the way they see themselves. Most of the members have more than one sexual identity. This may be true of most people, but the Ridiculous Theatrical Company lives this multiple sexual identity out on the stage.

Staged transvestism or theatrical sexual role-switching has been treated in countless plays, films, and community 'firehouse' reviews as a comic reaffirmation of strict sexual role division. 'Drag' is denigrated by showing how impossible it is for a man to create the role of a woman successfully (and vice versa) except for the purpose of derisive laughter. At the Theatre of the Ridiculous, the laughter is not derisive. They entertain the idea that strict biological/social sexual division may be a cruel joke that nature/society is playing on humanity. For them, and in their performances, pansexuality is a reality.

Yet there is no overt sexual 'message.' 'We are not a group,' states Ludlam, 'that is proselytizing one kind of an idea – ready-made content, like political theatre, or any group that takes on a cause. To us, this has always been a cop-out. We're involved in a certain kind of consciousness that does not permit codifying a specific philosophy and proselytizing it.' As Lola Pashalinski puts it, 'We express things from our sensibilities and our philosophy, but we don't give people "messages." We just reflect our own personal view of life.'

35

RIDICULOUS THEATRE
Scourge of human folly

Charles Ludlam

T68, 1975

AIM: TO GET BEYOND NIHILISM BY REVALUING COMBAT

Axioms to a theatre for ridicule

1. You are a living mockery of your own ideals. If not, you have set your ideals too low.
2. The things one takes seriously are one's weaknesses.
3. Just as many people who claim a belief in God disprove it with their every act, so too there are those whose every deed, though they say there is no God, is an act of faith.
4. Evolution is a conscious process.
5. Bathos is that which is intended to be sorrowful but because of the extremity of its expression becomes comic. Pathos is that which is meant to be comic but because of the extremity of its expression becomes sorrowful. Some things which seem to be opposites are actually different degrees of the same thing.
6. The comic hero thrives by his vices. The tragic hero is destroyed by his virtue. Moral paradox is the crux of the drama.
7. The theatre is a humble materialist enterprise which seeks to produce riches of the imagination, not the other way around. The theatre is an event and not an object. Theatre workers need not blush and conceal their desperate struggle to pay the landlords their rents. Theatre without the stink of art.

Instructions for use

This is farce not Sunday school. Illustrate hedonistic calculus. Test out a dangerous idea, a theme that threatens to destroy one's whole value system. Treat the material in a madly farcical manner without losing the seriousness of the theme. Show how paradoxes arrest the mind. Scare yourself a bit along the way.

36

FAMILY OF THE F.P.
Notes on the Theatre of the Ridiculous

Stefan Brecht

T41, 1968

This theatre has attracted little but unfavorable notice. [. . .] The lifestyle adopted is that of a *free person* [f.p.] as distinct from an authoritarian phony, the civilized adult.

The f.p. is erotic, socially self-assertive, playful and imaginative. [. . .] The battle is *play*. For the f.p. at all times (even in subjugation) feels free, feels creatively spontaneous. [. . .] The luck of war in conventional family life is apt to produce robots. For subjugation in erotic personality-conflict is a conditioning of will & imagination, destroys spontaneous creativity, & is achieved when the victim accepts a programmed will & imagination as his own objective reality, as what he is. He then acts out a role identity not his at all. He participates in an institutional 'theatre' with prepared scripts, mistakes the play for reality, his part for himself & the action assigned to it for his life. [. . .]

The theatre of the ridiculous is produced by a family or families of approximately free persons as part of their family life. Its members adopt & act roles as the f.p. playfully assumes his identity – without identifying & only for the sake of playing them. This freedom is conveyed by the de-illusionistic 'action' style of the roles: fantastic, romantic, & heroic dream-identities like those produced by the f.p.'s imagination, engaged in the erotic and imperialist activities of the f.p. The patent non-seriousness of these plays is underlined by a farcical and ironic performance style. [. . .]

The first essential point about the theatre of the ridiculous is that it's *de-illusionistic* as *conditio sine qua non* both for its lifestyle and for getting that lifestyle across to us. This is obligatory if the make-believe society represented by imitation (which is theatre) is to be utterly ridiculous. It suggests the fictions to which illusion might attach itself, but systematically prevents our escape into illusion by disorganizing both the representational mode & the fiction itself.

The tickets (club-memberships, contributions) all cost the same relatively little, the seats are not numbered, there are usually no ushers: thus the visitor [. . .] is not *assigned his place* in the theatre. [. . .]

A rabble of actors moves into, through, out of this space. They look bizarre &

shoddy. Their faces are apt to be highly made up (masklike, grotesque) in strong colors & bold streaks. Generally they appear dressed in rags (not picturesquely, not to make a point): underwear, torn shirts; or garish finery with a hint of the lovely, reds, sequins, nettings, trains, huge wigs, tiaras – a dream of courts, some handsome fellow in princely attire – parodies on stage-costumes, inappropriately put together – clownish clothes, baggy pants – much nudity – now and then a symbolic item (leather) – cod pieces, merkins, fake pricks, boas, veils, fans, swords, guns & whips (Ludlam, as 'emerald Empress' in *Whores*, uses a fly-swatter as a whip), secret weapons, the paraphernalia of romance & adventure. [. . .] Blatantly theatrical devices, daring & lovely, cheap. Dance, magic, acrobatics, clownery – skilled, mangled, inept. [. . .]

Though burlesque & melodrama predominate, a great variety of acting styles brings out the acting & stylization, [. . .] some of the actors going through ebb-tides of non-acting. [. . .] The most energetic physical interactions (fights, couplings) are the most simulated. Removal of cadavers, necessitated by the high onstage death-rate, is done with exaggerated clumsiness; the corpse does not cooperate – but mostly the dead just sit up after a while, walk off, reparticipate in the action. So many of the female parts are played by males & vice versa that it strikes one as peculiar when an actor plays his own sex. [. . .]

The characters in these plays are stereotypes from other entertainment media & daily life [. . .] yet the actors' appearance, speech, & action continually clash with their stereotypical lineaments. They are without personality in the sense that noth-ing they say or do would make us attribute to them a decision-making psyche. (Ludlam: 'Psychology must be banished from the theatre.') [. . .] Motivations are fragmentary, outside characters wander in, the main plot is ill-related to ill-explained sub-plots, & both are disrupted by actions apparently unrelated to either. The dialogue sabotages the characters & illusion by dadaist travesty. They *quote*: from dramatic & other classics, political heroes & movie vamps, advertisements. They speak in quotational styles: the emotional evocation of universal truths or sentiments, smart-alecky comebacks, loud 'presentational' delivery of burlesque dialogues. [. . .] The literary work's foolishness & clownishness obtrude – ridicu-lously ill-made plays reflecting an ill-made world. Their organization is left to the spectator.

[. . .] The fabulosity of the costumes & the science, spy, and crime adventure themes do not excite the escapist mechanisms of make-believe socialized existence for they are systematically undercut by the grotesque or mundane. Though the shows may entertain some determined queers who can swallow the fact that their camp is corny, a normal not-queer homosexual will have seen it all at many parties. Nor are the plentiful nudity, dirty language, & sexual acts & references very enter-taining: we live amidst hard-core pornography these days. The sex and 'obscenity' in these shows are done off-handedly, perfunctorily – anti-erotically according to the make-believe roots of eroticism. They clear the air. [. . .]

This theatre's techniques cut laughter short; unlike commercial comedy, it does not solicit appreciation of its wit. Its jokes are parodies on humor (Vaccaro used canned laughter in one production), destroying the innocent quality by not indicating that it is done in order to entertain. [. . .]

This theatre is resolutely opposed to art. It rejects the ideal of a formal integrity of the artwork in abstraction from the artist & his creativity; it rejects the ideal of

315

subordination of the artist's personality to his artistry; it intends aesthetic appreciation of its work only (if at all) as instrument to more important affective personal reactions. [. . .] However, sabotage becomes an artistic device & art as social sabotage in a social order as anti-artistic as ours is not precisely sabotage of art. In any event, the theatre of the ridiculous does not come on as art.

It's a ridiculous company: the opprobrium of the characters & plays they act attaches to the actors because they do not hide inside/behind the characters & yet (in hearty & not ostensibly motivated performance) assume responsibility for them. [. . .]

While the framework of reference of conventional theatre experience is the individual presentation of 'the' play, in this theatre it is the production of the play – the series of presentations, rehearsals, composition of the script: its making in development defines the individual evening's experience. The composition of the script appears as mere preparation of the *mise-en-scène*, almost incidental. Script and set are essentially by-products of the developing performance, collapsing into the activity of making the play. [. . .]

Each production is a three-way fight between the acting dramatist, the acting director, and the cast. Productions take the form of combat because onstage are *persons*, not actors. No abstract or generic identity is projected, not any private identity ('what I really am'). The performers project their personality by their parts. Whereas actors acting by empathy with the character give the impression of executing an internal compulsion – a zombie quality that is often thought of as naturalness   the actors in this theatre, having no viable stage personality to identify with, seem alive & themselves. [. . .] We seem to be watching the representation of the creative process. This sense would be destroyed if we experienced the play or any part of the performance as expression of personality. We don't.

[. . .] Fiction *not* turning into illusion – the act of buggery or fellatio merely indicated – our mind oscillates between the action of the performers & its significance to the fiction: the two never quite coincide. We cannot withdraw into the timeless meaning of the fiction. Each time we might, we are drawn back to this evening in this theatre – for since we oscillate *within* the intrinsic duality of an observation of role-adoption, the actual activity in actual time & space is our base-reference. [. . .]

Each performer concentrates on the business at hand with the intensity of circus & vaudeville performers, magicians & acrobats, the intensity of doing a trick. He is not acting *out* anything. Words & gestures have not been polished to mere expressions, but stand out freshly against the expressive functions we may attribute to them. Actions speak for themselves. We see what he does before or while we see what it means. [. . .]

All this is apt to get *boring* from time to time. Not just because of the failures of talent, skill, or effort but because the action-style of the play & performance so sharpen our awareness of the passage of time & the problem of its use that we become resentful of the foolishness & sterility as wasteful.

We are confronted with time by: lack of drive and direction; the absence of a sense of progress or continuity or development or achievement; inarticulation (no well-marked sub-sections or changes of direction in the line of action); deliberately slow-motion or speeded-up passages; frequent changes of rhythm & speed.

The capricious creativity of play & show makes one feel [the actors] could go on indefinitely. [. . .] Anything might repeat.

The basis of such boredom is anxiety, compulsiveness, the frenzy to keep busy so as not to face oneself, the habit of allocating time to particular purposes (tangible gains), tension or frustration, a general sense that one is wasting one's life – in short, an inability to play.

[. . .] It is in terms of original authorship that most theatre presents itself as expression & contribution. We are supposed to appreciate the invention of themes & characters. We experience the play as treatment of them. But this appreciation & form of experience are incompatible with the pose of ridiculousness adopted by the theatre & incompatible with its action-style. The theatre of the ridiculous foregoes the claim to original authorship.

The plays [. . .] draw on the mythologizing popular imagination reflected in and interacting with the folk art of vulgar commercial entertainment – the stereotyped imagination of the big city & small town poor, young, & male – lower- & lower-middle-class urban boys. They are *improvisations* on this material refracted through the alienating subcultures of queerdom & collegiate humanism which corrode the wild clichés of those oppressed, rebellious, but brought-to-heel dreamers, imbue them with irony but preserve their sweet poetry.

Scenarist, actors, & director all participate in this dream life. So do the audience. This makes it possible for the scenario to be a mere score for the actors & the spectacle similarly material for improvisation for the audience. The basic situation is that of Greek drama or any religious folk art. Not just because of the nature of the source but because the style of the theatre is to admit it, shamelessly. [. . .]

The sex is comic because of its flat guiltless naturalness: the characters don't beat around the bush. This directness makes it seem shallow but also administers a special shock of self-recognition: *ecce homo*. It's nothing special, just the bare essence of sociability – playful, unserious, unurgent: the opposite of D. H. Lawrence, Casanova, Genet . . . It is not a call for sexual freedom *à la* Henry Miller or naturalness *à la* Wedekind but mockery of the contemporary religion of this country: *pervert heterosexuality*. For ours is a historically unique culture dominated by a cult of sex to which it devotes the preponderance of its vast cultural efforts (advertising, films, advertising, musical comedies, advertising): a non-materialist & secular religion for corporation employees who are bereft of opportunities for free enterprise & so identify as consumers. [. . .]

The *ambiguity of sexual identity* is the basic variant of the theme of role-playing. Whether the male is defined as active principle (fucker) or by his genitals, the plays repeatedly point up the make-believe, free, role-playing character of sexual identity. By their grotesque display of male & female genitalia & secondary sexual characteristics, the productions starkly emphasize biological sexual identity. Then by their equally stark & repetitious exposure of sexual overtures & of acts of physical coercion paint a picture of a world in which an androgynous psycho-sexuality gives biologically male *or* female creatures a challenging choice between playing male or female roles.

The theatre leaves us with an image of social life in its most basic & most salient aspects: the relations between the sexes & political life or organized state power. It presents both of these as the playing of roles. And after showing us the arbitrariness

of all role-playing, it points out that the actual roles played (especially those basic
& salient ones which between them control the playing of all others) are both evil
& ridiculous. Furthermore, they are ridiculous not only by the actual way in which
they are played but especially (more basically) in being imposed role-identities,
straitjackets put on us in the bosom of the family & by the power of the state &
so transmitted from generation to generation – the inauthentic self-perpetuating
variants of one & the same figure, the authoritarian phony. [. . .]

37

IS THERE A TEXT ON THIS STAGE?
Theatre, authorship, interpretation

Gerald Rabkin

Performing Arts Journal, 1985

> The best possible play is one in which there are no actors, only text. I'm trying to find a way to write one.
>
> *Samuel Beckett*

> Interpretation is not the art of construing but the art of construction. Interpreters do not decode poems; they make them.
>
> *Stanley Fish*

> Never trust the teller, trust the tale.
>
> *D. H. Lawrence*

The question of the relationship between the play and its theatrical interpretation moved last year from theatres and the pages of books and critical journals into the realm of the news. The *New York Times* and the *New York Law Journal* asked respectively, 'Who's to Say When a Playwright is Wronged?' and 'Whose Play is it Anyway?' The occasions for these public questions were legal challenges by two esteemed contemporary playwrights – Arthur Miller and Samuel Beckett – to unauthorized and/or allegedly distorted productions of their work: the Wooster Group's *L.S.D. (. . . Just the High Points . . .)* – which incorporated long segments of *The Crucible* – and the American Repertory Theatre's version of *Endgame*.

The controversies never made it to court, where it would have been instructive to see the machinery of the law grapple with the complex critical questions involved. For the question of the relationship between play and performance is at the center of contemporary theatre theory. Artaud's emancipation proclamation of the director from the presumed tyranny of the playwright – 'No one has the right to call himself author, that is to say creator, except the person who controls the direct handling of the stage' – became one of the guiding principles of the advanced theatre of the 1960s and early 1970s. The written text as a sacred, inseminating source which commanded devout fidelity was overthrown in the name of a revolution of physical presence. The function of the playwright was spread among members of the ensemble or subsumed by the director-auteur. Or – as in the early work of Grotowski and Schechner – a classic originary text became the unprivileged ground from which a radical performance text was created.

This latter strategy persisted, and indeed increased, as a dominant model in theatre experiment, since collective playwriting waned in the face of the dissipation of the ideals of communality and the difficulties of the craft. Herbert Blau has noted that 'the polymorphous thinking body which had for a while in the theatre displaced the text . . . [came] to discover that along with the unreliable duration of group consciousness, it had a limited repertoire of ideas.' Even the most committed director-auteurs readmitted playwrights other than themselves, particularly playwrights not around to dispute radical interpretations (Breuer's *Tempest*, Foreman's *Don Juan*). The current controversies center on the fact that, even if their plays have achieved, by the frequency of interpretation, 'classic' status, the authors of *The Crucible* and *Endgame* are still around and possess legal rights over their literary property. The theoretical questions raised by Artaud's depriviDefleging of the playwright are still very alive in these controversies, for, though obviously crucial to the development of experimental theatre, the question of textual interpretation is fundamental to all theatre representation. Unfortunately – as much of the rhetoric in the recent controversies reveals – it is rarely discussed with critical rigor. What is the theatre text? Indeed, what is a text? How do we (theatre artists, critics, audience) read the meaning of the play and its performance interpretation? In the past generation there has been an explosion of theoretical concern with the literary aspects of these questions, precious little of which has found its way beyond the margins of theatre discourse.

JUST THE HIGH POINTS

The *L.S.D.* and *Endgame* controversies – which climaxed at the same time, in November and December 1984 – were legally dissimilar: the Wooster Group had never received the rights for *The Crucible*'s incorporation in *L.S.D.* from Miller's agents; ART [American Repertory Theatre], however, had obtained the rights from Samuel French for a standard stock production, but were challenged by Beckett's representatives for violating their contractual agreement to produce the play 'without changes or alterations.' The *L.S.D.* controversy was, all at once, simpler and more complex: simpler because the issue of license was clear-cut, more complex because *L.S.D.* never represented itself as Miller's *Crucible*. Not that it hid its indebtedness to Miller's play, which it conflated first into a fifty-minute work-in-progress, then into a twenty-minute segment of a multi-segmented work, and finally, in response to Miller's adamant refusal of rights, into a ten-minute, largely gibberish strand in a 110-minute collage: fewer and fewer of 'Just the High Points.' What the Wooster Group offered was not a production of *The Crucible*, but a new work in which substantial portions of the play – clearly too long for the fair use doctrine to apply – were embedded. Ironically, had the *Crucible* material indeed been 'blatant parody,' as Miller is reported in the *Village Voice* (12 December 1983) to have complained, it might have been legally appropriable, since the first amendment rights of satirists are often protected by the courts. And it is fascinating to speculate on what *L.S.D.* would have become if Miller had granted the rights the Wooster Group requested. For director Elizabeth LeCompte had welcomed Miller's participation, been willing to call the *Crucible* material in *L.S.D.* an adaptation, or whatever Miller desired. Miller's stubborn refusal shaped the subsequent development of *L.S.D.* which became in LeCompte's words 'on one level a conversation with Mr. Miller.' Had he indeed given permission, she dead-pannedly told this writer, 'I might be doing it at the Shubert.'

After having seen the initial autonomous fifty-minute version of his play in 1983, Miller advanced the dubious argument that to grant the Wooster Group rights would hamper a full-scale, 'major' uptown revival (presumably not directed by Ms. LeCompte). That Miller seemed desperate to fashion a way out of validating a production he did not understand is suggested by his reading as parody an interpretation that was manifestly an homage. So he fell back on his legal power as the play's creator as a means of confirming the aesthetic of authorial intent. 'The issue here is very simple: I don't want my play produced except in total agreement with the way I wrote it. I'm afraid people might see their version and not realize I never intended it to be staged that way' (*Village Voice*, 27 December 1983). Not all playwrights accept the inviolability of their intentions in the theatrical process (Strindberg and Pirandello are two giants who didn't), but Miller's plays, as Harold Clurman who staged *Incident at Vichy* has pointed out, are 'virtually complete in every detail by the time he submits his scripts.' As a playwright with a definitive productional vision he accepts the aesthetics of what Umberto Eco has called in *The Role of the Reader* the 'closed' text, texts which 'aim at pulling the reader along a predetermined path, carefully displaying their effects so as to arouse pity or fear, excitement or depression at the due place and at the right moment.' The problem is that the Wooster Group has always worked in accordance with Eco's alternative model of the 'open' text in which reader (audience) interpretation is demanded by the text in order to complete understanding. Open texts compel us to make the work together with the author, for they are open to 'a continuous generation of internal relations which the addressee must uncover and select in his act of perceiving the totality of incoming stimuli.' (We must note here that despite his postulation of this useful dialectic, Eco recognizes that on a broader level of analysis every work of art, whether or not produced by an explicit 'poetics of necessity,' is 'effectively open to a virtually unlimited range of possible readings.' More on this later.)

Eco's definition of the open text precisely describes the work of the Wooster Group, which has always consciously rejected the 'poetics of necessity' – authorial intent – in order to force its audiences' active participation, an aesthetic method insufficiently credited even by some who should know better. Erika Munk, for example, claimed in her review in the *Village Voice* that the randomness of *L.S.D.* 'disarms interpretation from the start.' On the contrary, as Eco's analysis reveals, interpretation is precisely what is armed. The commitment to the creation of open texts from highly charged material ('All our pieces,' says LeCompte, 'have been made by accumulating the texts around issues that evolve in the work') has gotten the Wooster Group into hot water before, most notoriously in the piece antecedent to *L.S.D., Route 1 & 9* (1981–2). In that controversial work, powerful but disturbing images of whites blackened from head to toe engaging in coarse vaudeville routines and trashing the set were perceived by many as part of an intentionally coherent closed text that could only be read as unsuccessfully satiric or racist. That the meaning of these images was consciously deferred within a vibrating system of theatre signification was not a methodology the readers of closed texts understood.

If *L.S.D.* developed in response to Miller's refusal of rights, it had its inception in the heat generated by the *Route 1 & 9* controversy. Hence the centrality of *The Crucible* with its narrative of historical persecution, its images of hypocrisy, hallucination, and hysteria. But to force *L.S.D.*'s contrasted exploration of counterculture consciousness experimentation into a closed system of enforced parallels is to falsify the Wooster Group's working aesthetic. The group's distinctive style coalesced in the third part of Spalding Gray's Rhode Island series, *Nayatt School*, in which a reading of Eliot's *Cocktail Party* was embedded in an assemblage of recuperated images from Nayatt's predecessors, 'junk' images from vaudeville and stand-up comedy, competing images from other media – phonograph records, film, disco music – all swelling to an apocalyptic proliferation which destroyed traditional relation between theatre representation and event. Thus the 'classic' play text – perceived as one of may kinds of texts – became a constant but destabilized element in LeCompte's work: *Point Judith* incorporated elements from O'Neill's *Long Day's Journey into Night* and in *Route 1 & 9*, long sections of Wilder's *Our Town* were played on TV monitors juxtaposed, with typical audacity, with pornographic film images. [. . .] Which leads us to *L.S.D.* and its appropriation of *The Crucible*. However seemingly unambiguous the legal dimensions of the controversy, the critical issues are complex. For the Wooster Group not only deprivileges the play while respecting its contribution, it explicitly challenges the identity of text with written text.

1001 ENDGAMES?

The Beckett–ART controversy differs in certain essentials from the *L.S.D.* dispute. First of all, ART applied for and received the rights to produce Beckett's famous play; second, it was neither embedding the work in a larger textual context, nor changing its title to assert its independence from its source. (Indeed, had it done the latter, the plaintiffs might well have been appeased.) According to the traditional theatre model, the production was meant to interpret with fidelity the 'text and spirit of the play.' The relationship between text and spirit was the sticking point. Director JoAnne Akalitis and the ART producers essentially adhered to the letter of the printed text despite a few cuts and alterations. Akalitis felt, however, that to be faithful to the spirit of the text it was necessary to find renovative theatrical strategies. In conformity with the tradition of the theatre collective of which she is a preeminent member, Mabou Mines (see Chapter 25), she sought, with designer Douglas Stein, to affirm her long-demonstrated commitment to the greatness of Beckett's vision through a resetting of the written text. Disregarding Beckett's laconic scenic instructions for a 'bare interior . . . two small windows . . . a door,' Akalitis and Stein set the play in a desolate length of subway tunnel replete with derelict cars and the detritus of modern technological civilization, a perfect contemporary equivalent, in their view, of Hamm and Clov's entrapment in the metaphorical Absurdist room with no escape. Mabou Mines' innovative strategies in resetting his work was not unknown to Beckett. Indeed, when, on an early European tour in the 1970s, Mabou Mines was denied the rights to perform his plays in

English by Beckett's French publisher, the group succeeded in contacting Beckett, who scrawled his permission on a napkin. We may note that these productions consciously 'violated' Beckett's aesthetic formulation: *The Lost Ones* was the group's environmental realization of a prose version of Dante's Purgatory, and *Cascando* – Akalitis's first directorial venture for Mabou Mines – was a multi-imaged transformation of a radio play in which Beckett had specifically exploited the purely aural resources of that medium. Indeed, even when Mabou Mines produced Beckett's plays – such as *Play* and *Come and Go* – it adopted strategies not called for in their published texts. In *Come and Go*, for example, the play's three actresses performed in a back of the house balcony while their reflected images were perceived on a slanted mirror set before the audience.

Given this knowledge of Mabou Mines' and Akalitis' consistent radical visual aesthetic and their long-proven commitment to his work (the movement of experimental theatre back to the playwright may well be said to have begun with them), why Beckett's fierce denunciation in the ART program of the production as 'a complete parody of the play as conceived by me . . . Anyone who cares for the work couldn't fail to be disgusted by this'? Assuming that Beckett was offered by his surrogates an accurate description of a production he never saw, I leave the psychological answers to Beckett's biographers; the aesthetic imperative seems rooted in Beckett's particularly possessive relationship to *Endgame*, in Ruby Cohn's authoritative judgment his preferred play. It is significant that the recent controversy is closely paralleled by Beckett's protest against André Gregory's 1973 production of the same play. Informed by his then and now American agent Barney Rosset of Gregory's 'unacceptable' environmental version which divided spectators into chicken-wire cages, Beckett, though alarmed by 'the omnipresent massacre and abuse of directorial function,' found it too difficult to intervene at long distance and let the production run in New York for the specified period of Gregory's contract. He promised, however, never again to renew it and applied subtle pressure so that the production never played in France where it was invited. Clearly, Beckett most keenly feels the crystalline achievement of *Endgame*, its precise distillation of language and image.

In the flurry of letters and accusations that went back and forth before the opening of ART's production in December 1984, Barney Rosset again acted as the defender of Beckett's intentionality and achievement, while ART's defenders focused on the centrality of freedom of interpretation in the theatrical process. Harvard law professor Lawrence Tribe insisted in the *Boston Globe* that 'freedom of speech is indivisible,' and deplored 'this latest attempt to establish an artistic orthodoxy by invoking federal judicial power to arbitrate a conflict of judgment between producer and playwright.' *Village Voice* critic Alisa Solomon defended the director's right to be wrong, since interpretation 'is what directors do' and new interpretation, even if reductive, 'teaches audiences something new.' Theatre Communications Group Literary Services Director James Leverett argued that to deny the interpretative contribution of theatre artists would negate 'the possibilities of a play's continued life on stage.' ART dramaturg Jonathan Marks offered Pirandello's admonition that the 'unwillingness to take up old works, to modernize and streamline for fresh production, betrays indifference, not praiseworthy caution,' and in his statement in the program (appended statements by Beckett, Rosset, and ART Artistic Director Robert Brustein were the compromise which withdrew the threat of legal action), Brustein insisted that while he yielded to no one in his acceptance of Beckett's genius, 'like all works of theatre, productions of *Endgame* depend upon the collective contributions of directors, actors, designers to realize them effectively, and normal rights of interpretation are essential in order to free the full energy and meaning of the play.'

The crux, of course, is the phrase 'normal rights of interpretation.' Beckett's defenders insist upon the fixity of his intentions as codified in the entire published text – dialogue and stage directions. Ironically Rosset began an angry cable to Brustein by noting how Alan Schneider (Beckett's favorite American director [see Chapter 8]) found on the left bank of Paris a battered second-hand volume called *1001 Endgames*, the perfect gift for the aficionado of chess and author of the play he and Rosset were in Paris to discuss in preparation for its American premiere. Rosset notes how *Endgame* 'merges the concept of infinite myriads of possibilities, moves, countermoves, evasions, attacks, and desperate defenses of the endgame in chess with its counterparts in our own human lives.' But he insists that these myriads of possibilities are reduced definitively to one unalterable strategy by Beckett's genius. Brustein and the defenders of interpretative freedom insist in turn that it is precisely the myriad possibilities of performance at different temporal and contextual junctures that make *Endgame* a masterpiece of theatre.

But what is interpretation and can it be normalized, legitimized? Beneath the impassioned parrying of what has been called the Brustein–Beckett brouhaha – as in the Wooster Goup–Miller controversy – lie questions that are anything but frivolous. The crucial axiomatic theatrical questions that demand interrogation are: who is the author of the theatre text, how is it 'legitimately' interpreted, and, antecedently, is there a text on this stage?

TEXT, SCRIPT, WORK

This last question, as those familiar with contemporary critical theory will doubtlessly recognize, is a playful variant on the title of Stanley Fish's essay 'Is there a text in this class?' which names his collection of reader-response criticism. As Fish points out, the problem of textual identity *begins* rather than ends with this question which arose in a typical academic situation: one of his colleagues was approached the first day of a new semester by a student who had taken a course from Fish. She asked the seemingly straightforward question of whether there was a text in the class, and the teacher replied, equally straightforwardly, '*The Norton Anthology of Literature.*' To which she annoyedly replied: 'No, no. I mean in this class do we believe in poems and things, or is it just us?' In other words, having been conditioned by Fish's theoretical preoccupations about the status of the text and the source of interpretative authority, she employed a notion of textuality far different from its familiar usage. If theatre people were more conversant with the explosion of critical scrutiny of the question of textuality for the last generation, they would be aware that the notion of the text is no simple thing. There is no universal agreement as to just what a text is: for some (Derrida par excellence) all reality is textual, and writing – *écriture* – is a self-conditioning mass whose limits are unknowable; for most Anglo-American literary critics, on the other hand, the text is the linguistic artifact that has been granted canonical privilege. And, if we move out of the parochial community of English professors to film, for example, we find the notion of textuality extended to the non-verbal. A recent article by Charles Wolfe in the film journal *Wide Angle* discusses 'The film publicity photograph as text,' noting that 'the text itself shifts in and out of view like an oscillation between figure and ground in an unstable optical illusion.' Not only is the text elusive, it is unstable.

In the performing arts the problem of textuality is complicated by the intermediary level of performance interpretation. The positions in the theatre controversies I have discussed turn precisely upon the definition of textuality, for, as we have seen, the text has been granted authority in our culture by the discourse of the law. Beckett's defenders insist that the text of *Endgame* is all language immobilized in the printed book: *Endgame*'s last line is '(Brief tableau.)' not 'You . . . remain.' The ART defenders insist that the history of theatre practice legitimizes a definition of textuality as the words the playwright intends the actors to speak. But this separation of stage directions from written text, though it seeks to liberate performance interpretation, still accepts the written text's privilege. That privileging, however, is not necessarily accepted by theatre discourse's truncation of 'manuscript' into the unique signifier, the script. Unlike critics, most actors and directors rarely talk about the text; they talk of the script which they hold in their hands as they rehearse. The script is inscribed, it may indeed be published, but it carries a provisional authority. The script is something to be used and discarded as its textuality is corporealized in performance.

One theoretical model of the performative process which privileges script over text has been provided by Richard Schechner in *TDR* (T59): his key terms are Drama, Script, Theatre, Performance. Text is not coterminous with, but one of the constituent elements – along with score, scenario, plan, or map – of drama, the smallest, most intense circle of performance, which is the broadest, most all-inclusive of the four terms. Script and Theatre are the intermediary circles in the hierarchy, with Script representing the basic code of the theatre event ('all that can be transmitted from time to time and place to place'), and Theatre the event enacted by a specific group of performers in concrete response to the drama and/or the script; Performance is the entire constellation of events that takes place *both* in performers and audience from the time the first spectator enters the field of performance to the time the last spectator leaves. In Schechner's model, then, text – defined as a function of language – is circumscribed by drama, the narrowest circle of performance which is privileged in its place. May I suggest in light of contemporary critical discourse that rather than accept this inversion that the concept of textuality be broadened so that the mediating level of performance is neither privileged *nor* deprivileged?

In hopes of clarification, let us backtrack a moment historically: the modern debate on the notion of textuality derives from Ferdinand de Saussure's post-World War I idea that all signs conjoin a form and a concept – a signifier and a signified – the relationship of which is arbitrary. To determine the meaning of the relationship, Sausssure insisted on the necessity of considering the system in which the sign functions, and language emerges as a largely unconscious system of hierarchical elements and forces defined always by their differences from and relations to one another *within a system*. It is necessary then to analyze different systems of signification to find how meaning is produced: the 'science' of semiology. [. . .] In sum, the text is the ensemble of messages we feel must be read as a whole, and, as the structuralists and poststructuralists who extended Saussure's linguistic insights recognized, the concept is not logically restricted to language systems. Nor is the text necessarily a function of artistic intent. Anything we can read as a coherent ensemble of messages constitutes a text. The canon of an author may represent a single 'true' text to a biographer; phenomena with no artistic pretensions, like the publicity photograph, or comic strips, or sports may similarly be endowed with textual meaning. It follows that since performance can be read, it constitutes its own textuality; but it is a complex textuality because it is created from the usually prior textuality of the play or score.

Even in the more common attribution of textuality to artifacts of language, the concept of the literary text has been pried loose from the concept of the literary work. The distinction, important for our purposes, is most eloquently expressed in Roland Barthes' classic essay 'From work to text,' which considers the implications of radical linguistic theory for literature: 'Over against the traditional notion of the work, for long – and still conceived of in a Newtonian way – there is now the requirement of a new object, attained by . . . overturning former categories. That object is the Text.' The Work, as Barthes defines it, can be seen in bookstores, in card catalogues, on course lists, it can be held in the hand, it is property and can be defended by law. It 'functions as a general sign and thus represents an institutional category of the civilization of the Sign.' The Text, on the other hand, exists only as discourse; it is *plural*, and 'expressed only in an activity, a production.' Since it can cut across a work or several works, it answers to 'an explosion' that commands the reader's active collaboration to confer meaning. The Work is an object that is *displayed*; the Text a methodological field that is *demonstrated*. If we accept the usefulness of this distinction, it is clear that Miller and Beckett were talking about their works and not their texts.

THE AUTHOR IS DEAD, *VIVE L'AUTEUR!*

Barthes draws conclusions from his crucial distinctions which unsettle the commonsensical reader, the most controversial being his announcement – seconded by many of his critical colleagues – of the Death of the Author. What is meant by this seeming absurdity? It's hard to dispute the opening clause of Arthur Miller's complaint in the *Crucible* controversy that 'I'm still around, and I should have a say about how the play is done as long as I am' (*New York Times*, 28 November 1984). Barthes' logic is as follows: the Work may indeed 'belong' to its author, but the Text, which exists only in discourse, 'defies filiation.' Once the text is released to the world of discourse, the Author-God who created it controls its meaning no more than any reader. The classic dramatic expressors of this paradox are, of course, Pirandello's *Six Characters* who, once placed on the stage of writing by the Author, act out their dramas independent of his presence. 'To give a text an Author' – that is to accept his/her intentions as its single 'theological' meaning – is to 'furnish it with a final signified, to close the writing.' So Barthes banishes the Author from his privileged domain: 'It is not that the Author may not "come back" in the Text, in his text, but he then does so as a guest.'

Barthes' argument is partly analytical, partly historical. He notes that the concept of the Author is a product of English empiricism, French rationalism, and Protestant individualist faith. That the Author-function, particularly as defined by law, is a modern historical creation, is a point made similarly by M. M. Bakhtin and Michel Foucault. The former writes: 'In the Middle Ages, boundaries between the other's words and one's own discourse were flexible, ambiguous . . . Certain types of works were constructed like mosaics from the texts of others.' (In dramatic history we are well aware of the anonymous authorship of mystery plays, and of Elizabethan wholesale borrowing from the common storehouse of available texts.) And in an essay asking 'What is an author?' Foucault answers that the traditional idea of the author as the creator of meaning must be reexamined. 'The truth is quite the contrary: the author is not an indefinite source of significations which fill a work, [but] . . . a certain functional principle by which, in our culture, one marks the manner in which we fear the proliferation of meaning.' Like Barthes and Bakhtin, Foucault historically notes that there was a time when the texts that we today call 'literary' were put into circulation and valorized without any question about the identity of their author. But once a system of ownership of texts arose the author became the 'regulator of the fictive,' a role reflecting the values of capitalist individualism. This has meant, asserts Foucault, that the writer who rebels against being placed in the system of property that characterizes our society must become in his work consciously transgressive.

An examination of the origins of copyright law confirms much of Foucault's historical analysis without necessarily accepting his ideological interpretation. Foucault asserts that the origins of the concept of writing as property – though propagated in the name of individual rights – arose in the late eighteenth, early nineteenth centuries as a means of controlling the dangerous proliferation of texts. Legal scholars do not dispute this analysis, and in fact trace copyright's emergence in English law even further back historically, to the establishment in 1556 of the Stationers' Company as a means of Tudor control of the press. The stationers – those who, with the rise of printing, bought from the printers the sheets which were then bound and sold as books – kept a company register in which all published works were listed. The register came to serve as evidence of the printers' title to the works included, and the idea of property and attendant rights and responsibilities was thus associated with literary work. But another originating strand of the idea of copyright arose from the royal practice of periodic special grants of monopoly. Significantly, crown grants of letters patent for particular works went to authors, not as with works registered with the Stationers' Company, to printers; and the rights granted were seen in the nature of privilege rather than as 'normal' property. Thus, competing tensions in the idea of literary ownership – which still undergird current copyright law – were present from the beginning: the tension between the 'inalienability' of personal property versus society's granting of special privilege which can be revoked in the name of the Greater Good, and the tension between the author's *personal* ownership versus the rights of those who *produce* his work.

So the rise of the author is perhaps less irresistible than Barthes and Foucault assert. 'Authority' may derive linguistically from 'author,' but historically the author's rights which emerge with capitalist individualism have always been rendered precarious by the marketplace. Barthes' insistence upon the disseminative power of the text does not logically abrogate the author's ownership rights over his work. Indeed, unless one is a confirmed Proudhonian, believing all property is theft, it is hard, in my view, not to agree that the cause of greater textual dissemination would be better served by the extension, rather than restriction, of author's rights; surely the more stringent the denial of the fruits of authorial labor the less likely the production of texts worth disseminating. The writer's legendary denigration in Hollywood is admonitory in this regard. Unlike the playwright – whose rights are carefully guarded by the standard Dramatists Guild contract, the American screenwriter, though more lavishly paid, works 'for hire.' This common law concept vests authorship and rights in the employer unless contractually speci-fied otherwise. (In France and other European countries, the *droit moral* insists that the author's work can be personally copyrighted regardless of employment.) The U.S. law comes down solidly on the side of economic interest; huge investments must be protected against the screenwriter's possible dilatory objections.

This structure raises interesting problems – noted by Elizabeth LeCompte in conversation with this writer – about experimental theatre. LeCompte admits the influence in her working method of the TV or film model in which the writer serves in the same way as the composer or choreographer. But she also agrees that the writer's subservience to a profit-making system creates a Gresham's Law in which the bad usually drives out the good. The screenwriter's inferior status, however, is not merely a function of the conflict between art and commercialism. French and American proponents of the *politique des auteurs* have deprivileged the writer aes-thetically by asserting that the true author of the film text is the director, who authoritatively 'writes' the film with the help of the narrative and thematic material provided by the writer. The dominance for a time of the auteur theory bred counterassertions of the significance, often preeminence, of the writer's contri-bution, notably by Richard Corliss in *Talking Pictures*, which notes the absurdity that the film of *Play it Again, Sam* – starring Woody Allen, screenplay by Woody Allen, from a play by Woody Allen – is heralded in the screen credits as 'A Herbert Ross Film.' Corliss notes that one reason for directorial supremacy in film is the virtual absence of the screenplay's validation in book form, while the total film is more readily accessible. In theatre, we may note, despite the lamentable decrease in the publication of plays, textual accessibility is reversed, hence the dramatist's greater authority.

These last remarks are cautionary: those of us sympathetic to the destabilizing of the author's patriarchal authority over his text must also recognize the importance of protecting the author's personal rights to his *work*. Can we deny that extending these rights in film and television would be aesthetically beneficial? The temporal compromise of his text by limiting the term of protection to the author's lifetime plus fifty years is not unreasonable. But deep legal problems remain in the law's inability to protect textuality that has not been tangibly fixed. Barthes's distinction remains vital to separating the strands of the interpretative debate. If the president of the Dramatists Guild compares *The Crucible* to Miller's automobile (*New York Times*, 23 December 1984), which cannot legally be driven off without his permis-sion, on one level he is right; but when it is asserted that the unit of discourse that is the text of *The Crucible* can only be 'legitimately' read according to the author's intentions, we must answer with moral persuasion that this is false both in theory and in practice.

THE ONLY GAME IN TOWN

'Fine word, legitimate.' If it is as valid to speak of performance text as of written text, the vital theatrical problem is the relationship between the two, for in the dominant hierarchical model in Western culture the performance text is offered as an interpretation – a reading – of the dramatic text. The rise of 'director's theatre' mirrors literary criticism's movement from the emphasis upon the immanent 'meaning' of literary texts to the acceptance of the processes of reading and interpretation which determine meaning. There has been during the past generation an enormous amount of critical theorizing on this problem, much too much to summarize here. These theories – some overlapping, some antagonistic – have been gathered under such rubrics as semiotics, structuralism, reader-response criticism, deconstruction, psychoanalytic criticism, hermeneutics, feminist criticism, *Rezeptionästhetic*. What all share, despite divergences, is opposition to the principle that the function of criticism is to let the text speak for itself. (How often the latter principle has been evoked against directorial (mis)interpretation led director–auteur Peter Brook to reply: 'If you just let a play speak it won't make a sound.')

If the text is that which is read, contemporary critical theory agrees, meaning is created by the dialogue between reader and text. The act of interpretation is not subsidiary to the production of meaning: it is central. The text cannot be read without meditation. The nature of this meditation is disputed by Marxist, feminist, psychoanalytic critics, but all accept the shift to what Bakhtin calls a 'dialogic' model of communication in which the interpretative process is primary. In German reception theory, for example, the concept of an objective and eternal work of art with a single, deterministic meaning is displaced by a model of the text as a never-completed unfolding of its effective history. In H. R. Jauss' aesthetics the text is never separable from its history of reception; it can be understood only 'in history rather than as a fixed entity.' Wolfgang Iser suggests that the reader's hunt for a truth buried in the text is foolhardy, for meaning is *not* to be dug out or pieced together from textual clues, but rather is reached by an interactive process in which the text is constituted *by* and *in* the act of reading. In American reader-response theory we find the same shift of focus: Stanley Fish insists that the question 'What does this mean?' must be replaced by 'What does this do?' He inveighs against the position best represented by Wimsatt and Beardsley's essay on the Affective Fallacy that the text is indisputably there and stable. Fish argues that it is the *developing* shape of meaning, rather than the *static* shape of the printed page, that should be the object of critical description. He substitutes the structure of the reader's experience for the formal structure of the visible text: 'The relationship between interpretation and text is thus reversed: interpretative strategies are not put into execution after reading; they are the shape of reading, and because they are the shape of reading, they give texts their shape, making them rather than, as is usually assumed, arising from them.'

Fish is aware of the danger of destabilizing the text, a fear which similarly troubles denigrators of director's theatre. Those who argue for the authority of a determinate core of meaning in the text fear that in its absence there is no normative way of construing what anyone says or writes (or produces), with the result that no interpretation can be said to be more or less valid than any other. Fish's answer (or answers, his position evolves on this problem) comes to rest on his model of 'interpretative communities,' groups who constitute the properties of texts through shared interpretative strategies which exist *prior* to the act of reading and therefore determine the shape of what is read. Meanings, then, are the property 'neither of fixed and stable texts *nor* of free and independent readers but of interpretative communities that are responsible both for the shape of a reader's activities and for the texts those activities produce.'

Fish's method of escape from the dangers of solipsism has remained the most challenged aspect of his criticism; nonetheless, it is as ingenious a way out from the formidable problematic as the Yale deconstructors' escape from their paradoxical equation of reading and misreading. To escape banal and reductive misreading, Paul de Man insists that a 'good' misreading must produce 'a text that produces another text which can itself be shown to be an interesting misreading.' 'Good,' 'interesting,' and 'strong' – Harold Bloom's criterion for a successful misreading – are notoriously vague aesthetic criteria; Fish's notion of interpretative communities at least explains why Arthur Miller and other theatre traditionalists found no meaning, or the meaning of parody, in *L.S.D.*

If we accept the insights of contemporary theory – whether in semiotic, deconstructive, or reader-response formulation – we can agree with Fish that 'like it or not, interpretation is the only game in town.' And if this is true with regard to the literary text, how much stronger the game in theatre, which posits another textuality between the written text and its receptors. Umberto Eco notes that though the intervention of the performer complicates the act of reception, for the purpose of aesthetic analysis the process is the same as reading, for 'every "reading," "contemplation," or "enjoyment" of a work of art represents a tacit form of "performance."' And conversely, every performance is a 'reading' or 'contemplation.' But we have in theatre two sets of readers – the theatre artists who traditionally 'read,' interpret, the written text, and the audience who read the new theatrical text created by the mediated reading. As the most privileged of mediating readers of the written text, the director, for the past century, has been made responsible for creating the performance text from the contributions of other interpretative artists. But there is no universal strategy for the production of the performance text; both in the traditional and experimental models the director may be more or less tyrannical or open to suggestions, more or less beholden to a preconceived notion of performance. In the manner of what Hollywood calls 'hyphenates' the director may combine multiple interpretative functions as director-actor, director-designer, even director-designer-actor; or the hyphenation of functions may overlap written and performance texts, particularly in the experimental model of ensemble playwriting.

Even in the traditional theatre, the playwright has often assumed the directorial baton. Both Miller and Beckett have done so, and it is instructive to examine the results, for if ever there should be an identity between the two levels of textuality it should be when the playwright and the director are the same person. Yet, as Ruby Cohn notes in *Just Play: Beckett's Theatre*, Beckett's productions of his own plays have strayed in many particulars from the literal wording of his texts – altering even spoken words as well as scenery, costumes, music. Though the changes have not been radical they reveal Beckett's *de facto* recognition of the dialectical interpretative function of the director. Miller, like Beckett, has occasionally assumed responsibility for the staging of his woks, but since he is a playwright with the strongest sense of intentionality, he has seen his directorial role as subservient to his role as playwright. And yet, he has changed textuality by not hesitating to revise his dramatic texts after initial production (*The Crucible, A View from the Bridge*), and he was not constrained by the playwright's intentionality in his version of Ibsen's *An Enemy of the People*, which eliminated all unsympathetic ambiguity from Stockmann's character.

How, then, do we – critics, audience – read the already read theatre text? How do we respect both the playwright's vital imaginative contribution – the most difficult of all theatre crafts – and the director's creation of the conjoined theatre text? Most essentially, by recognizing the paradoxicality and irreducibility of the theatre text, and by asking questions which illuminate rather than obscure the dynamics of the elements that constitute its plurality. In 'The world, the text, the critic,' Edward Said asks such questions about the creation of the critical text, questions that have clear applicability to theatre. Said offers three different but connected ways – 'modes of place' – the critical essay has of 'being the form the critic takes, and locates himself in, to do his work.' (Where Said talks about the critic we can usefully substitute 'director'; for 'essay' read 'performance.') The first 'mode of place' is the essay's (performance's) relation to the text (play) it approaches:

> How does it come to the text of its choice? How does it enter that text? What is the concluding definition of its relation to the text it has dealt with? The second mode of place is the essay's intention (and the intention presumed or perhaps created by the essay, that its audience has) in attempting an approach. Is the critical essay an attempt to *identify* or to *identify with* the text of its choice? Does it stand between the text and the reader, or to one side of them? . . . The third mode of place concerns the essay as a zone in which certain kinds of occurrences, events happen as an aspect of the essay's production. What is the essay's consciousness of its marginality to the text it discusses? . . . Finally, is the essay an intervention between texts, or an intensification of the notion of textuality?

The playwright's intentionality is, then, not irrelevant, but this intentionality is perceived within a complex matrix of interpretation. Had questions such as these been asked about the productions of *Endgame* and *L.S.D.*, the debates might have been just as spirited but far more productive. If we are to learn anything from these controversies, it is that while interpretation may indeed be the only game in town, it plays by many rules.

38

ISLAND HOPPING
Rehearsing the Wooster Group's *Brace Up!*

Euridice Arratia

T136, 1992

I'm not a theatre person, I'm not an acting coach, and I'm not a traditional
director. I think it is usually a traditional director who is trained to interpret a
play, while I'm making my own play even if I'm using someone else's play. I feel
that I'm making my own play which means that I have to develop my own
language. In standard theatre or a repertory company the actors are supposed to
bring a language with them and the director gives the actors the modus vivendi,
so to speak, the reason for coughing onstage and helps the actor to make that
language work on the stage. On the other hand, I'm working with many different kinds of training and ways of performing on the stage and all of them are
equally wonderful to me. I don't value one over the other, I value performance, I
value the stage.

Elizabeth LeCompte [1]

The process of shaping *Brace Up!* which opened in January 1991, underscores the
continuity and organicity of the Wooster Group's work and history. Many of the
characteristics present in LeCompte's early work continue to permeate the Wooster
Group's productions. To name the most obvious: emphasis of process over product; resistance to a univocal narrative through the creation of a nonlinear structure;
employment of diverse styles of performing, the overlapping of intricate aural and
visual elements, often mediated by sophisticated technology; and the recycling of
scenery, props, and costumes from earlier pieces.

The various elements or threads of *Brace Up!* intertwine to form a densely
patterned and textured cloth. Some threads can be disentangled with relative
ease, for example, the narrative throughline of Chekhov's *Three Sisters*. But even
then, sorting out the complex operations performed on the play is not easy. One
of the reasons is that the weaving of the performance text is an exceptionally
lengthy process. Another is that some threads were spun long before the piece as
such was conceived – the recycled props and scenery, and the autobiographical
references.

An additional challenge for anyone aiming to report on the Wooster Group's rehearsal procedures is presented by LeCompte's approach to the work sessions: when she directs, she is creating a language minute by minute. She is constantly recontextualizing. Sometimes it takes her weeks to be able to conceptualize her vision of a particular element of the *mise-en-scène*. Many times there is no attempt to verbalize a vision; material is brought in and/or generated onstage by the performers and, paraphrasing LeCompte, it is her task 'to recognize it when she sees it.' Some ideas are only temporarily valid. A word, gesture, or sound that works today can easily be discarded tomorrow, and the search begins all over again. Even when an overall structure has been shaped, modifications continue after the show opens. For the Wooster Group there is no such thing as a 'finished' product. It is only possible to say that one saw a version of *Brace Up!*

CASTING AND REHEARSING

Staging *Three Sisters* was suggested by Ron Vawter. Because all the main characters are female, *Three Sisters* appeared to fit the actual circumstances of the group; during the past few years the male performers have tended to be engaged in projects outside the group.[2] The performers collaborating in the project as it was listed in the New York program of January 1991 were Kate Valk as the Narrator, Peyton Smith as Olga, Joan Jonas as Masha, Beatrice Roth as Irina, Willem Dafoe as Andrei, Anna Kohler as Natalya, Roy Faudree as Kulygin, Jeff Webster as Tusenbach, Paul Schmidt as Chebutykin, and Michael Stumm as Solyony. Performing only on video were the child Jack Dafoe as Bobik, and Josephine Buscemi as Anfisa.

From the moment the text was chosen, LeCompte decided to call on outside artists and old friends to participate. This is not unusual for the Wooster Group. Ruth Maleczech, Joan Jonas, and Beatrice Roth were invited to play the roles of Olga, Masha, and Irina.[3] Selecting actresses much older than the young women indicated by Chekhov was an initial major departure from the text, one of many that subverted orthodox expectations of *Three Sisters*.

When I began watching rehearsals in October 1990, the Wooster Group's work routine was as follows: activity begins before 10 a.m. in the Performance Garage at 33 Wooster Street, New York. Onstage some performers organize their props while others chat and have coffee with members of the crew. Since most Wooster Group members do tasks other than performing, some go upstairs in the office to take care of administrative business or work on the props required by the piece. A little after 10 LeCompte enters the theatre and sits at a table set up for her and the assistant director. Using a wireless microphone she promptly begins the rehearsal. Rehearsals go until 3 p.m. with a half-hour break. Once the work-in-progress opens to the public, rehearsals are held from 2 p.m. to 5 p.m. and the public performance starts at 8 p.m.

During rehearsals it isn't unusual for an entire session to be devoted to three pages of Paul Schmidt's translation; long segments of the play are rarely worked on. What is to be rehearsed is discussed beforehand between LeCompte and assistant director Marianne Weems. Decisions are based on notes made during the last rehearsal. However, when asked how much of the creative work is done as 'homework,' LeCompte informed me that although she does a great deal of reading and thinks about the piece in a 'larger context,' she tries not to write down how the piece should look onstage.

> *LeCompte:* I never bring blind reading or ideas about the *mise-en-scène* or ideas about blocking, or even come with ideas. I never work on them outside. If I do, I don't even bother to bring them in. Inevitably they don't work. Sometimes if I'm stimulated by some idea that I think will look good, I'll write it down and then throw it away.

STAGE, PROPS, AND COSTUMES

The *Brace Up!* stage is a rectangular platform raised 20 inches off the floor and nearly as wide as the Performance Garage. Along the entire length of the upstage edge, there is a long table placed on the floor, with its top even with the stage. When seated at the table, performers' backs are against the theatre's rear wall and their lower bodies are hidden below the stage. Two ramps running along the left and right sides of the platform are used for entrances and exits. A step downstage center is another entry point. The stage is framed horizontally and vertically on all sides by metal tubing, giving it the appearance of a large cube. The audience is seated on risers directly facing the stage.

Asked about the history of the ground plan for *Brace Up!*, designer Jim Clayburgh explained that he first used this plan in *Nayatt School* (1970). It was reversed back to front for *Point Judith* (1979), moved to the left for *Route 1 & 9* (1981), and then returned to its original orientation for *North Atlantic* (1984), *L.S.D.* (1984), and Frank Dell's *The Temptation of St. Anthony* (1987). [. . .] As in all former pieces, no attempt is made to conceal the walls of the Performance Garage with flats or wings; performance space and theatre space have no delimiting borders – visible to the audience beyond the upstage left area is a small workshop where lights, tools, and equipment are hung. This area is connected to the stage by a ramp. Against the stage left wall are trunks containing costumes and props used in previous pieces, along with other paraphernalia. These trunks remain in place during the first months of the public performances but later are removed. In their place are three chairs for performers when they come down from the platform. Against the stage right wall are props for *Brace Up!* From this area, the stage manager operating in clear view hands props to the Narrator and other performers.

The main props are three standing lamps and a long-stem candelabra, two wooden coffee tables, three movable screens, several microphones (two on stands), three TV monitors (two of which are fixed on parallel tracks attached to the floor of the stage allowing them to be rolled up- and downstage), and two monitors hanging above the audience on which the cast watches the performance. On the left and right edges of the stage are two vertical panels of fluorescent light approximately two feet wide. [. . .]. Except for the light panels, all of the props are mobile. They are not only moved around the stage (especially by the Narrator), but are also taken on and off the stage. This occurs particularly with a pair of metal wheelchairs whose seats and backs are covered by fake fur.

> *Clayburgh:* After Liz started to think about going against the age in the casting of the three sisters, she talked about it as almost a hospital vision. There was a sense of great aging and almost illness and how the three sisters may get dealt with almost as

objects. Kate, who had worked in a nursing home, knew about those chairs and suggested them.

Weems: The sisters are kind of infirm and they are somehow trapped in these chairs, which are actually shower chairs for geriatric patients. People are strapped in and wheeled into the showers.

These wheelchairs are associated with Masha and Irina, but other performers sometimes sit on them.

Although some props, the wheelchairs for example, were generated especially for *Brace Up!* many objects are recycled from previous pieces, standing as referential signs of the Wooster Group's history.

Clayburgh: The lamps have been around for a long time. Naturally, the line of the lamp shade is reminiscent if not parallel to a red tent that was in *Rumstick Road*, *Point Judith*, and *Nayatt School*, and was sort of put together to mirror it, to be a negative image of it.

Using 'what you have in the closet' also applies to the costumes. Valk's man's gray suit was Willem Dafoe's for *Route 1 & 9*. Some costumes, such as Masha's kimono-like clothing, were conceived for *Brace Up!* When asked about this costume, Weems explained: 'That's definitely from noh. But it also is a reference to Yamamoto, that famous fashion store around the corner from the Garage.' The fusion of different styles is evident in all the costumes. Peyton Smith's stylish purple blazer is transformed by a wide purple belt tied at her back in a bow like an obi. Throughout the rehearsals and even after the opening, new elements are added to the wardrobe. For instance, for Acts III and IV Valk's jacket is replaced by a long sleeveless coat, and Stumm's costume is changed from a dress suit to a pair of calf-length culottes, a 1950s-style striped shirt, and black windsurfing boots.

PERFORMANCE OUTLINE

The structure of *Brace Up!* followed the narrative spine of *Three Sisters*. LeCompte said that, contrary to previous pieces, 'Now there is a much higher concentration on the play than on the framing of the piece. Usually it is pretty equal.' According to Clayburgh, 'this is the most accurate rendition of a script we've ever done. The folks in Europe jokingly said that it was because *Three Sisters* was so much better than the other scripts we have done that we couldn't tear it apart as much. I think it has more to do with the kind of work *St. Anthony* was, and how this, by comparison, is a relief.'

Although segments of Chekhov's play were skipped and scenes were condensed, what was performed adhered to Chekhov's order. To provide a general outline, I will list the events as they occurred. However, remember that the piece is a work-in-progress, so this scenario is not set.

Act I begins with the Narrator/Valk walking around the stage, delivering stage directions, introducing the performers and the characters they are playing. Most of the male performers are sitting at the upstage table facing the audience. Jeff Webster and Paul Schmidt are seated upstage at the right and left edges, with their backs to the audience; their faces are projected live on video on onstage TV monitors. Peyton Smith begins Act I seated on top of the back table. Her performance is most of the time seen on the stage monitors. Beatrice Roth and Joan Jonas are in wheelchairs (the latter behind a screen upstage right, which the Narrator thereafter removes). Throughout this first act Roth and Jonas walk around the stage as Vawter, Dafoe, Schmidt, and Faudree come downstage to deliver their lines using the standing microphones or Valk's wireless microphone. For Irina's birthday lunch scene, all the performers except Valk move to the upstage table area. By this time Anna Kohler has taken Webster's place and her performance is shown on the monitors. In this scene there is a 'photography session' and the performers' images are frozen in black and white stills on the monitors. Following the photo session, partners face off with long bamboo sticks, as in a martial arts exercise, and knock their sticks together to the accompanying musical beat. After the stick dance Kohler and Dafoe are left alone to play Natasha and Andrei's love scene, with Dafoe seated at the table facing the audience and Kohler seated with her back to the audience, her face seen only on the monitors.

There is almost no break between Acts I and II. Valk rearranges some props while Schmidt (seated as in Act I) summarizes events up to the point of Colonel Vershinin's philosophical speeches about life, some of which Vawter delivers sitting on the downstage center step or while walking around the space between the platform and the audience. After Vawter leaves, moments of calm are interspersed with accelerated scenes where several dialogs and songs overlap. There are abrupt changes of volume and speed. For instance, a frenzy is created by Jonas furiously walking around the stage shouting at the Narrator and the old nurse Anfisa (shown only on video); upstage the men softly sing a Russian song which crescendos along with an argument between Chebutykin and Solyony. At the same time, at center-stage Valk dances and mimics drinking vodka, as a loud recording of glass being smashed is played repeatedly. Then the performers place themselves in different areas of the stage (some on top of the table) for an increasingly energetic waltz. At Natasha's demand, the dance stops abruptly. The pace slows down, voices soften. Performers progressively leave the stage. Act II ends with Valk and Roth at stage right delivering Irina's 'I want to go to Moscow! Moscow! Moscow!' These two acts last approximately an hour and a half. The plan is to have an intermission between Acts II and III. Although excerpts of Acts III and IV are rehearsed, and in a few shows fragments of Act III are performed during spring 1991, their placement is still undecided by the time the Wooster Group leaves New York to tour in April 1991. Act III tends to concentrate on two moments of the fire scene: Olga giving away clothes to the fire victims and Masha confessing her love for Vershinin. Act IV begins to be shaped around the 'farewell song' with most of the performers singing and dancing, playing the street musicians and their roles at the same time.

SCORING

> *LeCompte: (to the performers)*   I make the frame. You have to make the picture within the frame.

In order to understand the dynamics of the rehearsal procedure (not only what happens but how it happens), one should bear in mind that the live performance, the mediated performance [performers videotaped live on stage], and the sound score are developed simultaneously. These were interdependent elements in the total score. Monitors, video cameras, and Christopher Kondek, the video operator, are at all rehearsals. As Clayburgh worded it, 'Since *Route 1 & 9*, microphones and video monitors have been like performers, part of the company.'

The Wooster Group does not work under the pressure of deadlines but in LeCompte's own words, 'things just happen.' Once Chekhov's play is chosen, the first step is to spend an initial period reading the play while roles are tentatively assigned. After these initial readings, the process of staging begins.

> *Weems:* I have to say that it was pretty much what you are seeing now. We started
> out with it being very open-ended – just trying to listen to the text and put different
> forms around it. We used to do game structures much more, big formal things, ways
> to get through certain sections. It took us around eight months to do Acts III and
> IV and approximately four months to do I and II.

Throughout the months I observed rehearsals, these 'game structures' were proposed by LeCompte at points when the rehearsal appeared to be stuck and performers seemed to be falling into what she defined as 'a kind of naturalism.' That is, when all the elements of the *mise-en-scène* began to function at the same level, threatening to cancel the multiplicity of readings. The game structures had the effect of making the performers refocus on the staging process, concentrating the scattered energy on new modes of dealing with material already familiar.

For example, late in November 1990, a couple of hours into a rehearsal that isn't producing the desired results, LeCompte divides the space into sections. When the performers move into each section, they have to adopt a different mode of performance. The back area becomes the area of 'most private performance.' Performers in the middle section put their dark glasses on and 'think pure dance.' While in this middle area, no one can finish their actions or lines looking at the audience. Finally, the front section is the place for 'a declamatory style, speaking to the whole room.' LeCompte also proposes that certain speeches be tried with different music. Music, she says, 'can be a co-performer.' In reference to the video score, LeCompte indicates that it 'has to be much simpler in the long stretches, the complications have to come in short spasms.' In this way, during the game, new sounds, chords, and fragments of footage are introduced at random.

In January 1991 Jonas as Masha and Roth as Irina are blindfolded. In order for the action to start, a blindfolded performer has to step on one of several 'x's made of black tape placed on the stage floor. Once the 'x' is hit, the production manager (Clay Shirky), sitting in the audience area, calls out numbered short sections of the play dubbed 'islands.' Once the number of the island is called out, Smith, standing on mike by the upstage table, cues the performers where exactly in the script to start. This is only the skeleton of the game, however. Besides these general guidelines, there are other rules and intricacies (many of them suggested by the performers) that develop. For example, if after a few minutes a blindfolded performer doesn't step on an 'x,' the narrator can do so. Also, time limits are set, and when the time is up, performers have to quit the island they are playing and pass to the next section. These games are to a degree improvisational and new elements are constantly introduced by the performers. New ways of dealing with the structure drive the performers to focus on formal aspects of the piece instead of on interpretation, or, as LeCompte tells the performers, 'on physical actions instead of emotion.'

From the outset, the *mise-en-scène* is flexible in order to cope with absent performers.

> *LeCompte:* There are very cued things that I start with, that with this piece, I knew may not happen. More than ever, we may have people coming and going because of the money situation. So I developed from the very beginning the idea that anyone could come and go without disturbing the piece. So that's a departure. On other pieces there has been that possibility obviously because Willem went in the middle of *St. Anthony*, and I substituted for him on video, but it wasn't an easy process. Same thing for *L.S.D.*, people went, and it was difficult to substitute them, so from the outset in this piece I said, 'I have to make a *mise-en-scène* where anyone could fill in anytime or someone else could read the lines, and it would not disturb the heart of the piece.'

One of the strategies to cope with absent performers is to focus on the elaboration of the islands. Although until the moment the Wooster Group goes on tour the Japanese material and sections of the video score are still undergoing a process of selection and placement within the piece, during the last five months of rehearsals the selected parts of Chekhov's play are to a great extent fixed. As the word suggests, islands are autonomous portions of the script as staged. If necessary, islands can be skipped. The links between islands are provided by the Narrator.

The Narrator is a sort of stage manager 'directing the actors' entrances and what they should do.' But more significantly, as in *Our Town*, the Narrator becomes the cohesive figure that exposes and links the multiple levels of reality being played out onstage. As Valk said, 'I am located in this piece as the free agent between the audience, which is now Liz, and the play.' At the opening of *Brace Up!*, the Narrator delivers the stage directions: 'The Prozorovs' house ... It is noon; the weather is sunny and bright.' She introduces each of the characters when it is their turn to speak (e.g., 'Irina the youngest sister . . .'). The Narrator not only introduces the character but also the performer playing the role (e.g., 'Peyton Smith in the role of Olga'). From improvisations, it evolves that during the initial scenes the Narrator will cue the lines of the performers by asking questions suggested by Chekhov's play itself (e.g., 'Olga, how was the weather the day your father died?'). Progressively this opening section takes on the style of a talk show. The Narrator introduces 'the theme' and asks questions while working the crowd, offering her wireless mike to the person answering.

Duplicating the elastic play between character and performer, and between script and the Wooster Group's reworking of the text, is the performance of Paul Schmidt in the dual role of Doctor Chebutykin and the translator of *Three Sisters*. Schmidt first intervenes as the translator when LeCompte suggests that he, upon the request of the Narrator, summarize the beginning of Act II up to the section where the scene is going to be performed. What began as a way to connect nonsequential scenes ends in an extended role for Schmidt. In Act I as Valk is introducing the men at the table, Schmidt interrupts, telling her she should say that 'the men at the back are all in uniform.' Later in Act II when Valk suggests that since 'we are running out of time we should cut and go to another scene,' Schmidt speaks up:

> *Schmidt:* No, Kate, let Masha say the lines; it is a beautiful speech where she talks about . . .
>
> *Jonas:* I remember, Paul, she says [reciting quickly], 'I think a person has to believe in something, or has to look for something to believe in, otherwise his life is empty, empty . . . Just to live, and not to know why the cranes fly, why children are born, why there are stars in the sky . . . Either you know the reason why you are alive, or nothing makes any difference.' Is that it?
>
> *Schmidt:* Yes, that's it.

[. . .] In the rehearsals much attention is given to physical actions. The smoothness and apparently effortless precision with which the actors perform their tasks (from energetic dances to complicated 'dialogs' where two or more performers speak at high speed, overlapping and stopping at the same time) is due to LeCompte's meticulous attention to detail. Even sloppy actions are the result of conscious choice. A clear example of this is the dance numbers where, after having mastered patterns of movements, actors are instructed to dismantle or fragment those actions in order to cancel the appearance of 'virtuosity.' This also applies to certain lines. LeCompte for instance asks Roth to 'build in a mistake': 'I want to go back to previous rehearsals where you would miss a line and Kate would give you the line; a mistake as a part of the text.' LeCompte refers to this device as a 'safety valve.' Building in a mistake interrupts the flow of the text, allowing the oscillation between acting and quoting the script.

Although LeCompte usually directs from the auditorium, whenever she feels it necessary she goes onto the stage to demonstrate how an action should be performed or to correct a performer's position – for example, the position of the feet of a performer sitting in one of the wheelchairs – or to watch closely some detail. According to LeCompte, 'every action must have its little thing.' Sometimes that 'little thing' – the detail that makes an action unique – happens almost by accident in activities initiated by the performers but singled out by LeCompte. LeCompte is especially attentive to what happens unexpectedly, an image randomly revealed on the TV monitors, an unplanned gesture. For example, during one rehearsal the Hollywood film *The Harvey Girls* (1946) was on TV. LeCompte saw the fire scene in the movie as material for the beginning of Act III, the fire in the Prozorov's town. Or, in one scene Jonas has to be sitting in her wheelchair while Vawter delivers his lines. Having missed her cue, Jonas hurried across the stage on her toes to reach the wheelchair. Everyone burst out laughing. LeCompte used Jonas' tiptoe cross as her entrance. LeCompte (to Jonas): 'Now do it again recreating the same thing. Your text is that you missed your cue. You need to get in without disturbing Ron's lines. [Half-jokingly] Your subtext is that you are pretending you are not acting.'

But at other times it is a painstaking process of trial and error. In the scene where Kulygin (Roy Faudree) kisses Masha (Jonas), LeCompte tells the performers that she is looking for 'a gesture that outlines that this is one of the few times where Kulygin kisses Masha.' Several ways of establishing physical contact between the actors are tried until it is decided that Masha will sit in the wheelchair upstage right in profile and not react to Kulygin's kiss. After several tries, LeCompte proposes that Kulygin have a coin in his mouth to put in Masha's ear as a gesture for an awkward kiss. In order to accomplish this, he has to hold Masha's head. This increases the difficulty and prolongs the action. Although the gesture was kept,

LeCompte was never fully satisfied with it. Months later she told the actors that 'the kiss doesn't work, it looks like a natural kiss, like you have a natural relation.'

One of the premises of the staging process was 'to have always something that amplifies or goes against' what is being said or done onstage. For this purpose, a substantial amount of time was devoted to the composition of 'framing devices': 'anything that punctuates, frames, emphasizes, or brings into the foreground any particular word, object, action, or position.' Many of the framing devices in *Brace Up!* were provided by the video work. For example, [. . .] after a lengthy rehearsal of a scene where Dafoe walks downstage and puts on a pair of white shoes using a fork as a shoehorn, LeCompte decides that the business should be videotaped and shown simultaneously with the live action. Furthermore, a close-up of a fork falling on the floor is videotaped and edited in throughout the tape.

Several framing devices are developed and used simultaneously and often overlap. A scene comprised of fragments from Act II, words referring to the weather, permeate the text. A dense aural and visual design is developed to accompany these key words: wind, snow, winter, etc. Throughout the scene, a new-age soundtrack mimicking the wind plays while footage of a man walking in a heavy snowstorm rolls randomly on the TV monitors. Also, at one point in the scene Michael Stumm comes forward playing a guitar and singing Bob Dylan's 'Blowing in the Wind.' (Later, in order to cope with Stumm's absence, his playing is videotaped.) [. . .]

LeCompte also experimented with enhancing some of the noises specified in the text. Speakers are distributed around the stage so that the sounds can be heard as coming from different locations and distances. For stage directions such as 'somebody knocks on the floor downstairs' loud noises and echoes are produced. These sounds were conceptualized by LeCompte as 'marks.' When she first asked the technicians for a door knock, and a perfect replica was delivered, she immediately objected: 'The knock on the door has to come louder, it is a mark, it is not real.' Also, 'unreal' sounds are sometimes added to punctuate the steps of entrances and exits. In another scene, the Narrator drinks vodka and after every drink throws her arm down as if smashing the glass against the floor. This gesture is repeated several times, and for every gesture the sound of glass shattering is added. In one rehearsal the sound was played before Valk had initiated the gesture. This accident is incorporated in the structure. Every time it occurs, Valk establishes eye contact with the sound booth as if to say, 'I didn't do it, did you do it?' thereby revealing the mechanism of the trick and forcing the audience to acknowledge the unnatural origin of the noise.

DIRECTING ACTORS

One of the most striking characteristics of LeCompte's work is the wide and eclectic vocabulary she uses. She expresses her directing in language drawn from film, visual arts, music, dance, and theatre. She acknowledges that out of a multiplicity of texts she is making her 'own play,' thus she has to develop her own language. Words like 'choreography,' 'naturalism,' 'task-oriented performance,' and instructions such as 'don't act' or 'report' are used frequently during rehearsals. LeCompte uses concepts such as 'functional entrance' or 'utilitarian exit' to prevent the performer from pushing a heightened level of emotion (simulated or real) while executing simple tasks such as exiting or entering. Functionality is also stressed for most of the Narrator's non-character walking and handling of props.

> *LeCompte:*   I use these [terms] sometimes as a shock thing. If I can sense that some-
> one's not connecting, I'll say different things just to shock the person into trying
> something else. So when I say 'don't act' it is often to people that have a certain
> facility to cover themselves, to repeat certain rhythms, and I get bored. I try to
> disrupt the patterns so they try something else, some other ways of doing. But it
> doesn't mean much more than that, believe me. It is that I want something to
> happen.

Throughout the rehearsals LeCompte warns the actors against filling their scores with emotion. The opposition action/emotion is a recurrent theme.

> *LeCompte:*   Everybody has to be aware I don't want anyone to fill any section with
> emotion. I want to fill it with your presence in the space. I want you to be who you
> are. I want physical actions, not emotions. The emotions would be given by the
> overall picture. Crying is an action not an emotion; don't manipulate your voice or
> feelings. If the play is boring let it be boring.

LeCompte's concern for clarity in every action and the performers' understanding of their role as a part of the overall structure are reflected in her experimentation with formalized ways of acting. During Act I, she asks Jonas (Masha) to break down her routine in 'Action–Line–Action–Line,' which created patterns; Masha walks, stops and then speaks; sits in the wheelchair, stands up, speaks; takes a fork, pauses, speaks, etc. LeCompte tells Dafoe (Andrei) 'not [to] confuse actions with words.' 'Don't confuse your sneeze with your lines. First you sneeze then you talk.' It's a quality in the performing unrelated to realistic theatre.

[. . .] LeCompte's method is to search among different strategies, and not every one produces the same results on different individuals. She searches, in her own words, for 'the path of least resistance.' Having very few preconceptions of how a performer or a character should look and be onstage, LeCompte is open to what-ever the performer offers. She is willing to explore and integrate things that ortho-dox theatre people would regard as obstacles or even handicaps. Thus, LeCompte advises a performer who is having a hard time learning the lines because of the constant blocking changes to use this 'distracted quality.' Later, in a meeting when another performer expresses confusion, LeCompte remarks that 'there is something, a quality achieved when people act not knowing what they are doing that really interests me.'

Two kinds of performance are thoroughly explored during the rehearsals. One imitates soap opera acting (images of 'real' soap operas such as *All My Children* are shown on the monitors). The other is a presentational style, less emotionally invested than the first. These two styles constitute two ends of a continuum, with many other styles in between. The soap opera acting is done mostly in the mediated parts of the performance, with the monitors showing exaggerated close-ups, a soap opera framing of images. This style had been explored in previous Wooster Group pieces (*Route 1 & 9* especially). It was introduced into *Brace Up!* while experimenting with video, searching for 'the strongest presentation that any person has.' For this type of performance, LeCompte requires the performers on camera 'to use a mask,' that is, 'to act' in the Western naturalistic tradition – for example, when

Webster uses a German accent for Tusenbach or Smith concentrates on playing up Olga's permanent headache. On the other hand, the presentational style, a Wooster Group signature, is related to reporting as opposed to reenacting. It requires of the performer a distance from the performance text, while maintaining great focus. It is most obvious in *Brace Up!* when someone comes to the microphone located down center. An example is the appearance of Vawter (Colonel Vershinin), whose first lines are: 'How do you do? I'm delighted to be here at last, delighted, believe me. Well, well! How you've grown!' Some of Vershinin's lines are delivered on the microphone to the audience, while others are to Masha and Irina onstage. Once the open rehearsals begin, these initial lines are delivered entirely to the audience, with Vawter overtly establishing direct eye contact with individual spectators.

Here and elsewhere LeCompte draws on the avant-garde tradition of blurring the boundaries between performer and role. She has no interest in 'creating a character' in the Stanislavskian sense. She stresses the effacement of character/ actor distinctions: 'Some of the work is improvisation. If you have some problems repeat your lines. Commit yourself because there is no difference between your role and yourself.' Or as she put it in a 1990 interview:

> [. . .] I use so many levels of performance style. For instance in one piece I'll have someone with a heavymask [*sic*] performing – acting – and at the same time I might have someone doing something that appears to be him or herself. It takes different kinds of skills I think. Some people are more natural on stage in a mask; some feel better on the stage without a mask. I'm just more interested in finding the place where the performer is the most alive, where I feel the presence is real.
>
> (in Phipps 1990: 33)

DANCING

LeCompte conceives her pieces as choreographies (see LeCompte 1985). 'I'm not really that interested in the stories because basically, I structure the pieces as music and dance' (in Phipps 1990: 34). The Wooster Group's dancing is made manifest throughout their work in the special attention to concrete time and space, the creation of solid physical scores which prevail over individual emotions, and the use of actual dances. These dances are non-linear and nonnarrative. LeCompte regards them as formal structures included mainly for the diversion they provide to herself and the group:

> *LeCompte:* I enjoy dances, so it's more like I have to include them for my own enter-tainment. We usually start out with dances. For *Brace Up!* Kate went down to a dance festival [Townsville, Australia, 1988] and brought back a videotape. So we integrated those with things that we had done over the past ten years and with some noh dances and a whole bunch of different dance structures that we had put together.
>
> (Phipps 1990: 33)

Valk's South Pacific dances functioned as sources from which the Wooster Group created something new. The dance numbers evolved under Valk's direction separately from the work on Chekhov's text. [. . .]

> *Shirky:* Jo [Andres, the show's 'dance consultant,'] and Kate got together and made those movements. [. . .] Then they took those dances they've been trying to rehearse

to the drumming music, which is not a-rhythmic but has no time signature: the drummers drum to match the dancers dancing, which is the exact opposite of the Western world. So, the drummers add to or subtract from the beat. Therefore, there is no measure or bars, it's a continuous drumming pattern with variations. They learned the dances accompanied by Japanese music, the movie music that was in 4/4 time. And then whenever we would get to a piece of the show where we would have a dance number, Kate would take the movements and make a pastiche between a Western time signature of 3/4, 4/4, and these learned movements from the Pacific tape.

[. . .] Although at a certain point the performers know the dances very well and can dance all together to the same beat with great precision LeCompte insists that the dance numbers have a rough quality. The sharpness achieved is partially dismantled in the last rehearsals before the New York opening, with the performers hesitating slightly between movements, purposely missing transitions, stopping for a couple of beats, etc. The dances oscillate between 'being right on the beat' and 'not knowing what to do,' between energetic exactness and an (apparent) relaxation, a contrast explored throughout the making of *Brace Up!*

JAPANESE MATERIAL

> If I want to imagine a fictive nation, I can give it an invented name, treat it declaratively as a novelistic object, create a new Garabagne, so as to compromise no real country by my fantasy . . . I can also – though in no way claiming to represent or analyze reality itself (these being the major gestures of Western discourse) – isolate somewhere in the world (faraway) a certain number of features . . . and out of these features deliberately form a system. It is this system which I shall call: Japan.
>
> (Barthes 1982: 3)

An identifying feature of the Wooster Group is the confrontation of classic texts with a wide variety of material – other written texts, interviews, autobiographical material, taped material, films, etc. In the case of *Brace Up!* some material comes from Japanese theatre and film. LeCompte's interest in Japanese theatrical forms predates the making of *Brace Up!* By fall 1989, as a separate track and without much idea of how it was going to be used, members of the group begin to pore over a variety of Japanese material including written texts, films such as Ozu's *Floating Weeds* (1934), samurai films, and videos of noh and kyogen. However, replicating a form was far from the goal of the Group.

> *Valk:* When we review the noh texts and the kyogen texts, when we watch Japanese theatre and Japanese movies, we are not going to try to reproduce their technique, we are not going to try and walk as they walk in the noh theatre. We make our own Japan, our own Japanese style, because it's culturally removed, it's existing in our heads [. . .].

Written texts serve as sources of information and inspiration. The readings range from technical aspects – how certain characters were supposed to move onstage in noh theatre – to philosophical problems such as 'inhabiting the stage' or the 'danger of reaching perfection.' On several occasions, LeCompte reads aloud essays on noh and kyogen theatre and from Barthes' *Empire of Signs* (1982). As LeCompte explains, the purpose of the material is 'to clarify herself,' to articulate something that she has been thinking of but has had trouble 'defining verbally.'

On another level, the material is explored as a framing device for Chekhov's *Three Sisters*, as another world permeating the Western classic. The main appropriation is from a documentary film about the life of the Ichikawa Santuro Geinin troupe, found early in the rehearsals. The opening narration of the documentary states:

> Kabuki plays and noh dramas are famous throughout the world for their refinement and delicately rendered sophistication. Kabuki and especially noh are the apex of Japanese theatre. Ranking somewhat below these [. . .] lies the gypsylike world of the traveling Geinin. For centuries, these troops of entertainers have been touring Japan, performing for the working classes and country peasants in cramped and often dirty theatres. With the advent of television and the closure of many of these theatres, a lot of these troupes have died out, and only the best of them have survived to entertain at modern hot springs, at hotels in Japan resort areas. Ichikawa Santuro troupe are such survivors.

The Geinin documentary is never intended to be used directly in the piece, but goes through a very sophisticated and lengthy process of appropriation.

> *Weems:* Liz's original conception is that there is a Japanese troupe that performs Chekhov. There is this traveling troupe in this burned-out hotel in the middle of New York, and they are performing this Western classic that may or may not be *Three Sisters*. So we need to develop the life of the group. That's the frame for the piece [. . .].

One of the steps to 'develop the life of the group' is the recreation of parts of the documentary by the Wooster Group. For this purpose a film is shot in 1990 and 1991 by Leslie Thornton in which Dafoe, Faudree, Kohler, Smith, Stumm, Valk, Vawter, and Webster play the principal members of the Japanese troupe. On the second floor of the Performance Garage the hotel where the Geinin troupe was staying is loosely reconstructed. There, the performers recreate some of the activities of the daily life of the troupe as shown in the documentary.

Thorton's film is not just a copy of the documentary. Fragments of the original film are intermeshed with new narratives, equally fragmented. One of these alien narratives weaves into the documentary autobiographical information concerning the Wooster Group people. A parallel is established between Dafoe and Sentaro, the Geinin troupe's star and the youngest brother of the family. [. . .]

Until the Wooster Group left to go on tour in March 1991, Thornton's film, as well as footage of a stylized samurai stick dance performed with costumes and makeup that resembled the Japanese warriors of noh theatre, was still in the process of integration into the piece. A few performances after the opening of the work-in-progress in New York in January 1991, some extracts of the film are shown on the TV monitors while Jeff Webster, sitting in the upstage right corner, reads extracts from voice-overs of the Geinin documentary. In subsequent performances, the reading of the voice-overs and almost all the images from the film are omitted.

Nonetheless, the search for images that echoed the Geinin troupe documentary is part of the rehearsal process. One of the images from the documentary introduced in *Brace Up!* is that of Sentaro demanding his shoes when getting dressed to perform. At the beginning of Act II, Andrei and Ferapont have a conversation which in *Brace Up!* happens over the phone. Andrei sits at the back table talking to a nonexistent Ferapont while, due to a 'bad connection,' the Narrator has to repeat aloud some of the old porter's lines. After this (fictional) conversation, Andrei delivers Sentaro's lines 'My shoes! Get my white shoes!' and walks toward the front microphone. Responding to the order, the Narrator brings out a pair of white shoes. Dafoe/Andrei/Sentaro puts the shoes on and leaves the stage.

While the conversation between Andrei and Ferapont is being rehearsed, images from different Japanese films are projected on the TV monitors. By chance, LeCompte's attention is caught by a song being chanted and she asks Dafoe 'to sing the song and at the same time to say the lines.' After a couple of attempts, he asked LeCompte to give him some time to write the song phonetically. Seeming to have found something that would work for the piece, LeCompte agreed, also asking him to 'imitate the whole body gesture and attitude' of the Japanese actor.

Japanese popular films are also used. One that is played throughout rehearsals is the popular sci-fi series *Godzilla*. Later on when Stumm (Solyony) leaves the piece, LeCompte decides that every time Solyony has a line the monitors will play scenes from *Godzilla*. The image has no more meaning than the one explained by the Narrator at the beginning of the performance: 'Since the actor playing Solyony cannot be here tonight, every time that he has to speak, we'll turn the TV loud.' Besides *Godzilla*, a scene from a highly stylized samurai film in which a child king and his court throw themselves into the sea rather than be taken prisoner by a conquering enemy is played during the stick dance. The film, with English subtitles, is shown without sound in slow motion while Valk dramatizes parts of the action, imitating phonetically the sound of Japanese at the front microphone while the rest of the performers dance at the back.

Another way of working with the Japanese films was the recontextualization of scenes from the films into *Three Sisters*. Thus, a group of women singing in *Gates of Flesh* becomes 'the carnival people' expected at the Prozorovs' house in Act II.

The Japanese films also provided the title for the piece. According to Valk, the group was puzzled and intrigued by the fact that in a number of Japanese films when the hero – often a samurai warrior – is defeated by the enemy, a disciple rushes to where the hero is lying in deep sorrow and delivers a long, intense speech which is consistently translated in only two words: '*Brace Up!*'

CONCLUSION

As I finish this article (in May 1992) *Brace Up!* is still evolving. Without a doubt some of the things described – blocking, dialog, sound and visual design among others – will change or be erased. For the Wooster Group, 'the final product is the last performance we do.' This, of course, is not news for anyone familiar with the group's work. LeCompte's methods defy solidification. In her own words, 'I can't stand it when something becomes perfect, enclosed. I like to leave the system open.' This approach permeates every element of the *mise-en-scène*, from embarking with a body of unrelated, sometimes antagonistic material to creating devices that disrupt virtuosity, to desynchronizing sound and gesture, and even to exploring in the same space a diversity of performance styles. Each bit, each layer of the performance text is submitted to endless testing. If some elements are discarded after the 'last performance,' others are recycled from piece to piece. *Brace Up!* has to be seen in relation to the Group's previous body of work, the product of a group of people committed to collaborative work based on deep trust in an ongoing project that has become a way of life.

> *LeCompte:* There is plenty of griping and complaining, you know, all these things that happen in rehearsal. But they know I'll get some place that they won't be ashamed of.

NOTES

1 Unless otherwise noted, quotes are from the following interviews conducted in New York: Kate Valk, 15 January 1991; Marianne Weems, 31 January 1991; Peyton Smith, 19 February 1991; Linda Chapman, 27 February 1991; Christopher Kondek, 1 March 1991; Jeff Webster, 9 March 1991; Elizabeth LeCompte, 5 April 1991; Anna Kohler, 12 April 1991; Clay Shirky, 2 August 1991; Jim Clayburgh, 17 September 1991.

2 The Wooster Group members [in 1992] are Jim Clayburgh, Willem Dafoe, Spalding Gray, Elizabeth LeCompte, Peyton Smith, Kate Valk, and Ron Vawter. Gray [. . .] has been working independently on autobiographical monologs. Dafoe [and Vawter have developed careers] as film actor[s].

3 Maleczech, a founding member of Mabou Mines, began rehearsing *Brace Up!* but due to other commitments couldn't continue. The role of Olga was taken over by Peyton Smith.

WORKS CITED

Barthes, Roland (1982) *Empire of Signs*. New York: Hill and Wang.

Chekhov, Anton (1990) *Three Sisters*, trans. Paul Schmidt. Unpublished manuscript.

LeCompte, Elizabeth (1985) 'The Wooster Group dances.' *TDR* 29, 2 (T106): 78–93.

Phipps, Wanda (1990) 'Two women: creating their own worlds: an interview with Wooster Group's Elizabeth LeCompte and Mabou Mines' Ruth Maleczech.' *High Performance* 13, 1 (Spring): 32–5.

Robinson, Marc (1991) 'Found in translation.' *Village Voice*, 17 September.

39

HAMLET AT WORLD'S END
Heiner Müller's production in East Berlin

Maik Hamburger

1994[1]

Rehearsals for a production combining Shakespeare's *Hamlet* and Heiner Müller's *Hamletmaschine* started at the Deutsches Theater in East Berlin in September 1989. At that time the eastern part of Germany seemed firmly in the grips of an old clan of Stalinist politicians, endeavoring to prevent the intrusion of *perestroika* from the East and of notions of democracy from the West. The opening of the sandwich show, called *'Hamlet/Maschine'* for short, occurred on 24 March 1990, one week after the people of the German Democratic Republic had in their first free elections installed a conservative, Christian-Democratic government. In the interim the country had seen in succession the downfall of the old state leaders, then the downfall of the 'new' state leaders that had replaced them, then of the government, then of the Communist Party, then of the transitional government, and finally of the Civic Movements that had initiated the whole process. Six months later, Germany was reunited.

Working at the same time that such phenomenal historic changes were occurring, the director of *Hamlet/Maschine*, Germany's leading playwright Heiner Müller, was constantly forced to reconsider and readjust his concept of the tragedy. Whether his production would in fact have differed substantially without the political rupture is something he himself probably could not say. However, this *Hamlet* became the crowning Shakespearean production of a doomed society and at the same time a foreboding of *Götterdämmerung* for humanity.

Let us look back a few decades. In 1945, in the bombed ruins of Berlin, the Deutsches Theater showed a conventional *Hamlet* directed by Gustav von Wangenheim, just returned to Germany from exile in the Soviet Union. The Prince was played by Horst Caspar, a beautiful actor with a mellifluous voice, whose heroic performance bore a message of hope for those liberated from fascism. In *Hamlet/Maschine* forty-five years later, a similarly graceful but less idealistic actor, Ulrich Mühe, repeatedly cites Müller's text: 'I was Hamlet. I stood on the shore and talked BLAH BLAH to the breakers, at my back the ruins of Europe . . .' For Müller, Europe is today more completely and irrevocably in ruins than Berlin was then. In 1964, Wolfgang Heinz directed *Hamlet* at the Deutsches Theater (with

Horst Drinda) as the story of an idealist who tragically failed to seize power when the opportunity came. In a vein of didactic enlightenment, Heinz turned the Ghost into a projection of Hamlet's fantasy and altered the ending to suggest a bright future for humanity, if only the champions of humanism assume command. Müller charges the Ghost with a sinister political meaning and also changes the ending, interpolating a poem by Zbigniew Herbert called 'Fortinbras' Lament,' which includes the words, 'Thus or any other way you were bound to fall, Hamlet, you were not fit for life, you believed in crystalline concepts and not in human clay.' Each of these productions proffered a comment on the historical attitude of the day, and Müller's staging is a reflection of his somber view that history has become disjointed and senseless.

The Shakespearean show that came into being alongside the downfall of a social- ist society is just as colossal as the monuments the socialist rulers had erected to mark their historical perpetuity. The performance takes seven and a half hours. In the overwhelming sets by the Viennese designer Erich Wonder, in which spatial architecture and vast cycloramas are cunningly fused, one of the most prominent features is a massive concrete shelter. Similarly the action of this *Hamlet* may be said to be embedded in concrete: it is monolithic and inexorable. Shakespeare's open dramaturgy is dispensed with. Spectators have no chance to make their own contribution; they sit there helplessly and watch the tragedy go by, a tragedy that is awaiting them as it awaits Hamlet. If Shakespeare's play can be regarded as a huge question, this production is an overpowering statement about the end of a civiliz- ation for which *Hamlet* was a central myth.

The program notes consist of three essays about time by Saint Augustine, John Donne, and Stephen W. Hawking. The lapse of time is a decisive feature in Müller's eschatology. The enigma of *Hamlet* arises in part from the fact that historical time intruded into the dramatic time when the play was written, argues Müller. This circumstance was reduplicated by the intrusion of historical time into the rehearsal process. Time has run away from Hamlet, as it has from a whole social era. Life punishes those who come too late, said Gorbachev. We all come too late, says this *Hamlet/Maschine.*

Ulrich Mühe's Hamlet is a slim, sensitive youngster wearing a double-breasted black suit too large for him. Although his hair goes gray by the end of the play, he never grows up to fill the suit, just as he is never willing to accept the political responsibility thrust upon him. He is Charlie Chaplin's tramp burdened by the curse of thought. Jörg Gudzuhn presents a Claudius who could be a Hamlet come to power. He is convinced of the pragmatic need to secure his position by ruthless means, but he lacks the capacity for ideological self-deceit. Thus he never achieves the demeanor of a professional politician like Polonius. He sees things too clearly, and deep down inside he does not believe in any justification for the power he exercises, so that at times he falls into quite inappropriate (and comic) bouts of flippancy.

In Horatio (Jörg-Michael Koerbl), Müller has put his alter ego on the stage: an ageless intellectual with a pinched face and spectacles who observes all the events from the fringe, who makes caustic comments through a throat microphone, one who is convinced of his own impotence in view of the power politics around him, and who, in the end, reacts to the destruction of his world with peals of sardonic laughter.

Hamlet in this production is made to traverse the history of the earth from Ice Age to Heat Death. Taking his cue from Francisco's lines, 'Tis bitter cold, / And I am sick at heart,' Müller sets the beginning of the play in a stage-high cube of stretched gauze to represent an enormous block of ice, whose melting produces a constant trickle of water and a pool in the middle of the stage, to be waded through by the characters at various points. The first lines heard when the play opens are Hamlet's dying words: already the end is a settled matter.

Over large stretches the action is presented in a ritualized style, many verbal passages being drawn out to great lengths and punctuated by weighty pauses. The ceremonial element is also emphasized when soliloquies are threaded back into the action and addressed to petrified listeners on the stage who should not normally hear them. On a second, more personal plane, the production depicts the conflicts individuals have to face when they get involved in political turmoils. Even those responsible for upholding inhuman rituals get caught up in them and suffer personally. Not only are Hamlet and Ophelia seen to be horrified at the injuries they inflict on each other under political exigency; even Polonius, drawn as a forceful, capable statesman, has an added passage revealing how much life he has wasted in the pursuit of his outwardly brilliant career.

On a third level, allusions to historical events provide suggestions for a contemporary orientation without being obtrusive or simplistic. Thus when the Ghost stalks across the stage (in the nude except for his helmet and codpiece), we hear a muted recording of the funeral ceremony at Stalin's death: it may be the 'Little Father' who is still haunting the realm, directing the murderous actions of coming generations. At various points, quotations from Müller's *Hamletmaschine* are interspersed in the action of Shakespeare's *Hamlet*. At the end of Act 1, for instance, after cursing the time that is out of joint, Hamlet adds the passage cited above: 'I was Hamlet . . . .' At this moment the historic span from Shakespeare to Müller, from the uneasy premonitions at the close of the Elizabethan era to the perturbed consciousness of the apocalypse now, is bridged perfectly. This exciting scenic moment is unfortunately followed by an overt Freudian passage when Ophelia enters silently and Hamlet reacts with the words (from *Hamletmaschine*) '. . . open your legs mamma. . . .' This fourth level, which reverts to a naïve psychological vocabulary, appears as an outmoded and (to me) redundant feature in an otherwise forceful production.

When the scene changes for the second part of the presentation, we witness the breathtaking vista of a tunnel through time. With astounding perspective effects, the arcades of a splendid renaissance façade upstage merge into a gigantic subway tube downstage. Between Ice Age and Heat Death this represents the epoch of human civilization. At some point in this tunnel Shakespeare must have written *Hamlet*, the 'Big Bang' of this stage cosmos that was born out of the play and has now expanded to an all-consuming universe. It is a long way from Shakespeare's 'wooden O' to Wonder's resplendent panorama conjured up with the aid of modern technology: an aesthetic correlative to a change in the perception of the individual from being subject to object of history.

The central part of the play up to Hamlet's departure for England is enacted in front of this monumental setting. The King's soliloquy 'O, my offence is rank! It smells to heaven' (3.3.36ff.) is turned into a dialogue with the Prince. Claudius gives Hamlet a piece of candy and pulls him onto his lap. In an idyllic family scene the uncle confesses to his stepson that unfortunate affair of having murdered his father. This turn of events (unexpected to Shakespeareans) calls to mind the kind of collusion that sometimes existed (unsuspected by historians) between the oppressors and their victims under socialist rule. It also has connotations with the contemporary situation of East Germans, who had lost their national father and immediately threw themselves at the new father figure imported from the West. The short-term reconciliation between Claudius and Hamlet suggests a complicity that soils the pure aspect of Hamlet's emancipatory endeavors. In the Queen's closet we again see an infantile prince drawing back like a naughty boy when his mother slaps his face and rolling back and forth on the bed with his hands clasped over his genitals.

After 4.4 ('My thoughts be bloody or be nothing worth') Müller's *Hamletmaschine* – a play-text comprising about ten pages of print – is performed as a block. As such it is less effective than the individual quotations previously inserted into *Hamlet*. Müller's lines are divided between various actors and actresses dressed in black, his somewhat grisly stage directions are frequently just read out aloud or ignored all together. There is a lot of play-acting of little scenic significance. The theme of the piece, the destruction of patriarchal myths surrounding Shakespeare's play, remains mostly verbal. Although a powerful text, *Hamletmaschine* is inadequately staged by its author so that it does not achieve the theatrical force needed to hold its own as a counterpoint to Shakespeare's play or, indeed, as the intellectual center of the evening. It seems that here again we have an instance of the endemic weakness of German drama – the divergence of the philosophic and the theatrical centers of gravity.

After the *Maschine*, the production presents the final part of Shakespeare's play as a last dreadful picture of a cosmic broadsheet. An array of bright metal plates is planted, maybe as mirrors, maybe as heat collectors or as tombstones, in an expanse of reddish sand. The final scene resembles a ritual act in the desert of lost time. Those about to die write their names on the gravestones. Hamlet knows that the rapier with the green blade is poisoned and forces Laertes to take it. The protagonists fight at a distance in slow motion. Then Hamlet stabs everyone present before he himself dies. His body hangs over the stage front. Ophelia enters the auditorium and carries the body lovingly onstage. Finally she is consumed by a blazing flame, speaking in the name of Electra, who retracts the world she gave birth to. Fortinbras enters wearing a golden helmet, obviously intending to gild over the gray prison of Denmark. While Zbigniew Herbert's verses over the loudspeaker reproach Hamlet for having taken the easy way out, Fortinbras covers Hamlet's face with a golden folder.

A couple of years ago, Heiner Müller declared that Shakespeare's plays could no longer be regarded as an adequate reflection of the world we live in. History has lost its meaning, he maintains, consequently we cannot expect any meaningful representation on the stage. With *Hamlet/Maschine* he has mounted an innovative allegory of a world totally out of joint, breaking theatrical conventions to do so. Although he has been accused of 'burying the theatre,' he seems to be carrying audiences with him since the production has run for a year and is still playing to full houses.

NOTE

1   This essay was originally published in *Shakespeare and Cultural Traditions*, ed. Tetsuo Kishi, Roger Pringle, and Stanley Wells. Newark: University of Delaware Press, 1994.

40

SUZAN-LORI PARKS AND LIZ DIAMOND
Doo-a-diddly-dit-dit

An interview by Steven Drukman

T147, 1995

> A continuous present is a continuous present.
>
> *Gertrude Stein (1990 [1926])*

The first time I read a Suzan-Lori Parks I flashed to Wittgenstein, not Gertrude Stein. There seemed to me to be a utilitarian focus to Parks' words – a surgical intensity – that belied her play's surface impression of hypnotic languor. Surely this is what Wittgenstein meant when he spoke of language games, I thought, and the contingencies of various meanings in languages' various contexts, words having uses and not mere dictionary definitions (see Hallett 1967), family resemblances of certain words, etc. Wittgenstein believed that the philosopher's task was to bring words back from their metaphysical usage to their everyday usage, and Parks' drama seems to play between the boundaries of both. There is a momentum in Parks' musicality, an aim in mind, a propulsion. But unlike surgical instruments, Parks' words do not seem sharp somehow, but blunt and easy: 'meaning,' it seemed, would come to the reader after the fourth downbeat, or maybe the fifth, head nodding, foot tapping. I couldn't conceive of actually seeing these dramas staged in the theatre; when, I wondered, would I get to close my eyes and listen?

Language does have an 'unearthing' function – *à la* Wittgenstein – in Parks' dramas, most explicitly in *The America Play* (1994). 'He digged the hole and the hole held him,' Parks writes in a footnote to the play, as 'History' itself is excavated from the 'great hole of history.' If it's taken for granted in our so-called postmodern condition that history is a narrative about the events of the past, then *The America Play* is, on one level, an example of a staging of that idea. But the play goes further: aware of the uses made of language, Parks suggests that – even if objective truth and knowledge are impossible – there are some discourses that are more powerful than others. This notion shows up in the detritus scattered throughout the great hole of history: the Lincoln-head pennies, the false beards, the stovepipe hats. All these historical fetishes (or 'tshatschkes,' as Parks likes to call them)[1] are themselves 'put to use' in what director Liz Diamond and Parks call a 'rep and rev' strategy. In *The America Play*, they are, in fact, the by-products of the repetitions and revisions of history itself. Following Jeffrey Mehlman's *Revolution and Repetition* (rev and rep?) which noted the 'absurdity [of] the history of a grotesque repetition' (1997: 14), Parks one-ups Marx: *The America Play* shows that historical events and personages happen first as tragedy, second as farce, and thereafter as Theatre of the Absurd.

Although Parks is clearly not, strictly speaking, an 'absurdist,' there is something like the myth of Tantalus (if not Sisyphus) going on when one is being swept away in her drama.[2] The 'rep and rev' strategy keeps the spectator/reader ever-vigilant, looking for something missed in the last repetition while scrutinizing the upcoming revision. Closure seems just on the horizon . . . where it remains. This narrative tease is then coupled with Parks' semiology: a conflation of usually discrete elements of the drama (e.g., character, line of dialog, stage action) into one package. The spectator is hyperaware of language, yet follows the traces of that language toward a narrative conclusion that never comes. It's like Gertrude Stein if Gertrude Stein liked to dangle carrots.

This is why I like to think of Parks' words as useful, or 'use-full': there's the melding of utilitarian words-as-tools with words packed full of suggestion and musicality. But what seems like such theoretical sophistication comes naturally to Parks, as she explains at the beginning of this interview in her discussion of 'meaning.' This ease with language adds lilt and up-front aplomb to her drama, still unmatched in the contemporary theatre.

Jazz is a useful (that word again) way of thinking about the theatrical collaborations of Parks and Diamond. Of course, director Diamond has already mentioned this in discussing Parks' 'rep and rev' strategy, but there's the complicated racial inflection of jazz that is relevant as well. As we discussed in the interview, Parks' drama is both about and NOT about the 'black experience'; it is concerned with the stories her figures tell to inhabit their experience as they speak their way into history. In the telling, identities (including, but not limited to, racial) are performed, reinhabited, reimprinted . . . but never for the first time. Jazz, as a genre, has always had both strains in its forming, reforming, and informing. Thelonious Monk, even as he played 'white' standards, wanted to forge a music that couldn't be appropriated by white folks, to 'create something they can't steal because they can't play it' (in Ross 1989).

Jazz is also analogous to Parks' peculiar use of puns. Just as tenor saxophone masters Dexter Gordon and Sonny Rollins were so fond of 'quotation' in their solos – momentarily weaving strands of the corniest white chestnuts into their free-blowing sessions – the 'Foundling' Father repeats and revises the assassination of Lincoln in *The America Play*. (Of course, the 'foundling' father is itself a fully packed pun, evoking both progeny and orphanage in one word.) If, during a solo, Gordon blows the main motif from 'Pop Goes the Weasel,' the strain is completely revised in the new context. But there is nothing extradiscursive about Gordon's new imprimatur: it is still the same ol' white standard . . . which is all he has to work with, after all. As Marc Robinson has noted, regarding *The America Play*:

> Every time the Foundling Father sits in 'Lincoln's Chair' at 'Ford's Theatre' and 'dies,' he is doing more than merely returning to a legendary moment. He is also forcing the past back into the present, and thus enabling himself to revise history.
>
> (1994: 191)

History, finally, is the discursive whirl/world of the 'worl'' (another loaded pun used by Parks in *The Death of the Last Black Man in the Whole Entire World* [1990]) in *The America Play*. While Alisa Solomon has correctly noted that the 'd'-less worl' of Parks' writing 'run[s] the risk of seeing white institutions wanting to fix that flattening –d onto her roun' writing' (1990: 80), my interview revealed that (for now, anyway) regional theatres are still unsure of how to absorb Diamond and Parks' collaborations into their subscribers' seasonal fare. To many artistic directors, it must seem as preposterous a disjunction as Ornette Coleman blowing with the local philharmonic. But as Diamond has noted elsewhere, the theatre needs – now more than ever – 'people who see their craft in the larger context of the cultural debate in the country' (in Pearce 1992: 39). Again, jazz seems an apt metaphor: the proto-American form that typifies our country's cultural debates, both in content (in its status as a genre) and in form (for what is a Gillespie solo if not a 'debate' of a standard?).

Finally, like Parks' plays, jazz keeps spinning out new black narrative. Contrary to Theodor Adorno's by-now notorious critique of jazz, wherein he states that 'the deviations are just as standardized as the standards themselves' (1967: 126), Parks' writing and jazz are the worl' of discourse from which all experience, black and white, is inscribed and exhumed. Where Adorno can only see that this 'method becomes trapped in its own net' (126) [. . .], Parks says that the net is all we have. 'Meaning' is never outside the net, so being trapped isn't ever an option. Parks figures that she might as well pack all the meaning she can into the words, charging them with (as she cleverly coins in this interview) 'plutonic' power.

I was intrigued by Diamond's and Parks' discussions of 'fullness,' as if texts were ingested, masticated, vomited. These ideas point to another aesthetic plane, one beyond the visual (*theatron*, meaning a place for seeing), and beyond jazz's aurality. This may be the next direction for their collaborations, although they may already be there, while the critics – myself included – are merely slow to catch on. I remain convinced that we still lack a critical vocabulary to discuss these collaborations, and offer this interview and introduction as yet another riff on the 'meaning' of these plays.

'A long complicated sentence should force itself upon you, make yourself know yourself knowing it' (Gertrude Stein, again . . . and again and again: 1990). This performative function of language – so pithily encapsulated by Stein – is at the heart of Suzan-Lori Parks' plays and, by extension (like a continuation of a sentence), the stagings of them by Liz Diamond. These theatre artists compel us to know ourselves knowing language, to reflect upon how meaning is performed, and to reinvestigate ourselves in the world of theatre as we reexamine the 'usefulness' of theatre itself.

Drukman: First, I want to say that it's surprising that nobody's ever interviewed you two together before because it seems to me that you're both artists dedicated to the same thing: that is, theatre texts and theatre productions that accrue meaning in the performance, that are performative in the sense that they give up some authorial hold on meaning. Do you agree with that assessment? Do you think that your productions together are collaborations in that respect?

Diamond: I think that, speaking of the productions, there's certainly collaboration. We've been able to be together on every production we've done. I mean, really together. Now, I exist very much outside of the writing process until the play has evolved quite a long way, but then we'll begin to do readings together and sometimes Suzan-Lori will read it out loud for me and I'll ask questions. We'll get images and ideas that pop up in the course of those oral readings and any rewrites and preliminary production ideas really take off from those first encounters, with the text in front of us, together. And then in the course of the production, Suzan-Lori will leave me alone as much as I need to be left alone. But there's an awful lot of conversation that goes on about what a moment's about, is it funny, is it something else? It's almost hard to describe the nature of our dialog because it's getting pretty fluent. I find that it's really in my work with Suzan-Lori that I've learned the most about the nature of poetry and poetic meaning and that has had a huge influence on the rest of my work. It's in discovering the ways in which a text is a three-dimensional thing, in terms of its reverberating meanings and my desire to find ways to make the stage space reverberate in a similarly complicated way that has really been, for me, the most exciting part of the collaboration.

Parks: It's interesting that you said something about giving up meaning; I realize that I don't understand that word 'meaning' as other people do. I think most people think that, say, for example, the Foundling Father means 'x' and if you figure out what that means, what he stands for, then that will enable you to figure out the play. People are welcome to understand the production in any way they choose, but I see that process as completely unhelpful. So I don't understand your notion of 'giving up meaning.' I mean, I don't understand that whole idea of meaning anyway, so I don't think we're giving up anything, I think we're together, giving meanings.

Drukman: Well, Foundling Father is a good example because one meaning is 'foundling father.' Another meaning is 'foundling' father, i.e., a father who is an orphan is a foundling. And that's just on the level of language, that's just the words. Already with one pun you've put into motion this idea of an origin-less father of our country's history! Then there's Liz's task: you have a person standing there as the foundling father, but he's only standing in as the foundling father, he's not really saying he *is* the foundling father. So all those different meanings sort of coexist, and they all sort of sprout from this one word.

Parks: Right. But I don't think you can do a play and not have that happen because the word is always there for me, and the guy would be there, so I don't think we'd be giving up 'meaning.' I guess what I'm saying is that I don't go in the direction saying, 'This is what this means, this is a metaphor for . . .' whatever. If I watch the production, I don't see that I've given up something, or lost something. Because I don't have that in mind, I don't lose anything.

Drukman: But do you see the text that you write as something that has full 'meaning' on the page? I ask this because your plays are both more literary, a better read than most plays, and yet, they're also like scores for a play, that can only be fully realized in a live performance. So, speaking about meaning now, can meaning be apprehended from just reading your plays?

Parks: Sure, I think there are meanings there. I mean, there's more if you do it, you know? I think there's meaning just in reading the play, and there's more meaning because it's a play and it's performed.

Diamond: When we first sit down and read the play together and talk about it, I don't ask what something 'means.' I'll often ask Suzan-Lori if she had an image in her head, if she sees it in a certain way, what the relationship of the figure is to the whole. I, as director, do concern myself very much with meanings, but I resist the temptation to impose one meaning on an event, a moment, a figure in the play. What I hope is happening in the course of the production is that the field of meanings that the play makes possible – the multitude of readings that a figure known as the Foundling Father and the Fo'/Faux/Foe Father will generate – are offered up by the particular way that figure's been cast, moves, speaks, etc.; that there will be a kind of wavelike effect so that one possible reading will be in the next instant contradicted by another and that all kinds of reverberating and clashing ideas will come up because that's very much the nature of this poetry. I do not agree with those directors who claim not to interpret the text when they direct. I think that one is always an interpreter if by interpreter we mean reader. All I'm offering the world is my own very partial perspective on this amazingly rich play that will have many, many, many, many other lives. But the act of reading is an interpretive act, and one has to be prepared to defend one's point of view at any step along the way. That's what makes directing an exciting and powerful enterprise. And there are stronger and weaker readings of the same text and if I were to judge a strong or weak reading of a play, the sort of play that Suzan-Lori writes, it would have to do with the ability of the production to set up those resonating waves of meaning, which I think the play does so magnificently.

Parks: I'd rather talk about the 'reading' of my plays than the 'meaning.' Every time I talk about meaning to people it sounds like they're trying to substitute something else for what I've written. I've had so many interviews where someone would say, 'So what does it mean? What does the Foundling Father mean? What are you trying to say?' And I'd say, 'Well, it's a guy and it's his life. I'm trying to show you guys what this guy's doing.' 'Yeah, but what does it mean?' That's basically saying, 'You're being obscure and why don't you tell us what you want, what you really mean,' thinking the writer has some sort of agenda that hides somewhere behind or underneath the text or behind the production somewhere.

Well, one meaning or reading is the fact that there are all black people in the play. And that's something I feel very strongly about, but it's not about just that. But then it's 'Oh, so the play's about black-on-black violence.' That's what I mean about meaning. It's like, oh shit, that's the little limit we get. (*Laughs*)

Drukman: Houston Baker says that African Americans are ultimately always theorists or theoretical because 'primary to their survival was the work of consciousness, of a nonmaterial counterintelligence' [1993]; I'm suggesting, as you're suggesting, that critics are resistant to seeing you as a formally innovative writer, a theoretical writer. You always have to be writing about, as you just said, 'black-on-black violence,' or something like that.

Parks: Right.

Drukman: I'm not quite sure why that is, what this resistance is of critics to seeing you as a formalist, or as formally experimental.

Parks: I can't figure it. I think it has something to do with what we allow ourselves – we, meaning the world, black people included – what we allow black people to do and one of them is not theory, despite what you just quoted. You can get away with it in the visual arts. Or if you're Houston Baker, whose work is fabulous. In theatre it's still . . . theatre's like the lag behind . . .

Drukman: As usual . . .

Parks: Yeah, so it's going to be the last thing to come around, after visual arts, after music. In theatre we still have more simplistic forms of representation that are still held up as examples of the best kind of theatre that black people can involve themselves in. (*Laughing*) It's just a long road, a long dumb road.

Diamond: Just jumping back for a second to this question of this thorny word 'meaning' and also sort of the secondary problematic term of 'interpretation': I think one of the reasons we struggle with it so much in this postmodern period is that the notion of a 'meaning' lying at the heart of a work – immanent and waiting to be unlocked – has been blown out of the water by theorists and artists themselves. Meaning is now understood to be a highly contingent artifact of the process of reading as opposed to something that exists in the text. And I think that most theatre people who want to talk about meaning still refer to a one-to-one interpretation as a translation: this means that, x means y, whatever. There's gotta be a more flexible, plastic way of thinking about 'meaning' that allows it to be as contingent, permeable, ever-changing as possible in the theatre.

Parks: Or just stick to the play. Instead of saying, 'What does that mean?' which is already a sentence that is outside of the play, ask you to fill in some blanks: it means this – that's an equation that's outside of the play. Stick to the play. So, let's see: you got a black guy onstage running around looking like Abraham Lincoln. If that's not enough for people to stick in their heads and go 'hmmmm.' Or, hey, you know, he talks in the third person, well that makes me think of . . . he's not comfortable with himself, he's alienated, he's left his family, he's living in a hole . . . If that's not enough already! But see, instead of digging there, they say, 'What does it mean?' which is a sentence that is outside of the play and already you're not talking about our play anymore. You want me to say something like 'black-on-black violence.' That is an answer to that kind of question, something that you saw on the news (people love that, you know). Or, the 'so your father left your family' – someone said to me once!

Drukman: It's pretty 'demeaning,' isn't it?

Parks: (*Laughing*) Good one.

Diamond: Sure, or you see black people picking up a gun, fake or not, and shooting a black man who's wearing a blond beard, and you know . . .

Parks: Yeah, yeah.

Drukman: [. . .] You've said somewhere else that you want your plays to be dense, leaden, which makes me think of . . .

Parks: I swear, don't put that in this interview! I cannot remember saying that and Liz keeps telling me I said it once but I'll be damned . . . (*Laughing*) I hate that!

Drukman: Well, I'm wondering . . .

Parks: (*Laughing*) It's like I want my cookies to be leaden, you know . . .

Drukman: Well, I was going to ask if you think audiences are too dense. I mean, you require a lot of audiences.

Parks: Yes! Well, sure. I think they are a bit. They only want something simple.

Drukman: Well, I wonder if we're so used to seeing mimetic art on television and film, that psychological realism just made us lazy . . .

Parks: Right, right.

Diamond: Well, this is where this whole rage about people taking your words and twisting them into something else drives you crazy: that 'lead' comment . . .

Parks: I must have said it, like maybe six or seven years ago . . .

Diamond: Exactly.

Parks: I cannot remember saying it . . . Plutonium! Plutonium is what, in my new enlightened state, I would say . . .

Diamond: Right, right.

Parks: That makes much more sense. Plutonium moves, it has a great half life, it's deadly.

Diamond: Yeah.

Parks: If it gets inside you, it can kill you. That's it. Lead is like something else . . . you think of cookies.

Diamond: No, but it's still a good quote, (*to Parks*) not because you want to torture people, because you want your plays to be lead, i.e., dense, i.e., unreadable, impenetrable. What I remember our conversation having to do with, which I thought was really powerful at the time and was why it was an idea I got excited about, was Suzan-Lori saying to me precisely that she wanted her plays strong enough to stand up to millions and millions of readings. (*To Parks*) That's what you were on about.

Parks: That's still the wrong word to use, let me tell you. I was not as good with words as I am now. Because lead is the wrong word! Lead is impenetrable . . .

Diamond: And it's inert. Too inert.

Parks: Yes. Plutonium is alive. Lead is dead.

Drukman: So may I use this if I include all this? (*Laughter*)

Parks: Why not? Go for it. It's your interview.

Diamond: But your question was about . . .

Drukman: If audiences are too dense.

Parks: If audiences are too . . . plutonic!

Drukman: I was wondering if audiences are lazy.

Parks: Yeah, probably. I think so. I mean, I can be . . .

Drukman: I have a hard time believing you're lazy.

Parks: Well, I'm lazy in certain areas. You just don't catch me when I'm being lazy. It's like a muscle – you don't exercise it and . . . I just wrote a recommendation for somebody and I wrote: 'You may think theatre is alive and well and that all these "special interest groups" are getting their work done and winning the big prizes, but actually it's a pretty pitiful place because it's a place of easy answers and easy questions and those are the kinds of works that are being lauded.' Easy question, easy answer, x = y, the meaning – go back to that word. (I can't think of another word to use; we'll kill this whole word.) But it shows in the form of new theatre. I heard a reading of a play a couple of months ago, it was all about, you know, someone kind of bursting out of their shell and going and changing the world. And it had some exciting ideas. The playwright obviously thought: 'Wow, I'm gonna say all this stuff!' But the structure of the play was a three-act play, you know with little scenes and a beginning, middle, and end and I thought, 'Jesus fucking Christ!' In no other art form would that be acceptable, you know what I mean? Nowhere else! People laugh at us in the theatre, other artists. And they should maybe. Yeah, we're lazy. I think we've all got big bellies. [. . . And] I think we should try harder as a theatre audience . . . it's hard. Because you think what's the payoff? You know you want something; you go to the show, you want something.

Diamond: But there's never been in theatre the kind of huge revolution in terms of orthodoxy that, say, there was in the visual arts in Europe at the turn of the century and in this country after 1945. I mean, it never really happened here in theatre, despite the Living Theatre, despite the Open Theatre, despite the Happenings and Fluxus and so on. Despite all of that, the fact of the matter is that the average American theatregoer likes it a certain way. In a sense, the modernist orthodoxy in painting is sufficiently strong that you can get an average American museumgoer standing in front of a painting by Franz Kline and be very upset about it and pissed off, but feel there is something worth dealing with here because he has been told there probably is. And you get people going to art lectures and talking about it and thinking about it . . .

Parks: Ah, wouldn't that be nice in the theatre?

Diamond: Plus, it's got the imprimatur of this giant institution that they all support with tax dollars which helps. Whereas, look at the regional theatre movement! I was told by an artistic director earlier this year that *Imperceptible Mutabilities* [*in the Third Kingdom*, 1989] might never be done in a regional theatre at this rate.

Parks: (*Laughing*) Don't name names!

Drukman: What reason was given?

Diamond: What reason? Accessibility! Inability for the audience to go along for the ride, to be there for it, to come out belching with satisfaction, you know? I mean, just . . .

Drukman: But this is a major regional theatre, on the level of . . .

Diamond: Yes, yes.

Drukman: That's a pity.

Diamond: Well, it sure is. Now, whole other topic but, how to deal with that issue? I don't know how to deal with that issue. It may be that we have to burn the regional theatres, I mean, not to be melodramatic. It may be that those aren't the places for this kind of work, you know . . .

Parks: Which is fine.

Diamond: Which is fine.

Drukman: Let's talk about *Imperceptible Mutabilities*, or not so much the play, but the use of photography in that play . . . Now this is a little reductive, but I sense in your writing, especially in that play, the notion (to rephrase Richard Foreman badly) that 'film is evil, theatre is good.' In other words, that the photograph fixes, freezes, fetishizes, and makes representation static – kind of like what critics do to you: they delimit your work this way by saying, 'She's African American, she's dealing with black-on-black violence' . . .

Parks: Right.

Drukman: And theatre, actually. Despite your complaints, you are really a lover of theatre, the way it re-presents, regenerates, recirculates (*Parks and Diamond mutter assent in unison*). So I'm onto something?

Parks: Yeah. Absolutely.

Drukman: I said it all, I should've let you say it.

Parks: (*Laughs*) No, no, no, because, again, you're the reader, that's what's so exciting, you're doing the 'meaning' thing, and that is your job in the recirculation. It is not mine, you know what I mean?

Diamond: Yeah, that's the other thing that's exciting about all this 'meaning' stuff: to hear people having huge discussions, debates, conversations about what it means. The problem that arises is when they don't trust their own experience of it enough to go on a journey of exploration with themselves and their friends about what they've seen or what they've read. But really, you can watch *The America Play*, you can look at that glistening black coal dust on the floor and look at those old columns all smeared with filth, you know, and look at Lucy wandering around and listening, listening, listening, for echoes of her husband and you can talk about those images for days and trust that the ideas that come up in you about those images are valid. Talking about those images – outside of the theatre – is part of the theatre.

Drukman: See, as long as we have audiences that are not allowed that experience by artistic directors who keep these plays out of the theatres and just want the 'belch factor,' audiences don't trust themselves to take that journey.

Parks: That's true. I know my plays aren't for everybody.

Drukman: Let's talk about history . . . Toni Morrison said in *Playing in the Dark* that what she calls American Africanism are the ways in which the Africanist presence or persona is constructed in the United States by literature, and the imaginative uses that this fabricated presence has served. Now it seems that when you make a stage figure or character, you start from that point, from the fabricated presence. In other words, you assume that the figure is a historical construction.

Parks: From the fabricated . . .

Drukman: From the fabricated presence.

Parks: From the fabricated absence, actually. It's a fabricated absence. That's where I start from. And that's where the Foundling Father came from. It's the hole idea.

Drukman: So, the figures are holes?

Parks: Well, yes and no, they come from holes, it's the fabricated absence. It's the story that you're told that goes 'Once upon a time you weren't here.' (*Laughter*) You weren't here and you didn't do shit! And it's that, that fabricated absence.

Drukman: So, like, the hole is the hole in Lincoln's head, the great hole in history, the holes in the gums of Aretha Saxton. These are all absences, holes . . .

Parks: Or abscesses!

Diamond: There's a gap . . . in 'Greeks' [the first part of *Imperceptible Mutabilities*, 1989] there's a gap . . .

Parks: Right, right. 'Overlap's uh gap,' it says.

Drukman: And to me, that's 'theatre' in your plays. The recirculation of meaning, the holes versus the closure of the photograph and the chronicle of another history by people who told the story.

Parks: Right, right. And whoever told the story, I mean, black people told stories and still do . . . it's not just 'evil white people out there.' They're two different stories but the same story, really.

Drukman: I think of jazz as an analog for the way you write, because, like you said, there are two stories. When I think of my favorite jazz standards, there's John Coltrane playing 'My Favorite Things,' Miles Davis playing 'Bye Bye Blackbird,' and Charlie Parker playing 'Laura' – black musicians playing white standards, as written by whites. But then, also in jazz, there's a completely different language – John Coltrane playing 'Naima,' Miles Davis playing 'So What?,' Charlie Parker playing 'Night in Tunisia,' and it seems that both those discourses are in your plays and that might be what people miss, that there are two stories that you're accounting for.

Parks: That's a good point. There's the standard and then there's the . . .

Drukman: The rep of the standard.

Parks: Right. It's like 'blubblubblub' or 'She be doo be waaah doo wah' – that's a great line from *Death of the Last Black Man* . . . but what does that 'mean'? You know, I've actually made a little dictionary – foreign words and phrases.

Drukman: You actually made the dictionary?

Parks: It's coming out in the spring (*laughs*), in the new book of my plays [1995³].

Drukman: Really?

Parks: Yeah, but I put a little thing in the book, 'Foreign Words and Phrases' and how to interpret the words, the pronunciation guide . . . we'll take care of all those people . . .

Drukman: Your invented glossary . . .

Diamond: The 'gloss' – ary! (*Laughter*)

Drukman: The gloss.

Parks: That's right, the gloss. No, they're words from the play that are, like, THEP (*makes inhaling noise*): I say how to do it and what it means . . . no not what it 'means,' why it's there . . . like 'doo-a-diddly-dit-dit' . . . that one means 'yes.' Actually, that's more like, 'yeah!' or, sometimes, 'yeah?' (*Laughter*) That's about it.

Drukman: See, that's what boggles me, Liz, how . . . when I read one of these plays, I don't . . . I feel like I wouldn't know how to stage it, but of course, I'm reading the play on my couch. Maybe if I had people listening, you know, or listening to people saying it, the 'THEP' or whatever would become very clear and I would just suddenly know in the performance how it's supposed to be and then *what* it means because I know *how* it's said.

Parks: But it's also about how we read, you know. We should read aloud. Definitely. Any book, not just a play. I think I write to be read aloud.

Drukman: What about all the hyphens and ellipses? How do you know how to stage the 'dash-dash-dash'? For example, the Lucy/Brazil scene when they're playing the location game and there'd be two dashes, and the next time there'd be four dashes . . .

Diamond: Well, that's just learning how to read the play as a musical score, determining that every single thing on the page is there for a reason. Again, it's like reading it formally, the way you would try to decode a map or the way you would read a poem. I think that periods and commas and semicolons and dashes and the distance between the heading and a line of text and the way it is written on a page are all full of rich clues for the director. I think what's fun is to experiment with it in rehearsal and Suzan-Lori and I will listen to it and we'll try having four dashes be one length of time and then we'll realize, well, you know, we've got eight coming up, we'd better shrink that. You just develop a sense of structure, a rhythmic structure.

There's clearly a difference between a moment when a writer has not given a character anything to say and that character's name doesn't even appear on the page and when that character's name appears on the page, has been given space, and says nothing. Something's happening there! That character is not speaking but is taking up space on the page and is taking up time on the page and must take up space and time similarly on the stage. Discovering exactly what the rhythmic shape of that space should be is what makes rehearsal so much fun, because you're just discovering what those musical, aural dynamics are, that are going to make it . . . pop. And you can't do that – you can't even do that reading out loud – you can only do that when everybody is up on their feet and their bodies are moving in space and you've got somebody fifteen feet away from somebody else. It's fascinating with these plays to see that.

Drukman: Do you think when you stage Suzan-Lori's plays that they change more or less during the course of the run? Do you feel like you need to 'set the score' and so they actually change less in the course of the run or, because there are so many textual clues, the performances change even more throughout a run?

Diamond: Boy. I don't know how to answer that. When I did 'Open House' in *Imperceptible Mutabilities*, I knew very much I wanted Aretha's bed to be just floating in space and I wanted it to be spinning around and I wanted her to be wrenched from the bed and I wanted those pliers over her head . . . the shape of the play felt like it had to be a really wild hallucinogenic, sort of nightmarish event. And I knew there was something about the stately rhythm of the sound of the text in 'Greeks' that made it feel – and the name itself, 'Greeks' – that made it seem that there needed to be a very strong choric quality to the family, and that the family somehow needed to have a military bearing. That was something that came from the rhythm of the way they spoke to each other. And in *The America Play*, you're given this amazing opportunity to have George Washington's wooden teeth on stage, it's completely irresistible. Staging these plays has to do with taking the text absolutely at its word. I mean, literally. It's finding stage directions embedded in the writing that is an enormous part of my task and it's through that process that the actors start to discover the code by discovering that (unlike traditional 'psychological' American acting training) *there is no code outside of what's on the page.* It's kind of an old-fashioned idea, really. This is what we're supposed to do when we direct or work on Shakespeare. But it's amazing how little American acting training prepares them for that kind of exploration of action in language! I guess that's what you mean when you say 'performative.'

My big breakthrough on *Death of the Last Black Man* was realizing that the so-called choruses took up more space on the page than the tableaux. There's the 'meaning' . . . perform that!

Drukman: (*To Parks*) You've said somewhere that you've gotten a lot of humor from Liz.

Parks: Yeah. I've become more socially acceptable since hanging out with Liz. (*Laughter*) It's true. When she met me, I was really, really weird. Now I'm only a little weird . . . Liz has an incredible sense of humor and (*to Diamond*) I've really learned from hanging around and working with you, 'cause my humor is so perverted . . .

Diamond: You're pretty funny yourself . . .

Parks: Mine's, like, twisted, and Liz's is, like, the kind of humor you can say in front of people, so we can get away with saying things like, 'the great hole' and 'prenuptial excitement,' and stuff that's unseemly. There are so many dirty jokes in *The America Play*. And Liz points them out to me, even though I've written them, I guess . . .

Diamond: Well, I maintain that it's there. I think the play is a riot. I mean, it's completely heartbreaking, but I think it's unbelievably funny, and I think when he reminisces about his honeymoon and says, 'We'd stand on the lip of that hole' . . .

Drukman: Most audiences miss the dirty joke there?

Parks: Yeah.

Diamond: And I think the idea of a woman listening for her husband's echo with an ear trumpet is brilliant and heartbreaking and extremely funny. For me, again, it helped me to be literal, so I started thinking about the echoes *qua* echoes, as stuff she was picking up. I liked thinking about the stuff that was coming into the hole. The Great Hole of History. It's like a wastebasket – there's gonna be crap that collects. And then, who are these people wearing these crazy outfits doing these shards from *Our American Cousin*?[4]

Parks: I mean, humor's a great way of getting to the deep shit, isn't it? Humor is a very effective way of saying something that you probably could never say ordinarily. And, you know, we do it everyday. I say all kinds of bizarre things with a little laugh, or as a joke.

Drukman: What are you working on now?

Parks: I'm working on a film. I am. I just finished the first draft of it. It's due this week.

Drukman: What is it?

Parks: It's . . .

Diamond: . . . top secret! Top-secret stuff!

Parks: It's my first feature-length film and it's with Spike Lee, and the other night Liz and her husband, Ralph, helped me . . .

Diamond: . . . figure out what it meant. (*Laughter*)

Parks: It's the first time I actually sat down and said – because films are written in a completely different way – you need this plot point and those things to happen at certain times, and you need to say, 'So what does this mean to you guys? OK, that's a good reading of that, I'll put that in the pressure cooker and make it produce popcorn on page 96.'

Drukman: And what about you, Liz?

Diamond: I'm working on a children's musical, by Mac Wellman, called *Tiger, Tiger, Tiger* and we're going to do it out at Sundance and Michael Roth is composing the music.

Drukman: And your newest play, *Venus*? I couldn't find . . .

Parks: Because it's not written.

Drukman: It's not written yet?

Parks: I mean, it's written, but I have to write some more. It's the new play . . . it's um . . . I'm even worse talking about plays before they're done. It's a play about love and fame and . . . and . . . somebody's ass. (*Laughter*) No, it's a play about this woman called the Venus Hottentot who had a big butt and exhibited it in the nineteenth century.

Drukman: Do you mean . . . she really did?

Parks: Yeah, yeah. And she had a large butt.

Diamond: And a large following.

Parks: And a larger following. (*Laughter*)

Diamond: Her rear end was only exceeded by the . . . size of her audience. (*Laughter*)

Parks: That's right. Like me, maybe, someday.

NOTES

1 As quoted in Pearce (1994:26).

2 As I have written elsewhere (1994:191) Parks' plays are almost unbearably tantalizing because meaning, it seems, is always just around the bend.

3 The dictionary was published under the heading 'foreign words and phrases' in 'Elements of Style' in Suzan-Lori Parks, *The America Play and Other Works* (New York: Theatre Communications Group, 1995). (Editors' note.)

4 *Our American Cousin* is a popular nineteenth-century American comedy by Tom Taylor. It was made famous by Laura Keene's production, which starred Joseph Jefferson and E. A. Sothern, and by the fact that it was in performance at Ford's Theatre in Washington, D.C., when Abraham Lincoln was assassinated.

WORKS CITED

Adorno, Theodor (1967) 'Perennial fashion – jazz.' In *Prisms*. Cambridge: MIT Press.

Baker, Houston, Jr. (1993) *Black Studies, Rap and the Academy*. Chicago: University of Chicago Press.

Drukman, Steven (1994) '*The America Play*.' *Women and Performance* 13, 7:1.

Hallett, Garth (1967) *Wittgenstein's Definition of Meaning and Use*. New York: Fordham University Press.

Mehlman, Jeffrey (1977) *Revolution and Repetition: Marx/Hugo/Balzac*. Berkeley: University of California Press.

Pearce, Michele (1992) 'Liz Diamond.' *American Theatre*, May: 38–40.

—— (1994) 'Alien nation: an interview with the playwright [Suzan-Lori Parks].' *American Theatre*, March: 26.

Robinson, Marc (1994) *The Other American Drama*. New York: Cambridge University Press.

Ross, Andrew (1989) *No Respect: Intellectuals and Popular Culture*. New York: Routledge.

Solomon, Alisa (1990) 'Signifying on the signifyin': the plays of Suzan-Lori Parks.' *Theatre*, Summer/Fall: 73–80.

Stein, Gertrude (1990) 'Composition as explanation (1926).' In *Selected Writings of Gertrude Stein*, ed. Carl Van Vechten, 511–23. New York: Vintage.

41

THREE SISTERS AT MILLENNIUM'S END
Richard Schechner's production at La Mama

Rebecca Schneider

Theatre Journal, 1997

What does it mean to want to get to Moscow from 1997 America?

Several friends and I huddled in the cold outside of LaMama in New York City waiting to be ushered into Richard Schechner's production of Chekhov's *Three Sisters*. For the end of January, it was not really as cold as all that. Not as cold as it might be had we been, as we waited to imagine, in Russia at the turn of the last century. Once inside the theatre we sat beside each other in rows. I sat with my companions. As I glanced about, I recognized several others, then noticed that even strangers were familiar: New York art patrons. No one seemed out of place. Our seats all pointed forward toward a curtain and it was safe to say that we all knew where we were: the theatre.

The curtain underscored it. Schechner had hung a vast map of the Moscow Art Theatre set design for Stanislavsky's 1901 production of the drama Chekhov had written the year before. As we rifled through our programs and chatted with each other, we looked at the design. It was the first indication that this production would be as much about the history of the theatre as it was about the drama (or 'comedy') of three unhappy women at the seeming close of a way of life. The lights dimmed and we hunkered down.

When the curtain was drawn aside, we were treated to a first act (see fig. 41.1) staged according to the tenets of naturalism. Masha (Maria Vail Guevara), in a black period dress, sat center stage on a pink chaise-longue. Her depressed and sarcastic glances anchored the scene that followed. Irena (Shaula Chambliss), in white, glowed in her youth and resolute high spirits. Olga (Rebecca Ortese), in dark green, paced about prim and anxious and tired-looking. All was as it should be, as it has so often been. Chandeliers dripped soft light. Plush rugs, a striking clock. The brick walls of LaMama were visible, but when Irena came to the front of the stage to look out of an absent window, she had us believing that she was seeing the Russian landscape, not our New York faces peering back at her. Lines were delivered over top of each other, pauses were allowed as 'real life' would have them. Yes, we might indeed have been guests in the Prozorovs' living room, as Stanislavsky would have liked. Yet, true to form, we were comfortably unacknowledged guests –

**Fig. 41.1 Act I of *Three Sisters*, directed by Richard Schechner.
(Photo by Richard Schechner, courtesy of Richard Schechner.)**

no one greeted and welcomed us, as Olga greeted Vershinin (Frank Wood) when he
arrived with his stories of Moscow. Rather, as guests, we were ghosts – specters who
could pass through fourth walls. Looking back at the scene – listening to Vershinin
say, 'Someday folks will think of our lifestyle as insignificant' – we were ghosts from
the future. And we were accustomed to our haunts.

Schechner's direction of this production, however, aimed to acknowledge us, as
act by act it dragged itself across the twentieth century to something vaguely dis-
cernible as the present. The first act was Stanislavsky's, the second was Meyerhold's, the third was set in a Gulag prison camp, and the fourth act . . . well, by
the time we were at the fourth act the actors were standing at four microphones,
looking audience members squarely in the eyes, quoting their characters, replaying
the first three acts silently in the background, yet still brimming with emotion and,
now and then, bursting into full-bodied song. As performance forms changed and
even challenged each other across the acts, one thing remained constant: the desire,
across 100 years, to get back to an absent future marked 'Moscow.'

I was impressed by Schechner's cast. In this production, Chekhovian despair, most
exquisitely manifested in Masha (who also did a wonderful job expressing the giddy
joy of a lover's passion), is punctuated by hearty ensemble renditions of stirring
Russian folk songs. These songs underscore a consistent passion and even investment that courses through the production. Indeed Schechner never depletes the
emotion of the play, even when emphasizing biomechanical gesture in the second
act, or radically altering the context of the drama in the third, or whispering the
text into microphones in the last. Something remains throughout the alterations of
form. Indeed the alterations of form punctuate such Chekhovian lines as Andrei's
'Why can't things remain the same?' We are able to see, through all the upheaval of
twentieth-century performance experimentation, like the upheaval of revolution,
something of the resolute desire and despair at the base of Chekhov's play: if
things do not remain the same, they also do not alter as radically as all that.

In the second act, set just after the Bolshevik Revolution (see fig. 41.2), drawing-
room finery is replaced by uniform grey worker tunics, as Meyerhold's actors had
worn in his constructivist period. A small, red hammer and sickle is pinned at each

Fig. 41.2 Act II of *Three Sisters*, directed by Richard Schechner. (Photo by Richard Schechner, courtesy of Richard Schechner.)

chest. The chaise-longue remains center stage, and the chandeliers remind us of the first act, but almost all other trappings of the living room have vanished. In this act, most objects are mimed. An actor breaks the fourth wall and addresses the audience. Gestures are exaggerated, and some of the actors, especially those playing Vershinin and Irena, have mastered a symbolist monotone delivery interrupted now and then by passionate outbursts of song. With the theatricalism of Meyerhold interrupting the naturalism of the first act, we realize that it is not only Russian history and Prozorov family history we are traversing on this stage, but theatre history as well. With this move, Schechner underscores the relationship between representational form and our social, political, and personal histories. That is, Schechner's (Stanislavsky's) Chekhov becomes at once a history of representation and a representation of history.

In the Gulag prison camp which sets the third act (see fig. 41.3), the chandeliers are piled on the floor, still lit. They have become fires, and actors (characters?) try to warm their freezing hands by their glow. Stamping and coughing, the actors are also busy moving piles of cinder blocks, and we soon realize that they are building a wall at the front of the stage. The wall never gets high enough to block our view because as some actors stack it up, others dismantle it and build elsewhere. Thinking of the theatre lineage Schechner is charting, I wondered if the half-wall is a gesture toward Brecht (who was gesturing toward Asia). I was also reminded of Grotowski's *Akropolis* in which actors built a gas chamber out of piles of junk. Indeed, in this act, the attempt either to reinforce or dismantle, underscore or challenge the fourth wall is made literal as a kind of debate (did not Meyerhold lose his life over just such an issue? Did not Schechner make his name over it?). Of course there is also a foreshadowing of the fall of another wall – the Berlin Wall – which will be rubble by the time the fourth act, set in the present, takes place. Interestingly, even while building and destroying the wall, naturalism has a place here, though it is often against the text. When Natasha says, 'Who says I'm getting fat? It's not true!' as fellow workers fight over a shard of bread, Chekhov's meaning is altered – almost, but not quite. When Irena, in another fit of longing and now dressed in work-camp rags, cries that she misses the 'life they had,' Chekhov's

Fig. 41.3 Act III of *Three Sisters*, directed by Richard Schechner. (Photo by Richard Schechner, courtesy of Richard Schechner.)

Fig. 41.4 Act IV of *Three Sisters*, directed by Richard Schechner. (Photo by Richard Schechner, courtesy of Richard Schechner.)

meaning is altered – or is it? The narrative, like the wall, has crumbled, but not fully. True, it is hard to follow the precise storyline in the midst of camp life. Does the scandal Olga is concerned about have any validity here? Is the town fire the group speaks of a fantasy born of Siberian desperation? Are they warming themselves by replaying shards of Chekhov for their amusement? Are they replaying it for memory? For survival? Are we?

In the fourth act (see fig. 41.4), the chaise-longue has returned center stage, but now it is turned around. The chandeliers are piled on the floor like trash, their lights out. The actors, who had worn ragged overcoats in the third act, now enter in their own street clothes and speak their lines into four microphones downstage. We are given to think we're present at the reading of a radio drama. When Natasha plays the piano, the sound is prerecorded. When the soldiers kiss Irena goodbye, they make kissing sounds into the microphones. Interestingly, however, this act does not become a meta-statement about the tyranny of technology, the impossibility of 'real' interaction in a mediated, late capitalist age. There is no saying, with

Beckett's Krapp, 'Farewell to love' – even as Masha loses Vershinin, and Irena loses Tuzenbakh. Nor is this act slick enough to be quoting a Wooster Group meta-textual commentary: there's still a resilient sense of investment in the drama and no attempt to avoid the flush of presence, character, and emotion. Shaula Chambliss stands as Irena at the mic. She looks out at the audience from the same spot she had stood to look out of the window in Act I. This time she looks me fully in the eye and speaking Irena's line says, in effect, 'Tell me what happened at the theatre.' With Chekhov she is speaking of Tuzenbakh and Solyony, but also with Chekhov she is speaking more broadly. She still wants to get to Moscow, but she's becoming resigned to its impossibility. I wonder if I am as well. Or will the fourth act revert, again, like theatre always does, to the first act, as somewhere, in another city, in other countries, in other millennia, *Three Sisters* are mounted again.

I take a cue from Schechner and consider that the 'cool down,' or what happens 'after the theatre,' is as important as what happens in the theatre. I trundle back into the cold with my companions. True to a post-theatre ritual to which we've become accustomed (famished ghosts that we are), we try and find a restaurant we'll enjoy. I imagine that many of the patrons of LaMama are doing the same. Our first choice for dining has too long a waiting list. We resign ourselves to the impossibility – we'll never get there – and find another spot. Our dinners and our conversation are both expensive and nourishing. We discuss Moscow and impossibility, history, and investment. Then, one of us orders a 'flaming banana' for dessert. Huddled around its fire, I am moved by the ironies of our desire. What does it mean to enact and reenact the desire for Moscow from the seat of our post-Soviet privilege as this turning century marches toward its conclusion? What do *we* not see just beyond our horizon? The banana is delicious as the flame subsides. So is the conversation. 'If we only knew,' says Olga at the close of the play. 'If we only knew.'

INDEX